T0398335

LEADERSHIP AND MANAGEMENT IN PHARMACY PRACTICE

SECOND EDITION

CRC PRESS
PHARMACY
EDUCATION
SERIES

RECENTLY PUBLISHED BOOKS

Leadership and Management in Pharmacy Practice, Second Edition
Andrew M. Peterson and William N. Kelly

Basic Statistics and Pharmaceutical Statistical Applications, Third Edition
James E. De Muth

Basic Pharmacokinetics, Second Edition
Mohsen A. Hedaya

Pharmaceutical Dosage Forms and Drug Delivery, Second Edition
Ram I. Mahato and Ajit S. Narang

Pharmacy: What It Is and How It Works, Third Edition
William N. Kelly

Essentials of Law and Ethics for Pharmacy Technicians, Third Edition
Kenneth M. Strandberg

Essentials of Human Physiology for Pharmacy, Second Edition
Laurie Kelly McCorry

Basic Pharmacology: Understanding Drug Actions and Reactions
Maria A. Hernandez and Appu Rathinavelu

Managing Pharmacy Practice: Principles, Strategies, and Systems
Andrew M. Peterson

Essential Math and Calculations for Pharmacy Technicians
Indra K. Reddy and Mansoor A. Khan

Pharmacoethics: A Problem-Based Approach
David A. Gettman and Dean Arneson

Pharmaceutical Care: Insights from Community Pharmacists
William N. Tindall and Marsha K. Millonig

Essentials of Pathophysiology for Pharmacy
Martin M. Zdanowicz

Quick Reference to Cardiovascular Pharmacotherapy
Judy W. M. Cheng

Essentials of Pharmacy Law
Douglas J. Pisano

*Please visit our website **www.crcpress.com** for a full list of titles*

LEADERSHIP AND MANAGEMENT IN PHARMACY PRACTICE

SECOND EDITION

Edited by

Andrew M. Peterson, PharmD, PhD
John Wyeth Dean
Mayes College of Healthcare Business & Policy
University of the Sciences
Philadelphia, Pennsylvania, USA

William N. Kelly, PharmD, FISPE Professor
Pharmacotherapeutics & Clinical Research
College of Pharmacy
The University of South Florida
Tampa, Florida

CRC Press
Taylor & Francis Group
Boca Raton   London   New York

CRC Press is an imprint of the
Taylor & Francis Group, an **informa** business

MIX
Paper from
responsible sources
FSC® C014174

CRC Press
Taylor & Francis Group
6000 Broken Sound Parkway NW, Suite 300
Boca Raton, FL 33487-2742

© 2015 by Taylor & Francis Group, LLC
CRC Press is an imprint of Taylor & Francis Group, an Informa business

No claim to original U.S. Government works

Printed on acid-free paper
Version Date: 20141014

International Standard Book Number-13: 978-1-4665-8962-9 (Hardback)

This book contains information obtained from authentic and highly regarded sources. While all reasonable efforts have been made to publish reliable data and information, neither the author[s] nor the publisher can accept any legal responsibility or liability for any errors or omissions that may be made. The publishers wish to make clear that any views or opinions expressed in this book by individual editors, authors or contributors are personal to them and do not necessarily reflect the views/opinions of the publishers. The information or guidance contained in this book is intended for use by medical, scientific or health-care professionals and is provided strictly as a supplement to the medical or other professional's own judgement, their knowledge of the patient's medical history, relevant manufacturer's instructions and the appropriate best practice guidelines. Because of the rapid advances in medical science, any information or advice on dosages, procedures or diagnoses should be independently verified. The reader is strongly urged to consult the relevant national drug formulary and the drug companies' printed instructions, and their websites, before administering any of the drugs recommended in this book. This book does not indicate whether a particular treatment is appropriate or suitable for a particular individual. Ultimately it is the sole responsibility of the medical professional to make his or her own professional judgements, so as to advise and treat patients appropriately. The authors and publishers have also attempted to trace the copyright holders of all material reproduced in this publication and apologize to copyright holders if permission to publish in this form has not been obtained. If any copyright material has not been acknowledged please write and let us know so we may rectify in any future reprint.

Library of Congress Cataloging-in-Publication Data

Managing pharmacy practice.
  Leadership and management in pharmacy practice / [edited by] Andrew M. Peterson, William N. Kelly. -- Second edition.
    p. ; cm.
  Preceded by Managing pharmacy practice / edited by Andrew M. Peterson. c2004.
  Includes bibliographical references and index.
  ISBN 978-1-4665-8962-9 (hardcover : alk. paper)
  I. Peterson, Andrew M., editor. II. Kelly, William N., editor. III. Title.
  [DNLM: 1. Pharmaceutical Services--organization & administration. 2. Pharmacy--organization & administration. QV 737.1]

RS98
615'.4068--dc23   2014039469

Visit the Taylor & Francis Web site at
http://www.taylorandfrancis.com

and the CRC Press Web site at
http://www.crcpress.com

Contents

SECTION 1 *Leadership*

SECTION 2 *Management*

Preface

This is the second edition of a text originally designed to introduce students to the managerial side of pharmacy practice. When William "Bill" Kelly joined with Andrew Peterson as the coeditor of the second edition, he instilled the idea that the focus of this text should be on the *leadership* of pharmacy, supported by the management principles. The changing nature of pharmacy practice must be led, not just managed. It was with this concept that we reorganized the book, placing the leadership chapters first followed by the management chapters, emphasizing the need for leadership first.

This text is designed for students in the professional years of their pharmacy curricula and those promoted recently into pharmacy leadership or management positions. The purpose of this book is to introduce a variety of leadership and managerial issues facing pharmacists presently and in the future. References are made throughout the text to changes occurring internally and externally to the profession. Much of the material applies to all settings of pharmacy practice—community, hospital, industry, ambulatory care, and long-term care. Readers should not confine themselves to one area of practice; rather, when a particular setting is used as a platform for discussion, they should also see how the issue manifests itself in another setting. The concepts and skills underpinning the management of human resources, drug distribution systems, formularies, and drug use evaluations are transferable among the variety of practice settings.

Effective leadership in pharmacy is critical to having an innovative practice setting, and to advancing the practice of pharmacy. Thus, the first six chapters of the text focus on this critical skill. Knowing how to manage a smooth-running pharmacy practice department is another skill that is mostly learned from others. In this regard, the authors of the 10 management chapters have broad and deep experience in pharmacy management.

The chapters are written by contributors from within and outside pharmacy practice. As such, the style of writing and presentation of information will vary among chapters. This diversity of contributors, as well as the diversity of writing styles, should not be considered a distraction, but rather a reflection of the complexity of management in pharmacy settings. Cases are added to each chapter that are thought provoking and promote critical thinking and problem solving—two skills that are critical in being an effective pharmacy leader or manager.

The overarching intent of the authors is to give students of pharmacy and new pharmacy leaders and managers a broad overview of the complexities and intricacies inherent in managing and leading the profession. Regardless of students' ultimate practice setting, knowledge of the leadership and management skills contained herein will aid them in serving their profession throughout their careers.

Editors

Andrew M. Peterson, PharmD, PhD is the John Wyeth Dean of the Mayes College and Professor of Clinical Pharmacy and Health Policy at the University of the Sciences, Philadelphia, Pennsylvania. Before joining USciences in 1996, Peterson was Assistant Director of Pharmacy and Clinical Services at Thomas Jefferson University Hospital, Philadelphia, Pennsylvania, and Associate Director of Pharmacy, Drug Information, and Clinical Services at Crozer-Chester Medical Center, Upland, Pennsylvania.

With more than 20 years of research experience in pharmacy management, managed care pharmacy, medications compliance, and, more recently, medications in the environment, Peterson's accomplishments span scholarly research, innovative programming, and securing significant grant funding. Recognitions include several awards for excellence in teaching and learning innovation.

A speaker at conferences around the world on issues related to pharmacy and health policy, Dr. Peterson is coauthor of an authoritative text for mid-level practitioners and a contributor to numerous peer-reviewed publications. He is active in the academic and research communities and has served on the boards of many professional organizations.

Peterson earned his PharmD from Virginia Commonwealth University, Richmond, Virginia, and his PhD in Health Policy at USciences. He also completed an advanced residency in Hospital Pharmacy Administration at Thomas Jefferson University Hospital and a residency in Hospital Pharmacy Practice from Rush-Presbyterian St. Luke's Medical Center, Chicago, Illinois.

William N. Kelly, PharmD, FISPE is Full Professor at the USF College of Pharmacy (Tampa, Florida) and is President of William N. Kelly Consulting and Publishing, Inc. (Oldsmar, Florida), providing consulting on pharmacy and medication management services nationally and internationally. He is also Vice President and Senior Vice President of Scientific Affairs of Vivace, Inc. (West Chester, Pennsylvania). He was previously Chairman of Pharmacy Practice and a tenured professor at the Mercer University School of Pharmacy, and a guest researcher at the Immunization Safety Branch of the Centers for Disease Control and Prevention (CDC), both in Atlanta, Georgia. Prior to that, he was Assistant Vice President and Director of Pharmacy at Hamot Medical Center, a 500-bed hospital in Erie, Pennsylvania.

Dr. Kelly earned a BS in pharmacy from Ferris State University and a Doctor of Pharmacy (PharmD) and residency certificate in clinical pharmacy from the University of Michigan. He also completed a fellowship in executive management at the Leonard Davis Institute of Health Economics at the University of Pennsylvania. He completed graduate work in pharmacoepidemiology and biostatistics at McGill University (Montreal, Quebec, Canada), Emory University (Atlanta, Georgia), and the University of Michigan, and is a Fellow of the International Society for Pharmacoepidemiology.

Kelly has published over 100 peer-reviewed manuscripts, 15 chapters in books, and has presented his work nationally and internationally. He is the author or co-author of three other books on pharmacy: *Pharmacy: What It Is and How It Works* (2011, CRC Press, Boca Raton, Florida), *Prescribed Medication and the Public Health: Laying the Foundation for Risk Reduction* (2006, CRC Press), and *The Good Pharmacist: Characteristics, Virtues, and Habits* (2011, with Elliott Sogol; William N. Kelly Consulting, Inc., Oldsmar, Florida).

Contributors

Patricia R. Audet, PharmD
Chair
Department of Pharmaceutical and
  Healthcare Business
Mayes College of Healthcare Business
  and Policy
University of the Sciences
Philadelphia, Pennsylvania

John E. Clark, PharmD, MS, FASHP
Assistant Professor and Director
Experiential Education and Residency
  Programs
Department of Pharmacotherapeutics
  and Clinical Research
University of South Florida College of
  Pharmacy
Tampa, Florida

David A. Ehlert, PharmD, MBA, FASHP
Vice President
Health Systems Product
  Management
McKesson Health Systems
San Francisco, California

Gene A. Gibson, PharmD
Associate Director of Pharmacy
Hospital of the University of
  Pennsylvania
Philadelphia, Pennsylvania

Steve Gilbert, MBA
Director of Pharmacy
Hampton Behavioral Health Center
Philadelphia, Pennsylvania

Mei-Jen Ho, PharmD, MSPH
Assistant Professor
Department of Pharmacotherapeutics
  and Clinical Research
University of South Florida College of
  Pharmacy
Tampa, Florida

James M. Hoffman, MS, PharmD
Associate Member, Pharmaceutical
  Sciences
Medication Outcomes and Safety Officer
St. Jude Children's Research Hospital
Memphis, Tennessee

James A. Jorgenson, RPh, MS, FASHP
CEO
Visante, Inc.
St. Paul, Minnesota

William N. Kelly, PharmD, FISPE
Professor
Department of Pharmacotherapeutics
  and Clinical Research
University of South Florida College of
  Pharmacy
Tampa, Florida

Michael J. Magee, MS, RPh, FASHP
Vice President of Pharmacy Services
BayCare Health System, Hospital
  Division
Tampa, Florida

Melanie Oates, MBA, PhD
Assistant Professor of Business
Chatham University
Pittsburgh, Pennsylvania

Andrew M. Peterson, PharmD, PhD
John Wyeth Dean
Mayes College of Healthcare Business
    and Policy
University of the Sciences
Philadelphia, Pennsylvania

**Gary E. Sloskey, BSc Pharmacy,
PharmD, BCPS**
Associate Professor of Pharmacy
Philadelphia College of Pharmacy
University of the Sciences
Philadelphia, Pennsylvania

Sarah J. Steinhardt, PharmD, JD, MS
Assistant Professor
Department of Pharmacotherapeutics
    and Clinical Research
University of South Florida College of
    Pharmacy
Tampa, Florida

**Dennis A. Tribble, PharmD,
FASHP**
Director, Healthcare Industry
    Operations
CareFusion, Inc.
San Diego, California

Robert J. Votta, MBA, PhD
Assistant Professor of
    Business
Mayes College of Healthcare
    Business and Policy
University of the Sciences
Philadelphia, Pennsylvania

Stephanie A. Zarus, PharmD
Managing Director of
    Innovation
Avancer Group, Inc
West Conshohocken, Pennsylvania

Section 1

Leadership

1 Principles and Characteristics of Leadership

Andrew M. Peterson

CONTENTS

Learning Objectives: After reading this chapter and working through the case, the reader will be able to:

1. Compare and contrast leadership and management
2. State three prevailing theories of leadership
3. Describe the four domains of emotional intelligence (EI)
4. Discuss how the four domains of EI relate to six leadership styles
5. Provide three examples of how to successfully influence others
6. Demonstrate three strategies for successful negotiation
7. Provide three ways you can develop your leadership skills

INTRODUCTION

From the pharaohs leading Egyptians and slaves to construct the pyramids, to Jack Welch leading the United States' largest corporation into the new millennium, leadership has been the subject of considerable discussion. For centuries, theorists have attempted to determine what it takes to be a leader. All of us know a leader when we meet one, but this seemingly easy concept eludes external identification of the absolute qualities of a leader.

Leadership, the ability to influence the actions of others, is based on the interaction of three elements: the leader, the person or persons being led, and the situation in which both coexist. All three elements change, almost on a daily basis. A good leader understands each of the changes and develops strategies to work with and through others to accomplish goals.

Leaders are not always managers, and managers are not always leaders. Those who display characteristics of both are typically best for organizations. According to Bennis and Nanus (1985), "Managers are people who do things right and leaders are people who do the right thing" (p. 21). Managers typically focus on performing the job on behalf of the organization, routinely invoking the five functions of planning, organizing, directing, coordinating, and controlling. In contrast, leaders consider the needs of the organization as well as the needs of the people they are leading.

The purpose of leadership is to help individuals, groups, and organizations grow and develop. Individuals need leadership to aid in their personal and professional growth, whereas groups need leadership to promote teamwork, cohesion, and attainment of mutually desired goals. Corporations and organizations, including professions, need leadership to assure that activities are continually aligned with collective visions and expectations.

The need for leadership in pharmacy is growing as the profession expands its horizons and takes on more patient-focused responsibilities. The rapid changes within and outside the profession require visionary leaders to help followers cope with and adjust to these changes so as to maintain and grow its professional role within society.

This chapter considers some of the theories of leadership. It is not a comprehensive analysis of the leadership literature, but instead reviews basic leadership theories and describes one model of leadership for the practicing professional.

SELECTED THEORIES OF LEADERSHIP

EARLY LEADERSHIP THEORIES

Leadership studies have varied over time. Research in the early twentieth century attempted to identify the traits that separate leaders from followers. The inherent traits studied include, among others, intelligence, birth order, and socioeconomic status. The learned traits, such as ambition, energy, honesty and integrity, and self-confidence, were also studied. Although many were considered quality attributes of leaders, no single trait or combination of traits fully characterized leaders. This incomplete characterization led to the investigation of other theories attempting to differentiate leaders from followers. Such theories were typically based on the task-relationship approach; that is, they looked at the situation in which the leader and the follower coexisted and then examined the interaction between the two. From this approach, theorists delineated a series of learnable behaviors that leaders exhibit in different situations.

Two of these theories are the situational leadership theory and the contingency theory, in which the organizational environment is considered a major factor in leader effectiveness. The path-goal theory adds another extension to these situational theories—the concept of the leader as a coach and mentor. The concept of situational leadership as developed by Paul Hersey and Kenneth Blanchard helps participants identify their own leadership styles, helps them understand the four preferred styles available to them, and matches leadership styles to the needs of their followers (Bennis and Nanus 1985).

The situational leadership theory suggests that leaders assume a variety of different roles depending on the situations with which they are faced. Situational leadership is based on the premise that followers are at different readiness levels for different tasks they perform. Readiness is defined as the willingness, confidence, and ability to do a particular task. The situational leadership theory espouses four major styles that a leader assumes, depending on the readiness of the followers, both motivationally and functionally, and the resulting needed relationship. Leadership styles vary depending on the relationship the leader has with the follower as well as the complexity of the task. These styles are telling, selling, participating, and delegating. The telling style is best for inexperienced followers requiring direction and encouragement. The selling style is best used for more seasoned individuals requiring a retooling of skills, coupled with some convincing that the new way is better. The participating style is more supportive, providing a higher level of encouragement to complete a task, but the skill set is already present. Last, the delegating style is useful when group members are willing and able to take responsibility for completing the task.

The situational theories, both the situational leadership theory and the contingency theory, involve examining the employee's perception of the complexity of the task, which then leads to the relationship the leader must assume; that is, the relationship between the leader and the employee is contingent on the complexity of the task (Figure 1.1). If the task is highly complex, the leader must assume a higher-level relationship with the employee; if the task has a low level of complexity, the leader should have a low-level relationship with the employee. If the task has a low level of complexity and the leader assumes a high relationship, this mismatch can lead to the employee

FIGURE 1.1   Task complexity and relationship complexity grid: outcome of matches and mismatches of complex and noncomplex situations.

feeling scrutinized or micromanaged. For example, an experienced pharmacist processing a routine prescription would not need her boss to check her work at each step of the process—the complexity of the task (prescription processing) is low and does not require a high-level relationship. In contrast, if an inexperienced pharmacist is given significant responsibility without the manager around to help, this mismatch could leave the pharmacist feeling overwhelmed or swamped. The situational theories stress the complexity of the leader-follower relationship. However, these theories are unable to predict which leadership skills are necessary; they do not help identify what makes a good leader, but only how a good leader should behave.

CURRENT LEADERSHIP RESEARCH

Because situational theories were unable to predict which individuals would be good leaders, theorists revisited the concept of personality traits as determinants of leadership ability. These studies gave rise to the differentiation between leaders and managers and identified organizational vision as a characteristic strongly predicting leadership potential. The results indicate that good leaders have not only a vision of what the organization should be doing, but also facilitate the development of a shared vision among members of the organization.

The research suggests that leaders best accomplish facilitating the shared vision when they value the human resources of their organizations. At least two contemporary theories work with this principle of valuing human resources: the transformational leadership theory and the theory of emotional intelligence.

Transformational Leadership

In the 1970s, the concept of transformational leadership developed. According to this theory, researchers assert that leaders do not exhibit specific behaviors, rather there is a process by which the relationship between the leader and the follower raises both to higher levels of motivation and ethical behavior. Simply put, transformational leadership is a process through which individuals are transformed and changed. This transformation is guided by a desire to seek equality, justice, and fairness within the organization. By striving for these higher values, leaders become appealing to others and therefore develop followings. Transformational leadership goes beyond individual needs by focusing on shared visions and meeting self-actualization needs.

The transformational leadership theory focuses on the need for consensus development among followers and achievement of organizational goals. In this model, the leader must balance the aspirations and goals of the workers with the goals of the organization. This theory of leadership concentrates on the actions and behaviors of the leader in the process of developing individuals and the organization.

Transformational leadership helps build high-quality, highly effective relationships between leaders and followers. To that end, transformational leaders display conviction to mutual goals and emphasize trust. Leaders and followers take a stand on difficult issues by presenting principles and standards relevant to both. The emphasis of the interaction is on the ethical consequences of decisions. Transformational leaders become role models for followers, inculcating pride and confidence around a shared purpose. These leaders facilitate the development of a shared purpose by creating a vision of the future that is attractive to followers. Then, leaders challenge followers to perform better to achieve this shared vision. This challenge is both intellectual and emotional, often coupled with serious questioning of long-standing beliefs and traditions. By challenging these beliefs, transformational leaders encourage the development of new ideas, thus creating commitment and loyalty among workers. At the same time, these leaders treat others as individuals and consider their individual needs, abilities, and aspirations. This approach allows transformational leaders to further employee development through purpose, directed coaching, and advising.

EMOTIONAL INTELLIGENCE AND LEADERSHIP

Daniel Goleman introduced the concept of emotional intelligence (EI). This concept merits some elucidation as it relates to leadership. Goleman and others describe EI as the "emotional needs, drives and true values of a person." EI research is akin to the trait theory of leadership, in which the core elements of successful leaders are identified. Researchers have then taken these traits and identified leadership styles in which these traits are dominant, thus allowing a person to begin using particular traits in particular situations.

Purportedly, EI largely determines the leaders' success in both their careers and relationships with others. Goleman describes EI in four separate domains: self-awareness, self-management, social awareness, and relationship management or social skill. The first two domains are personal. The last two are more externally related, characterized by an appreciation and respect for others through effective and clear communication. Each EI concept and how it relates to leadership styles is detailed in the following.

Self-Awareness

Self-awareness is characterized by recognizing and understanding personal emotions and motivations and how they affect others. This understanding allows leaders to assess accurately their personal strengths and weaknesses as well as their personal value systems. This assessment allows them to know, and be comfortable with, their limitations. Armed with this knowledge, people who are self-aware become more self-confident, and therefore develop strong personal goals for self-improvement.

Self-Management

The next step in the ladder of EI is self-management. Managing emotions, particularly disruptive emotions, is not a natural consequence of self-awareness. Individuals must make a conscious effort to control emotions when presented with a variety of situations. For example, a pharmacist confronted by an irate patient regarding the high cost of a medication needs to control the natural impulse to become defensive and irate as well. Self-management, not allowing disruptive emotions to interfere with professional interactions, creates an environment of trustworthiness and integrity. These are key elements to a successful leadership relationship.

Social Awareness

After being able to identify and control personal emotions, a true leader also has the ability to sense the emotions of others. This skill, empathy, applies not only to the individual but to the organization as well. Understanding the organizational climate is a key political skill that can be learned through proper mentoring and guidance.

Relationship Management or Social Skill

Social skill is the culmination of the other dimensions of EI. It involves building relationships, developing teams and collaborative work relationships, and using communication as a tool for influencing and developing others to become catalysts of change. It is also key for managing conflicts. The following section applies the concepts of EI to various leadership styles.

Whereas many theories help an individual understand how to lead, there remain styles of leadership that a person can adopt to influence the actions and behaviors of others. Many of the theories discussed earlier describe some form of leadership behavior. The work of Goleman in EI provides a nice framework for describing various leadership styles.

EMOTIONAL INTELLIGENCE AND LEADERSHIP STYLES

The four EIs described by Goleman can be important traits for a leader to possess, but they alone are not useful in identifying a good leader. These traits must be

---

TABLE 1.1

Styles of Leadership and Associated EIs

Affiliative

1. Social awareness
2. Social skill

Authoritative

3. Self-awareness
4. Social awareness
5. Social skill

Coaching

6. Self-awareness
7. Social awareness
8. Social skill

Coercive

9. Self-management

Democratic

10. Social skill

Pacesetting

11. Self-management

---

coupled with a repertoire of leader behaviors, or styles. Goleman has developed six styles of leadership that make use of some or all of the EIs previously described. Table 1.1 lists the leadership styles and the primary EIs associated with these styles.

In *Leadership That Gets Results*, Goleman (2000) describes the six leadership styles and provides empirical data showing the correlation between leadership style and overall organizational climate. The data suggest that the authoritative style has the overall most positive effect, with the affiliative, coaching, and democratic styles also positive, with little distinction among these three. Conversely, the coercive and pacesetting styles have, in the long run, a negative impact on organizational culture and climate. Goleman cautions that no particular style should be used exclusively, and each has at least a short-term use. The following descriptions elucidate the strengths and weaknesses of each of the styles.

Affiliative Style

The affiliative style creates harmony and builds emotional bonds. This style primarily uses the external EIs of social awareness and social skill. This people-come-first style works well when teams are dysfunctional or stressed (e.g., because of downsizing). The affiliative style helps create a feeling of belonging and security through feedback and reward systems. This focus on praise and belonging, though, does not help when there is poor individual performance that needs correction. The affiliative leader tends not to deliver bad news to a person, thus not allowing the employee to grow or change bad habits. The affiliative leader who lets employees arrive late to work every day without admonishing them will allow bad habits to continue and create mistrust among other employees. Therefore, the affiliative leader should, at times, employ other styles such as the authoritative or coercive style, depending on the situation.

Authoritative Style

The authoritative style, although sounding "bossy," is one of the most positive styles a leader can employ. It is characterized by the self-awareness, social awareness, and social skill EIs. Individuals using the authoritative style display self-confidence, empathy, and the ability to develop cooperation and teamwork when leading the organization. A leader using this style motivates the team toward a new vision by providing a trusting environment in which individuals know their roles in achieving organizational goals. The authoritative leader develops the end vision while allowing the team to determine how to achieve the vision. This style works well in most situations but fails when the leader is working with experts in a field who already know the vision and how to achieve it. For example, a director of pharmacy in a hospital should not typically employ an authoritative style when leading highly qualified clinical pharmacists (i.e., he or she should not tell the experts what the vision should be, but should instead use another style to help the clinical pharmacists develop their own vision of patient care).

Coaching Style

Similar to the authoritative style, the coaching style uses the EIs of self-awareness, social awareness, and social skill. The focus of the coaching style is to help employees improve performance over the long term. The coach delegates responsibility to subordinates for the dual purpose of achieving outcomes and encouraging employees to develop new skills. The coach knows, though, that the task may not be accomplished quickly or, at least at first, very well. Instead, the coach uses the opportunity to provide feedback and instruction to employees. The obvious issue that exists is the leader's need to accomplish business objectives, the immediate needs versus the employees' needs for growth and development. Balancing these two conflicting priorities takes the skill of social awareness—understanding the organization's climate and needs as well as the employees' needs. The coaching style works well when employees are ready to be coached and have identified areas for improvement. It does not work well when employees are resistant or if the business climate requires immediate results.

Coercive Style

Individuals practicing the coercive style of leadership demand immediate compliance with orders and directives. This style is primarily associated with leaders displaying a strong sense of self-management, but focusing little on others. These leaders may not lack social awareness or skill; they merely do not employ these EIs routinely. When habitually used, the coercive style typically has a negative impact on employee morale and eventually productivity. The do-as-I-say attitude does not allow for employee creativity and therefore employee commitment. This creates an environment of mistrust and disrespect, which erodes the cooperation and teamwork a leader typically needs to further an organization and its people. Because of the negative impact the coercive style has on an organization, it should be employed only sparingly, such as in a crisis situation or when a poorly performing employee is not responding to education and training.

Democratic Style

Democrats are participative consensus developers. They work primarily under the participative management style. Democratic leaders use social skill as the primary means for directing the activities of a group. The democratic style uses collaboration and teamwork to gain buy-in from constituents. Overall, this style has a positive impact on the climate of the organization and should be considered on par with the affiliative style in terms of effectiveness. It can be most effective when the leader is unsure of the best course of action to achieve a vision or when the leader does not have the expertise to evaluate the situation effectively. It too, though, has its drawbacks. Using a consensus-driven approach may lead to endless meetings, delayed decision making, and confusion among employees seeking a direction that the team has not developed.

Pacesetting Style

In contrast to democratic leaders, pacesetters are more autocratic in their leadership style. Pacesetters set high standards of performance for themselves and expect others to have the same high standards. In this case, the pacesetting leader predominantly uses the self-management skill. The pacesetting style works well with highly motivated and competent teams in which there is a strong commitment to the work at hand. This style should be employed sparingly because constant pressure to keep up the pace can drive down morale. When productivity lacks because of depressed morale, pacesetters often step in and micromanage the work, indicating to the employees that they are not capable of performing the job, further eroding morale.

Newly promoted supervisors, typically well-intentioned and capable employees, tend to adopt the pacesetting style. In a short period of time, they attempt to fix every problem they encountered before the promotion. This can be disconcerting for the staff being supervised because the perception may be that the leader has become power hungry.

In summary, the authoritative and coaching styles appear best and should be used as the primary tools for leading groups and individuals. The democratic and affiliative styles are also effective but may present additional challenges when used. Last, the coercive and pacesetting styles may be effective but should be used sparingly because they have an overall negative impact on the culture when employed routinely.

Case Study 1

After graduating from pharmacy school, I joined a regional chain as a pharmacist in a store near my hometown. I had always wanted to go back to my hometown and live with my parents for a few years to save money and pay off my loans. I had three years of experience as an intern with another chain while in pharmacy school, and I felt the new chain offered better career prospects, as they were implementing new medication therapy management (MTM) programs. Knowing that this would give me a lot of experience, besides looking good on my resume, I was quite excited about the new job.

I joined the busy store as the second evening pharmacist, rotating every third weekend into a day shift. I met the manager, Divyish, during the interview, and I was looking forward to working for him. On my first day, I was introduced to my colleagues and was shown around the store by Divyish. My colleagues, both pharmacists and technicians, seemed warm and friendly, and comfortable with their workplace. After about an hour of reviewing policies about attendance, schedule, paychecks, and so on, Divyish partnered me with the pharmacist working the shift, Janice. Janice was busy but took time to show me the ropes as best as she could. I picked up pretty quickly but had lots of questions regarding process and policies. At the end of the day I was tired, but I felt as though I learned something. The next day, it seemed to work similarly, Janice was helpful and I felt a bit more comfortable with the process. Divyish noticed and complimented me by saying "good job—looks like you are getting the hang of this."

The third day, Janice called out sick. Divyish came up to me and told me that I would be working alone that day, but he would be available for questions. The day was rough, being the first time that I was "responsible" for all the prescriptions that went out that day. I did ask lots of questions—most of which Divyish did not seem to mind—but I was looking forward to Janice returning the next day.

Unfortunately, she did not. Apparently, she would be out for about two weeks due to a medical condition. Divyish explained that he had a lot of responsibilities to take care of, but he would be around to help like he was yesterday. I felt uncomfortable, but what could I do?

Divyish was not around much that day, or any of the remaining days during Janice's absence. I felt overwhelmed and began to resent Divyish—why did he not get another experienced pharmacist in to help? Why was he not helping more? Even though I have three years of experience as an intern in another pharmacy, I do not have experience as a pharmacist yet! I said, "They don't pay me enough for this." I soon left that job and found a small independent pharmacy to work at where the owner was there regularly, knew his customers, and cared about his employees.

EXERCISE

1. Identify at least two things you could have done differently and explain why you may not have done them in the first place.
    a. What are the consequences for you if you took each of the actions?
2. Identify where Divyish believes you are in the relationship/task complexity grid. Identify where you think you are in that grid.
    a. Identify at least three assumptions of Divyish when he chose that situational leadership style.
        i. Challenge each of the assumptions with your own rationale.

  b. What type of style (affiliative, authoritative, etc.) does Divyish display in the beginning? Does the style change over time?
3. If you were Divyish's boss, how would you recommend he change his actions the next time a similar situation arises?

LEADING AND MANAGING HEALTH-CARE PROFESSIONALS

DISTINCT QUALITIES WITHIN HEALTH CARE

Health care is distinct from other industries in that it involves the care of human beings. Because human beings are involved, the stakes are appreciably higher, and there is an absolute necessity for a high level of quality in the work performed. Health service organizations are also unique in that a wide range of human resources is deployed in the delivery of the care, from some of the most highly trained and educated professionals and scientists to manual laborers. A high technology base and the coexistence of automated and manual work methods also help distinguish health care from other industries (Longest 1990).

The basic contribution of health professionals is intellectual in nature in that they produce, apply, preserve, and communicate knowledge. The word *profession* literally means to "testify on behalf of" or "stand for something." Health professionals profess their commitment to serving society. Pharmacists not only profess to be experts in medication use therapy but are also committed to helping improve patient quality of life through achieving optimal outcomes in medication therapy. Mrtek and Catizone describe the work of professionals as being public, special, and exclusive (as cited in Buerki and Vottero 1996). The work of professionals is public in nature because they must demonstrate an unselfish concern for, and serve the needs of, others. The functions performed by professionals are special in nature in that they are more complex than what can be observed. For instance, there is much more to filling a prescription than what can be directly observed. Whereas an outsider could observe the acts of entering a prescription and dispensing a medication, the cognitive component of filling the prescription (e.g., screening the prescription and dose for appropriateness, checking for drug–drug, drug–disease, drug–lab, and drug–food interactions) would be indiscernible. The exclusive nature of the functions performed by professionals stems from regulations and authority granted by state and federal agencies (e.g., licensure) that determine who is permitted to practice and under what conditions.

CLASSICAL MANAGEMENT THEORY

How does one integrate and apply an understanding of the characteristics of professionals and the unique needs of health care into the development of effective management techniques for health-care professionals? To answer the question, it is essential to review classical management theory. Simply put, management is a process in which inputs, such as human and physical resources and technology, are transformed under the influence of management into desired outputs (Longest 1990). The five functions that comprise the management process are planning, organizing, directing, coordinating, and controlling. When studying the different functions of the management process, it is helpful to think of each as an independent step. However, the five steps are *not* a series of independent steps, but instead part of a continuous process with each step overlapping the other.

COVERT LEADERSHIP

Although directing and controlling are frequently thought of as critical functions in the management of human resources, the distinguishing characteristics of professionals dictate a slightly refined management approach. For instance, because of their independence and knowledge base, professionals generally require little direction and supervision. Readers are cautioned from interpreting the preceding statement as saying that the supervision of professionals is completely unnecessary. Instead, when managing professionals, the manager must apply what is known from classical management theory and apply a sense of nuances, constraints, and limitations. Henry Mintzberg (1998) uses the term *covert leadership* to describe this concept of managing with a sense of nuances, constraints, and limitations.

Mintzberg (1998) further explains that the art of managing professionals is analogous to the work of an orchestra conductor. He suggests that "the symphony orchestra is like many other professional organizations ... in that it is structured around the work of highly trained individuals who know what they have to do and just do it" (p. 141). Instead of the manager providing the coordination, much of the coordination and structure comes from the profession itself. Because they are secure in what they know and how to do it, professionals, like musicians, do not need empowerment. Instead, they require an infusion of energy to help spark the inspiration necessary to complete the objectives.

Even though the profession provides some coordination and structure, management and leadership of professionals are still necessary. Without them, the system will break down. To continue the analogy of a symphony orchestra, fragmented music could result in the absence of any leadership. How then does a manager engender the support of professionals to help meet the needs of the organization?

IDENTIFYING INFLUENCERS

One skill that managers of professionals need to master to be successful is the ability to identify and enlist the support of the influencers within the group. Influencers are those individuals within an organization or society to whom others turn for counsel or guidance, even though the particular individual is not identified as being in a leadership role. Bassett and Metzger (1986) describe seven strategies to identify influencers:

1. *Identify vocal people to whom others seem to listen.* The second part of this statement is critical. Vocal individuals who are frequently dismissed or ignored are not considered influencers.

2. *Identify persons who seek others out.* These individuals will often be those who greet and welcome new employees or comfort a distressed employee.
3. *Identify persons whom others seek out.* These individuals are those to whom employees turn with questions or issues.
4. *Identify the trendsetters.* People generally tend to imitate those whom they respect.
5. *Identify those who seem to reflect the consensus.* Certain individuals often stand out as representing the opinions and values of those around them.
6. *Identify those who set the work standards.* Certain individuals often set the pace for how the work is performed.
7. *Identify persons with a certain spark or charisma.* Certain individuals often emanate a certain charisma. However, it is important to note that such a spark is not always positive.

Mastering techniques to help enlist the support of influencers is as important as identifying influencers. Bassett and Metzger (1986) describe four strategies that can be used to engender the support of influencers:

1. *Ask influencers for advice or opinion.* Generally, people find it very flattering when someone in authority asks for their advice or opinion, yet it is important that advice should be sought from influencers only if there is a chance that the advice will be followed. Sometimes it may be safer to seek an opinion on a potential course of action because the obligation to follow what is suggested is somewhat mitigated.
2. *Give or share responsibility.* Because there are risks associated with giving or sharing responsibility, it is important not to ask for help on matters for which failure or error is unacceptable.
3. *Keep influencers in on things.* Keeping individuals in the loop about what is going on and what is being planned is critical in helping individuals respond to stress and anxiety. When people know what is going on, they generally develop an improved outlook and favorable feelings toward those who give them the information.
4. *Match motive and reward.* One of the motivational factors for influencers is a need to be acknowledged as leaders. When influencers are recognized and respected as leaders, they are more likely to provide additional support to meet the overall objectives and goals.

Motivating Professionals

The concept of motivation is a key determinant in influencing human behavior. At its core, motivation theory revolves around needs, actions, and goals. According to Bassett and Metzger (1986):

When you have a need (a wish, a desire, a want, a life requirement), it moves you into action. You stay in action, in one form or another, seeking to reach a goal that will satisfy the need. Yet action ceases when the need is satisfied, and no action takes place until the need surfaces.

Because what another person specifically needs or wants is rarely known, applying this theory is difficult.

Understanding what motivates people and applying that knowledge can facilitate the development and maintenance of a strong and loyal workforce. What people want from their work has changed remarkably little through the years. Surveys reveal that employees desire appreciation for the work done, a feeling of being in on things, interesting work, and job security. Interestingly, good wages was not the highest ranked factor for employees, but instead ranked fifth (Bassett and Metzger 1986).

A challenging job is a key motivator, especially among professionals, because it allows for a feeling of achievement, growth, responsibility, advancement, enjoyment of the work itself, and earned recognition (Longest, 1990).

REWARDS AND REINFORCEMENT

In 1911, Edward L. Thorndike proposed the first major theoretical treatment given to the concept of rewards and reinforcement. His law of effect states that behavior that is followed by satisfaction (reward) is more likely to recur, and behavior that is followed by discomfort (punishment) is less likely to recur. Rewards or reinforcements "are external to individuals in that they are environmental events that follow behavior" (Muldary 1983, p. 155). Reinforcement is therefore different from motivation in that the latter is considered an internal phenomenon. Positive reinforcement involves the presentation of something pleasant, whereas negative reinforcement involves the termination or removal of something unpleasant. Both positive and negative reinforcements serve to increase the probability that a given behavior will recur (Muldary 1983). Managers should attempt to create situations where their employees are influenced more by positive reinforcement than by negative reinforcement.

To help satisfy employees' key needs for recognition and for feeling important, it is critical that managers acknowledge employee accomplishments. Recognition of accomplishments helps employees believe that they are accepted and approved by the institution and by their managers. It also shows them that they are doing useful work, and it tells them that their managers understand and appreciate their contributions (Bassett and Metzger 1986).

In addition to recognition and praise, employees can be rewarded through a variety of tokens including raises, promotions, bonuses, vacations, flexible scheduling, privileges, continuing education, training, equipment, and supplies. The opportunity to improve their skills through formal training and continuing education can be a powerful token for professionals (Muldary 1983).

In granting reinforcements and rewards, managers need to be cognizant of several points. First, reinforcements and rewards need to be granted consistently and applied systematically. However, this should not be interpreted as saying that all individuals should be rewarded the same. In fact, rewarding all people the same tends to encourage mediocrity because high performers perceive that the organization does not value their extra efforts. Inaction by managers can also serve as a reinforcer. Therefore, if rewards are withheld for any reason, managers need to explain why. Continuous reinforcement is usually suboptimal because if the reinforcer is ever removed, the behavior is likely to cease quickly. As a result, the use of different schedules of reinforcement is a highly efficient way of enhancing the quality of work life and facilitating greater job satisfaction (Muldary 1983).

The Importance of Communication

Communication can be a key determinant in an organization's ability to achieve its objectives. Unless a manager can effectively communicate what, how, by whom, and when a task or job is to be done, the likelihood of the objective being completed as desired is diminished (Longest 1990). The process is complicated because each communication involves at least six messages: what one means to say, what one actually says, what other people hear, what other people think they hear, what other people say, and what one thinks other people say (Bassett and Metzger 1986). Distortion in any of the six messages can impair the communication process.

Willard and Merrihue describe four principles that managers can use to ensure effective communication with their employees (as cited in Basset and Metzger 1986). First, managers should seek to gain the confidence of their employees by being impartial and consistent, fulfilling commitments, addressing and answering any problems or concerns, representing employees' interests to others within the organization, and making it clear that the institution has an effective grievance process. Second, managers should seek to gain the respect of their employees by showing sincere interest in issues that are important to the employees, being considerate and helpful, and displaying enthusiasm about their progress. Third, there should be good upward and downward communication between managers and employees. Listening, talking, and selling skills must be developed and cultivated. Last, because half of communication is active listening, it is important to listen carefully to achieve a full understanding of the information received, take action quickly based on this understanding, and communicate the results of such action. It has been said that the better the manager listens, the more the manager will inspire.

WHEN PROFESSIONALS BECOME MANAGERS

Very few people begin their careers as managers. Usually, a person is offered a management position because of past performance in some specialty or functional area. However, past success in one area does not guarantee that the person will be an effective manager. The Peter Principle states that "in a hierarchy, every person tends to rise to his [sic] level of incompetence" (McConnell 1997, p. 40). Laurence Peter, for whom the Peter Principle was named, recognized that good performers within a functional or specialty area tend to be singled out for promotions. He posited that "the outstanding worker at any level is likely to be promoted to the next level in the hierarchy. This process may continue until the individual reaches a level where performance is mediocre at best" (McConnell, p. 40). Although Peter paints a rather grim picture; the situation for newly promoted managers is not as bleak as one might think. After all, management is an art, and for the most part, "the art of management is learned on the job" (Longest 1990, p. 35).

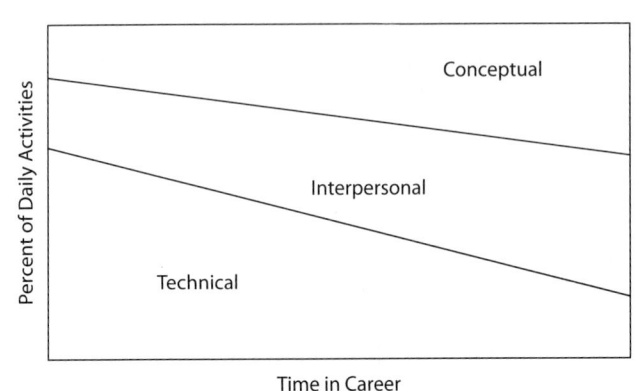

FIGURE 1.2   Relative application of management skills over time.

To be effective in the practice of management, new managers need to optimize their skills within three broad domains, identified by Katz as technical, human, and conceptual. Technical skill includes the ability to use the methods, techniques, and processes of a particular field. Human skill involves "the ability to get along with other people, to understand them, and to motivate and lead them in the workplace" (as cited in Longest 1990, p. 37). Conceptual skill involves the ability to visualize the factors and various interdependencies within a situation and an organization. Conceptual skill allows the manager to understand the various issues within a situation, how they fit together, and how they interact with one another. The relative use of these skills changes over time along with the position one holds (Figure 1.2).

THE MANAGER'S ROLE

Individuals must learn how to recognize and control the stresses of their work, monitor their responses to these stressors, and adapt their behaviors accordingly (Muldary 1983). Even though individuals are ultimately responsible for coping with burnout, managers must also play active roles and recognize their own influences as potential sources of stress for staff.

Availability and accessibility are critical so that staff members feel that they can approach their managers with problems. When approached with employee problems, managers need to exercise different skills. Listening is perhaps the most important strategy that a manager can use to address an employee's problems. When a staff member's problem is related to conditions within the organization, the manager must take an advocacy role on behalf of the employee. Being an advocate demonstrates a powerful message of support and respect for staff.

Confrontation is another technique that managers can use when employees need to see the role that they play in creating some of their own problems. Sometimes managers may need to impart information that challenges underlying assumptions of employees. Suggestions and guidance can also be given in response to employee problems; however, advice should be doled out with caution. According to Muldary (1983, p. 154), managers should answer the following questions before giving advice: "What will be the consequences of providing bad advice? What will be the consequences of giving good advice? Will the individual become dependent on the [manager] for solutions? Does the [manager] know enough about the person, the problem, and the solution to give advice? Is giving advice the only recourse?"

In addition to being accessible and available, managers can help combat burnout by granting time off from work. However, this strategy can be difficult to execute at times because of the characteristic stereotypes of certain healthcare professionals. For instance, one of the characteristics of compulsive personalities is that "leisure does not come easily … because it must be worked for and planned … [Moreover,] the compulsive person does not tolerate 'doing nothing,' so even during times away from work, the person works. In many cases, the individual will often postpone vacations and leisure activities" (Muldary 1983, p. 106). Effective managers need to be vigilant about this tendency and intervene when necessary to ensure that their employees have adequate time off from work.

CONCLUSION

The literature reveals that effective leadership in an organization is critical. Early examinations of leaders reported differences between leaders and followers. The early trait theories failed to predict accurately the inherent qualities of a leader. Subsequent leadership studies differentiated effective leader behaviors from noneffective leader behaviors. As such, leadership was recognized as a complex interaction among the leader, the follower, and the surrounding situation. More recent studies assert that a shared vision and collaboration with followers are important characteristics of effective leaders.

The concept of transformation leadership and the EI theory allow one to see how the behavior of the leader affects the behavior of the follower. Valuing the human aspect of the follower—that is, identifying with and appreciating the emotional and professional needs of the follower—is a key aspect of an effective leader. The transformational theory of leadership espouses a moral and ethical balance to leadership, whereas the EI theory supports the recognition of the emotional connection between the follower and the leader. According to the EI theory, there are at least six different styles of leadership, with the authoritative style typically the most effective when consistently applied. However, the coaching and affiliative styles of leadership are also effective. The pacesetting and coercive styles are effective only when used sparingly and in specific situations.

Although this chapter has discussed both theory and practical applications, there is no simple strategy for managing professionals. The management of professionals seems to follow the contingency theory of management, which states that what works best for one group in one setting may not work for another group in another setting. Part of the art of management is to use whatever methods work to draw out the strengths of those who are managed and to direct them toward achieving objectives (Longest 1990).

BIBLIOGRAPHY

Abramowitz PW. Nurturing relationships: an essential ingredient of leadership. *Am. J. Hlth.-Syst. Pharm.* 2001; 58: 479–484.

Bass B, From transactional to transformational leadership: learning to share the vision, *Organ. Dynam.* Winter 1990.

Bassett LC, Metzger N. *Achieving Excellence: A Prescription for Health Care Managers.* Aspen, Rockville, MD, 1986.

Benderev KP. The emerging leader. *Top. Hosp. Pharm. Manage.* 1986; 6: 41–45.

Bennis WG, Nanus B. Leaders: the strategies for taking charge. Harper & Row, New York, 1985.

Bolman L, Deal T. *Reframing Organizations.* Jossey-Bass, San Francisco, 1991.

Buerki RA, Vottero LD. The purposes of professions in society. In: *Pharmaceutical Care.* Chapman & Hall, New York. 1996, chap. 1.

Chalmers RK, Adler DS, Haddad AM, Hoffman S, Johnson JA, Woodward JMB. The essential linkage of professional socialization and pharmaceutical care. *Am. J. Pharm. Educ.* 1995; 59: 85–90.

Code of Ethics for Pharmacists. American Pharmaceutical Association. www.aphanet.org/pharmcare/ethics.html (accessed June 14, 2003). Goleman D. Leadership that gets results. *Harv. Bus. Rev.* March/April 2000, 78–90.

Goleman D. What makes a leader? *Harv. Bus. Rev.* November/December 1998, 93–102.

Heffler S, Smith S, Keehan S, Clemens MK, Won G, Zezza M. Health spending projections for 2002–2012. *Hlth. Aff.* 2003; 21: 207–218.

Kouzes JM, Posner BZ. *The Leadership Challenge.* Jossey-Bass, San Francisco, 1987.

Longest BB. *Management Practices for the Health Professional*, 4th ed. Appleton-Lange, Norwalk, CT, 1990.

McConnell CR. *The Effective Health Care Supervisor*, 4th ed. Aspen, Gaithersburg, MD, 1997.

Mintzberg H. Covert leadership: notes on managing professionals. *Harv. Bus. Rev.* 1998; 76(6): 140–147.

Muldary TW. *Burnout and Health Professionals: Manifestations and Management.* Appleton-Century-Crofts, Norwalk, CT, 1983.

Northouse PG. *Leadership: Theory and Practice.* Sage Publications. Los Angeles, CA 2013

Simmons S, Sommons JC. *Measuring Emotional Intelligence: The Groundbreaking Guide to Applying the Principles of Emotional Intelligence.* Summit, Arlington, TX, 1997.

Starr P. *The Social Transformation of American Medicine: The Rise of a Sovereign Profession and the Making of a Vast Industry.* Basic Books, New York, 1982.

Tannenbaum R, Schmidt WH. How to choose a leadership pattern. *Harv. Bus. Rev.* 1973; 51(3): 162–172.

Case Study 2*

You are the assistant director of pharmacy at a 750-bed hospital, where more than 5 million doses of medications are dispensed per year from the central pharmacy. The hospital pharmacy employs more than 50 full-time pharmacists and 50 technicians. It was recently decided that the hospital pharmacy convert to a bar code–assisted medication dispensing process. This pharmacy initiative

---

* This case was based on a published case by Nanji and colleagues (Nanji KC, Cina J, Patel N, Churchill W, Gandhi TK, Poon EG. Overcoming barriers to the implementation of a pharmacy bar code scanning system for medication dispensing: a case study. *J Am Med Inform Assoc.* 2009 Sep-Oct; 16(5): 645–650). The case can be seen at http://www.ncbi.nlm.nih.gov/pmc/articles/PMC2744715/

occurred as part of the implementation of a bar code scanning system at the bedside, and the project was a major joint initiative between the pharmacy and the nursing staff.

You are charged with directing the pharmacists during the implementation. You are walking into the meeting now at which you will be announcing to the staff that this system will be implemented during the next year. Recognizing that the last major technological implementation—a robotic dispensing system—did not go well, you are concerned that you will get resistance from the pharmacists. Read through the following actions and (1) decide which type of leadership style it represents and (2) decide which you would take and why.

SCENARIO 1

"All—thank you for coming here today. I have some news for us. Some of you will consider this good news and others will not, but here goes. Within the next year, we will be implementing a bar code system to further automate the medication dispensing process. I know this is change and none of us have real expertise with barcode systems, but if we implement this well, and I know we can, systems such as these have decreased medication errors, both in the pharmacy and the nursing side, by as much as 50%. I know we don't have a lot of medication errors to begin with, but any reduction in medication errors is a good reduction. Within the year, I see the technicians doing things very differently and freeing up time so that they can take on some of the pharmacists' tasks. To that end, I see the pharmacists having more time to interact with the nursing and medical staffs, as well as the patients. However, I also see some challenges—these workflow changes will result in an increased need for communication, teamwork and mutual support. Each of us will have a role and a responsibility. I will be working with you, our director, and the technicians to develop a workflow and schedule for us to follow so that we can all work together on this."

SCENARIO 2

"All—thank you for coming here today. I have some news for us. Some of you will consider this good news and others will not, but here goes. Within the next year, we will be implementing a bar code system to further automate the medication dispensing process. I know we have had trouble with implementing new systems in the past, but this is for better patient care, which is why we are here. I am seeking your cooperation and support for this. I am looking for a team of volunteers to help develop the work plans for implementing this process during the next year. The team will have to address the inevitable challenges these workflow changes will create—an increased need for communication, teamwork, and mutual support."

2 Understanding and Working in the Organization

Andrew M. Peterson and David A. Ehlert

CONTENTS

Learning Objectives: After reading this chapter and working through the case, the reader will be able to:

1. Demonstrate knowledge of organizational structure
2. Discuss how high-performing organizations work
3. Name the titles of the top seven positions in a hospital or corporation
4. Articulate the importance of demonstrating leadership ability to the C-suite
5. Discuss five ways the pharmacy leadership of an organization can be successful with the C-suite
6. Provide three ways to be successful with others' organizational leaders
7. Compare and contrast what can happen when there is effective and poor communication within a pharmacy department

INTRODUCTION

Organizations come in a variety of shapes and sizes. Many are organized according to specialty, others by matter of convenience. The manner in which organizations are put together clearly affects how they function. There are several theories on which companies are organized, and this chapter reviews some of these theories and focuses on applications of them in professional pharmacy practice.

An organization is a group of individuals structured to work together to achieve common goals. The organizing function is designed to make the best use, in terms of efficiency and effectiveness, of the organization's resources to achieve these common goals. The organizational structure is the framework in which people are assigned jobs and responsibilities. The formal organizational structure is usually depicted by an organizational chart (Figure 2.1) that displays the job titles and corresponding departments of the people within the organization. Through this graphical depiction, one can readily see the relationships and lines of authority among people and departments.

CLASSICAL ORGANIZATIONAL THEORY

The classical organization, the bureaucracy, was first described by Max Weber in the early 1900s. Several concepts underlying the bureaucracy are specialization of labor, departmentalization, unity of command, and chain of command. These concepts, originally developed by Weber and further expanded by Henri Fayol, are based on the scientific method of analyzing processes and procedures to provide the most efficient and effective means of organizing individuals for maximum productivity. There are 14 points of organization and management outlined (Table 2.1). The salient points for our discussion are *specialization of labor, unity of command,* and *scalar chain (of command).*

SPECIALIZATION OF LABOR AND DEPARTMENTALIZATION

Specialization of labor, the placement of individuals into categories based on job functions, leads to increased productivity. This increased productivity is seen by (1) an improvement in a worker's ability to do a task, resulting from a worker's concentration

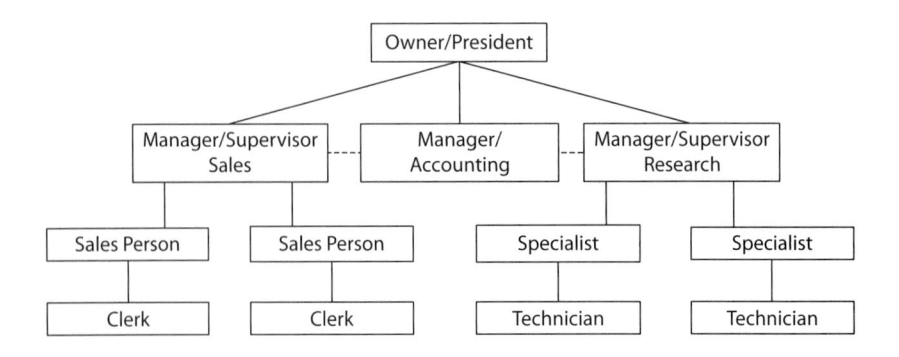

FIGURE 2.1 A typical organizational chart.

TABLE 2.1

Fayol's Principles of Management

Authority	The right to direct and control actions of employees
Centralization	A single, central source for decision making; decisions are made from the top
Discipline	When actions are governed by a strict set of rules and compliance is mandatory
Equity	Fairness to all; does not imply equal treatment, only fair treatment
Esprit de corps	Camaraderie; enthusiasm for a common goal
Initiative	Taking on work without prompting
Order	When each person has responsibilities and proceeds in a usual and customary manner to carry out work activities
Personnel tenure	Dedication to the job and workers; mutual desire to stay and work at the company; longevity
Remuneration	Fair pay for work completed
Scalar chain (line of authority)	Formal chain of command
Specialization of labor	When workers are organized according to specialty in work function to improve productivity
Subordination of individual interests	When workers are to focus on work
Unity of command	When each employee has one and only one boss
Unity of direction	Relates to centralization, when orders come from the top and subordinates are to follow

Source: Adapted from Rodrigues CA, *Management Decision* 39:10;880–889, 2001. With permission.

on one or a few tasks; (2) time saving due to minimized need for physical relocation or from adapting, or orienting, a worker to the new task; and (3) concentration on one or a few tasks increasing the likelihood of discovering easier and better methods.

Within pharmacy, there is often a specialization of labor. Specialization works not only with employees but departments as well. In pharmacy, this is seen on a large scale because there are pharmacists specializing in hospital pharmacy work and those specializing in community practice, with the subspecialization of independent versus chain stores, and even long-term-care or managed-care pharmacy. Even within a given setting, pharmacists are divided based on their specialties. In hospitals, there are unit-dose pharmacists and IV pharmacists. The IV pharmacists can be further divided into chemotherapeutic and nonchemotherapeutic.

Managers have the responsibility of coordinating the efforts of each division or department to produce a comprehensive work product. Weber's model suggests that such specialization is necessary and that the specific boundaries separating one department or division from another must be guided by rules, regulations, and procedures.

Unity of Command and Scalar Chain

It is evident that coordinating the departments of large organizations requires clear lines of authority arranged in a hierarchy. This means that all employees in the organization must know who their boss is, and all persons should always respect their boss (i.e., a chain of command). Further, there should be only one boss (i.e., unity of command). This means that only one person should be able to give orders to subordinates, and people should receive orders only through their own immediate supervisors. In this way, everyone knows where the responsibilities lie, and there is assurance that orders are carried out by the best person possible. The concepts of command and power form the basis for organizational design and function. The following section will discuss power and authority more in depth.

POWER AND AUTHORITY

Before considering specific relationships presented by an organizational design, a basis is required on which to discuss power and authority.

Sources and Types of Power

The literature is replete with definitions of power. Max Weber defined power as "the possibility of imposing one's will upon the behavior of others" (as cited in Fuqua et al. 2003). It has also been suggested that "power is the ability to obtain compliance [or cooperation] by means of coercion, to have one's own will carried out despite resistance" (Liebler and McConnell 1999).

Within the context of organizations, Cangemi asserted that "power is the individual's capacity to move others, to entice others, to persuade and encourage others to attain specific goals or to engage in specific behavior; it is the capacity to influence and motivate others" (as cited in Fuqua et al. 2003). Cangemi believed that successful leaders move and influence people through their power toward greater accomplishments for themselves and their organizations. Power allows organizations to function efficiently and effectively.

French and Raven classified five types of power: reward, coercive, legitimate, expert, and referent (as cited in Fuqua et al. 2003). Reward power is based on a willingness and ability to reward. Those having the ability to deliver jobs, money, or anything else that people seek will derive power. Coercive power, on the other hand, depends on the ability to administer punishment or give negative reinforcements. Legitimate power is inherent in the position and its function—hiring and firing, giving raises or discipline is up to the boss—s/he has the legitimate power over the group. Expert power is based on expertise, information, and special knowledge in a given area. Part of the power of pharmacists originates in society's dependence on them for their knowledge and competency as medication use experts. Referent or charismatic power occurs when people try to emulate an individual or when they show great admiration for that person.

Legitimate, reward, and coercive powers are powers of position, or formal power. Expert and charismatic powers are considered informal or personal powers, derived from personal interactions and not by virtue of position (Table 2.2).

Formal Power

Legitimate power is power based on one's position. It is a formal power, bestowed on a person through appointment, selection, or election. Legitimate power allows

TABLE 2.2
Formal versus Informal Power

Position (Formal) Power	Personal (Informal) Power
Legitimate	Expert
Reward	Charismatic (referent)
Coercive	

superiors to hire or fire a person, dictate job responsibilities, and control the work of an individual by virtue of their position. In an organization, the boss has legitimate power.

Reward and coercive power are related. Reward power is based on the distribution of rewards. It involves compensating the recipient with something of value in return for work or favorable stance on an issue. For example, a manager of a pharmacy may reward a worker with a bonus for good performance. The person giving the reward holds the power, provided that the reward is of value to the recipient. Typically, managers give rewards to employees in the form of bonuses, raises, increased vacation times, and special recognitions. If the reward is of no, or little, value in relationship to the job requested, there might be no power. Conversely, coercive power involves withholding something of value, or distributing punishments, until an action or a behavior is displayed. For example, an employee reprimanded for persistent tardiness would be experiencing a form of coercive power.

Informal Power

Expert power is power derived from a person's knowledge or expertise in a given area. Pharmacists have expert power related to drugs, particularly drug–drug interactions and adverse events. Pharmacists exercise this type of power when they call a physician to request a change in drug therapy because of a life-threatening drug–drug interaction. The pharmacist, however, must use good interpersonal skills, or charismatic power, to get the message across effectively.

Managing with Power

Bennis and Nanus note that one of the major problems facing organizations at present is that individuals are reluctant to exercise power: "These days power is conspicuous by absence." Without power, leaders are unable to lead. After all, "power is the basic energy needed to initiate and sustain action," or, put another way, "the capacity to translate intention into reality and sustain it" (Bennis, cited in Pfeffer 1992, p. 13).

Despite the fact that more time is spent living with the consequences of decisions, many organizations spend an inordinate amount of time and energy in the decision-making process. Rather than getting unnecessarily bogged down in this process ("paralysis by analysis"), organizations must ensure that sufficient time is given to implementing decisions and dealing with their ramifications. As Pfeffer explains, "The important actions may not be the original choices, but rather what happens subsequently, and what actions are taken to make things work out" (p. 40).

Various strategies have been attempted to counteract this powerlessness phenomenon present in health-care organizations. Health-care literature is replete with efforts to empower the frontline health-care practitioner. Empowerment is the sharing of power with those who actually do the work. For example, much has been written on the topic of shared governance within the nursing literature. There also has been recent discussion of shared governance within the profession of pharmacy.

To increase organizational power, successful leaders must develop their own personal power and be effective implementers. Power and influence are the tools required to get things done. The following strategies should be considered in managing with power:

- *Manage through a shared vision or organizational culture.* Such a practice will minimize the effects of hierarchical authority. Moreover, it will help engender a team spirit.
- *Identify the various interests within the organization.* Determine the points of view of the various individuals identified. According to Pfeffer (1992), "The real secret of success in organizations is the ability to get those who differ from us, and whom we don't necessarily like, to do what needs to be done" (p. 46).
- *Enlist the cooperation and support of others outside the chain of command.* Remember that formal authority is not an absolute requirement for a leader to wield power and influence.
- *Understand where power comes from* and how these sources of power can be developed and utilized within organizations. Recognize that politics is involved in innovation and change.

Line and Staff Authority

The bureaucratic model has led to the traditional use of lines and boxes in an organizational chart. Within the organizational chart, the reporting relationships are depicted by solid or dotted lines. The solid lines, referred to as line authority, indicate the direct authority a superior has over a subordinate. Persons with line authority over a subordinate have the ability to use all forms of power (i.e., legitimate, reward, and coercive power). The manager in this position has the ability to hire and fire a direct report, give raises to the person, or reprimand the person. In contrast, staff authority is advisory to line authority. For example, an accountant who prepares reports for the district manager has staff authority over the pharmacists within that district but can only make recommendations to the district manager regarding actions. The accountant cannot hire or fire a pharmacist because of poor financial performance. Staff authority is usually depicted on an organizational chart as a dotted line (see Figure 2.1).

Focus of much of the classical organizational theory is on output and productivity—refining the process to be the most efficient means of producing a product. Although this was attractive to most managers, many employees felt disenfranchised with the process. Often, considerations of the employee were not taken into account. From this recognition of the human factor arose some of the modern organizational theories.

MODERN ORGANIZATIONAL THEORIES

Modern organizational theories take on a more behavioral management flavor—managing people instead of processes. In this vein, Douglas McGregor developed, in *The Human Side of Enterprise*, his dual theories of management: Theory X and Theory Y. The underlying messages in these theories are that managers maintain certain beliefs about their employees, and these beliefs affect how the managers deal with employees. Consequently, employees react to managers, at times, in manners that bring about self-fulfilling prophecies; that is, employees become what managers think they are.

Theories X, Y, and Z

Theory X states that people inherently dislike work and need to be coerced into performing a duty. Further, the theory indicates that people attempt to avoid responsibility and have relatively little ambition. They wait to be told what tasks to perform and have little or no control of or direction in their work lives. Overall, employees seek money and job security only. Theory X is considered a strict authoritarian style of management.

McGregor recognized that Theory X works best in some situations. Those cases include repetitive tasks in which a high volume of output is required. Further, where following orders is important to the well-being of the organization, Theory X management style is important. Often seen as the prototype, the US military is a Theory X organization. The soldiers are required to follow their superiors' orders without question.

Conversely, Theory Y states that people want to exercise self-direction and control and seek to expand their spheres of influence and accept additional responsibility. People operating under the influence of this theory tend to see job commitment as a function of rewards rather than merely of job security.

If Theory Y holds, an organization can take advantage of the motivation of its employees. By delegating authority and power, decreasing the number of levels of management, each manager will have a greater span of control and be more productive. A participative management style that involves employees in the decision-making process will also tap their creativity and provide them with more control over their work environment. Through this, employees have a greater sense of job enlargement, where the broader scope of job responsibilities adds variety and opportunities to satisfy ego needs. If properly implemented, such an environment would result in a high level of motivation and enhance employee productivity and satisfaction.

In 1981, William Ouchi developed a related motivational theory labeled Theory Z (Ouchi 1981). This theory is similar to Theories X and Y but emphasizes more the attitudes and behaviors of the worker than the manager. The theory places a large amount of trust and responsibility with the worker; that is, responsibility for success or failure is shared between employees and management, and not only management. In many Japanese companies, employees are guaranteed a position for life, which ideally increases their loyalty to the company. Further, Japanese companies tend to take a greater interest in their employees' lives outside work. Companies operating under

Theory Z tend to have more stable employment, taking care of the job security issue, and managers who tend to care about their employees, satisfying Theory Y needs.

In conclusion, Theories X and Y both work, but in different ways. On the proper occasions, Theory X can produce better short-term results. However, if people are subjected to Theory X management style consistently, it could lead to disharmony and dissatisfaction, which is counterproductive in the long term. To maintain a healthy, viable organization, managers need to keep people happy and motivated.

Using these theories about human functioning in work environments and the concepts of power and authority addressed basically, we can now explore a few organizational designs that have arisen in the past century.

ORGANIZATION DESIGNS

One of the first steps in designing an organization is to determine which jobs belong in which department. This process, called *job classification*, allows one to determine the similarities and differences and allows jobs to be organized into larger segments, such as departments. Creating these departments allows for individuals to be grouped into manageable units. There are at least four methods to group work activities:

1. *Departmentalization by function* organizes jobs by the functions to be performed. For example, in a hospital, the department of pharmacy is created to maintain all medication-related functions for the hospital. This form of departmentalization allows the organization to gain efficiencies from combining people with similar skills, knowledge, and purposes together in common units. Figure 2.2 shows a typical hospital organizational chart, grouping workers together by function.
2. *Departmentalization by product* organizes all functions needed to make and market a particular product under one person. For example, in the pharmaceutical industry, the brand manager for a product is in charge of the marketing, research, and development functions related to the product. This allows for a coordinated and directed effort in the sales and development of the brand. Further classifications also exist, in which the company may have several cardiovascular products and may have several brand managers within the cardiovascular group.
3. *Departmentalization by geographical regions* groups jobs on the basis of territory or geography. For example, a pharmaceutical company may have its sales force organized regionally, into the northeast, southeast, midwest, southwest, and northwest. This creates jobs such as regional manager for cardiovascular products (Figure 2.3).
4. *Departmentalization by customer groups* jobs on the basis of type of customer. In pharmacy, home-care or long-term-care patients represent this type of departmentalization. Within this customer segment, the trend is to use cross-functional teams, which allow various group members chosen from different functions to work together to interdependently provide a service. Home-care organizations usually have pharmacists, nurses, pharmacy technicians, medical assistants, and others to provide the patient with the needed care.

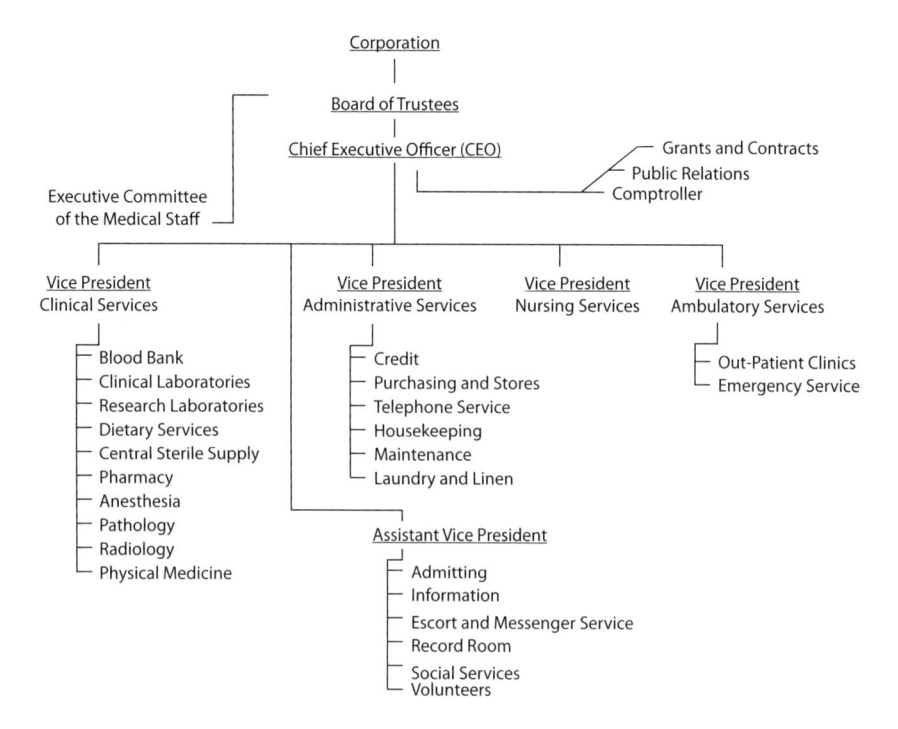

FIGURE 2.2 Example of a hospital organizational chart.

Structure Types

Organizations can be rigid, with significant structure and formality, or they can be loose, with little to no formal structure. The mechanistic organization, inherently a rigid organization, is the traditional and probably the most common structure used in medium- to large-size organizations. Mechanistic organizations have many rules and procedures, well-defined tasks, and a clear hierarchy of authority. The prototypical mechanistic organization is the bureaucracy. In mechanistic organizations, there are often multiple levels within the hierarchy, creating a "tall" organizational structure. The benefits of this type of organization are clear delineation of tasks, centralized

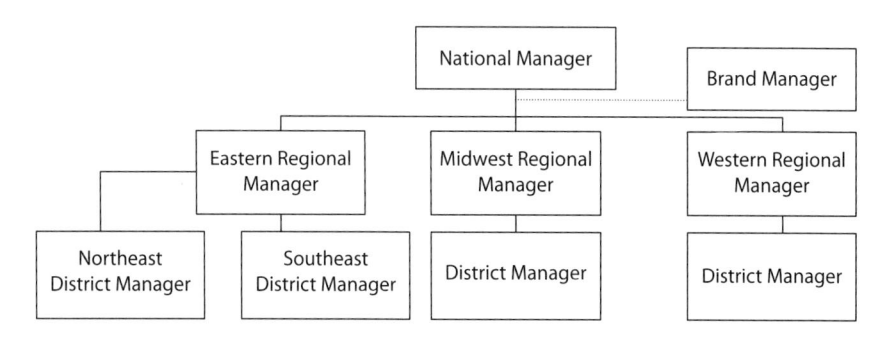

FIGURE 2.3 Example of a geographical organizational chart.

decision making, and potential for a career ladder by which employees can progress and be promoted. Further, the specialization of labor and the functional control over the output by managers typically results in consistent productivity—up to a point. The multiple layers seen in bureaucracies, coupled with centralized decision making, make this model slow to adapt to change. This fact, coupled with the many rules and regulations associated with these organizations, creates employees who are often disillusioned by the lack of timely response and the lack of independent decision-making capability. This mentality then perpetuates Theory X characteristics. In response, managers moving up the ladder continue this Theory X mentality and further perpetuate negative aspects of this style of management.

Another form of mechanistic organization is the matrix organization. A matrix organization has a dual authority system. Employees are organized along both functional (project) and departmental lines (Figure 2.4). As such, employees report to two or more managers. Project managers have authority over activities geared toward achieving organizational goals, whereas departmental managers have authority over promotion decisions and performance reviews.

Matrix structures were developed from the aerospace industry in an effort to take advantage of employee skills when solving a difficult problem or developing a new product. This structure assigns specialists from different functional departments to work on one or more projects led by project managers. However, the matrix organization violates the unity of command principle of bureaucracies, thereby potentially creating communication and decision-making conflicts as well as confusion in employee evaluation and accountability. Matrix structures may not work well as long-term strategies.

In contrast to mechanistic structures, organic structures are more flexible and more adaptable. Organic organizations use participative management as a style and are often less concerned with a clearly defined structure. Organic organizations are typically flat, with only one or two levels of management. Flat organizations emphasize a decentralized approach to decision making and encourage employee involvement in decisions. These types of organizations work well when there is a need for quick decision making and change due to the environment. In these organizations,

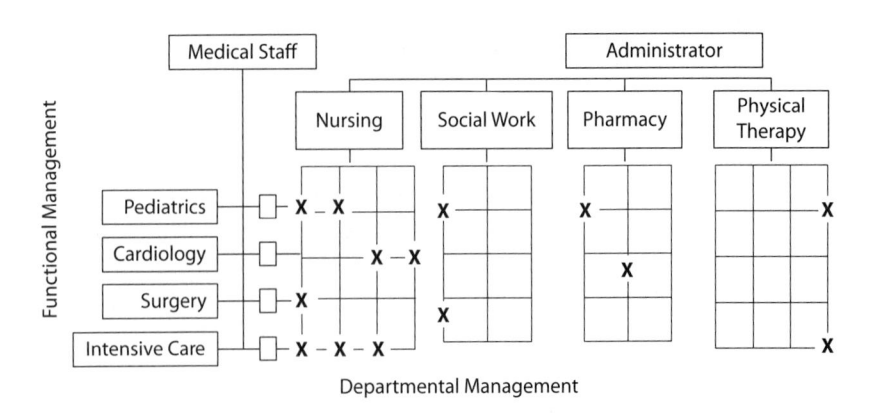

FIGURE 2.4   The hospital as a matrix organization.

the manager must maintain a more personal relationship, thereby adopting Theory Y characteristics, to allow for the development of trust and respect.

Professionals often work within an organic-type setting. Consider, for example, the medical team on rounds at a hospital. Typically led by a physician, multiple professions are represented on the team—medicine, nursing, pharmacy, social work, respiratory therapy, and others. In some ways, this represents a bureaucracy; that is, the physician is in charge, with staff authority over the other professionals. However, the team differs from bureaucracy in that as the team sees patients on "rounds" throughout the hospital, decisions are made regarding the care of patients. This decentralized decision making, standardized more by the professionals themselves than by policy and procedures, allows for more flexibility and adaptability in the decision making when needed. In addition, even though these decisions are often costly, none of the professionals ask their bosses for permission. This professional bureaucracy is a means of allowing professionals discriminatory decision-making power yet allowing the manager to maintain some semblance of control.

In professional bureaucracies, the patient is the central focus. All members of the organization, or team, have a primary goal in mind—for health-care professionals this is improvement in the health and well-being of the patient. As such, health-care professionals and not the managers develop the standards by which the patient is cared for. However, one of the drawbacks to this model is the potential for conflict among the professionals themselves, because many of the professionals will exercise expert or charismatic power, and (most likely) the physician has primary legitimate power.

THE C-SUITE

The C-suite, a term derived from the initial notion that all chiefs (chief executive officer, chief operations officer, etc.) were all housed in the same office suite, now refers to a group of individuals at the top of the organization who make key decisions regarding business strategy and organizational vision. The members of the C-suite in each organization differ, but there are some common C-suite members that need to be discussed. See Table 2.3 for a list of common C-suite titles and a brief description of their roles.

In hospital and health systems, the C-suite is likely to contain the chief medical officer (a.k.a., chief of staff) and the chief nursing officer (director of nursing). As one can see, the C-suite oversees the organization from a variety of aspects—personnel, financial, strategic, clinical, and even legal.

The pharmacist, and more importantly the director of pharmacy, must be aware of the C-suite executives' priorities and be sure to position the department such that it is viewed as an essential component to achieving organizational objectives. To accomplish this, the leaders in pharmacy must constantly keep competent within the field of pharmacy as well as other areas such as finances and regulatory compliance. The pharmacist needs to be sure that s/he continually sees the "big picture" and is part of the administrative team as well as the clinical team. Table 2.4 lists some of the C-suite priorities as applied to pharmacy practice. Not every organization will have all of these leaders, and many organizations have a single individual manage several of these areas. It is incumbent on the pharmacy leader to routinely communicate with the C-suite leaders in each of the areas pertinent to pharmacy and the organization.

TABLE 2.3
C-Suite Roles and Functions

C-Suite Title and Abbreviation	Role in an Organization
Chief executive officer (CEO)	Highest-ranking corporate officer in charge of organzations; reports to a board of directors (or other authority) and is the primary decision maker, leader, and manager
Chief financial officer (CFO)	Senior manager responsible for overseeing the financial activities of an entire company
Chief human resource officer (CHRO)	Senior manager who oversees all human resource management and employee relations for an organization
Chief information officer (CIO)	Senior manager responsible for overseeing the information technology and computer systems throughout the organization; CIO can report to the CEO, COO, or CFO
Chief marketing and sales officer (CMSO)	Senior manager responsible for sales, product development, marketing, and distribution of products; CIO can report to the CEO or COO
Chief operating officer (COO)	Senior manager responsible for overseeing operations of the entire organization; usually reports to CEO
Chief legal officer (CLO)	Also known as general counsel, the CLO oversees the legal and policy issues for an organization

TABLE 2.4
C-Suite Priorities Applied to Pharmacy

1. Sound business practices are applied at all levels of the pharmacy organization.
    a. Medications and associated supplies are purchased using best practices.
    b. Personnel are recruited, retained, rewarded, and managed in conjunction with the human resource department and best practices within the industry.
    c. Insurance and patient billing and other sources of revenue are conducted ethically and support the mission of the organization.
2. Patient safety and health outcome are the primary concerns of the practice.
3. All practices involving the practice of pharmacy are monitored and assured to be in compliance with all local, state, and federal laws and regulations.

INFORMAL ORGANIZATIONS

Organizations come in a variety of shapes and sizes. The outward structure, depicted by the organizational chart, can demonstrate some of the relationships that exist. However, there is also an informal organization inherent within any formal organization. This informal organization arises within the formal structure because of the social interaction among the organization's members. This interaction leads to the formation of groups, both large and small.

Small groups are the central component of the informal organization, and membership is strongly influenced by social acceptance. Further, management has no control over the formation of these groups, but it must recognize the negative and positive impact these groups may have on the performance of the organization.

One of the main negative aspects of the informal organization is its ability to thwart the efforts of the organization. It is well recognized that what is good for the organization may not be good for the employee or a group of employees. Increasing the prescription volume of a pharmacy without increasing staffing may seem to be a logical managerial decision, but the pharmacist and technicians required to implement this increase might see this as a poor decision. As such, this informal group may take steps to impede the implementation of this objective. A good manager will take a Theory Y approach and attempt to involve the employees in this decision-making process, tapping the resources of the informal organization to gain support and trust.

In contrast, the informal organization can complement and even enhance the formal organizational structure. If there is a good relationship between the manager and the leader of the informal group, the manager could use this as a means to gain support for new programs, enhance communication, and fend off rumors and misinformation. Further, the informal organization can supply the much-needed social interaction and human contact to perform work efficiently and effectively.

CONCLUSION

As one climbs the corporate ladder, one finds that technical and functional expertise is less important and the soft skills such as leadership and interpersonal communication and an understanding of the organizational dynamics become increasingly important.

BIBLIOGRAPHY

Anon. Bureaucracy. www.analytictech.com/bm021/bureau.htm (accessed December 16, 2002).
Anon. Classical Organization Theory. The HRM Guide Network. www.hrmguide.co.uk/history/classical_organization_theory.htm (accessed March 10, 2003).
Anon. Theory X and Theory Y. Net MBA Business Knowledge Center. www.netmba.com/mgmt/ob/motivation/mcgregor/ (accessed December 29, 2003).
Fuqua HE, Payne KE, Cangemi JP. Leadership and the effective use of power. *Natl. Forum Educ. Admin. Superv. J.* 2003; 20E. www.nationalforum.com/12FUQUA.htm (accessed June 25, 2003).
Groysberg B, Kelly LK, MacDonald B. The new path to the C-suite. *Harv. Bus. Rev.* March 2011; 60–69.
Laschinger HK, Sabiston JA, Kutszcher L. Empowerment and staff nurse decision involvement in nursing work environments: testing Kanter's theory of structural power in organizations. *Res. Nurs. Hlth.* 1997; 20: 341–352.
Liebler JG, McConnell CR. Organizing. In: *Management Principles for Health Professionals.* Aspen, Gaithersburg, MD, 1999.
Longest BB. Modern health services in an organized setting. In: *Management Practices for the Health Professional*, 3rd ed. Reston Publishing, Reston, VA, 1984a, chap. 1.
Longest BB. Organizing: the framework for management. In: *Management Practices for the Health Professional*, 3rd ed. Reston Publishing, Reston, VA, 1984b, chap. 5.
McGregor D. *The Human Side of Enterprise*, Reprint edition. McGraw-Hill/Irwin, New York, 1985.

Ouchi, William G. *Theory Z: How American Business Can Meet the Japanese Challenge.* Avon, New York, 1981.

Pfeffer J. Understanding power in organizations. *Calif. Manage. Rev.* 1992; 34: 29–50.

Pharmacy Advisor. Engaging the C-suite to Advance Pharmacy Practice. http://pharmacyadvisor. com/engaging_the_c-suite_to_advance_pharmacy_practice/ (accessed January 17, 2014).

Richards B. Reflections of power. www.conncetiveintelligence.com/reflections.html (accessed March 10, 2003).Tootelian DH, Gaedeke RM. Organizing and staffing the pharmacy. In: *Essentials of Pharmacy Management.* Mosby, St. Louis, MO, 1993.

Venn P. Theory X, Y, and Z. http://members.tripod.com/PeterVenn/brochure/complete/xyz. htm (accessed December 29, 2003).

Young D. Shared governance builds leaders, aids patient care. *Am. J. Hlth-Syst. Pharm.* 2002; 59: 2274, 2278.

Case Study

Medication errors continue to be a concern for your hospital, partly due to recent news headlines that highlight errors occurring in other regional institutions. The chief operating office has called a meeting with you, the director of pharmacy, asking for a detailed discussion of steps your department is taking to minimize medication errors.

1. List the potential stakeholders in the C-suite and how you will address their concerns.
2. Describe how you intend to use your positional and personal powers to influence the stakeholders also jointly involved in the medication use process to minimize medication errors.
3. Find a recent story in the news about a medication error and describe how you would explain to a newspaper reporter the organizational changes you would make to prevent the error.

3 The Importance of Vision, Inspiration, Strategic Planning, and Getting It Done

William N. Kelly

CONTENTS

Learning Objectives: After reading this chapter and working through the case, the reader will be able to:

1. Discuss the importance of creating a vision and some ways it is created
2. Compare and contrast the terms *innovation, quality*, and *value*
3. Define the term *stakeholder*

4. Explain the preferred way to do strategic planning
5. Explain the term *SWOT*
6. Explain one method of reaching a consensus
7. Define the term *entrepreneurship* in the context of working within an organization

INTRODUCTION

Why are some pharmacy departments innovative and exciting places to work, some above average but not great, and some downright boring? Everyone wants to work on a winning team—be part of something exciting. This chapter focuses on the critical ingredients that leaders use to make a team a winner, or a department or a company first-rate.

OUTSTANDING LEADERSHIP

Much has been written about what constitutes outstanding leadership, and some leaders have volunteered their answers:

> A leader is best when people barely know he exists, when his work is done, his aim fulfilled, they will say: we did it ourselves.
>
> **Lao Tzu**

> A good leader is not the person who does things right, but the person who finds the right things to do.
>
> **Anthony T. Dadovano**

> If your actions inspire others to dream more, learn more, do more and become more, you are a leader.
>
> **John Quincy Adams**

> The art of leadership is to say no, not yes. It is easy to say yes.
>
> **Tony Blair**

> Outstanding leaders go out of their way to boost the self-esteem of their personnel. If people believe in themselves, it's amazing what they accomplish.
>
> **Sam Walton**

There is much truth in what these leaders have to say; however, a better way to discover what constitutes outstanding leadership is by examining the characteristics of some outstanding leaders:

Adventure Leaders—The Wright Brothers: These brothers made history on December 17, 1903, as they flew their Flyer at Kitty Hawk, North Carolina. What made these men succeed when others had failed?

Business Leader—Steve Jobs: What magic did Steve Jobs have that made Apple an industry leader?

Changed the World—Susan B. Anthony: A pioneer of the women's suffrage movement, she greatly influenced the creation of the nineteenth amendment, giving women in the United States the right to vote. How?

Military Leader—General George Patton: The most controversial, yet most effective, general for the allied forces in World War II. His men loved him. Why?

Political Leader—Nelson Mandela: A leader in the fight against South Africa's racial policies of apartheid—he was imprisoned for 27 years and then became president of South Africa in 1994. How could this happen?

Science Leader—Albert Einstein: He was one of the greatest and most famous scientists of the twentieth century. He brought forth one amazing discovery after another. Sure, he was smart, but was this all?

Spiritual Leader—Mohandas Gandhi: He was renowned for his doctrine of nonviolent protest. He was the leader of India's fight for independence and single-handedly brought the British Empire to its knees. Astounding!

Sports Leader—John Wooden: He is considered the greatest coach in the history of US college basketball. How did he inspire his players?

Pharmacy Leader—Donald C. Francke: He became the champion for "clinical pharmacy"—a vision that changed the practice of pharmacy. His inspiring writings were the basis of the *Journal Clinical Pharmacy*, now known as the *Journal of Pharmacotherapy*. What drove him to achieve this?

What characteristics did these great leaders have in common? The evidence shows that great leaders are not necessarily charismatic, have a participative leadership style, or are lucky as some believe. Leadership is more about setting a vision, being inspirational, and achieving the vision. Leaders, of course, also develop a team and define the values of the organization they lead.

GREAT LEADERS CREATE A VISION

DEFINITION AND IMPORTANCE

Merriam-Webster defines visioning as "the act of forming mental images." When these mental images are pleasant and highly desired, they become dreams. And when dreams become firmly implanted in our minds, and there is commitment to achieve them, they become goals.

Some believe imagining, visioning, or dreaming is pure foolishness—that it is unproductive, unrealistic, and a waste of time. And yet all the great leaders dreamed and practiced visioning. It has been said that what the mind can conceive, the mind can achieve. Tiger Woods uses visioning every time he hits a golf ball. Before he strikes the ball, he sees the perfect shot and tries to duplicate what he saw in his vision.

Visioning and dreaming are powerful. Think of how long the people of East Germany dreamed of tearing down the Berlin Wall. How much longer will the Chinese and Egyptians just visualize freedom?

If you want to lose weight, you should concentrate more on the vision of how good you will look, how good you will feel, and how others will view you when you achieve the weight loss you are seeking, rather than just focusing on the food you are eating.

Boss Kettering

There is a story about Boss Kettering, the inventive genius and a head of research at General Motors for 27 years. He wanted to prove the power of imagination and visualization, so he invited a friend over and made a wager. He bet a large sum of money that if his friend put a beautiful, ornate birdcage in the foyer of his home, that by and by, he would put a bird in the birdcage. Well, the friend accepted the bet and put a beautiful, ornate birdcage in his foyer. Friends would come over and say, "my, what a beautiful birdcage—where did you get it?" And he would say, "Well we went to the furniture store and looked through some pictures, and selected this one. It fits nicely with our décor, don't you think?" And his friends would say, "Well, where is your bird?" And he would say, "Well, I don't have a bird. No, he didn't die. No, I don't intend to get a bird. I don't know, I guess everyone is hung up on something—with me it is birdcages." Well, he kept seeing the birdcage, seeing the birdcage, and seeing the birdcage. He even saw it in his sleep. Finally, he gave in and put a bird in the birdcage and lost the bet.[1]

So, be careful what bird you put in your birdcage, you might just get it. Visionary leaders spend most of their time thinking about their vision, getting others to buy into the vision, and making sure the vision is achieved.

CREATING A VISION

Being visionary means having the ability to identify what is most important, to see what others may not see, and to understand and communicate why the vision is worth pursuing.

The process of visioning is simple but demands discipline. The first step is to create time to spend sitting and thinking with a pencil and paper. The second step is to discover a private space with no distractions. And the most important step is—you should begin with the end in mind.

Steven Covey's book *The 7 Habits of Highly Effective People* (1990) has had an effect on how I do things, and it changed my career path and career goals almost overnight. Part of it has to do with Covey's Habit 2: begin with the end in mind. If you have not read the book, you should, if you want to be a dynamic leader.

A tool for visioning would be to say, "By (date), this headline about our organization/department/profession's efforts and/or outcomes will be published in the newspaper or talked about on CNN News." What would your headline say?

Beginning with the end in mind removes barriers and restrictions and allows the dreamer to freely create what most others cannot see. You avoid negatives and naysayers who say "it can't be done," "we tried that before and it did not work," or "that is a waste of time."

Bell Telephone

In the late 1970s, the CEO of Bell Telephone called his top managers to an 8 a.m. meeting at a local hotel. They were waiting for him to arrive and it was now 8:10 a.m.

Then suddenly, the door to the room slammed open. The CEO, looking disheveled, walked quickly to the front of the room and with a troubled face and in a loud voice said, "there has been an accident at the office—it is completely destroyed—no one is hurt, but there is nothing left."

At this point, no one in the audience knew what to think. The CEO then said, "of course, that did not really happen, but for a moment you thought it did, didn't you? If it did happen, we would have to start from scratch, and that is exactly what I want you to do today—create a new phone and new phone system. The ones we have now have not changed much since it was invented over 100 years ago. Now get to work on a new one!"

The rest of the day, Bell's top managers worked to create a new telephone and new telephone system that was the initiation of touch phones, call waiting, conference calling, and other services we take for granted today.

There are some parameters to follow when visioning. For example, the vision needs to be consistent with the mission and values of your organization, and what your stakeholders (like your board, boss, clients) value. For example, a director of pharmacy's vision needs to be consistent with the hospital's mission and values, and with those of the profession.

Write It Down—Not only must you start with a clean sheet of paper, but you must write the vision down.

John Goddard

One rainy afternoon, an inspired 15-year-old boy named John Goddard sat down at his kitchen table and wrote three words at the top of a yellow pad: "My Life List." Under that heading he wrote 127 goals. Some goals were easy, while others were challenging, like: #82, make a parachute jump; #73, become an Eagle Scout; and #117, milk a poisonous snake. Some seemed near impossible: #21, climb Mt. Everest; #73, visit every country in the world; #109, read the entire *Encyclopedia Britannica*; and #125, visit the moon.[3]

In all, he accomplished 109 of these quests and logged an impressive list of records in achieving them. He visited all but 30 countries. And his rocket science expertise helped the United States put a man on the moon.

"When I was 15," he told *Life* magazine, "all the adults I knew seemed to complain, 'Oh, if only I'd done this or that when I was younger' (Goddard 1972). They had let life slip by them. I was sure that if I planned for it, I could have a life of excitement and fun and knowledge." Surely, if he had not carefully recorded his goals, few if any would have been accomplished. He achieved what he did by creating a "life list" rather than a "bucket list." Of course, in achieving fulfillment, it helps to know who you are and your purpose in life.

To many, John Goddard's feat of achieving 109 of his 127 life goals seems difficult, if not impossible. Yet Goddard admitted that he would not have been able to be successful without a written plan. Writing a goal makes it visible—makes it real—makes it a possibility. Goddard's vision was to be a life-adventurer, and he did it because he had a vision and wrote it down.

Reviewing the vision for your pharmacy or practice, mulling it over in your mind, and revising it provide clarity on what you need to do. But it will never happen unless you write it down.

GREAT LEADERS INSPIRE AND GET "BUY-IN" TO THEIR VISION

OK, I have a vision—how do I inspire others to "buy in" to my vision? The others are your stakeholders—your staff, boss, C-suite (CEO, CFO, CMO, COO), or stockholders. To move forward, someone (your board or boss) needs to approve you moving forward. After that, you must achieve "buy-in" from your team, as they will be the ones to make it happen.

Therefore, before discussing getting buy-in with your team, it is important to list the steps for building a successful team:

- A clear purpose
- Team members chosen carefully
- Strong measurement of progress
- Timely and effective communication
- Celebration of success

Buy-in is all about the "why" of the vision, rather than the "what" and the "how" of what you want to do.[5] People buy in to the reason for the vision. For example, Dr. Martin Luther King, Jr. did not say—"I have a plan"—no, he said, "I have a dream." Here is an example for pharmacy:

Weak Approach—I want to design a study measuring the impact of pharmacist interventions on the 30-day hospital readmission rate for heart failure. Will you help?

Strong Approach—I want to design a study measuring the impact of pharmacist interventions on the 30-day hospital readmission rate for heart failure *because* positive results will elevate practice, increase the public image of pharmacy, and help pharmacists become paid providers. Will you help?

See the difference?

Great leaders create vision and inspire others to buy in to their vision.

COMMUNICATING AND ENFORCING THE VISION

Leaders must communicate their vision effectively to others without many words. For example, can you effectively communicate your vision in 60 seconds or less if that was all the time you had to convince a key stakeholder, like the CEO of the company, if you saw him on an elevator?

The key elements of the 60-second elevator speech are as follows. Fill in the blanks:

- Picture—The vision of the pharmacy service is …
- Purpose—Our key objectives (or challenges) are (from the audience perspective) to …
- Plan—Our plans are to …
- Request—What we need from you is …

You need to make your elevator speech about the listener, challenging and actionable. Make sure you are clear, concise, and compelling. Most of all, make it easy for the listener to buy in.

The leader should plan and find opportunities to reinforce the importance of achieving the vision as often as possible with all stakeholders, especially the leader's team who is working to achieve the vision.

CREATING A STRATEGIC PLAN TO ACHIEVE THE VISION

Alice in Wonderland

Remember what happened when Alice came to a fork in the road? "Which road do I take?" she asked. "Where do you want to go?" responded the Cheshire Cat. "I don't know," Alice answered. "Then it doesn't matter," said the cat, "any road will take you there" [author addition].[6]

A big part of being an effective leader, manager, or supervisor is promoting teamwork and enthusiasm to accomplish an important goal. Many times, the goal is set by the leader or manager and is not important to the worker. Thus, the worker tries to look like he or she is excited about accomplishing something that he or she couldn't care less about.

It is the team's responsibility to create the strategic plan, but there must be a manager accountable for activating, monitoring, and making adjustments to achieve the vision. A strategic plan provides a road map and *action plans*, creates teamwork, and helps with buy-in.

SWOT ANALYSIS

In developing a strategic plan, it is traditional to perform an environmental scan that summarizes the organization's strengths, weaknesses, opportunities, and threats (SWOT). The SWOT analysis lays out the challenges to getting to the vision easily and quickly. But it also provides clues on how to do it. Figure 3.1 shows an example

Strengths	Weaknesses
Pharmacists	Budget
Clinical knowledge	Staff support
Enthusiasm	Computer support
Facilities	Rapport with
Communication	infectious disease
	physician
Opportunities	**Threats**
Recent infection control report	Increasing antimicrobial
Recent media reports	resistance
on "super bugs"	Increased use and cost of
Support of the P&T	antibiotics
Committee	

FIGURE 3.1 Example of a SWOT analysis to implement an antimicrobial stewardship program.

of a SWOT analysis for implementing an antimicrobial stewardship program in a 250-bed hospital.

REACHING CONSENSUS

The strategic plan starts with the end in mind—the leader's vision—then works backward in a straight line to the present. What lies along the line is the plan—the work that needs to be accomplished to achieve the vision. Those ideas are generated by the team. Many ideas are usually generated, but the process gets bogged down in deciding which ideas are the most important and worthy of being included in the strategic plan. It is important to use a process where every person's idea is considered equally and where there is consensus on which ideas are the best. One way to do this is by using the nominal group technique (NGT). Figure 3.2 explains how the NGT works.

DRAFTING THE PLAN

Someone (usually the project or clinical pharmacy coordinator, or another pharmacy manager) drafts the first version of the strategic plan. It is best to have the person who will be accountable for implementing the plan do this.

Strategic plans start with a written statement of the vision and a date for obtainment of the vision. The next step is to develop major goals or mile markers along the way to achieving the vision. Goals are the big things that need to be accomplished and always start with the word "to," are listed in chronological order, and have dates for achievement.

Under each goal are objectives—steps, in chronological order, that need to be accomplished to achieve the goal. Managers can also list a person who is accountable for achieving the objective.

What does a strategic plan look like? An example is presented in Figure 3.3.

Nominal Group Technique

1. The leader explains something that needs to be done or solved and explains why.
2. There is brief, open group discussion.
3. If most people understand and agree that something needs to be done, everyone silently (privately) records ideas on how to solve the problem or do what needs to be done.
4. After a few minutes, the first person states a solution. The recorder writes the suggestion as #1 on a large flip (post-up) sheet. At this point, no one may ask questions or critique the idea.
5. The next person provides their idea. This person's solution is #2. Keep going around the room. If a person is out of suggestions they say "pass."
6. Once all the sheets are posted, it is time for clarification. People may ask others to clarify what they mean. However, no one can speak negatively or against anyone's idea. This point is important.
7. The next step is to see if any ideas are similar and should be combined.
8. Each person has a set of points (3 points, 2 points, and 1 point). Each person votes for ideas they think are most important by placing their points next to the ideas. You may spread the six points or place all on one idea.
9. Declare a short break while someone adds up the points for each item.

FIGURE 3.2   Rules for performing nominal group technique.

Strategic Plan

Vision: By November 1, 2015, we will: (1) counsel each patient newly diagnosed as having diabetes mellitus, hypertension, or hyperlipidemia on: (a) their disease, (b) their medication, and (c) the importance of compliance, and (2) on the first refill we will check on: (a) the effectiveness of the medication, (b) the safety of the medication, and (c) compliance, and (3) make any necessary recommendations concerning improvements in therapy to the patient's prescriber.

Goal 1: By 9/1/15 construct a small semi-private counseling room near the dispensing area.

Objective 1 - To identify three carpenters to submit a bid for renovation (6/1/15)
Objective 2 - To have bids submitted by 7/1/15
Objective 3 - To plan (by 9/15/15) how to dispense medication with the least amount of disruption during the construction process

Goal 2: By 9/10/15 train all pharmacists and non-pharmacy staff on the new service.

Objective 1 - To develop (by 7/1/15) educational handout material for patients
Objective 2 - To set up (by 7/15/15) the procedure to be used in counseling patients
Objective 3 - To train (by 8/15/15) the pharmacists on each disease state, procedure, and expectations.
Objective 4 - To explain to each non-pharmacist employee the "whys" and "hows" of the service and what their role is in the service. (9/30/15)

Goal 3: By 9/1/15 develop a marketing and communication plan for the new service.

Objective 1 - To identify (by 7/10/15) doctors within two miles of the pharmacy that should know about this new service
Objective 2 - To develop (by 7/20/15) a brochure for doctors explaining the new service
Objective 3 - To develop (by 8/1/15) a brochure for patients explaining the new service
Objective 4 - To develop (by 10/1/15) a simple press release for the local newspaper on the new service

---

FIGURE 3.3   A strategic plan to implement a new patient counseling service.

GETTING IT DONE

As a leader, not only must you have a vision and get buy-in, but you must keep it simple, focus, and be determined on achieving your vision. This leads us to Steve Jobs, a.k.a. "Mr. Focus."

Focus

After Steve Jobs' death, people started wondering what made the founder and CEO of Apple so successful. Walter Isaacson's biography of Jobs was written while Isaacson was in close contact with Jobs during the last 18 months of Jobs' life. Some feel Isaacson painted a much rosier picture of Jobs in the biography than some of Jobs' employees (a few thought he was a real jerk!). Isaacson made up some lost ground when he published "The Real Leadership Lessons of Steve Jobs" in the April 2012 edition of the *Harvard Business Review.*[7] Jobs cofounded Apple in his parent's garage in 1976 with $2000, was ousted as Apple's CEO in 1985, and returned to rescue the company from bankruptcy in 1997. Isaacson's claim is that Jobs' number one secret to his and Apple's success was his ability to focus.

Steve Jobs

In 1997, Apple was producing a random array of computers. After a few weeks of being back at Apple, Jobs declared, "This is crazy." In front of his top managers, he drew a 2 × 2 grid and said "This is what we need." Above the two columns he wrote the words "pro" and "consumer." In the next two rows he wrote the words "desktop" and "portable." Their job, he told the group, was to focus on producing those four products—all other products should be canceled. The group was stunned.[7]

Computer/User	Pro	Consumer
Desktop		
Portable (Laptop)		

As he righted the company, Jobs liked to take his top people on a retreat each year, and would ask them to "develop the top ten things we should be doing next." People would fight to get their suggestions on the list. After a day of much jockeying, the group created a list of ten ideas. Then Jobs would come in the room, quickly look at the list, slash the bottom seven and announce "we can only do three." Were these top three the iPod, the iPhone, and the iPad?

DETERMINATION

Besides focusing on the vision, leaders are determined to achieve the vision.

The Persian Prince

There is a story of a Persian prince[1] who had a hunchback. His twelfth birthday was approaching and his father, the King, came to him and asked, "What would you like for your birthday, son?" Without a second's hesitation, the son replied, "Father, I would like a statue of myself, and I would like it placed outside my bedroom window in the courtyard." At that point, his father wished he had not come to his son's room—he was sorry he had even thought of it. A statue of his poor crippled son! His son further instructed, "I want it made not as I look now, but as if I could stand straight and tall." Well, the King thought this was even worse, and that the son was mocking him. But after some thought, the King granted his son's wish. Several times a day the young prince would go to the courtyard and stand beside the statue. He would stretch and pull, and stretch more, even until it hurt. He did this several times a day, every day for nine years. And, on his twenty-first birthday, that young prince stood with his shoulders erect, and his head high, and he looked at the statue eyeball to eyeball, and looked just like the statue. That is the power of vision, focus, and determination.

ASSIGNING RESPONSIBILITY

It is critical that the leader appoint a manager to be responsible for achieving the vision. In corporate organizations, this person is usually the chief operating officer (COO). In large pharmacy services, it is usually the associate director of pharmacy or the clinical coordinator.

Monitoring Progress

Great leaders create a vision, inspire others to buy in to their vision, focus, and are determined to achieve the vision. Therefore, they constantly think about the vision and monitor progress closely. They look forward to when the vision reaches a tipping point and when the vision is achieved, and they live by the motto "we manage what we measure."[8]

An effective tool for monitoring and communicating progress is a simple spreadsheet with five columns: goal, accountability, scheduled date to achieve, progress, and comments (see Table 3.1). Color coding the progress section is essential for the leader to get a quick handle on progress, where the bottlenecks are occurring, and where he or she needs to lend support when needed.

Coaching and Counseling

A great leader knows when to prod and when to praise and does both effectively to move people toward achieving the vision. Both forms of communication can be done effectively in one minute but must be done with style.[9]

Celebrating Success

Another hallmark of great leaders is they recognize the team and those individuals contributing the most toward achieving the vision, and know how to celebrate success. This boosts morale and team building. This step is often missed in many organizations but is essential in establishing a positive culture where people like to work.

TABLE 3.1

An Example of a Simple Tracking Document to Assess Progress on Achieving a Leadership Vision

Goal	Accountability	Date to Achieve	Progress*	Comments
1. Fully inform staff on the project	A Jones	2/30/15		Completed 2/29/15
2. Reconfigure the dispensing process	C Smith	3/15/15		Almost done
3. Redesign the dispensing area	K Morse	4/1/15		Working through issues
4. Train all pharmacists and technicians	W Williams	5/15/15		Not started

*Blue (1) = complete; green (2) = on track; yellow (3) = some progress; red (4) = no progress

---

SUMMARY

Great leaders are visionary, inspiring, and get the job done. They do this by:

- Creating a vision
- Inspiring others to buy in to the vision
- Recording and enforcing the vision
- Approving a strategic plan to gain the vision
- Assigning accountability
- Focusing and being determined to achieve the vision
- Monitoring progress closely
- Recognizing team members' contributions to achieving the vision
- Celebrating success with his or her team

Questions for pharmacists in leadership positions include the following:

- Do I have a clear vision for my department?
- Can I explain my vision in a one-minute elevator speech?
- Is my vision in writing?
- Does my team understand the vision and why it is important?
- Has the team bought in?
- Is there a strategic plan in writing to achieve the vision?
- Do I have
  - The correct organizational structure?
  - The right people in the right positions?
  - Knowledge of the person accountable for following the strategic plan?
- Are we making progress?
- Are we on track?

REFERENCES

1. Meyer PJ. *Power of Goal Setting*. Success Motivation Institute, Waco, TX, 1972.
2. Covey SR. *The 7 Habits of Highly Effective People*. Simon and Schuster, New York, 1990.
3. Goddard J. John Goddard's Life List. www.johngoddard.info/life_list.htm (accessed November 14, 2012).
4. Goddard J. One Man's Life of No Regrets. *Life*. March 24, 1972; 66–68.
5. Sinek S. *How Leaders Inspired Action*. TED. May 4, 2010. www.ted.com/talks/simon_sinek_how_great_leaders_inspire_action.html (accessed October 29, 2013).
6. Carroll L. *Alice's Adventures in Wonderland*. Random House, New York, 1946.
7. Isaacson W. The real leadership lessons of Steve Jobs. *Harvard Bus. Rev.* April 1, 2012.
8. Gladwell M. *The Tipping Point. How Little Things Can Make a Big Difference*. Little Brown, New York, 2002.
9. Blanchard KH, Johnson S. *The One Minute Manager*. Blanchard Family Partnership and Candle Communications Corporations, New York, 1982.

Case Study

1. In a small group, (a) create a vision and (b) put it in writing by completing the following:

   By (date), (pharmacists/my pharmacy/the profession) [select one], will

   _____.

2. In a small group, based on Exercise 1, perform and record the SWOT analysis.

3. In a small group, based on Exercises 1 and 2 above, use the NGT by using Rules 1 through 9 in Figure 3.2, and create ideas on how to achieve the vision. Highlight the top five ideas.

4. In a small group, based on Exercises 1 through 3, create a simple strategic plan to achieve the vision you created, using Figure 3.2 as a guide.

4 Leading Culture, People, and the Strategic Plan

William N. Kelly and John E. Clark

CONTENTS

Learning Objectives: After reading this chapter and working through the case, the reader will be able to:

1. Explain the importance of organizational culture and how it is set
2. Explain how to achieve a culture where people are productive and feel appreciated
3. Explain the importance of an organizational structure for a pharmacy department
4. Provide three examples of how top leaders build their leadership teams

5. State three strategies for effective departmental leadership communication
6. List five principles of running an effective meeting
7. Provide an example of how to let employees know what you expect
8. Explain the importance of managing by walking around
9. Explain how to do one-minute goals, praises, and reprimands
10. Explain the importance of holding people accountable for their responsibilities/assignments and how to do it

INTRODUCTION

Leaders set visions, obtain buy-in, and inspire others to achieve the vision. They also lead the culture, the people, and the strategic plan that directs actions toward achieving the vision. They do this not only because it is their charge, but because they are highly motivated achievers who are goal and results oriented. This chapter is about how they lead the culture, people, and strategic plan to produce desirable results.

LEADING THE CULTURE

ORGANIZATIONAL CULTURE

Every organization has a culture. Organizational culture is the belief and behavior that determine how an organization's employees and management interact and handle outside transactions. An organization's culture is reflected in its dress code, business hours, office setup, employee benefits, turnover, hiring decisions, treatment of its customers, and customer satisfaction.[1]

For example, Google is a company that is well known for its employee-friendly corporate culture. It offers perks, such as telecommuting, flex time, tuition reimbursement, free employee lunches, and on-site services like physicians, oil changes, massages, fitness classes, car washes, and hair stylists. Thus, it ranks high consistently on *Fortune* magazine's list of "100 Best Companies to Work For."[1]

However, organizational culture is more than perks. It also sets the tone for the organization and indicates to its employees what it values and how it expects employees to act.

LEADER'S ROLE IN ORGANIZATIONAL CULTURE

The leader sets the values and expectations for the organization. Therefore, the ideal organizational culture is directly related to the characteristics of the "ideal leader," the main characteristic being the leader's priority for honesty and ethical behavior.[2]

The importance of developing a department of pharmacy culture explicitly, rather than by default, cannot be underestimated. An ideal departmental culture promotes productivity and employee happiness; increases longevity of employment (employees want to continue working there); increases cooperation, communication, and teamwork among employees; allows employees to take pride in their work; and instills the desire to achieve more.

CREATING THE IDEAL WORKPLACE

Creating the ideal workplace involves five ingredients:

Having a Clear Vision—This is discussed extensively in Chapter 4. The benefits include motivating employees, challenging employees to work toward a common goal, and providing a sense of respect and ownership.

Consistency in Expectations—It is important to have a set of expectations for pharmacy employees so they understand their roles within the department. Keeping these expectations consistent among all employees allows for a feeling of fairness.

Setting Standards—There should be a written set of standards or rules that define the regulations and policies of the pharmacy department. These can be found in a policy and procedure manual that is updated routinely, with significant changes communicated to all employees.

Providing Access to Resources and Training—As a pharmacy leader, you want to alleviate any feelings of "being lost" when first hired. A support system needs to be in place for further training and to provide opportunities for people to advance within the department or organization.

Employee Recognition—Employees need to be acknowledged and receive consistent feedback that they are valued. More on this important ingredient is provided later in this chapter.

In the end, building an ideal pharmacy departmental culture and workplace is mostly about trust, communication, and treating people like people, not employees.[3]

LEADING THE PEOPLE

There are many aspects of leading people effectively, but here are ten important ones.

HIRING THE RIGHT PEOPLE IN THE RIGHT POSITIONS

Pharmacy departments are complex operations that need to be organized efficiently and strategically. They need to be staffed with highly skilled employees to achieve peak results. So, when being selected as the pharmacy manager, Director of Pharmacy (DOP), or Chief Pharmacy Officer (CPO), two key questions should emerge: (1) What is expected of me? and (2) Do I have the correct organizational structure to achieve the expected results?

In general, most organizations provide a "honeymoon period" for newly appointed pharmacy managers, DOPs, and CPOs to reorganize, make changes in positions, and hire some people with needed skills. This honeymoon period is often short, certainly less than one year. So, as a new pharmacy manager, DOP, or CPO, you need to assess your area of control and reorganize quickly based on a strategy to achieve the desired results.

The first step is revising the organizational chart. This takes more thought, and time to accomplish this. Be careful to get it right. Positions may need to be reassigned, eliminated, or added. The second step is asking if you have the right people in the right positions. This aspect of reorganization can be difficult, as you may be affecting people's security when you increase, reduce, or eliminate their responsibilities. But you must proceed with the end in mind, your vision. The critical part of this is not what you do, but how you do it. Be kind and respectful, but firm.

In making new hires in strategic positions, it is critical that the position description is carefully constructed with desired expectations and outcomes explicitly stated. Then, when interviewing, make sure to dig deep to discover whether the candidate has the skill sets and experience you desire.[4] Next, is the candidate honest, optimistic, reliable, efficient, and a team player? Some skill sets and experiences need verification by previous supervisors.

TEAMWORK

Once in place, your pharmacy team needs cultivation—attention, grooming, direction, and your genuine interest. Team building is an art that divides true leaders from wannabes, and it takes time, but the payoff is excellent. Here are some ways to build a team:[5]

> *Give Clear Expectations*—People operate best when they are clear on the expected behaviors and expected results you are seeking.
> *Commitment*—Are they clear on your vision, and have they "bought in"?
> *Understanding and Respect for Other Team Members*—Do they respect and understand the strengths of other team members and their roles?
> *Control*—Do they understand how much freedom they have?
> *Collaboration*—Making collaboration an honored action pays dividends.
> *Creative Innovation*—Let people know that thinking outside of the box is encouraged as long as it is productive.

It is said that "teamwork makes the dream work." Building an effective team is much more than what is written here. Therefore, it is recommended that the reader pursue more information on this important subject.

EFFECTIVE COMMUNICATION

There is a lot to be said for pharmacists to have effective communication skills in relating to patients and other members of the health-care team, like physicians and nurses. However, communication within a pharmacy department is also important but is often neglected in teaching and in practice. The common problem within pharmacy departments, identified by outside pharmacy consultants, is people working in "silos," resulting in poor or no communication. Here are some tips to keep department communication effective:[6]

- Make sure communication is routine, important, and timely.
- Make sure it fits the audience.
- Be sincere, simple, short, specific, and summarize what is said.

- Ask for questions and feedback.
- Check to see if the communication is effective, and if not, find out why not.

RUNNING AN EFFECTIVE MEETING

Sometimes memos, e-mails, and newsletters are not enough or not fast enough to communicate effectively, and thus a meeting is necessary. The responsibility for making this happen is the person who organizes and runs the meeting. Effective leaders know when and how to run meaningful meetings. Here is how they do it:[7,8]

- Know if you really need a formal meeting. Meetings are expensive. Can this be done another way?
- Have a clear reason for the meeting. Setting expectations is vital, and everyone invited to attend the meeting should know these reasons before the meeting begins.
- Establish objectives and expectations.
- Have a tight agenda. List a person's name after each agenda item.
- Set out the ground rules. These ground rules need to be discussed up front.
- Facilitate the meeting well. Keep the meeting running smoothly and on task.
- Beware of Parkinson's Law: "Work expands so as to fill the time available for its completion."
- Give everyone a voice. Be watchful to see who has not spoken and provide opportunities for them to speak.
- Have a stand-up meeting. To get business done more quickly, remove the comfort zone of the chair and table that makes it more likely that people will talk less and get to the point quicker.
- Leave time to sum up. Allocating time at the end of the meeting to summarize so everyone is on the same page is critical.
- Assign action steps. Assign someone to each action step, and set deadlines and follow up.

Tip: Never call a meeting unless it is absolutely necessary.

TAKING INTEREST AND EMPOWERING PEOPLE

Most people work best when they know what is expected of them and are empowered to accomplish the expectation with freedom to act. Leaders who know how to do this well are truly exceptional. The main steps in doing this are (1) getting to know the people you are empowering, (2) making them feel important, and (3) letting them know you have confidence in them.

SETTING EXPECTATIONS

A common mistake in management is expecting an employee to do something according to the specific expectations of the manager. When this does not happen, the employee is not rewarded, when it was the manager's fault for not making the expectation clear to the employee before starting the assignment. Here is how to make your expectations clear:[9]

- Make sure the employees understand what the end result is that you expect.
- Do not set too many expectations.
- Explain the importance of the task—the reason for the assignment. Do they buy in?
- Show you have confidence in their abilities to accomplish the task.
- Explain what is in it for them.
- Let them know how much freedom they have to act.
- Set a firm deadline for completion of the task.
- Let them know you are available for questions, direction, and help.
- Let them know how often you want an update on their progress and how you expect it?

One way of letting employees be aware of what is expected is by setting a one-minute goal.[10] This is how it works: A manager meets with an employee and states what needs to be done and why, and confirms that the employee is fully invested in achieving the goal. The employee records the goal (the outcome expected and when) on one page using no more than 250 words (the amount that can be read in one minute). The employee and his or her supervisor each have a copy.

Since 80% of important results come from 20% of a person's goals, each employee has one-minute statements of their goals for that 20%—usually three to six goals. It is critical that each goal excludes attitudes and feelings. State what is happening in observable, measurable terms. Last, the manager should explain what he or she would like to see in behavioral terms—what is actually happening now and what you desire to happen.

MANAGEMENT BY WALKING AROUND

In the television series *Undercover Boss,* chief executive officers (CEOs) of major companies go undercover, in disguise, to see what really goes on in the everyday world of their companies. Bosses discover both good and bad. Rewards and reprimands are handed out after a week, and needed changes in policies and procedures are put in place after the week of sleuthing. To most viewers, the CEO–worker disconnect is no surprise. However, the problem runs much deeper, even in pharmacy departments.

Many managers, including pharmacy managers, directors, associate directors, assistant directors, and supervisors, are guilty of spending most of their time in their offices and going to meetings, and are only aware superficially of what actually goes on daily in their areas of responsibility. More importantly, they are not digging deep enough to understand what kinds of problems people are experiencing on the job, what ideas workers have for improvement, and if any personal problems are interfering with the workers' ability to do their best work.

The remedy for this is to manage by walking around (MBWA). Here are six tips on how to do this well:[11]

1. Make MBWA part of your routine.
2. Do not bring an entourage—just yourself.
3. Visit everybody.
4. Ask for suggestions and recognize good ideas.
5. Follow up with answers.
6. Do not criticize.

Number 7 may be to ask employees what kinds of problems they are experiencing on the job, either with what they do or with the organization's policies and procedures. MBWA takes time, but it has proven to produce big dividends. It can even be fun!

HOLDING PEOPLE ACCOUNTABLE

Let us go back for a moment to the meeting action assignments discussed in "Running an Effective Meeting" and the one-minute goals in "Setting Expectations." Each of those items was assigned to someone to complete within a stated time frame. Following up to see if these goals have been completed is called "holding people accountable," and this action is perhaps the most underused management tool, and the reason progress gets stymied.

Leaders and managers who hold people accountable obtain the fastest and most desirable results, compared to those who only occasionally use this tool or do not use it at all. Making an assignment or a goal and not asking for progress reports between the time the assignment or goal is made and when it is due, is poor management. Progress reports and updates are vital to make sure the project is on track. Table 3.1 provides an example of how to design effective progress reports.

COACHING AND COUNSELING FOR SUCCESS

There is no question that coaching (being a cheerleader) and counseling employees costs less than hiring new employees, but it is more than that. Supervision includes expressing confidence, sharing observable behavior, and pointing out when an employee has done well. Employees appreciate positive feedback that tells them they are on track and doing well. Positive feedback can turn an average employee into a peak performer. Letting employees know they are doing well can be done with "one-minute praises."[10]

One-minute praises work by letting employees know when they are hired that as their manager, you will be telling them when they are doing well and when they are doing poorly. It is important for employees to know where they stand. "Catching" them doing something right results in instant gratification and motivation, and is a win-win scenario.

It is important to respond quickly to mistakes made by employees, once you have verified the facts. This can be done by using one-minute reprimands.[10] This process involves counseling the employee in private, looking them straight in the eye, and letting them know that what he or she did was wrong. It also involves sharing with the employee how you feel about it, and how competent you think the employee normally is. At the end, state how much you look forward to seeing the employee in the future as long as he or she does not make the mistake again.

RECOGNIZING, REWARDING, AND RETAINING EMPLOYEES

Peak performing pharmacy services know how to recognize, reward, and retain employees.

Recognizing Peak Performers

Like discipline, recognizing top performers in an organization is an underused tool.[12] Recognizing each employee's unique skills is one of the best ways for an organization to improve dramatically, as those recognized become highly motivated to do even better. In addition to one-minute praises, which are done privately, peak performers need to be acknowledged formally through processes like public recognition for a job well done, being the employee of the month, or a write-up in a newsletter or organizational publication.

Rewarding Employees

In addition to traditional rewards like merit increases, perks commonly available include a parking place for one month close to the building where the employee works, cash bonuses, time off, better shifts or schedules, a better office, more support, additional training, higher-level assignments with more responsibility, and promotion.

Retaining Employees

The way to retain peak performers in your organization or pharmacy department involves multiple processes such as:

- Hiring the correct people to begin with
- Providing an effective orientation process for new employees
- Making sure everyone knows, understands, and buys into the vision
- Achieving "teamwork that makes the dream work"
- Communicating effectively
- Taking an interest in and empowering individuals
- Leading by walking around
- Using one-minute goals, praises, and reprimands
- Holding people accountable
- Recognizing and rewarding employees

Using these tools increases the chance that employees will know they are working for an exceptional organization and will want to continue working there.

LEADING THE STRATEGIC PLAN

In addition to making sure the wheels do not come off the pharmacy department, the number one job of the pharmacy leader is to make the department successful, which means achieving the vision. To achieve the leader's vision, there must be a strategic plan. To be successful, the leader (for pharmacy, the pharmacy manager, DOP, or CPO) must have a process in place for tracking and assessing progress, and a constant focus and determination to achieve his or her vision. More detail on how to do this is provided in Chapter 3.

SUMMARY

Leading the culture, people, and strategic plan of an organization, like a pharmacy service, is not an easy task. It takes knowledge, time, and commitment to do it correctly. However, those who do it well will be highly successful, as measured by motivated and happy employees, and achievement of the pharmacy leader's vision.

REFERENCES

1. Investopedia. Definition of corporate culture. www.investopedia.com/terms/c/corporate-culture.asp (accessed December 16, 2013).
2. Faris RJ, MacKinnon GE, MacKinnon NJ, et al. Perceived importance of pharmacy management skills. *Am J Health-Syst Pharm.* 2005;62:1067–1072.
3. Hindle B. Building blocks to corporate culture. *Industry Week/IW.* 2013;262(11):26.
4. Mink M. Hire the right people. *Investors' Business Daily.* Page A03. March 26, 2013.
5. Coker J. 12 tips for team building. 2009. www.slideshare.net/ajcoker/12-tips-to-team-building-presentation (accessed December 26, 2013).
6. MacLeod-Glover N. Communication in pharmacy practice: An overview. 2006. www.tevacanada.com/pdfs/CCL—June-2006.aspx (accessed December 26, 2013).
7. Anderson P. Holding effective meetings. *Middle East Economic Development Digest.* 2013:Supplement;12.
8. Kelley J. Top ten tips for running a great meeting. *Am Salesman.* 2012;57(11):24–27.
9. Wiley S. Guidelines for setting expectations. *CPA Pract Manage Forum.* 2013;9(11):9–10.
10. Blanchard K, Johnson S. *The One-Minute Manager.* Blanchard Family Partnership and Candle Communications Corporation. Harper Collins, New York, 2003.
11. Fisher A. Management by walking around: 6 tips to make it work. *CNN Money.* August 23, 2012. http://management.fortune.cnn.com/2012/08/23/management-by-walking-around-mbwa/ (accessed December 27, 2013).
12. Williamsen M. Recognition: the underused tool. *Pit and Quarry.* 2013;106:54.

Case Study

You are newly appointed into your first manager position at a large, 24-hour chain-store pharmacy where you have never worked. Your plan is to work and observe the pharmacy operation for six weeks before you make any substantial changes, but you find this difficult as you see so many things and people that need correcting. After three weeks you become frustrated, because the employees are not working as an efficient team, one employee is clearly not up to par, and you know things can be much better. At four weeks of observation you say enough is enough.

ASSIGNMENT

1. What will be your initial approach to making things better?
2. How will you get others to buy in to your vision?
3. How will you get everyone working together efficiently?
4. What will you do with the subpar employee?

5 Leading Change and the Pharmacy Enterprise*

James A. Jorgenson

CONTENTS

---

* This chapter uses the framework for change published by Elaine Biech in her book, *Thriving Through Change,* and the framework for "Effective Influence and Advocacy" published by John A. Daly in his book *Advocacy,* coupled with pharmacy specific examples to provide pharmacy leaders with an effective tool set to successfully advocate for and drive change.[1,2]

Learning Objectives: After reading this chapter and working through the case, the reader will be able to:

1. Identify key drivers of change in healthcare
2. Identify common pitfalls in making successful organizational changes
3. Apply the principles of the CHANGE model to any change initiative
4. Identify critical elements to garner organizational support and exert influence for pharmacy change initiatives
5. Craft a persuasive presentation

INTRODUCTION

One constant we can all agree on is that change is a daily facet of our practice, and the rate of change is continuing to accelerate. The S&P 500 stock market index, maintained by S&P Dow Jones indices, measures performance of 500 large-cap American companies covering about 75% of the American equity market by capitalization. Consider that the life span of an S&P 500 company is down from 75 years in 1937 to just 15 years today.[3]

The world is changing faster than ever before, and companies must keep up with this pace. Hospitals and health systems are in essence healthcare companies that must also adapt and change to the environment, and it is important to recognize that healthcare is changing almost faster than it is able to reorganize. Organizations or individuals that cannot or will not adapt to keep pace with the accelerating rate of change will undoubtedly be left by the wayside. Pressures forcing change are probably the greatest they have ever been.

With US healthcare consuming upward of 17% of total gross domestic product (GDP) and climbing toward 20%, financial pressure to curb this unsustainable trend is enormous.[4] In addition, the United States continues to provide a "two-tiered" healthcare system with unequal access and care for all Americans. Estimates are that prior to implementation of the Affordable Care Act more than 45 million people in the United States were without health insurance.[5] Approximately 30 million Americans in 2014 will become eligible for some form of healthcare insurance which will help improve equitable distribution of care but will also significantly stress the current delivery models.[6]

Despite the enormous investment in healthcare, which is more than the entire GDP of every other country in the world, the United States is still producing less than stellar outcomes. The World Health Organization (WHO) ranks the United States thirty-seventh overall in health outcomes, two places above Cuba which spends roughly $250 to $300/citizen/year on its healthcare, while the United States spends in excess of $7,000, with life expectancy in the two countries virtually identical.[7] Life expectancy at birth increased by almost nine years between 1960 and 2010 in the United States, but that is less than the increase of over 15 years in Japan and over 11 years on average in Organisation for Economic Cooperation and Development (OECD) countries.[8] Clearly we have to do better in terms of access, quality, and cost.

You can look at this from the "glass-half-empty" or the "glass-half-full" perspective. The pessimistic viewpoint would say that this problem is too big and complex for pharmacy to tackle, and it would be easier to keep our heads down and hope this passes us by. Unfortunately that mentality has not gotten us anywhere in the past and will do even less for us in the future. Instead it should be acknowledged that yes, this is a huge problem, but with big problems come big opportunities and pharmacy needs to step up and take full advantage of the opportunity.

On the individual hospital and health system level these issues are manifesting in a variety of challenges. Future government reimbursement for hospitals is being cut by roughly 30%, and virtually every healthcare organization is scrambling to identify and implement cost reduction measures to try and offset these impending reimbursement cuts.[9] Expenses for supplies and equipment continue to rise. Quality and safety continue to underperform. Clinical outcomes are being challenged daily to do better—no more hospital-acquired infections, no more readmissions within 30 days, and patient satisfaction driving additional payments are just a few examples.

A NEW MANDATE FOR CHANGE

When all of the above challenges are considered, it is obvious that there is a greatly increased demand for new ideas and change. Stepping back and looking at overall performance in terms of healthcare delivery, it is clear that almost no one is happy with our current system.

The United States spends the most, quality is not universally paid for, most Americans do not have a regular physician, care is not convenient and as a result is not accessed consistently, and doctors do not typically have enough time to listen to patients and therefore there is limited communication. There are high rates of chronic conditions, and these chronic conditions are not being treated properly and consistently. There are frequent medical and medication errors. And as noted earlier, everything costs too much. As a result there are high levels of dissatisfaction. All of these add to the burden of the issues being faced by our hospitals, and pharmacy is pivotal to each of these issues. Organizations need all the help they can get and all the ideas they can gather to cope with these pressures and changes. There is great opportunity for pharmacy to help address these issues and to advance pharmacy practice initiatives in the process.

LEADING CHANGE

Effectively addressing these change initiatives in our organizations is an important skill set for leaders, yet literature would suggest that over half of all major change efforts result in failure. Pharmacy leaders need to ensure that pharmacy changes are not among the failures when attempting to drive change initiatives in our organizations. There are literally hundreds of different change models, theories, and strategies. It is possible to spend years studying all of the different efforts to address change management.

With all of these theories, models, and plans for change, why do over half of all change initiatives still fail? In large part, people fail to recognize that the change process goes through a series of phases that in total requires time. People tend to get impatient and rush or skip steps, and while this may create the feeling that the change process has been accelerated, it really results in a loss of satisfactory results. Critical mistakes in any phase can have a negative impact on the change initiative as a whole, reduce the change momentum, and negate or reverse any gains. John

Kotter's *Leading Change* is one of the seminal works on change failure, and he details eight primary reasons that change efforts fail:[10]

1. Not having a great enough sense of urgency
2. Not having a guiding coalition with enough power
3. Lacking vision
4. Undercommunicating
5. Not removing obstacles
6. Not planning for and creating short-term wins
7. Declaring victory too soon
8. Not anchoring changes in the organizational culture

SENSE OF URGENCY

Creating a sense of urgency for a change is the most basic first step in the process. Without motivation for a change, people will not get involved and the initiative is unlikely to move forward, yet many organizations fail in this first basic step as a result of paralyzed senior management. This often comes from too many managers and not enough leaders where the focus is on minimizing risk and keeping current systems operating instead of recognizing the need to change.

Change by definition is about creating new systems which demand leadership not management. It is also a common mistake for leaders to fail to recognize how difficult it is to get employees out of their comfort zone. For almost all people change is neither sought after nor welcomed—no matter how good the idea is. As a leader it is critical to recognize that for a major change a new compact is being created between employees and the pharmacy service. It is important to remember to answer these four key questions for change for employees to get them involved:

1. What is happening?
2. Why is it happening?
3. How will it affect me and my job (what is in it for me)?
4. What is the plan for getting this done?

GUIDING COALITION

Not creating a powerful enough coalition also builds on the first error with a sense of urgency. A powerful enough coalition to continue to drive the change forward is needed. In any organization there will be a bell curve in terms of change readiness as depicted in Figure 5.1. In his 1962 work *Diffusion of Innovation*, Rogers estimated that 2.5% of employees will be *change innovators*—they are constantly looking for and leading efforts to change and improve and 13.5% of employees will be *early adopters*.[11] Early adopters are influenced by the innovators and quickly embrace a change when they perceive the positive value.

About 34% of employees are an *early majority* and take some convincing, but easily adopt the change once the concept appears proven and sound. About 34% are the *late majority,* and you have to work a little harder to get them to embrace the change but with the right motivation and support they will move forward with it.

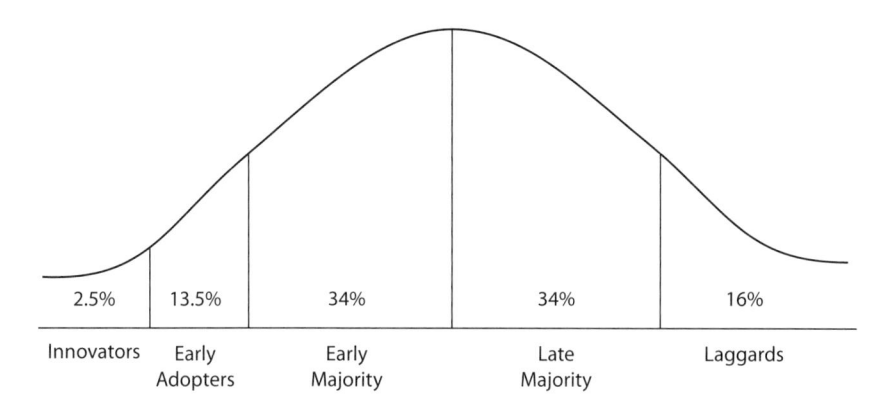

2.5%	13.5%	34%	34%	16%
Innovators	Early Adopters	Early Majority	Late Majority	Laggards

FIGURE 5.1 Adopter categorization.

Finally, 16% of employees are *laggards*.[12] *Laggards* actively and passively resist change no matter how good it is. They are stuck on the status quo and are big proponents of keeping the "way we do things around here" in place. These are the people who generally are not happy unless they are unhappy. Long-time football coach Bill Curry coined a great term for these people: "the fellowship of the miserable." Leaders often make the mistake of spending too much time on this group when there is little chance they will ever move much higher on the curve. Leaders' time is better spent with people on the front end of the curve where all of the innovation, creativity, and change are happening.

For the laggard group, the change should be clearly and definitively spelled out with the pros and cons of the change defined, and then all employees should be held accountable for the change. If the "laggards" cannot or will not make the change, then leaders need to be prepared to quickly remove them and replace them with more productive people.

VISION

If the vision for the change is lacking, this will cripple the change effort from the start. The vision has to go beyond just numbers, and it has to really say something to clarify the direction in which the organization needs to move. It has to appeal to employees' hearts and minds, and it has to offer them something better than they have now. It should not be full of big words and abstract verbiage. Leaders need to be able to clearly communicate the vision to any employee in less than five minutes and get a reaction that demonstrates understanding and interest.

COMMUNICATION

Even with a powerful vision for change, if it is undercommunicated, the change will be in jeopardy. Employees will not change even if unhappy unless they believe useful change is possible and worth the effort. To accomplish this it is important to establish a persuasive communication campaign. Leaders need to clearly communicate to employees that change is imperative, and demonstrate why the new direction is the right one. Leaders should position and frame plans positively and gather feedback and incorporate good feedback ideas. The employee morale should be monitored through constant communication and reinforcement.

OBSTACLES

With any change a variety of obstacles may present themselves during the process. Employees may be perfectly positioned, understand the vision, and committed to making the change happen but something gets in the way and prevents them from moving forward. Leaders must be cognizant that no matter how good the planning has been there will always be unexpected contingencies that arise during the change process, and the leader must be continually on the lookout for these obstacles and remove them to maintain credibility for the change effort.

CELEBRATE

It is important to celebrate short-term wins as the change initiative progresses. Short-term wins keep the momentum moving forward and keep employees engaged. Failure to celebrate short-term wins reinforces the laggard position and the desire to return to the status quo. Leaders need to build in and actively work to develop short-term wins. It is not enough to just hope for them. Good change processes plan for wins to keep the staff engaged and motivated and keep the change moving forward. Leaders need to be sure to celebrate and promote these wins when they happen.

DECLARING VICTORY

It is also important as a leader not to relax and declare victory with a change too soon. Leaders must make sure the change is embedded in the organizational culture as the new norm so that employees do not lose focus and change resistors are not provided an opportunity to regress and bring things "back to the old ways."

ANCHOR

In the final analysis, change sticks when it becomes "the way we do things around here." Until new behaviors are embedded in organizational norms and values, they are subject to degradation as soon as the pressure is off. Leaders must ensure changes are firmly anchored and are the new norm for things to get done. The people who model the new change should be recognized and rewarded, and any behavior that hints at backsliding should be immediately addressed and corrected.

THE CHANGE PROCESS

To begin the change process, someone must decide to make a change and someone must drive change to be successful. Pharmacy leaders will find themselves in both roles, and while both are important to the change process, they are different. In general, the change leader has to be able to create the vision and sense of urgency for change, and the change agent must be able to develop and facilitate the actual implementation of the change.

Leader/Sponsor	Change Agent/Facilitator
Develops vision	Collects and analyzes data
Establishes sense of urgency	Builds a business case
Communicates the vision	Facilitates teams
Holds others accountable	Coaches team leaders
Removes barriers	Coordinates implementation
Delivers implementation plan	Designs communication plans
Institutionalizes the change	Evaluates change effort
Implements rewards and consequences	Identifies rewards and consequences
Committed to the change	Displays credibility to the workforce

With the need for change established and roles in the change delineated as we learned, there are still multiple opportunities for things to go wrong with the change. How can these issues be avoided to make sure the change is in the half of changes that are successful? At its simplest, to be effective in change management, you need two things: a plan that translates concepts into concrete steps that your team can carry out, and performance of all of the steps in your plan. That involves getting everyone involved who has a stake in the change.[12] In essence you need to "plan your work and then work your plan," and using a defined repeatable change model is an ideal way to accomplish this.

THE CHANGE MODEL

A goal of this chapter is to provide a workable change model that you can use quickly and effectively in any change situation. The CHANGE model by Elaine Biech is one of the most streamlined and straightforward models that captures this simple philosophy and provides the structure to effectively lead and facilitate change.[1] The CHANGE model utilizes six defined sequential steps:

1. Challenges the current state
2. Harmonizes and aligns leadership
3. Activates commitment
4. Nurtures and formalizes a design
5. Guides implementation
6. Evaluates and institutionalizes the change

CHALLENGE THE CURRENT STATE

The first step is to challenge the current state. This involves thoughtful preplanning as well as action. In this step, the leader collects and analyzes data to support the new position, determine organizational readiness for the change, establish change management roles, and build a solid business case to support the change idea. A good example of this is work done by multiple organizations to establish specialty pharmacy programs that include a pharmacy specialty billing unit.

This is a unique concept that involves a tremendous amount of change for pharmacy and on the organizational level. Specialty pharmacy billing does fit the model used for inpatient billing and it also does not fit the model of on-line claims adjudication used for outpatient prescription billing. However, with over half of drugs that are currently in phase III development falling into the specialty category and with the high cost for these drugs (estimates are that spending for specialty drugs will increase by 67% at year-end 2015), it is worth considering a different approach.[13]

Traditional hospital billing and revenue cycle programs are not geared toward the complexity of specialty pharmacy billing and collections. By challenging the current state and effectively moving this concept through all of the steps in the change process, organizations have been able to build on the "business within a business" concept for pharmacy and create a specialty pharmacy billing unit that has significantly improved billing and collection efforts on these high-cost/high-revenue drugs.

HARMONIZE AND ALIGN LEADERSHIP

It is important to align change initiatives with the overall organization's strategic plan, but it is equally important to ensure that the leadership that will sponsor and drive the change has also been aligned. Things rarely go exactly as planned in change initiatives, and having the leadership team on board and committed goes a long way toward improving the odds of success. To accomplish this, Biech notes the best leaders build this coalition by having a VIEW (visionary, inspiring, enthusiastic, wise).

Visionary leaders can articulate the vision for change and paint a picture that everyone can understand. They are big picture thinkers (and that may frustrate some people by not having all the details worked out), and they are comfortable with the ambiguity of the process. Inspiring leaders can sell the vision and its benefits. They can speak spontaneously and with conviction and can motivate others. Enthusiastic leaders look for the best in situations and encourage positive learning opportunities. And wise leaders exude confidence. They are competent and credible in their approach.

A change implementation team is also an important element here and provides guidance for the change. It defines strategies, sanctions processes, and provides needed resources, and it should be selected early in the process to help initiate and drive the change. This will be the key support tool for the change facilitator.

It is very important to get the right people on the team (people who can provide credibility and expertise) from the right areas (most critical areas and stakeholders) and with the right attitude (those who are positive, problem solvers, enthusiastic, and persistent). For example, a pharmacy automation project and implementation team might consist of informatics, pharmacy operations, facilities and engineering, and purchasing people. From the pharmacy it would be important to include not only managers but also pharmacists, techs, and support personnel who would be intimately involved with the systems.

ACTIVATE COMMITMENT

At this point in the change process a fundamental description of a desired change is in place, a business plan to support the change has been developed, leadership is aligned behind the vision for change, and a change implementation team has been selected. Now it is necessary to activate commitment and fill in the details of the implementation and actually move the change forward.

The implementation plan is the roadmap to take the change from beginning to end in the process—it is the tool to estimate time and resources needed to accomplish the change, it is a communication tool whereby something tangible is provided to the rest of the organization about the change, it is the organizer that lays out who will do what by when, and it creates credibility for the effort by clearly demonstrating that thought and effort went into the initiative.

A solid plan removes any doubt that you are just "winging it." It is important to make sure the initial data and business case tell the whole story and sell the reason for the change. State the change goals and a clear description of the end state, identify specific actions needed to achieve these goals, identify completion dates for each action, identify and allocate dedicated resources/experts/consultants, and assign responsibility and define accountability for each step.

Decide whether to conduct a pilot program or to benchmark and establish a monitoring plan and a regular reporting process. Identify choices people have, ensure opportunity for candid dialogue, be concerned about losses people may experience, identify preferred behaviors, and provide necessary training/coaching.

Make sure the plan establishes a communication mechanism that includes ways to obtain employee feedback. Use multiple communication methods—e-mail, newsletters, staff meetings, and focus groups. In a change initiative it is impossible to overcommunicate.

Celebrate short-term wins and major milestones in the process as well as long-term wins. As an example, for a pharmacy automation project it would be wise to spend time developing detailed statements of work and work plans. The project could be split into phases, with the first six months dedicated to the planning step. Specific people could be assigned to this process to ensure that every step in the plan was clearly articulated, responsibility for metrics captured, and reporting delineated.

NURTURE AND FORMALIZE YOUR DESIGN

With an implementation plan established, a look at the steps that have been detailed is beneficial to assess their impact on other areas of the organization to identify and alter any structures, processes, or procedures that might hinder the change effort. The design must be formalized and nurtured.

The workforce should be reviewed in terms of their skills (do they need more training?), time (do you need added resources?), and current priorities—any new change will automatically compete with existing priorities and stress employees in terms of time management. Even the best implementation plan will struggle if it is poorly timed.

Metrics should be revisited to ensure that they are realistic, timely, and meaningful. A risk assessment of the change effort should be performed—what might go wrong, what might happen if the plan fails? All of the potential things that might occur to prevent achieving the desired change outcomes should be identified and analyzed. A risk rating can be created such as high, moderate, and low to help prioritize risk. It is important to have options ready to minimize risks, and a process to monitor and address risks as they change should be established—in essence, have a contingency plan.

For a pharmacy automation project, initial and ongoing training to complement hardware and software upgrades would be an issue, as would expanding staff needs. Keeping the database clean and synchronized would also be a major risk that would need to be addressed. Detailed backup plans to handle hardware and software failures would be required and contingency plans ready.

Guide Implementation

Finally, select the tools you will use to monitor and guide the change process (e.g., Gantt charts, Pert charts, action maps). Guiding the implementation is where the leader needs to be actively involved with the change to ensure that it keeps moving forward. Particularly in complicated, difficult, or long-term projects, it is easy to lose enthusiasm and motivation for the change.

Careful attention should be paid to hand off points so nothing slips through the cracks; promote short-term wins to senior leadership and to staff; keep the informal leaders informed and engaged; keep all the stakeholders up to speed and engaged, even those on the periphery of the change; remember to thank staff who are doing great work to advance the change; deal with rumors and naysayers up front (post a FAQ tool, have a rumor-of-the-week posting; find out what is really bothering people and address it).

The bottom line is to *not* lose momentum for the change. For a pharmacy automation change, often nothing is going to look or work the same for staff in terms of daily operations, and it can be a constant challenge to keep staff and management positive about the project and engaged.

Evaluate and Anchor the Change

The last step in the process is where the change is evaluated to ensure it is valid and becoming "the way business is now done." Change agents or organizations often skip this step, but it is important to learn from each change process to do better with future initiatives, and it is important to make sure the change has "taken." If attention is not focused on this step, people will be tempted to return to the way they were doing things as soon as the spotlight is off them. This is also a great opportunity to bring closure to the change teams and to celebrate success.

For a pharmacy automation project it would be important to keep detailed project metrics such as turnaround time, missing orders, phone calls from nursing, dispensing/pick errors, and inventory values, to demonstrate value. It would be key to regularly update senior leadership and staff on progress and outcomes and take time to celebrate wins to reinforce the new way of providing service.

INCREMENTAL VERSUS TRANSFORMATIONAL CHANGE

It is important to recognize that not all change is the same and many organizations are struggling with this difference. Given the magnitude of the issues facing healthcare today, what is required to be successful is transformational change. Unfortunately, what most organizations have relied on for the past 20 years is incremental change methodology.

Incremental change means using the same thinking but focusing on driving change in behaviors to achieve new levels of results. Software upgrades would be a good example of an incremental change. There is no change in thinking—people do not need to think differently to capitalize on new systems—they just need to learn new screens and keystrokes. As noted by Marilyn Ferguson in *The Aquarian Conspiracy,* "If you continue to think as you always thought, you will continue to get what you have always gotten."[14] In an evolving market, organizations that achieve the same results they have in the past will eventually fall behind and incremental change will take an organization only so far. To achieve breakthrough results requires a change in thinking to drive new behaviors, as illustrated in Figure 5.2. Changing thinking produces that breakthrough level of performance or transformational change needed for future success. In healthcare today the classic example of transformational change is the movement to accountable care. We are changing the way we think from a volume-driven environment of care to one focused on improved outcomes and accountability.

THE BUSINESS OF PHARMACY—THE NEED FOR CHANGE

With a viable change model in hand, an understanding of the need for transformational change, and major problems confronting our organizations, what is it that pharmacy needs to change? Consider that if our organizations want to materially

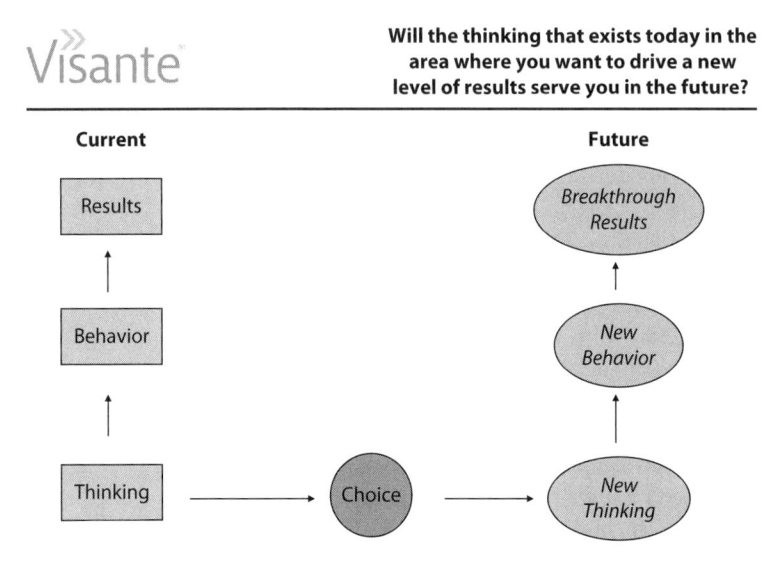

FIGURE 5.2 Transformational change.

impact expense, revenue, clinical quality, and risk, what service can have a greater impact than pharmacy? What is one of the fastest growing expense lines in any organization—drugs. What is one of the primary sources of revenue for any organization—drugs. What is the primary treatment modality for over 80% of patients in an organization—drugs. And, if we are going to seriously injure someone through medical error, other than in the operating room, where is the greatest source of risk? It is with millions of doses of drugs dispensed annually.

Put all of that together and we should be in a very strong position to help our organizations address these big problems while we also advance our pharmacy practice model initiatives (PPMI). But we continue to struggle. In his book, *Good to Great,* Jim Collins notes that great companies have defined and understand the drivers of their economic engines and they do everything they can to nurture those drivers.[15] There is no "one-size-fits-all" mentality in these companies. As healthcare organizations struggle they would do well to consider this strategy. Pharmacy is an obvious driver of success for all the reasons just noted, but in general little is done from the hospital executive level (C-suite) to nurture and grow that driver.

There are notable exceptions, but by and large pharmacy is not viewed by the C-suite as the material, clinical, and business operation that it really is. The overall impact of pharmacy is underappreciated, undervalued, and underutilized. There is a pharmacy brand challenge—the C-suite typically sees pharmacy as an ancillary support service. Pharmacy gets lumped in with the usual cast of characters—radiology, dietary, laboratory, respiratory, and physical therapy, where its unique contributions may not be recognized.

Pharmacy leadership typically is not part of the C-suite and may report up through a variety of different structures from associate administrators to chief nursing officers to various vice presidents, but the bottom line is pharmacy does not have a seat at the decision-making table, and as a result tends to get managed as a commodity. The average hospital administrator is unaware of the opportunities in pharmacy.

They certainly see the drug spend and often have a laser-like focus on that aspect of practice. However, the clinical impact of pharmacy is undervalued. There is rarely an understanding of the relationship between having the right skill mix and numbers of pharmacists and the impact on the drug spend and clinical care of patients. It is not recognized that pharmacy is a departmental outlier—it does not look like any other department in the hospital. Pharmacy is part clinical and part business, but the major expense, unlike every other department, is *not* people.

Personnel costs account for only 18 to 20% of the average pharmacy budget, while drugs are closer to 75 to 78%, with everything else in the 2 to 5% range. Pharmacy is a critical player in the care delivery process but not typically present at the C-suite table, and we have extremely complex operational systems and exception processes that do not "fit" the average departmental model. Unfortunately this often comes to light only *after* critical issues such as medication incidents, drug shortages, or financial crises trigger doubts regarding operational and financial controls. There is a bit of a "black hole" mentality at the C-suite level when it comes to pharmacy. They see resources going into the department in terms of head count, salary expense, and drug expense, but they do not see or understand what is coming out.

CHALLENGE/CHANGE THE CURRENT PHARMACY BRAND

Pharmacy needs to change its brand in our organizations. Our brand should be familiar such that there is immediate brand recognition in the organization. It should be captivating so that our C-suites pay more attention to the brand, and it should be preferable to other brands in the organization so that when tough choices have to be made the natural tendency will be to select the pharmacy brand. Pharmacy should mean quality so the perception is a better brand that is valued, and there should be cache or status associated with the pharmacy brand. Pharmacy should ensure that its brand is held in high esteem by the C-suite and that they are knowledgeable about what pharmacy does and what the brand stands for.

In each organization pharmacy needs to understand how it is currently seen and then decide what it wants to be seen as and also what it does not want to be seen as. Clearly, there is a need to aggressively educate the C-suite on "the business of pharmacy." There is a need to establish the pharmacy as a positive contributor to the challenges faced by our organizations and to create the perception that the pharmacy is material to the organization's efforts in terms of financial management, patient safety, and clinical care.

A redefinition of C-suite expectations for pharmacy is in order in terms of creative and innovative solutions that align with organizational goals and direction; clear and defined roles for pharmacy expertise to be available at the point of care; pharmacy accountability for all facets of the medication use process across all points of care; redefinition of the basic pharmacy systems and services required to meet the changing organizational model; and leadership that recognizes the balancing act between clinical and business outcomes and that can deliver new skills and collaboration.

SELLING THE CHANGE

So how does all of this happen without formal authority in the current organizational structure? Using the CHANGE model and employing better utilization of influence and advocacy skills to challenge the current state and harmonize and align leadership gives pharmacy its best chance to drive transformational change. It is not enough to have great ideas. Pharmacy has to be able to effectively sell those ideas through better advocacy.

There are hundreds of examples of people who have come up with great ideas without the formal authority to implement those ideas but have been able to challenge the current state and convince the right people through effective advocacy to move forward with those concepts. This involves being able to persuade the decision makers in the organization to listen to pharmacy and care about the issues, and to include pharmacy at the table when decisions are being made. Pharmacy needs to do a better job of speaking and writing in more compelling ways to overcome resistance by decision makers and make them want to support and adopt our ideas.

It is important also to note that advocacy is not an endeavor reserved only for those with titles like director or manager. Everyone in the pharmacy from the entry-level tech to staff pharmacist to pharmacy leader can be an effective advocate for the profession. And being an advocate does not mean always having innovative or creative ideas yourself—you can certainly sell the ideas of others to decision makers. Also, while this skill may come more naturally to some than others, anyone can learn to become a more effective advocate. How can this be accomplished? In his book *Advocacy*, John Daly provides an exceptional look at effective influence and advocacy, and this chapter uses his work as a framework for some key elements that can help pharmacy leaders.[2]

COMMUNICATE CLEARLY AND MEMORABLY

Start by knowing exactly what it is that needs to be understood by decision makers. Presentations are often cluttered with dialogue that is not germane to the main point, and this confuses decision makers. Can you convey the idea in less than 100 words? What is your two-minute "elevator speech"? It does not take a lot of words to communicate a memorable idea—the Gettysburg Address had only 272 words. It is important to stay on message and reinforce the message through repetition and redundancy.

Everyone dislikes political ads but think back to the successful campaigns and how they stayed on task with key messaging. Use multiple examples to reinforce the idea as well as different modalities. Remember that some people are auditory learners while others are visual or kinesthetic. Do not underestimate the value of visual reinforcement of an idea.

For example, what is the number one way to help reduce hospital acquired infection—everyone knows it is the simple act of hand washing. We have regulatory standards for this and hospital infection control standards, but it still remains less than optimal. One hospital took cultures of the hands of their top physicians and made the results available in very striking photos showing large colonies of bacteria. These photos became the screen savers for the hospital, and hand washing compliance shot up immediately. People knew the message, but they really got it when they saw the visuals.

FRAME YOUR MESSAGE

People like to categorize things and automatically sort information in their head into different categories or schemas. People with well-developed schemas around a topic will have an easier time understanding and remembering new information on that topic, while people with less-developed schemas will find it harder to grasp and remember the same material.

Most people have experienced reading something and at the end having no idea what they just read. The article was likely on a topic for which they did not have a well-developed schema. This rarely happens on topics on which people are expert. Think back to the C-suite—what is their schema around pharmacy? Are they experts? Probably not. If it is automatically assumed that they have well-organized and highly detailed schemas around high-performance pharmacy, then as advocates it is possible to quickly lose them if in reality their schema is much less complex.

To have the best chance of success, pharmacy should work to communicate ideas in ways that fit the C-suite schemas, and that means listening to and doing some homework on these decision makers. What is their background and training, where did they work before, what are their hobbies and interests, what are some of their major accomplishments? If selling a new clinical pharmacy service that improves patient outcomes, reduces overall hospital risk, and generates new income, how is this best framed? For a decision maker with a legal background the most important schema may be risk, while for someone with a financial background it may be the enhanced margin. A good advocate finds and matches the idea with the decision maker's schema.

BE PERSUASIVE AND MAKE SURE THE IDEA RESONATES

Often only one shot is possible at promoting an idea for change, and pharmacy leaders need to make sure they are at their most persuasive and that the idea resonates with senior leaders to have the best chance for success. The most successful coaches in sports always follow a game plan, and pharmacy leaders should have their own game plan for success. Presentations should do the following:

- Demonstrate a need
- Offer viable solutions to that need
- Stress the positives associated with the change
- Highlight the potential negatives that can happen if the change is not adopted
- Make the change easy to say yes to
- Use credible data sources for support
- Recognize and play into any emotion involved with the change
- Build on a positive track record and a positive history of success

SUMMARY

As Charles Dickens said, "it was the best of times, it was the worst of times."[16] The current challenges facing healthcare include access, quality, and cost, and while these may seem overwhelming, visionary pharmacy leaders will recognize these challenges as unique opportunities to put pharmacy forward as a solution to many of these issues. However, to take full advantage of these opportunities pharmacy leaders will need to be effective advocates for change as well as successful change leaders, and this demands a new way of thinking and new skill sets.

REFERENCES

1. Biech E. *Thriving Through Change: A Leader's Practical Guide to Change Mastery*, ASTD Press, Alexandria, VA, 2007.
2. Daly JA. *Advocacy: Championing Ideas and Influencing Others*, Yale University Press, New Haven, CT, 2011.
3. Vellmere B. 2010. Average Life Span of an S&P 500 Company, www.brianvellmere.com (accessed November 13, 2012).
4. Kane J. Healthcare Costs: How the US Compares to Other Countries. *PBS NewsHour*, www.pbs.org/newshour/rundown/2012/10/health-costs-how-the-us-compares-with-other-countries.html (accessed August 26, 2013).
5. Young J. Uninsured Americans 2012: More Than 45 Million Lacked Health Insurance Last Year, CDC Reports. *Huffington Post*, www.huffingtonpost.com/2013/03/21/uninsured-americans-2012_n_2918705.html (accessed August 26, 2013).
6. Collins SR, Robertson R, Garber T, Doty MM. Insuring the Future: Current Trends in Health Coverage and the Effects of Implementing the Affordable Care Act. The

Commonwealth Fund, www.commonwealthfund.org/Publications/Fund-Reports/2013/Apr/Insuring-the-Future.aspx (accessed August 26, 2013).

7. Kiem B. What Cuba can teach us about healthcare. *Wired*, www.wired.com/wired-science/2010/04/cuban-health-lessons (accessed August 26, 2013).

8. Tandon A, Murray CJL, Lauer JA, Evans DB. Measuring Overall Health System Performance for 191 Countries. GPE Discussion Paper Series: No. 30 EIP/GPE/EQC World Health Organization.

9. Barry D, Luband C, Holley T. The Impact of Healthcare Reform Legislation on Medicare, Medicaid, CHIP, www.healthlawyers.org (accessed August 26, 2013).

10. Kotter J. Leading change: Why transformation efforts fail. *Harvard Business Review*, March–April 1995.

11. Rogers EM. *Diffusion of Innovations*, Free Press, New York, 1962.

12. Bradford RW, Duncan JP. *Simplified Strategic Planning*, Chandler House Press, Worchester, MA, 2000.

13. Stettin G. Healthcare Insights 5.21.13, Specialty Drug Spending to Jump 67% by 2015, http://lab.express-scripts.com/prescription-drug-trends/specialty-drug-spending-to-jump-67-by-2015 (accessed August 26, 2013).

14. Ferguson M. *The Aquarian Conspiracy: Personal and Social Transformation in Our Time*. Tarcher, Los Angeles, CA, 1987.

15. Collins JC. *Good to Great*, Harper Collins, New York, 2001.

16. Dickens C. *A Tale of Two Cities*. Chapman and Hall, London, 1859.

Case Study

You are the director of pharmacy at a well-respected tertiary care facility. The organization has both an adult and pediatric hospital. The adult hospital offers high-risk obstetrics, and a pediatric hospital provides a level-one neonatal intensive care unit (NICU) with 65 beds. You are concerned that you have only one clinical pharmacist deployed in the NICU. This person is not able to adequately cover all of the desired medication needs for this patient population on a daily basis, and you have been continuously approached by pharmacy, medical, and nursing staff about increasing the pharmacy staffing and support in the NICU.

However, your hospital is also struggling with finances and just announced that they are launching a major cost reduction effort to cut 30% of total operating expenses over the next three years. You must present a persuasive argument to the budget committee to approve new staffing for the NICU in the face of cost reductions, and you have 15 minutes on their agenda to do it. How do you craft a successful case, and how do you present this persuasively?

- State Your Case
  - What do you lead with to let your audience know right up front what you want to accomplish?
- Use Experts
  - Who are important people in your organization that you can enlist to help to make your argument more credible?
- Use Data
  - Facts and numbers used well can be very convincing in support of your argument. What kind of data will you use to support your position?

- Use Emotion
  - Getting people emotionally involved can help your case. How will you leverage the emotion around "sick and at-risk babies" to help your presentation?
- Build on Trust
  - Having a track record that your audience is familiar with and trusts can greatly assist your presentation. What other successful initiatives have you produced that would help to reinforce your competence and engender trust in your ability to deliver on this request?
- Use Timing Concerns
  - Stress the time-sensitive nature of your proposal to create a greater sense of urgency for action. How will a continued delay in service impact the organizational risk profile?
- Use Supporting Facts and Research
  - Using reliable and familiar data sources to support your proposal is very powerful and consistent with the "evidence-based medicine" theme. Are there recognized benchmarks for staffing you can use? Are there examples of serious medication errors from other organizations in this patient population you can use to show the impact of a negative outcome in this population?
- Close Effectively
  - Close your presentation and get a commitment. Given all of the positive evidence and support for improving the care of this high-risk population, how can you get a commitment to move forward with creating additional neonatal clinical pharmacist positions before you leave the committee meeting?

6 The Leader in You

Stephanie A. Zarus

CONTENTS

Learning Objectives: After reading this chapter and working through the case, the reader will be able to:

1. Give details regarding the context in which leadership takes form
2. Identify behaviors that foster effective leadership
3. Explain the importance of professional relevance, including physical and virtual profiles
4. Incorporate methods for decision making and prioritization
5. Outline the pros and cons of having a mentor or leadership coach
6. Provide strategies for career promotion
7. Develop a plan to avoid burnout

WHY IS LEADERSHIP A MYSTERY?

If only it were easy to address this question. Academics and corporate executives continue to banter the polemics of both the theory and practice of leadership. Defining it is as elusive as defining love. Perhaps it is because both love and leadership involve people functioning together to achieve something other than and perhaps better than they can as individuals.

Conceptually leadership requires adaptation to a shared vision. It requires trust in one another and trust in the mutual ability to make difficult decisions. Leadership also requires the resiliency to thrive in an ever-changing environment. Your leadership success depends on the ability to communicate a future state that is physically, emotionally, financially, and spiritually sound. Leadership is about a future state with the promise of something better than the present state.

WHY IS LEADERSHIP IMPORTANT FOR YOU?

Countless self-help books have been written on leadership development. Amazon. com lists an inventory of over 100,000 leadership books as of August 2014. Add to this leadership arsenal the many news feeds, blogs, and tweets that share minute-by-minute suggestions on how to lead better, be more effective, or make a difference. You need not look far to witness the many available resources touting the secret to personal and professional success. Personal leadership development tools are everywhere for a reason—life requires the leader in you to be present at any time and any place, but as in life, there is no one recipe for leading well in every situation.

We have enough examples of leadership that need an injection of extra help. Consider the commercial or public service debacles that have occurred throughout pharmacy's history because people in positions of leadership failed to rally a team for the cause or failed to manage the lure of self-interest. Recall the meningitis outbreak that emanated from a Framingham pharmacy. Over 400 people experienced serious infection that resulted in hospitalization and death across 19 states. Where was the leadership breakdown in the compounding pharmacy? At what point did the pharmacist, technician, and staff lose sight of their role in patient safety? Why did the board of pharmacy not act, even after receiving a notice of concern? Why did leadership fail?

LEADERSHIP VERSUS LEADING

Leadership is a process by which people work toward an improvement over the current state by using or inventing resources. In pharmacy practice, a leadership opportunity exists each time a patient is confronted with a new or worsening ailment for which a therapeutic intervention is possible. The pharmacist is one expert in a line of many trained health-care intermediaries who share the goal of returning the patient to health. Each person (practitioner, administrator, support personnel, payer, researcher, regulator, etc.) has a core responsibility that is important to the patient's well-being.

Leading is the action that is being performed at a given time to achieve the leadership outcome. Health care in America requires leading to occur across many disciplines. Each discipline takes responsibility for some part of the care process. The more people involved in the care process, the more critical leadership becomes to the health outcome. This requires honest, persistent, smart people with courage to do what is right and to do it well.

As you develop and mature your ability for leading, you will attract these capable and competent people. A strong personal and professional network builds your resources for leadership success.

LEADERSHIP CONTEXT

In this chapter, leadership is viewed through the context of purpose, process, and outcome. Purpose clarifies why a change is necessary. Process describes how to rally people for the cause. Outcome defines the resultant future state for which the leadership work is necessary.

Leadership starts with understanding yourself within the context of personal and professional purpose, process, and outcome. Mark Moir, currently vice president of human capital for the Colorado Permanente Medical Group, studied the social forces and processes that attribute to leadership in a health-care setting. In his dissertation research he found that "context and situation are important factors in determining the success of both individuals and initiatives."[1] The success of your leadership work depends on your understanding of the context and situation in which your leadership is applied.

Leadership "work" begins with the way you answer the following five questions:

1. What is my purpose in this situation—what am I trying to do?
2. What is it that I will request of others in pursuit of this purpose?
3. How is this purpose in line with the organization's mission?
4. What process(es) will I use to achieve my purpose?
5. What outcomes will be realized in pursuit of this purpose?

These questions outline the context in which the "work" you are asking others to perform will occur. The answers become the narrative to communicate your vision and strategy. The answers also establish the baseline from which to evaluate ongoing performance. Leadership requires ongoing consideration of purpose and adaptation of process to achieve targeted outcomes.

In pharmacy practice this can present as evaluation and reevaluation of targeted health outcome occurring while the patient brings his or her medical condition under control. In the case of an infection, the patient can understand the value of taking an antibiotic to treat the infection. Taking the first dose offers promise of relief. By the fifteenth dose on day 8 of a 10-day regimen the relief has been realized. Once feeling better, the person's desire for adherence wanes. A leadership opportunity for the pharmacy staff is to enable the patient to see the value of taking the full 10-day regimen.

KNOW YOUR LEADERSHIP STYLE

LEADERSHIP BEHAVIORS

More often than not, you will lead with a behavior that is comfortable to you. Your approach might be to focus on the task at hand or the people involved as you strive to get it done, get it right, get appreciated, or get along.[2] In any given situation these four elements of leadership are important to the way you are perceived by others. A nimble leader understands the value of each behavioral trait and how to ignite the best in people. They also recognize behaviors that are attributed to stress, resulting in derailment of the purpose, process, or outcome.

You have already participated in many leadership challenges, whether in your family, in school, on the field or courts, and perhaps even at work. Outline a situation where you were called upon to engage people to do something different from what they were doing. Take a minute to reflect on the behaviors you used to get the group to act.

Often, we keep using the same behaviors even when the situation calls for something different. Do you have a hard time getting something done? Do you ever derail what someone else is trying to get done? Have you ever irritated someone or driven someone away when you were trying to get that person to do something?

When you begin to see a pattern in the way others respond to you, it is time to experiment with other leadership approaches. The skill in leadership is to achieve a positive outcome in support of the overall purpose. This is achieved by drawing upon what you do well, drawing out what others do well, and controlling the behaviors that derail the desired results. It is especially important when the behaviors are yours.

PSYCHOMETRIC TOOLS TO IDENTIFY YOUR LEADERSHIP ASSETS

To develop effective leadership behaviors, it is prudent to know your leadership strengths. Social scientists have been developing tools to assess behaviors for decades. There are many psychometric tools available to evaluate leadership traits or behaviors. Table 6.1 outlines a selection of tools used in leadership assessment.

Assessment tools used in leadership development enable us to categorize, prioritize, and give language to the different ways we behave in a given situation. How we behave, how we learn, how we treat others, and how we communicate who we are and what we know impact our leadership performance.

The leadership assessment tools used in psychometric analysis tell us, in comparison to others in similar situations, how likely we are to behave or act. For example, are you quick to speak out or do you listen to what others say? Do you begin looking for solutions or making a list of what you see is working? Do you research an opportunity or get an idea and go with it? Does it bother you when a colleague talks on about an issue or do you generally understand where your colleague is coming from? Would you rather read the manual or try your intuition?

Psychometric tools are often available through the career center in an academic institution, your community workforce office, or your personnel department. You can find valid assessment tools online; some are free of charge.

Take a few minutes to perform a basic psychometric analysis on yourself to assess your leadership behaviors. If you use the tool provided by the Kellogg Institute,[3] this tool considers leadership from the perspective of how a person gathers and evaluates information as the basis for decision making. This tool labels the leader behaviors for gathering information as intuitive or sensing, and labels the way a leader evaluates information as thinking or feeling. All leaders are capable of using intuition, sense,

---

TABLE 6.1
Tools Useful in Leadership Assessment

Tool	Internet Site	
Myers-Briggs Type Indicator[4]	www.capt.org/take-mbti-assessment/mbti.html	
DiSC[5]	www.discprofile.com/discclassic.html	
Kellogg School of Management[3]	www.kellogg.northwestern.edu/faculty/uzzi/htm/teaching.htm	Free
	Select the option for Leadership Assessment Tool Inventory, and then choose the link for the Cognitive Style Instrument.	
Online diagnostic tool in the article "Do You Play to Win—or to Not Lose?"[6]	hbr.org/2013/03/do-you-play-to-win-or-to-not-lose/ar/2 or available directly at http://yourfocusdiagnostic.com/	Free
Strengthsfinder 2.0 based on information from the Gallup database[7]	www.gallupstrengthscenter.com/?utm_source=googadwords&utm_medium=web&utm_campaign=newhomepage&gclid=CIqb9Y-M6LoCFTRk7AodOT0AHQ	

thought, and feelings to make decisions. The tool helps us measure, in relation to other men and women, how likely we are to use which of these behaviors most often.

How Does a Psychometric Evaluation Tool Help You?

With your evaluation results you are able to understand how you will approach gathering and evaluating information as well as understand that others around you might do it differently. If you typically lean toward being intuitive, you may pay extra attention to sensing what the data are portraying or ask others what they are sensing about the situation. The same can be applied to balancing thinking and feeling. Understanding more about your cognitive style helps you see how others perceive you as a leader. The perceptions others have about the way you make decisions are important to building your brand.

LEADING REQUIRES OTHERS

We all have behaviors that enable effective leadership. The way you behave impacts others and in some instances this impact is predictable and reproducible. As shown in Table 6.2, some people perform favorably when they are given specific data about a situation and the outcome that is expected. Others are motivated by understanding how the consequences of change will impact relationships and feelings, others respond to following laws and rules, and still others are motivated by a good story. A pharmacist might use this behavioral information to apply tactics to impact medication adherence, such as antibiotic compliance.

Our greatest behavioral assets can turn ineffective when under stress.[2] Review the behaviors in Table 6.3 and identify which you use when you are under stress. How might these behaviors impact your leadership abilities?

TABLE 6.2
Behaviors That Motivate People to Be Compliant with Taking Antibiotics

Behaviors That Motivate People to Act	Tactics for Antibiotic Compliance
Person performs favorably when given specific data about a situation and the outcome that is expected	Review the cause and consequence of the infection. Clarify the role of the antibiotic. Be specific about the regimen and what to expect if it is not followed.
Person is motivated by understanding how the consequences of change will impact relationships and feelings	Present the therapy and scenarios that occur when noncompliance results in reinfection that leads to missed time with friends and family. Suggest how others might feel about their relapse.
Person responds to laws and rules	Show the package insert that outlines the dose and frequency. Be specific about the regimen.
Person motivated by a good story	Share success stories of other patients who have benefited from this regimen. Tell of ways they overcame obstacles to achieve adherence.

TABLE 6.3
Ten Different Behavior Patterns Often Exhibited by People under Pressure

The Steamroller (or Tank)	Aggressive and angry; victims can feel paralyzed, as though they have been flattened
The Sniper	Uses sarcasm, rude remarks, and eye rolls; victims look and feel foolish
The Know-It-All	Wields great authority and knowledge; cannot stand to be contradicted or corrected; will go out of his or her way to correct others
The Grenade	Explodes into uncontrolled ranting that has little, if anything, to do with what has actually happened
The Think S/he Knows It All	A cocksure attitude often fools people into believing phony "facts"
The Yes Person	Wants to please others; never says no
The Maybe Person	Procrastinates, hoping to steer clear of choices that will hurt feelings; avoids decisions, causing frustration of others
The Blank Wall (or Nothing Person)	Offers a blank stare, no verbal or nonverbal signals
The No Person	Spreads gloom, doom, and despair when new ideas arise; saps energy from a group
The Whiner	Helpless most of the time; overwhelmed; wants things to be perfect; nothing seems to go right; wants to share his or her misery

LEADERSHIP PURPOSE, PROCESS, AND OUTCOME

Leadership forms out of an urgency to do something. A purpose must exist at some level for leadership to take hold. Once the purpose is envisioned, the one leading can implement processes to achieve the targeted outcome.

PURPOSE

As a pharmacist, the foundation of your purpose stems from the oath you take at graduation, "I promise to devote myself to a lifetime of service to others through the profession of pharmacy."[8] Your purpose is also formed by the contract you agree to in accepting licensure by your state board of pharmacy. Your purpose is further refined by the roles and responsibilities you accept in your employment agreement. The pharmacist's *purpose* in the purest sense is to ensure optimal medication use. The *outcome* of a pharmacist's work is to improve the health and well-being of patients. The *process* applied is from your moral and ethical being, within the rules, regulations, and acceptable practice standards established in your state of licensure, the company in which you are employed, and the position that you hold (Figure 6.1).

Technically, it sounds easy for a pharmacist to develop, refine, and apply effective leadership skills. Pharmacists have a clear purpose, guidelines, and expectations that define success. Society has a purpose for pharmacists: to enable a person to best use medication to resolve or manage a health issue. The people and resources available

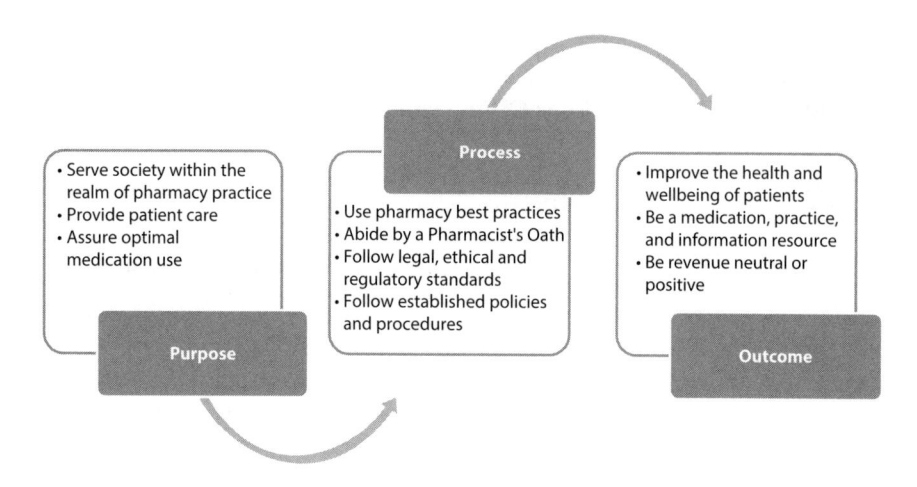

FIGURE 6.1   The pharmacy leadership purpose, process, and outcome.

to rally for this cause are fairly well defined. So why is this not easy? Your ability to lead effectively is confounded by many variables in conflict with your purpose, process, and outcome—starting with you.

Process

Leadership is a process that relies on social interactions. It is a social phenomenon that depends on many variables impacted by how a person behaves. Leadership behaviors used in one situation may be different from behaviors applied in another. These variables include how you feel about the issue, your belief in your ability to garner resources to make an impact, and the abilities of others to work with you. Ultimately, your behavior impacts the behavior of others, your access to resources, and your ability to navigate barriers to success. This social phenomenon of leadership results in either a positive or negative influence on your ability to lead.[9]

No one is able to predict exactly what leadership behavior or specific process is needed at any given time. More effective leaders are competent in their technical knowledge and are socially nimble. They understand what they bring to the table as well as how others can add to or distract from the desired result. They try different approaches. They have the discipline to reflect on what works and what needs adjustment. Leadership requires the courage to take action, even when the action may be unpopular.

Leadership process requires adaptation to happen within a mutually satisfactory cultural context. The parties involved become part of a new culture, sharing the belief that the vision is important and their actions are warranted. Leadership work rarely takes place in a protected environment. People have conflicting agenda, their moral and ethical positions differ, and there is competition for limited resources. People have ego needs, environments change, and fear of adapting to a new state causes people to question the validity of the vision. Once you consider these factors, it quickly becomes evident how teams, organizations, and entire systems are filled with leadership obstacles.

OUTCOME

The outcome of the work done is a reflection of the leadership provided. Consider this: you work in a pharmacy with two interns, two pharmacists, and a clerical assistant. Each person has a cadre of primary and secondary responsibilities. When the work is done collaboratively, the result is an efficiently run pharmacy. Systems are in place to assure quality prescription processing and medication management that result in satisfied patients, engaged staff, empowered prescribers, and positive cash flow.

Think of the dynamics under way when just one person on the team slows down. Perhaps he is repeatedly distracted by texting or taking personal calls. Perhaps she only does the work she likes and is otherwise less than productive for the team.

A one-time event that diminishes the standard process can generally be overcome by others who pick up the slack. What results after this behavior becomes the normal culture in the pharmacy?

WITHOUT LEADERSHIP, PEOPLE GET RESTLESS

It stands to reason that continued lack of realization of purpose and disregard for process yield poor outcome. Good employees become conflicted, as they struggle with the way they want to perform and the performance that is accepted. Continued lack of performance expectations causes a negative impact on the other staff physically (as they pick up the slack); emotionally (as they wrestle with the work imbalance, morale issues, try to "fix" the problem themselves, etc.); financially (the cost of lost productivity and re-work from errors); and spiritually (as they struggle with the poor performance in themselves and others).

Staff grows resentful, some act as entitled to certain things as payback, and others become entrenched in what they think is right. Left without leadership intervention, more negative behaviors begin to spread across the workplace. These behaviors lead to more mistakes, disorganization, and negative morale. There is erosion of the purpose, process, and outcome across the pharmacy, until no one is clear why things are not working anymore.

You can begin to see the nuances that make leadership challenging. Knowing the behaviors you and others use to navigate through getting things done will help you temper behaviors to optimize leadership opportunities. Of course it is not just about modifying people's behaviors. Effective leaders keep the purpose clearly visible. They ensure people (including themselves) are always learning. They build skills and competencies to support personal and professional growth. They encourage a culture of innovation and problem solving.

Every time you make a request of another person to support the purpose you are trying to achieve, there will be a moment of reconciliation where that person determines if the benefit of fulfilling your request is in his or her best interest. Leadership happens only with people who are willing and able to be involved. Left without leadership, people become restless. They question the value of being involved. They construct their own concept of purpose and implement their own process. The resultant outcome is nothing you envisioned.

BUILDING YOUR LEADERSHIP BRAND

A leader makes requests of other people. The more challenging the situation, the greater risk the leader is requesting people to take. In order for people to take great risk (that is putting their all into it) to fulfill a request from another person, they need to feel safe, and they need to believe that the risk is worth it—either for themselves personally or for what they believe in.

The way you show up—your leadership brand, impacts the way others react to you. It also impacts their willingness to take risks for you and their willingness to fulfill your request with their greatest skill and competency. Building a network of people who believe in you and are willing to give your request their best effort, going above and beyond what is expected to deliver on your request, is exactly what a successful leader achieves.

Your brand, made up of factors like the roles you play, your position, the way you appear, act, work, treat others, deliver on your word, communicate, and are "believable" (what one expects) are all considered by the people around you as they formulate their responses to your requests.

As a pharmacist you will be expected to be conservative, professional, and service oriented. The degree to which you need to be conservative, professional, and service oriented will depend on the culture where you work, whom you wish to lead, and the authority that is provided to you by the position you have. Four domains of leadership strength (executing, influencing, relationship building, and strategic thinking) are beneficial to team performance.[10] Figure 6.2 provides a framework of strategies used by leaders to achieve career progression.[11] Consider how you can build your professional brand to include these domains.

Building a strong brand is good for career development. When a career seeker intentionally creates a personal "brand image," he or she is set apart in a positive manner from other competitors and is more likely to achieve career advancement.[11]

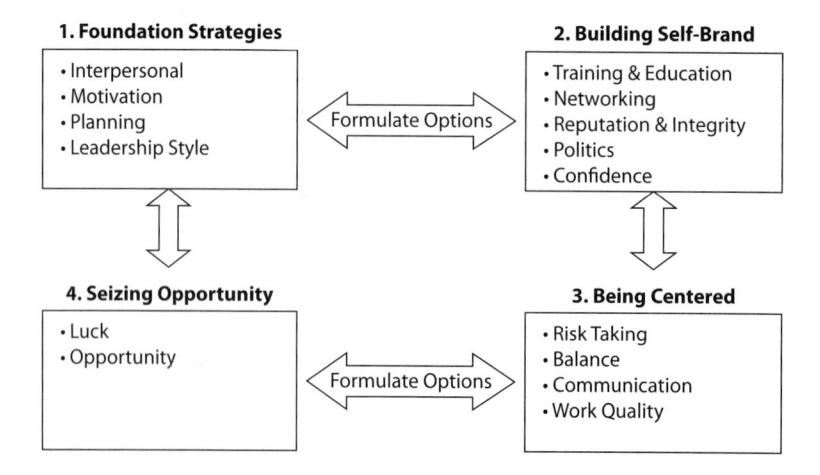

FIGURE 6.2 Framework of groupings of the 15 upward mobility tactics. (Reprinted from R.L. Laud and M. Johnson, *Career Development International.* 17(3): 240, 2012. With permission.)

Physical Profile

Why does the way you appear matter to your leadership ability? Your dress may not change what you know about leadership, but it can change the process by which others engage with you. Recall how leadership requires people to fulfill a request you are making of them. In order to comply with your request, they need to have a relationship with you. The way they relate to you has everything to do with how they perceive you.

Picture this: An 80-year-old woman enters the pharmacy to pick up her medication. It is a new prescription that requires specific instructions to be followed. You ask her to join you in the counseling area. She stares at your mohawk hair cut and tattoos with apprehension. While she follows you to the seating area, she gets more suspicious. The entire time you are talking, she sits stiffly and wonders if your tongue piercing hurts. She cannot imagine that you would understand her health issues or medication she needs.

For better or worse, people are programmed to judge what they see, hear, smell, feel, and taste. From these inputs, people make assumptions about the legitimacy of what is presented to them. Are you a threat or will you help them? A 2008 survey conducted by CareerBuilder.com showed that 41% of employers admitted to promoting people who dressed professionally.[12] These people looked like they would perform well on the job. In the case of leadership, does what they see in you meet their expectations of a person they want to consider "a leader," or more specifically "their leader"?

Consider the same elderly woman who enters the pharmacy. This time you greet her (mohawk and all) with a smile. You tell her that you realize your look is not in line with her expectations. You let her acknowledge this. You show her your pharmacist license and tell her of other people you have taken care of. You work hard to develop a trusting relationship. It takes several visits for her to warm up to you and trust you to be her pharmacist. You can break down the barriers caused by an unexpected appearance. It requires extra work.

You can make the leadership process easier on yourself and the people around you. Provide the visual that projects a person worth trusting—a person who is believable, and a person deserving of an honest response. You need to be genuine and prepare yourself, your work product, and your work environment to project the highest level of professionalism for the position. Align your persona with what the community in which you operate expects. Do not require people to have to figure you out before they are willing to work with you.

Your dress, work environment, and work product support or distract from your personal leadership brand. Be authentic and follow what Bill George calls your "True North."[13] You should prepare yourself, your dress, and your behaviors to emulate what you stand for. Check that your appearance is consistent with your message and respects the people with whom you wish to relate.

Professional Profile

Like a ballplayer, your professional metrics demonstrate your experience and value. Today, professionals maintain a current profile or résumé that is published on a business networking site like LinkedIn. Business networking sites provide a standard format to showcase a person's past experiences, education, and accomplishments. Often there is an option to create a print version or to e-mail your resume or curriculum vitae (CV) directly from the site. Figure 6.3 provides a template you can use to get started on your résumé.

Networking sites allow you to join groups of professionals with similar interests. You can build a global professional network and remain connected to colleagues, even those who change employers. People can seek your advice or offer you opportunities. Online professional forums provide quick access to information and introductions you may not get on your own. If you do not yet have a professional profile, search the Internet for different sources. Schedule a time to create one for yourself.

SOCIAL PROFILE

Do you have a social media site? Take a minute to flip through the pictures you have posted. Do they portray the brand you want projected about you? Is your cyber image current and relevant?

Provide your social media links to two family members, two good friends, two professional colleagues, and two recent acquaintances. Ask them to view your sites and send you five words that describe you as a result of what they see. Review and compare the responses you receive. Are there any patterns in the way you show up to these different people? Is this the leadership brand that you want? Will this leadership brand do well for your career or will it hinder you? What can you do specifically to update your social profile? How can you positively influence the way others think about your leadership ability when they interact with you through social media? While you are thinking about your presence in the electronic world, take a minute to update your voicemail message, e-mail address, and electronic signature line.

STAYING ON TRACK AS A LEADER

It will not come as a surprise to you to learn that leading takes time. Leaders solve problems for which solutions are not readily apparent. This problem solving often requires many actions. Intelligence gathering, data collection, and evaluation are used to clarify vision and strategy. Once there is clarity regarding the promise of a future state, the leader moves to articulating the vision so that each person is able to understand his or her role. The leader delivers this information to individuals in time for their use when needed. Leadership requires ongoing research, prioritization of actions, information sharing, teaching and learning, monitoring, and reporting.

MAKING TIME WORK

Leaders spend time efficiently. Leaders are particularly effective at allocating resources, prioritizing needs, and addressing issues in time to keep the people and processes on track. When you take a leader stance, knowing your purpose (your leadership goals) in the context of the situation will enable you to be aware of how

Name

Address, email, cell phone/contact number

Profile:
- Short paragraph describing who you are, your purpose, and your value—your two-minute elevator pitch.

Skills:
- Technical, scientific, medical, or other expertise (e.g., pharmacy intern)

Abilities:
- What you can do (e.g., inventory control)

Knowledge:
- What you know (e.g., WorkflowRx Pharmacy Inventory Management Software)

Education:
- Degree and major, school, year graduated or will graduate, any important course work/projects/research, and so forth

Certifications:
- Industry-recognized credentials

Languages:
- Proficient in speaking, reading, writing, and so on—be specific

Professional affiliations:
- Associations, societies, memberships

Publications:
- Manuscripts, presentations, and so on

Research:
- Manuscripts, presentations, and so on

Professional (include volunteering or unpaid research as an experience) experience:
- Company name, city, state
- Title:
- Begin Year to End Year:
- Open paragraph—In the first sentence describe what the company is; second sentence describe your responsibility/accountability; and then after in bullets describe your results/accomplishments:
- Project specific #1 (Begin Year to End Year) – Summarize what you did and results
- Project specific #2 (Begin Year to End Year) – Summarize what you did and results

FIGURE 6.3 Sample résumé template.

effectively you are prioritizing your time. President Eisenhower was famous for bringing clarity to time management with his quote, "What is important is seldom urgent and what is urgent is seldom important." Eisenhower was reflecting on the fact that there are many things that appear urgent that only marginally impact what a leader is trying to achieve. If you are able to cull those items with the highest importance and the highest urgency, you will be most effective in achieving the stated purpose.

IMPORTANCE VERSUS URGENCY

This "Eisenhower Principle" sums up the concept of the urgent/important matrix later introduced to business practice by Steven Covey.[14] The concept is straightforward. Create your list of professional and personal things that you believe need to be done to further your professional and personal leadership goals. Assign each item a value of 1 to 5, representing, respectively, least to most important to achieving your goals. Assign a second value of 1 (least urgent) to 5 (most urgent), requiring timely attention. The urgent items generally require your participation to further someone else's agenda.

Creating a task matrix brings to light the items of greatest value to your leadership efforts. The items ranking highest in both categories—importance and urgency— are the ones you want to tackle first. Those with the lowest ranking are most appropriate to reschedule or delegate.

TURNING ON URGENCY

Items with a single high ranking in either urgency or importance have the greatest risk and return for your leadership efforts. When taking action is important, but not urgent, you risk procrastination. It seems a level of urgency stimulates action. Think about ways you could build urgency into your important items. Create greater visibility and accountability on important items that lack immediate urgency. This tactic provides an ongoing sense of urgency. This is also where breaking a complex item into a series of items with more urgent deadlines can help to pace leadership work.

DOING THE IMPORTANT STUFF

Finally, the items of high urgency and low importance tend to distract us from what is really important to our leadership purpose. The fact that there is a level of urgency means that there is some risk associated with not acting on the item immediately. For the highly urgent items of low importance look to (a) handle the item once—do it immediately, (b) delegate it quickly, (c) put it away and negotiate a new deadline, or (d) find an alternate way to mitigate the risk of delaying. You can reduce leadership stress by setting expectations regarding how you will prioritize items that may be urgent but are not aligned with your goals.

There are a number of time-management tools available to you. New tools are being introduced to the market regularly. Personal communication devices come with sophisticated applications to establish timelines, manage schedules, and send alerts. Pick a time-management system and use it faithfully.

DECISION-MAKING TOOLS

Leadership can be modeled. *Leadership Is for Everyone* introduces the L.E.A.D.E.R.S. Method, a framework developed by Peter Dean for leader decision making.[15] The L.E.A.D.E.R.S. Method suggests that in any given situation, if a person is actively engaged and willing to (1) listen to learn, (2) empathize with emotions, (3) attend to the aspirations of others, (4) diagnose and detail the situation, (5) engage for good ends, (6) respond with respectfulness, and (7) speak with specificity, they are more likely to enroll others in taking the risk of fulfilling a request.[15] This method provides fundamentals to be an effective leader.

The ideas of this model are further supported in the work done by Kouzes and Posner in their book titled, *The Leadership Challenge*, where they outline research done to identify the 20 most desirable characteristics of leaders.[16] Such characteristics as honesty, farsightedness, competency, intelligence, and fair-mindedness are supported when one interacts with others using the L.E.A.D.E.R.S. Method.

Using the L.E.A.D.E.R.S. Method as a framework, give yourself a check in each box that describes how you approach making a request to another person or denying a request that is made of you. Declining a request is just as much a part of leadership as saying "yes." Complete Table 6.4 to learn what behaviors are positioning you well for decision making.

EFFECTING CHANGE

Experiencing a positive leadership moment comes when you understand the situation (know the purpose), can determine the leader abilities needed from yourself as well as from others in such a way (processes) to mobilize yourself, other people, and the necessary resources to achieve a desired outcome, and then you act on it all. Michael Useem, in *The Leadership Moment*, suggests that your leadership moment is the "critical point where the fate or fortune of many or a few can be changed by you," the point where your actions "whether small or large shape the future of others." Useem considers leadership the "act of making a difference."[17]

In *Leadership on the Line*, Ronald Heifetz and Marty Linsky characterize the complexity of leadership to span a spectrum of situations from those requiring a technical intervention to those requiring an adaptation of human behavior.[18] When people have the necessary know-how and procedures to do what needs to be done, then they have a technical problem. When there is no known solution and something within a person requires changing, then an adaptation of behavior is required.

For example, when a pharmacist is confronted with a patient who does not adhere to his or her medication regimen, it can be considered a technical problem. Figure out why the patient is not taking the medication and set up a system to enable the patient to adhere to it and you have the solution.

You already know that compliance is not that easy. If it were, everyone in every situation would be compliant. Patients may have underlying reasons for their

TABLE 6.4

Leadership for Everyone: How to Apply the Seven Essential Skills to Become a Great Motivator, Influencer, and Leader

Apply the Leader's Methodology as You Formulate a Request	Visual Leader Queues When Making a Request	Verbal Leader Queues	Vocal Leader Queues	What Specific Personal Behaviors Do You Need to Add or Eliminate from What You Currently Do?
Listen to Learn	Look the audience in the eye, diminish interruptions, and remove barriers to acceptance.	Press for clarity, accuracy, and secondary agenda. Use valid references to clarify points and correct misinformation. Demonstrate your determination and competency.	Use calming, even tone and volume; remain interested in the speaker and the content; provide safe environment in which to share information.	
Empathize with Emotions	Understand and clarify how the person is feeling about fulfilling the request; look for emotional responses and other visual cues resulting from your request.	Acknowledge the reactions you perceive and resist immediate action. Show self-control. Speak to the emotion you see; recognize it verbally and provide a safe way to move forward. Demonstrate your integrity.	Be patient and resilient. Demonstrate your empathy. Build trust over problem solving.	
Attend to Aspirations	Look for clues that show you what motivates the individual. How do they dress, act, and communicate? What is important to them in the workplace? Whom do they listen to? What are they aspiring to achieve and how does this connect with your request in the past, present, or future?	Address these factors as you make your request. Position your request within the context of their aspirations.	Be inspiring. Show excitement for their aspirations and ways these aspirations can be further supported through the request at hand or recognize the aspirations will not be addressed at this time, but as a result of success achieved in pursuit of the purpose, their aspirations can be addressed at a later time.	

Diagnose and Detail	Gather and evaluate information; take notes, release relevant notes and research; request feedback on assumptions; and require data to have integrity.	Ask pressing questions; require honest answers; curb hearsay; support a culture of honesty and integrity; and refrain from taking sides or talking about others.	Remain open minded and straightforward in your approach; treat all information as potentially valuable until proven unlikely to be; and refrain from making quid pro quo side deals.
Engage for Good Ends	Clarify the value of your request in support of the purpose or mission. Confront what you will personally receive from the request or the resultant outcome of the request. Willingly make transparent any personal gains you or others will receive.	Communicate the value the request brings to the mission. Assure all understand each other's part and the value to the overall mission in comparison to any personal gain. Recognize that everyone may not have an equal stake in the outcome.	Be transparent about the integrity of decision making and the perceived and actual outcome expected. Guard against the potential for a conflict of interests.
Respond with Respectfulness	Demonstrate how you honor individual worth, rights, and values. Expect the same behavior of others.	Be honest and patient. Resolve conflicts with fair process. Be forward looking and provide necessary and full background to position your request in the context of the overall mission. Assure recipients have adequate time and information to make an informed decision to your request.	Be dependable, responsive, honest, and straightforward.
Speak with Specificity	Your spoken, unspoken, and written word reflect what you intend. Minimize leadership risk and speak with specificity. Refrain from distractions (toying with objects, facial expressions, and flowery words). Be mature and self-controlled.	Prepare before you make your request, and select word choice and delivery method. Request feedback; assure clear communication and full understanding. Demonstrate intelligence, dependability, courage, and loyalty.	Breathe evenly. Speak with volume tone and pace that convey your belief in the message and the result you anticipate from the request you are making.

Adapted from Dean, PJ. (2006). *Leadership for Everyone: How to Apply the Seven Essential Skills to become a Great Motivator, Influencer, and Leader. The L.E.A.D.E.R.S. Method.* New York: McGraw-Hill. Copyright © 2013 Peter J. Dean. All Rights Reserved. Used with permission.

inability to be adherent. Perhaps they emotionally do not want to take the medication, perhaps their family does not want them to take it, perhaps culturally there is a stigma attached to the disease or the medication, maybe someone they know had a bad reaction, maybe they like the attention they get from their illness and taking the medication may eliminate this attention, the possibilities are endless. Values, attitude, and behavior impact compliance on par with technical obstacles like access.

The pharmacist is called to lead the person to understand the purpose of the therapy and the processes necessary to be compliant, including adjusting their lifestyle and behaviors. Of equal importance, the pharmacist should lead the patient to want the desired outcome. The patient should be able to see that the desired outcome (health with medication) is better than his or her current state.

The pharmacist's leadership challenge in patient compliance is in understanding the nuances that exist at the intersection between the technical ability of a person to adhere to a regime and that person's desire to adapt his or her beliefs and behaviors to do it. Competence in pharmacy and therapeutics alone will not enable the pharmacist to support the patient in achieving optimal compliance. Impacting patient adherence requires the pharmacist to be competent in medication management. It also requires the pharmacist to demonstrate emotional and social skills to enable the patient to adapt to what is required to achieve compliance.

Activity: Consider a noncompliant patient situation. Using the L.E.A.D.E.R.S. Method table, outline how you would lead a patient to comply and remain compliant on a new therapeutic regimen for managing hypertension.

THE VALUE OF STRESS

Did you ever feel so uncomfortable with a situation or were prodded enough that you stood up and took action? Turning on the heat or stress for yourself or others can be an effective way to overcome the status quo and initiate a change or action. Change causes a degree of tension. The tension is good to get action.

In contrast, have you ever been in a situation where you felt paralyzed to act or you acted badly? Perhaps you felt the risk of appropriate action would have a negative impact on you in some way. As a leader, you want to watch for hidden conflicts and control the temperature, assuring that the tension is enough to get people to pay attention and act, but not so much that stress causes bad behavior or fear and paralysis set in.[18]

When you recognize that a person is behaving ineffectively, you can help to identify the reason and address the behavior. You can enable the person to redirect energy to the purpose, the process, or the outcome toward which you are leading. Diagnosing the cause of stressed behaviors can be straightforward or deeply entrenched and complicated. The leader's challenge is to turn on just enough stress to cause a positive reaction and to modify a situation to de-stress behaviors that are distracting.

Consider again the texting pharmacist who was distracted and underperforming. In the margin of the page, write down how you would react to this pharmacist. In an environment with effective leadership, the fellow staff members would be empowered to speak honestly and respectfully to the offending pharmacist about his behavior. This confrontation would cause a degree of tension. Done well, this confrontation will modify the texting behavior and restore a culture of accountability.

DO YOU NEED A LEADERSHIP COACH?

You are on your way to leadership when you (1) understand the change that needs to be made; (2) can create and deliver the underlying narrative that enables others to commit to making the change happen; (3) can navigate the dynamics of working with people; and (4) are able to measure, monitor, and make changes along the journey to the future state.

Leadership requires problem solving. Mumford and colleagues suggest that the key to leadership effectiveness is the generation, evaluation, and implementation of reactive and proactive solutions. They suggest that leaders solve complex problems in dynamic settings with limited information in real time.[9]

It is nearly impossible to be an effective problem solver in a vacuum. Effective leaders surround themselves with people who provide feedback and test the leader's assumptions, skills, competencies, and behaviors. Leadership stays relevant when those leading can see themselves and their actions from differing perspectives.

VALUE OF A SOUNDING BOARD

Advisors, mentors, and coaches provide a trusted place in which the leader can reflect on past experiences. With a sounding board, an individual can experiment with new leadership ideas and "what if" scenarios without going public. The leader can talk through potential options before implementing a course of action. A coach also keeps a leader's ego in check and keeps pressure on the leader to focus his or her efforts on the purpose, thereby reducing distractions and conflicts.

INFORMAL MENTOR OR FORMAL COACH

Consider a difficult assignment you have had in the past, particularly one in which the directions were sketchy and the stakes were high. You may have gone to a teacher or one who assigned the project to get clarification of expectations. You may have spoken to peers or colleagues to learn how similar projects were conducted. As you formulated your own details, you may have tested your theories on others or had a respected colleague review your completed work before submitting it.

This informal way of seeking mentoring and advice is effective. It engages others to improve the outcome. As your leadership responsibilities gain complexity, a professional coach can work with you to navigate challenges, empower others, and align resources to achieve and celebrate the outcomes being pursued. A professional coach is contracted to assist you in working through your leadership challenges.[19]

SELF-APPOINTED COACH

As you exercise your leader abilities, you may find people with conflicting agenda and self-interests who are eager to present their ideas to you and offer to "coach" you through problem solving. Be cautious of a person who presents him- or herself to you. Select your mentors, advisors, and coaches based upon their proven record of competency in the area in which you are seeking clarity. Request a résumé and check references. You want to work with a coach who understands your purpose, process, and outcome and is passionate about enabling you to serve as an effective leader. Everyone has a purpose—be sure you understand the purpose of your advisors, coaches, and mentors. Do not let the purpose of others derail your purpose.

PATHWAY TO PROMOTION

With your professional profile polished, your mentor in place, and your ever-growing number of leader experiences under your belt, you may be thinking about short- and long-term strategies for promotion. Taking control of your career management has been shown to result in career advancement.[11]

SELF-PROMOTION

Are you comfortable promoting yourself? People generally feel uncomfortable talking about their accomplishments. Most people are not aware of how valuable self-promotion is to career promotion. Laud and colleagues identified 15 key factors (Figure 6.2) reported by leaders to contribute to upward mobility, one category of which included Building Self-Brand.[11] Promoting yourself with humility is effective and valuable to career progression.[20] Consider the strategies for self-promotion in Table 6.5 and outline what you can do to promote yourself over the next 30 days.

TABLE 6.5
Strategies for Self-Promotion

- Be visible
- Be prepared
- Take pride in doing a good job
- Avoid belittling accomplishments
- Accept compliments gracefully
- Avoid self-discounting language
- Be free to share accomplishments
- Weave accomplishments into the conversation
- Avoid repeatedly mentioning accomplishments
- Avoid exaggeration
- Speak positively of others
- Dress for success
- Take an active role in mentoring

Adapted from Self-promotion: a strategy for career advancement. Davidhizar R; Lonser GY; *Health Care Manager*, 2004 Jan–Mar; 23(1): 11–14. With permission.

The Elevator Speech

You may want to begin your self-promotion by perfecting your elevator speech—that is, the introduction of yourself and your qualities that can be shared during a two-minute elevator ride. An elevator speech begins with an introduction that includes connecting with your listener. Share your name and perhaps where you are from. This can be a geographic location, department within a company, or area of study in a university. Next provide a quick statement about your purpose. What are you interested in? What do you stand for? Then make your request or outline what you would like the listener to remember about you. The elevator speech is meant to be an introduction of yourself, your concept, and a request of the listener. Usually the request is to meet at a scheduled time for a more in-depth discussion or permission to call upon the listener at a later date. It gets your foot in the door, so to speak.

Practice your monologue to eliminate hesitation and awkward moments. To conclude the conversation, work an interesting, engaging question or two into your ending. This also provides an opportunity for the listener to share something about him- or herself or the company with you.

Every time you exchange or share something with someone you are building a relationship. Making a request of someone who has some relationship with you improves the likelihood that your request will be answered favorably.

Seek New Responsibilities

Use the "elevator speech" approach to identify new or different responsibilities that you might tackle at your present workplace. Having broad experience across differing roles is valuable to your career progression. Working, volunteering, or participating in different roles within work and your community enables you to hone skills, meet people, practice leadership behaviors, and build your professional network. A strong and varied network provides many resources. Your network can serve as a sounding board when you need advice, can provide access to people or places you may not have been able to reach on your own, and can often provide you with an opportunity for career advancement. Reflect upon your professional narrative. Write an elevator speech about yourself. Practice it on three people and refine it until it is clear, concise, and impactful.

AVOID BURNOUT

Immersing in endless hours of work can lead a person to become isolated, exhausted, and disengaged. A leader can become emotionally reactive instead of proactive. Continual draw on emotional and energy reserves results in poor decision making and reduced performance.

Of equal importance to getting work done is to schedule time to celebrate and recharge. Know how you best recharge yourself. Review the psychometric analysis you did earlier in the chapter. If you are a person who relaxes through internal activities, have books or games around. If you recharge with external stimuli, join a local club where you can learn or experience something with others.

Nurture Interests

External interests enable you to relate to people on many levels, have the energy to tackle whatever issues arise, and base decisions on elements of life beyond the workplace. Leaders engage in opportunities outside work that stretch their competencies and provide opportunities for growth and mastery. Outside activities add to a leader's ability to be agile and innovative at work.

Leadership provides never-ending opportunities to problem solve, engage people, allocate resources, and meet business expectations. Take a moment to outline how you can avoid leadership burnout. Think about what matters to you physically, socially, emotionally, and spiritually. How will you nurture these facets within yourself? How will you nurture these facets in others?

Protect Against Burnout

In a blog published by Entrepreneur.com, Nadia Goodman notes that burnout is best kept at bay by protecting against it up front.[5] She recommends three considerations for every leader: (1) engage, train, and inspire employees to lead effectively within the organization, empowering others and ensuring shared responsibility; (2) bolster your confidence by taking the time to continually learn and build your network of people who can support you, answer questions, and provide direction. As stated earlier, seek mentors who will provide honest and timely feedback, rather than placating or misdirecting you; (3) make your health and well-being a priority. Be with your family and friends. Exercise, eat well, and get sufficient sleep. Travel to new places. Do things you enjoy. Meet people. Build your personal and professional network. Participate in sports, arts, or theater. Teach and learn. Mentor and reflect.

Leadership is not about working endless hours or doing it all yourself. On the contrary, effective leadership requires people who are engaged and aligned. Leadership requires effective use of time and resources. Strong leaders are relevant, interesting, and believable. They are able to enroll, inspire, and engage people to perform—not just any people, but the right people (those who give their best effort to bring change to fruition).

SUMMARY

You are your greatest asset. What you know, whom you know, what you can access, how you behave, and how your behaviors impact others determine your ability to formulate a purpose, construct and communicate effective process, and realize an accomplished successful outcome. These are the components of your leader skills. Commit to learning more about your leader skills. Use valid psychometric tools to assess your natural tendencies. Seek a mentor to provide you with honest feedback.

Practice refining the way you lead. Each time you imagine a better experience than the one you are in, a way in which the lives or fortunes of someone could be improved by something you can do, then you are poised on the edge of a leadership opportunity. Formulate your purpose for making a change. Plan out a process that includes identifying and engaging the people needed to make the change and those touched by the change. Test your assumptions regarding the outcome with your trusted advisors. Practice your elevator speech (and your texts and tweets) to let others know what you are doing. Continue to invest in refining and maturing your leader abilities. Your ability to lead enhances your workplace, your community, and the profession. Your ability to lead also enhances your career opportunities, including advancement.

It is possible to study, practice, and be mentored to develop effective leadership behaviors. With study, practice, and feedback you can develop greater leadership competency and agility, improving the success of your involvement in teams, in organizations, and within society. Leadership, like life, has a lot of moving parts. More often than not, we do not get it right. This is why reflecting on past experience, refining present decisions and practice, practice, practice further hone leader skills. Your leadership maturity will come with leadership experience.

ACTIVITIES

ACTIVITY 1

Which of these statements best describes you: (a) I strive for perfection. (b) I am better able to assure positive outcomes if I am in control of the situation. (c) I perform better when people approve of me. (d) I like working with people and helping everyone succeed.

From the following list, select the way you most often act out under stress:

1. I whine and complain, say "no way" or say nothing at all; it is OK if I get it done myself as long as it is right.
2. I get aggressive and try to bully my way through; generally I know exactly what we should do; it bothers me that no one listens; it does not matter too much because I get it done.
3. I have outbursts that I regret or I pick at people; generally I think I know what we should be doing; I am often frustrated because it takes so long to get things done, but it is OK as long as I get credit for what I do.
4. I say yes and go along with the plan or say nothing at all; I do not like to make waves; things do not always get done, but it is OK as long as everyone gets along.

   a = perfectionist; b = controlling; c = attention seeking; d = getting along

Which one best describes you? Which best describes the person you most often work with or to whom you report?

ACTIVITY 2

List three times you were placed in a situation to lead people and how many people you were with. This can be a team you worked with in school, a project you shared at work, or a sporting game. The criteria for this "leadership moment" are that you worked with other people to achieve a successful outcome.

Leadership Environment (e.g., School, Work, Sports, Camp)	Situation (Describe the Leadership Scenario of Whom You were Working with to Get What Done)	Number of Other People Involved
a.		
b.		
c.		

1. In the three scenarios above, describe how you felt about the situation and how you behaved.
2. How do these behaviors differ or match your responses from Activity 1?
   a.
   b.
   c.
   Describe how effective you believe your leader behaviors were in each of the situations you described above. Justify why you believe this.
3. Share this information with the class. Take note of the different ways other people address leadership opportunities and the results that are achieved. Ask classmates to consider one of your scenarios (or a leadership challenge that is frustrating you today) and how they might address the situation and why. What possible outcomes could result from the different leadership behaviors applied to the same situation?

ACTIVITY 3

Leadership requires understanding, practice, and receiving feedback:

1. Where have you learned about leadership? What books, websites, programs, or courses do you recommend and why?
2. Provide examples where you have practiced leadership in the last two weeks. What roles did you play?
3. Who has provided leadership feedback to you? What type of feedback have you received and how critical has it been?
4. What have you learned from the feedback? Are there any patterns in the way you lead?

ACTIVITY 4

1. Prior to class, come prepared to identify one change you would like to see in your institution. Present to your group (a) the change you wish to see, (b) why it is important to the organization, and (c) why it matters to you.
2. After each person in the group has presented his or her desired change and all changes have been reviewed, have all members in your group rank the

options for both overall value and feasibility. Select the one recommended change that the group will work on together.

3. Working in your group map out the different individuals and or positions (factions) who are decision makers in enabling this change as well as those individuals, departments, or positions who will be impacted in any way (positive and negative) by the change you are suggesting. Include the reason why they are on your map and what concerns you have.

4. Use the leadership model from "Leadership for Everyone" to think through how you might approach each faction to achieve a positive outcome.

5. Present your findings to the greater group/class, including justification for your findings.

6. Rank the other groups in the class based on the degree of thoroughness they performed in their idea selection, justification or feasibility, and mapping.

REFERENCES

1. Moir, M. Contextual Leadership: The Social Construction of Leadership in a Comprehensive Healthcare System. Electronic Thesis or Dissertation. Antioch University, 2009. *Ohio LINK Electronic Theses and Dissertations Center*. August 1, 2013.

2. Brinkman R, Kirschner R. *Dealing with People You Can't Stand: How to Bring Out the Best in People at Their Worst*. New York: McGraw-Hill; 2002.

3. Kellogg MBA & Executive Teaching. *Brian Uzzi*. N.p., n.d. Web. November 15, 2013.

4. The Myers & Briggs Foundation. *The Myers & Briggs Foundation*. N.p., n.d. Web. November 15, 2013.

5. DiSC® Classic Profile. *Test (DiSC 2800 Series)*. N.p., n.d. Web. November 15, 2013.

6. Halvorson HG, Higgins ET. Do You Plan to Win—or to Not Lose? *Online Harvard Business Review*. March 2013. http://hbr.org/2013/03/do-you-play-to-win-or-to-not-lose/ar/2 (accessed August 2, 2013).

7. Rath T. *StrengthsFinder 2.0*. New York: Gallup Press; 2007.

8. American Association of Colleges of Pharmacy (AACP). *Oath of a Pharmacist*. www.aacp.org/resources/studentaffairspersonnel/studentaffairspolicies/Documents/OATHOFAPHARMACIST2008-09.pdf (accessed December 9, 2008). [The revised Oath was adopted by the AACP House of Delegates in July 2007 and has been approved by the American Pharmacists Association.]

9. Mumford MD, Zaccaro SJ, D Harding FD, et al. Leadership skills for a changing world: solving complex social problems. *The Leadership Quarterly*. 2000;11(1):11–35.

10. Rath T, Conchie B. *Strengths Based Leadership: Great Leaders, Teams, and Why People Follow*. New York: Gallup Press; 2008.

11. Laud RL, Johnson M. Upward mobility: a typology of tactics and strategies for career advancement. *Career Development International*. 2012;17(3):231–254.

12. CareerBuilders.com. Forty-One Percent of U.S. Employers More Likely to Promote Employees Who Wear Professional Attire. Survey 2008. www.careerbuilder.com/share/aboutus/pressreleasesdetail.aspx?id=pr438&sd=6%2F17%2F2008&ed=12%2F31%2F2008. (accessed August 2, 2013).

13. George B, Simms P. *True North*. San Francisco, CA: Jossey-Bass; 2007.

14. Covey M. *The 7 Habits of Highly Effective People*. New York: Fireside; 2003.

15. Dean PJ. *Leadership for Everyone: How to Apply the Seven Essential Skills to Become a Great Motivator, Influencer, and Leader. The L.E.A.D.E.R.S. Method*. New York: McGraw-Hill; 2006.

16. Kouzes JM, Posner BZ. *The Leadership Challenge*. San Francisco, CA: Wiley; 2007.

17. Useem M. *The Leadership Moment. Nine True Stories of Triumph and Disaster and Their Lessons for Us All.* New York: Three River Press; 1998.
18. Heifetz R, Linsky M. *Leadership on the Line. Staying Alive through the Dangers of Leading.* Boston: Harvard Business School Press; 2002: 107–108.
19. Granko R, Morton C, Schaafsma K. Role of executive coaching in pharmacy management. *American Journal of Health-System Pharmacy* [serial online]. November 2013;70(21):1883–1885. Available from CINAHL with Full Text, Ipswich, MA. Accessed November 13, 2013.
20. Davidhizar R, Lonser GY. Self-promotion: a strategy for career advancement. *Health Care Manager.* 2004; Jan–Mar; 23(1): 11–14.
21. Goodman N. *3 Skills to Prevent Leadership Burnout.* Entrepreneur.com. www.nbc-news.com/id/51301470/ns/business-small_business/t/skills-prevent-leadership-burnout (accessed August 28, 2014).

Case Study 1

The manager of a busy pharmacy where you have been interning for over a year is struggling to communicate effectively with a technician who was hired three months ago to support added patient volume. It appears the technician has been slow to perform to the expectation of the manager. You witness a conversation that is going wrong between the pharmacy manager and the technician. The technician appears withdrawn and quiet. The pharmacist is loud and fast paced, multitasking between speaking, checking, taking calls, and tracking inventory. You are intrigued by the discourse. You know you can take action to improve the situation between them and improve the overall performance of the pharmacy. Using the L.E.A.D.E.R.S. Method as your framework, demonstrate your leadership ability in this situation. Your goal is to improve performance of the technician and the pharmacy manager by making two requests:

1. First make a request of the pharmacist to allow you to mentor the technician.
2. Next, make a request of the technician to perform to the demands of the position.

Case Study 2: Finding Your Leadership Voice

One day you arrive to work in the pharmacy and witness a technician ignoring a patient who is obviously looking for assistance. Using your leadership learning you greet the customer with respect and attend to his needs. When the customer interaction is complete, you find the technician, and you:

A. *Give the technician a piece of your mind.* You know the technician has been spoken to previously by the pharmacist regarding patient service. You look the technician squarely in the eyes and say, "That was not a good way to take care of the patient. Are you looking to lose business?" The technician gets red-faced and snipes back, "mind your own business!"

B. *Approach the technician with concern.* You know the technician has been spoken to previously by the pharmacist regarding patient service. You approach the technician and say, "Hi, how are you today?" (Allow time for an answer.) "I noticed the patient was waiting for your attention when I arrived. I know the pharmacist spoke to us about attending to patient needs first, before other work. Is there a reason why you kept working while the patient waited?" The technician replies that he is uncomfortable speaking to patients and prefers to be behind the counter filling prescriptions and supporting the pharmacy in other ways.

You take your concern to the pharmacist.

A. You are upset that you were sniped at and feel the technician owes you an apology. You approach the pharmacist with your concern about being treated improperly. The pharmacist agrees that you should be treated with greater respect and asks you to settle your differences directly with the technician.

B. You are concerned for the benefit of the patients and the performance of the technician. You share with the pharmacist what you learned and offer to do some role-playing with the technician to help ease his discomfort. The pharmacist shares that she has noticed a shift in behavior ever since she asked the technician to get more involved in working with the patients. She likes your approach and thanks you for taking the initiative. She asks how you would like to proceed. Together you decide on a staff meeting during a slow period to address the situation and offer the role-playing option.

Review of Case Studies

In Case 1, the direct approach is received as an attack. The technician is confronted and protects his position by sniping back. This situation becomes uncomfortable enough to shift focus from the patient care issue to a personnel issue. The pharmacist is provided with a scenario that appears to be two disgruntled employees who need to work out their differences.

In Case 2, approaching the technician with the intent to learn more about the situation and understand potential opportunities for improvement yields new information and possible ways to solve the problem. Once the problem is articulated, the pharmacist is in a position to enable staff to work together to formulate a solution.

Section 2

Management

7 Principles and Characteristics of Effective Pharmacy Management

Michael J. Magee and William N. Kelly

CONTENTS

Learning Objectives: After reading this chapter and working through the cases, the reader will be able to:

1. Describe the differences between leadership and management
2. List three key responsibilities of a pharmacy manager
3. Explain what new managers should accomplish during their first year
4. Compare and contrast managerial skills and behaviors that produce results
5. Explain how to manage and measure success

INTRODUCTION

For sure, the responsibilities of leaders, managers, and supervisors overlap, yet each one has its specific characteristics. Most people have a fair understanding of the responsibilities of a leader (the top person, where the buck stops) and of supervisors (they get the everyday work done). However, the duties and responsibilities of managers get a bit murky for some people.

This chapter is about understanding how to become an effective manager. Why read it? If you hope to one day become a manager, are receiving formal management training, or are a newly appointed manager or even a veteran one, this chapter is your basic survival manual. If you are a pharmacy student, this chapter will provide insight into management, and what you need to know to transition from a staff or clinical pharmacist position into a management position.

The chapter covers management responsibilities, what to do during your first year as a manager, what skills and behaviors are most effective, how to report to document improvements, and putting everything altogether.

AM I A MANAGER, SUPERVISOR, OR LEADER?

There may be an official definition of manager, but the easiest one to understand is having overall accountability for a department, section, or organization. Supervisors are responsible for seeing that the daily work gets done efficiently but do not have the overall accountability for the entire operation. Leaders are responsible for setting the vision, values, direction, and results of an organization.

Can managers be supervisors and leaders? Yes they can be and often are. The best example of this is a hospital director of pharmacy. They lead the professional aspects of the department and set a vision for the department to achieve. They are also supervisors to their direct reports, like associate/assistant directors, managers, coordinators, supervisors, and secretaries. They are considered a "middle manager" of the hospital—responsible for a department.

While most hospital directors of pharmacy are managers with some leadership and some supervisory responsibility, the next level up, a chief pharmacy officer (CPO), has more leadership responsibilities since the CPO is expected to set the vision, values, direction, and results. By comparison, associate and assistant directors of pharmacy are managers with some supervisory responsibility. Pharmacy supervisors and clinical coordinators supervise other staff members. In general, the more staff directly reporting to you, the more you act as a supervisor.

People at the top (leaders) of an organization have few people reporting directly to them.

A manager is accountable for specific areas within the organization and is part leader, part supervisor, but mostly a manager.

MANAGEMENT RESPONSIBILITIES

So, what am I a manager of? The answer to that question is in your job description—read it. If still unclear, work with your boss to rewrite it. To be an effective manager, there must be a clear understanding of what the boss expects. Some bosses give managers freedom, while others are "micromanagers" who will closely watch what you do and how you do it, and critique along the way.

But in general, what do managers manage? The answer is (1) the day-to-day operation of your area of responsibility; (2) the leader's or boss's vision; and (3) resources like people, budget, and time.

MANAGING IN PHARMACY

Before going into specifics about managing, let us look at the mindset and general aspects of managing specific to pharmacy. The following tips are based on the thoughts of some of the John Webb Lecture Award recipients based on the theme of "Achieving Excellence in Pharmacy Management"[1]:

- Managers must have a strong commitment to patient care.
- Managers must design systems that achieve comprehensive drug-use control and appropriate drug therapy outcomes.
- A departmental organizational structure should recognize, empower, and encourage the growth of practitioners and practice leaders.
- The department's culture must reward innovation, nurture human interaction, and result in a thoughtful, creative vision.

MANAGING THE EVERYDAY OPERATION OF YOUR AREA OF RESPONSIBILITY

This responsibility is mostly about achieving results. Good leaders provide clear expectations and hire managers who have insight into how to work with a team to achieve the desired results for the organization. Progress is reported and discussed routinely between the two, most commonly with one-on-one meetings or in a group meeting every week or two.

The key responsible areas for a director or manager of a pharmacy are as follows:

- Safe and effective drug use control—Are drugs secure, in-date, and available when needed?[2]
- People—Do you have the right people in the right positions?[3]
- Productivity—Are people being used effectively and efficiently?[4,5]
- Fiscal resources/budget management—Are you spending too much? Too little?[6]

- Compliance—Are you practicing consistently with applicable laws, rules, regulations, standards, and guidelines?[7]
- Vigilance—Do you know what is going on in your area? Learn to manage by walking around.[8]

These responsibilities are addressed for pharmacy practice in the best practices published by the American Society of Health-System Pharmacists (ASHP).[9]

MANAGING THE LEADER'S OR YOUR BOSS'S VISION

The boss is looking for effective, efficient, and innovative management of the operation by the manager. When this is done well, the leader will often provide the manager with additional opportunities to help achieve the overall organizational vision. Rewards for the manager include more generous evaluations/raises and valuable experience that will make the manager more marketable for a promotion.

The most skilled managers have mastery over their area of responsibility and ask the leader what else they can do to help achieve the overall organizational goals.

MANAGING TIME

Like a river, time marches on with nothing to stop it. There is only so much time available for a manager to get things done. A good manager understands the difference between what is *important* and what is *urgent*, and knowing when to do which one first.

Although there are many good readings on time management, perhaps the most practical is what is contained in *The 7 Habits of Highly Successful People*.[10]

All tasks that need to be done can be put into a 2 × 2 table and assessed and revised at the start of each day (Figure 7.1). In the first box in the figure (upper left)

	Urgent	Not Urgent
Important	I ACTIVITIES: Crisis Pressing problems Deadline-driven projects	II ACTIVITIES: Prevention, PC activities Relationship building Recognizing new opportunities Planning, recreation
Not Important	III ACTIVITIES: Interruptions, some calls Some mail, some reports Some meetings Proximate, pressing matters Popular activities	IV ACTIVITIES: Trivia, busy work Some mail Some phone calls Time wasters Pleasant activities

FIGURE 7.1 The Time Management Matrix. (Covey SR. *The 7 habits of highly effective people*. Simon & Schuster. New York, 1990, Reprinted with permission.)

tasks are listed that are *important* and *urgent*. In the second box (upper right) tasks are listed that are *important* but *not urgent*. In the third box (lower left) tasks are listed that are *not important* but *urgent*, and in the fourth box (lower right) tasks are listed that are *not important* and *not urgent*. Covey recommends spending the most time on activities in box I; keeping the time spent in items in box II to a minimum, and spending little to no time in boxes III and IV.

So what do you do if a needed task is very important and at the same time another task is very urgent? The usual answer is who is asking? If it is your boss or the leader, you should do the one he or she wants done.

SUMMARY

Managers must be organized, use time wisely, achieve efficient and quality results, and help achieve the vision of the leader or boss.

IF YOU ARE A NEW MANAGER, THIS PART IS FOR YOU

So, you are a newly appointed pharmacy manager, now what? In addition to praying for external guidance, you need to figure out a plan. That plan may call for some remedial didactic training in management or putting into practice the lessons learned from pharmacy residency training. Regardless of the starting skill set, improvements will be needed and may be organized in the following systematic fashion.

THE FIRST FOUR MONTHS

The skills you need to master right away are organizational management, and relating to and managing people. This book can help in the area of organizational management, but for managing people, you will need the help of your human resources department, the staff of which should become your best friends. Many corporations support this training with competency-based training either on-site or in corporate training centers. While the first months in a new position may seem daunting, a new manager must make time to become knowledgeable about the skills and expectations as a new manager.

Beyond this, it is recommended that the first two months be spent gathering facts and assessing your area's operations without making many changes, and working on interrelationships.[11] During months 3 and 4, emphasis should be on understanding your extent of authority, developing working relationships with others, and assessing the pharmacy team and their ability to achieve the vision.

MONTHS FIVE THROUGH TWELVE

Any reorganization and personnel changes should be completed and you should have a top-notch management team. Strategic planning (see Chapter 3) as a team should take place during this time and an action plan with buy-in created.

THE FIRST YEAR

During the first year, the following tasks should be completed:[12]

- An assessment of pharmacy services, staff, and customers—the good, the bad, and the ugly
- A regulatory and accreditation review
- Assessments of pharmacy leadership, information services, and clinical services
- Charts of workflow
- Setting priorities and work plans to address issues
- Development of reporting systems and metrics

These timelines provide general guidance, but the new manager must be in tune with expectations of the leader and adapt accordingly.

IF YOU BECOME DIRECTOR OR MANAGER OF A PHARMACY

If you become the director of pharmacy, it is recommended that you read carefully the chapters in this text on leadership. If you become a pharmacy manager of a community pharmacy, it is recommended that you also read *Getting Started as a Pharmacy Manager*.[13] If you become a chief pharmacy officer, you should read the American Society of Health-System Pharmacist's (ASHP) statement on *The Role and Responsibilities of the Pharmacy Executive*.[14] Another recommendation for all is to find a mentor, as this has been found to be a critical step in being successful.[15]

SUMMARY

Taking on a manager role within your organization can be overwhelming, but it is best to remember that this is a journey and not a destination. The new manager must be intentional and thoughtful in his or her approach. This section outlines some key points to being successful including understanding the authority and responsibilities of your position, getting a mentor, and learning about organizational and personnel management. Together with a strong dose of self-awareness for areas where personal "skill set" improvements are needed, the areas identified above will set you off in the right direction.

MANAGEMENT SKILLS AND BEHAVIORS THAT WORK

COMMITMENT

Being a pharmacy manager or a director of pharmacy is a complex job. To manage successfully, certain behaviors and skill sets are needed. For sure, planning, communicating, networking, listening, and motivating are essential skills. However, being committed to pharmacy practice and patient care and always being professional are more important.

YOUR MANAGEMENT STYLE

The manager sets the tone for the values and culture of the areas being managed. The vision, culture, values, and management style of the manager control how well the team functions, behaves, and produces results. Pharmacy managers should lead by example and display a strong ethical foundation, honesty, integrity, and a strong work ethic.[16]

BEING IN TOUCH WITH YOUR PEOPLE

Because of the complexity and diversity of pharmacy work, the best management style is to manage by walking around, rather than by staying in offices most of the time. You do not need to be an "undercover boss" to be effective. Developing strong people skills—showing interest and trust in your employees and fellow workers, communicating effectively, following through on promises, getting back to people on issues—all work to your advantage and elevate your esteem among your employees.

THE HARDEST PART

The most difficult skills for new managers are decision making and understanding organizational behavior and politics. Autocratic management is efficient but harsh and often unappreciated by staff. Participative management allows for input from your staff, which is appreciated, democratic, and sometimes adds new information or ideas that make decision-making easier. The problem is that it can be slow.

Knowing when to use which style comes with experience, and how much time you have to make a decision. In general, participative management is preferred as it builds teamwork. Regardless of the manner in which a decision is made, there is usually both support and opposition. Of course, not making a decision usually creates universal opposition. For managers to manage, you must make the hard decisions, recognizing that universal agreement is not always achievable.

ORGANIZATIONAL BEHAVIOR AND POLITICS

Dealing with organizational behavior and politics can be bewildering—there are no primers or encyclopedias on how to handle these situations, as almost everyone is different. This is why a mentor is so important to a new pharmacy manager. They most likely have run into similar situations. In general, make sure you have enough background information and both sides of any issue before you act.

ALLIANCES

The importance of aligning the pharmacy with other important departments and people is key to organizational survival and moving a program forward. A strong alliance or partnership with nursing and the medical staff should be on every pharmacy manager's agenda. Understanding where decisions are made in the organization and being part of that process is key to effectively weaving the pharmacy processes into the organization and providing great value for the organization and the patient.

Take every chance you have to get to know others you work with—it can actually be quite rewarding and can make the manager much more effective at getting things done within a complex organization. Also be prepared for meetings where you are asked to identify needs for the area you manage or a story that will highlight the contributions your team makes to the overall success of the organization. Keep it simple and balance humility with the true need or success. This is often referred to as an "elevator" speech.

KEEPING UP

Pharmacy managers who are disciplined to keep up with the literature (pharmacy and drug therapy) have a decisive edge on others.[17] Knowing innovative and evidence-based services that strengthen pharmacy and patient care services moves pharmacy programs along at a faster pace.

BEING PERSUASIVE

Pharmacy managers who present compelling data and convincing arguments are the managers who move programs forward. Justification is an art that needs to be learned and improves with time.

SUMMARY

Pharmacy managers who are committed to patient care, have strong ethical behavior and interpersonal skills, can build strong alliances and partnerships, keep up with the literature, and can justify new services or more personnel when needed are the managers every organization and every pharmacy employee wants to have as their managers.

WE MANAGE WHAT WE MEASURE

You cannot manage and will not spend much time on what you do not measure. Unless you measure something, you do not know if it is getting better or worse. You cannot manage for improvement if you do not measure to see what is getting better and what is not. The question is not if you measure, but what you measure. The answers to "what you measure" are as follows: What is important to you, your boss, or your organization? Are you trying to show compliance with a standard? Are you trying to prove something is working or not working? The questions are endless, but selecting the most important ones and doing a superb job of collecting, analyzing, reporting, and making changes or recommendations is what is important. Do not collect information unless it is meaningful and useful.

Select key metrics to measure your area's progress.

REPORTING PROGRESS: WHAT HAVE YOU DONE FOR ME LATELY?

Knowing what information needs to go to whom, how often, and in what format is key to doing this important function well. The answer is to ask. In general, upper managers like routine progress updates from their direct reports in a format that is quick and easy to understand. A picture (tables and graphs) is worth a thousand words. Study the format suggested in Chapters 3 and 14. If a long report is required, master the art of writing an executive summary.

SUMMARY

Learn to make short and interesting reports that grab attention and solicit action.

PUTTING IT ALL TOGETHER

Being a pharmacy manager is a complex job and the learning curve is steep. Having an attitude toward learning and being a student of management help make the journey easier and more exciting. Pharmacy managers who have a good mentor and develop the right behaviors and skill sets are those who will personally excel and move their programs forward. The essential element of leaders and managers is trust.

REFERENCES

1. Gouveia WA. The contemplative manager. *Am J Health-Syst Pharm.* 2007;64:1299–1300.
2. Manasse HR, Andrawis MA. Accepting accountability for the medication-use system. *Am J Health-Syst Pharm.* 2011;68:1444–1448.
3. Petra T. What it takes to attract and hire winners. *The Fordyce Letter.* 2013;XLX.1,18–19.
4. Rough SS, McDaniel M, Rinehart. Effective use of workload and productivity monitoring tools in health-system pharmacy, part 1. *Am J Health-Syst Pharm.* 2010;67:300–311.
5. Rough SS, McDaniel M, Rinehart. Effective use of workload and productivity monitoring tools in health-system pharmacy, part 2. *Am J Health-Syst Pharm.* 2010;67:380–388.
6. Cmelik T. Financial analysis of drug management and pharmacy costs. *Pharmacy Purchasing and Products.* 2012;9:12–16.
7. Patil NP, Vargas R. Pharmacy Accreditation 101. *Pharm Times,* published online, June 4, 2012.
8. Fisher A. Management by walking around: 6 tips to make it work. *CNN Money.* August 23, 2012. http://management.fortune.cnn.com/2012/08/23/management-by-walking-around-mbwa/ (accessed December 3, 2013).
9. ASHP. Best practices by topic. *Pharmacy Management.* www.ashp.org/menu/PracticePolicy/PolicyPositionsGuidelinesBestPractices.aspx (accessed January 6, 2014).
10. Covey SR. *The 7 habits of highly effective people.* Simon & Schuster. New York, 1990.
11. Nold E. Role of the director of pharmacy: the first four months. *Am J Hosp Pharm.* 1982;39:1702–1706.
12. Nold EG, Sander WT. Role of the director of pharmacy during: the first six months. *Am J Health-Syst Pharm.* 2004;61:2297–2310.
13. Bradley-Baker LR. Getting started as a pharmacy manager. Washington, DC. American Pharmacists Association; 2012.
14. American Society of Health-System Pharmacists. ASHP statement on the roles and responsibilities of the pharmacy executive. May 7, 2008. www.ashp.org/DocLibrary/BestPractices/MgmtStPharmExec.aspx (accessed December 21, 2013).
15. White SJ, Tryon JE. How to find and succeed as a mentor. *Am J Health-Syst Pharm.* 2007;64:1258–1259.

16. Faris RJ, MacKinnon GE, MacKinnon NJ, et al. Perceived importance of pharmacy management skills. *Am J Health-Syst Pharm.* 2005;62:1067–1072.
17. PR Newswire. Oregon State University launches new online earning system for pharmacy managers. June 15, 2012.

Case Study

You are a new pharmacy manager and have spent the first two months observing and assessing the pharmacy area you now control. It seems obvious that the organizational structure needs adjustment, several pharmacy supervisors are in the wrong positions, and one supervisor is weak. You want to make changes.

- What would be your approach to changing the organizational structure?
- How would you tell your people what you think and what you would like to do?
- What would be your approach to having some people change positions?
- What will you do with the weak supervisor?
- How will you handle any negative feelings about the changes?

8 Managing Projects to Achieve Desired Results

Patricia R. Audet

CONTENTS

Learning Objectives: After reading this chapter and working through the case, the reader will be able to:

1. Explain the term "project management" and its importance
2. Outline the process of developing a project, its scope, and its plan
3. Outline the primary responsibilities of the project manager
4. Explain the proper way for project managers to assign responsibility and hold people accountable for getting work done and keeping the project on time and in budget
5. Explain the importance of project updates and a well-written final report

PROJECT MANAGEMENT DEFINITION

Project management is a process for planning and implementing a complex, temporary, and unique task. Projects are often the mechanism for implementing organizational changes, improving processes, and developing new products. Projects have the potential for significant impact across the organization and often require cross-functional collaboration.[1] It is crucial to define the scope of the project and the necessary outcomes or deliverables. Project managers with their teams develop a plan that includes start and end dates, resources including personnel and funds available, and the proposed actions needed to complete the project.

Project management is an essential skill for pharmacists. It is a required element in postgraduate year 1 (PGY1) pharmacy residency programs.[2] Having this skill can be critical in developing interdisciplinary, patient-centered therapy management programs, implementing automation for distribution technologies, and preparing accreditation reports for institutional reviews. It is also helpful in other management responsibilities, such as construction projects and process improvement roles within pharmacy practice organizations, including hospital or community pharmacies. These skills enable the pharmacist to progress from direct patient care, to system management for health-care organizations, and ultimately to deliver improvements for overall public health.[2]

PROJECT CHARTER

When project managers accept responsibility for a project, they should meet with the key project sponsors or champions to agree to a charter. Figure 8.1 illustrates a sample project charter. The champions should discuss the business needs, goals, and necessary outcomes for the project and confidentiality requirements, if any. The project should be "SMART" (i.e., Specific, Measurable, Agreed upon, and Realistic within a Time frame). An example of a SMART project is provided in Table 8.1.

The sponsors should provide budget guidance with defined project boundaries. They should assist the project manager to obtain the necessary people, equipment, space, and/or supplies. Although it may be a challenge to complete the project on time and within budget, the project manager must be committed and convinced that it is an achievable goal. It is critical that the project outcomes are measurable.

PROJECT MANAGEMENT ROLES

Project leaders are responsible for overseeing the deliverables, project resources, timelines, communication, and conclusion. They are not responsible for

---

PROJECT CHARTER

Project Name:
Project Sponsor (s):
Project Leader:
Business Needs:
Project Deliverables:
Project Scope (what is included and excluded):
Resources:
    People: team members and internal resources
    Budget
    Space
    Equipment
Timelines
Constraints

FIGURE 8.1 Sample project charter.

TABLE 8.1
SMART

Specific	
What is needed?	Develop a stable, attractive, good tasting, reasonably priced liquid product line extension for a specific antibiotic X made by your company or pediatric use
Measurable	
How do you know if your project is successful?	• Assay to measure antibiotic concentration • Demonstrate bioequivalence to existing solid dosage form • State range of volume needed for likely doses • Determine product stability under varied conditions over time, measure degradants, contaminants, etc. • Conduct taste testing for acceptable colors, flavors, and palatability
Agreed upon	
Who will be judging the success of your project?	Stakeholders: • Pharmaceutical development executives • Manufacturing organization • Marketing department • Pediatricians • Insurance companies • Patients and parents
Realistic	
It must be achievable with the resources provided	• Doses in range of 0.5–5 mL • Cost of goods not more than 50% higher than solid dosage form • Does not infringe on existing patents
Timeline	
Indicate the timing from start to finish and other dependent variables or checkpoints	• Complete formulation development within one year after project initiation for product to begin Phase I testing • Formulation needs to be developed for clinical testing (e.g., seven years before composition of matter patent expiration, or within one year of product launch of solid dosage formulation, or two years before planned Phase 2 pediatric trials for otitis media)

completing the project by themselves. Project leaders should get the project work done through their team. Leaders motivate their team to drive for changes. They inspire them to use their knowledge, skills, and dedication for the good of the organization. Successful project leaders are resilient problem solvers who are results oriented with good communication skills. They must be detail oriented but remain focused on the positive, overall vision of the alignment of the project with the organizational goals. Other terms for the person who leads the team can be project director, project executive, or project manager. For some very lengthy, large, and complex projects (e.g., developing a new drug for a pharmaceutical company), there may be both a project leader and a project manager. The project leader will usually focus on the strategic direction of the team while the manager will be the person implementing the project management tools to track timelines, budgets, and resources.

PROJECT MEMBERSHIP AND RESPONSIBILITIES

Membership in the project team should be defined. Ideally, project managers should have input into who will be participating as team members. For a multiple-task process, it is important to include a team of people with the necessary knowledge and training to enable successful completion of the project. Project managers should assess the capabilities and potential weaknesses of their team members. Sometimes team members are accountable for the project in addition to their normal work responsibilities. Stimulating the team members to do their best when the project may be a temporary diversion from their full-time jobs can be difficult.

INITIATING THE PROJECT TEAM

There are five core processes for a project. These include project initiation, developing a project plan, executing the plan, monitoring progress, and closing the project.[3] When beginning a project, it is important to have a kickoff meeting with an agenda. This meeting should include a presentation about the project charter, introduction of team members, ground rules for the team operation, and performance responsibilities. This meeting should include discussion of background materials, meeting frequency, and time commitments for project participation. Project managers should be open and honest with their team. It is imperative that the team believes that the manager appropriately represents the best interest of the project and team members. The team should have a strong sense of purpose in an open, cooperative, noncompetitive environment. At the initial kickoff meeting for the team, the sponsors should attend part of the meeting to describe the vision for this project and what it means to the organization.

Functional managers of the team members must understand the time commitment for their staff to participate in this project and not obstruct the project deliverables. These managers are critical for ensuring that the project manager has participants who can provide the expertise needed for the team's success. Although confidentiality may be important, it should not be used unnecessarily. Transparency across the organization for these complex projects can enhance alignment with the team members, their functional managers, the project manager, and sponsors. Support by senior leaders in the organization is a vital factor for a successful project. Great project managers are influential negotiators. They handle the organizational politics, both formal and informal, using shared points of view to gain support for their team's tasks.

DEVELOPING THE PROJECT PLAN

When the team convenes, they should work to develop a detailed plan. Project managers are often generalists who must rely on their team members for technical knowledge for components of the project. A well-functioning project team does not remain in silos of their areas of expertise. During a brainstorming session team members meet to discuss tasks, make constructive suggestions, and understand the dependencies for the activities to develop an optimal plan. The team should identify fixed milestones and duration needed to complete each task. The duration should be calculated based upon realistic, not overly optimistic or severely pessimistic, estimates for completing a task. A project timeline that has been determined using all optimistic deadlines is unlikely to succeed; a plan with all pessimistic timelines may cause unnecessary delays for an important project for an organization. It is helpful for a team to determine the critical path activities. These are the rate-limiting events for project completion. The team should focus on these tasks and closely interrogate these figures to determine what can be done to improve this timeline. The team should use its own expertise, reference previously relevant projects, consider industry benchmark data, and/or seek the advice of consultants or other technical experts. The project plan should include assigning team members accountable for specific actions, timelines, resources for these tasks, and specific deliverables for each task.

An often overlooked component for plans is consulting outside experts to complement internal knowledge. They can bridge technical gaps and knowledge for the company. External consultants can provide unbiased recommendations. They may also have had experience with a similar project for other organizations. Some companies employ consultants to assist with major projects. External forces should not lead the projects without internal commitment, participation, and insight.

Projects need to be assessed regularly to determine progress for the team's activities and resource utilization. It is helpful to have a graphic representation of the tasks and subtasks for overall completion of the project. A variety of information technology tools is available to assist in developing and monitoring the project. These include Microsoft® Project, QuickGantt (Aicos), Microsoft® OneNote, TurboProject, Oracle® Primavera, and Microsoft Excel. When selecting the tools the project manager should focus on the need for sharing data or the confidentiality of information, the cost and compatibility of the tool, and experience or training needed to use the project tool. Project management tools and templates are readily available on the Internet. Many of these resources are free. There should be an organized, accessible location for project-related materials such as Google Docs, shared areas, or databases. A Gantt graph is the most commonly used tool for describing project tasks, durations, and overall timelines. Examples for many projects can be illustrated by searching on the intranet using the key term "Gantt chart images." Figure 8.2 shows a sample Gantt graph.

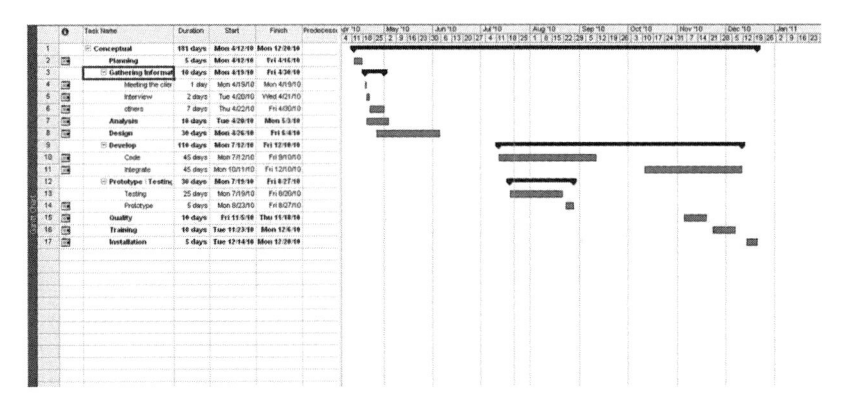

FIGURE 8.2 Sample GANTT chart. (From www.Photobucket.com. With permission.)

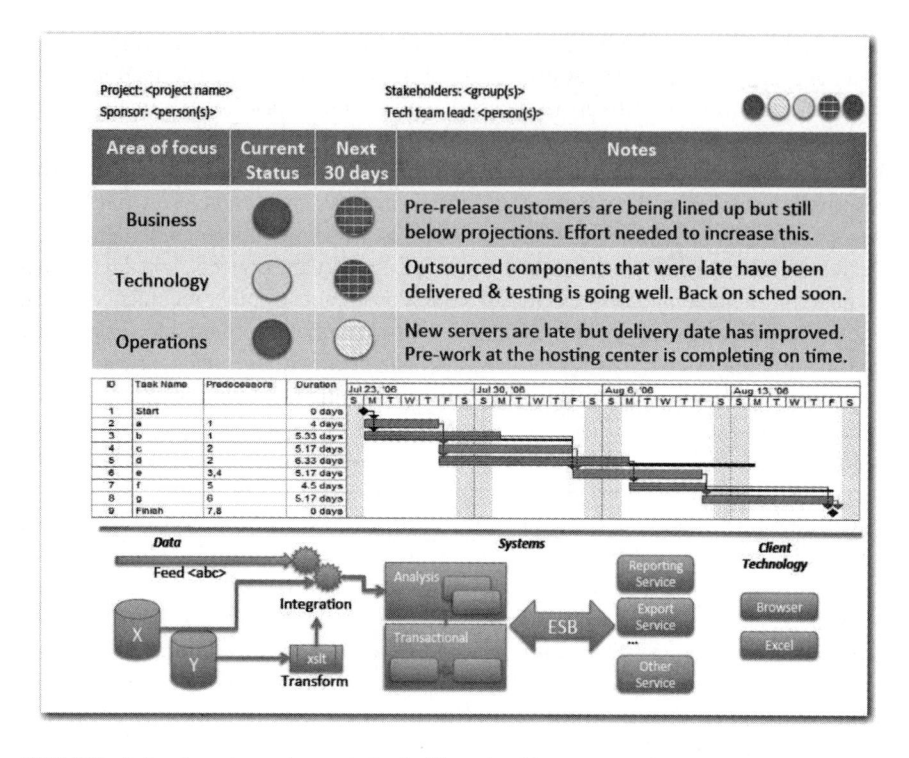

FIGURE 8.3 Sample color-coded dashboard. (From www.images.yahoo.com. With permission.)

Gantt graphs show the timeline and dependencies for work to be done. In this example which could be for developing a smartphone application to link to your pharmacy services (e.g., refilling prescriptions, making prescription deliveries, or obtaining receipts for tax filing or health-care spending accounts). There are tasks under the basic heading of planning, gathering information from stakeholders, designing the web page and applications, testing a prototype, checking quality, training pharmacy personnel and testing with sample patients, allowing downloading and installation of applications from the pharmacy website.

A dashboard for milestones using green, yellow, and red lights can provide a simple visual representation to summarize the project's progress. Figure 8.3 demonstrates a color-coded dashboard to a team's progress. This example shows areas of concern to be able to meet expected timelines for a project.

PROJECT PLAN EXECUTION AND MONITORING

Following project plan approval, the implementation phase begins. At this point, the project leader should publish the agreed responsibilities, resources, and timelines with the team and the team's sponsors. An often overlooked part of the plan is preparing a communication plan for the team and its sponsors. It should include communication methods, reporting intervals, level of detail, and what constitutes a significant event for the team and the project champions. Communication should occur at planned intervals (e.g., weekly, monthly, or quarterly), not only when there are problems with the plan. A key responsibility is for the project manager to communicate regularly with his or her team members to identify project status, remind them of upcoming tasks, and congratulate them on the project accomplishments. It is helpful to regularly schedule meetings for each participant to update the actions each is accountable for delivering for this project. The agenda for these meetings should specify what information and the actions expected from each participant. Meeting minutes will summarize the team decisions, clarify further actions and responsibilities, assist absent team members, help new team members if turnover occurs, and provide information for retrospective project evaluation. Team leaders must encourage open communication from their team. Team members should not rely only on scheduled meetings for communication. The project manager ought to be approachable so that the team will readily seek assistance from him or her and promptly identify potential issues, concerns, or deviations from the plan. The project manager should frequently reinforce the overall project goals and importance to the organization.

Because these are complex projects, they often deviate from the initial proposal. Few projects are completed without encountering any difficulties or revisions. It is important to consider risks and contingency plans for your project and the need to avoid project creep. Adjustments may be necessary. Changes can be very troublesome to the team. If the project scope changes, this may impact quality, timelines, people, or budget needed to complete the project. If new demands are imposed upon a team without additional resources, then this may result in missed deadlines or compromises in the delivery of a quality product from the project team. Any change in the balance of specifications, resources, or timelines may require revisions in the project charter with the sponsor to ensure delivery of a product of similar quality.

The team should discuss technical issues, analyze potential and actual problems, propose solutions, and recommend actions to mitigate vulnerabilities for the team or this project. The team must evaluate the impact to the previously described plan. Often additional requirements are added to a project after the initial charter has been agreed with the project champions. This may jeopardize the ability for the project completion on time and on budget. If necessary, the project charter may need to be adjusted (i.e., a change in deliverables, resources, or timelines). It is critical to keep sponsors informed about problems with the project and proposed changes to the project charter quality, and to obtain approval for the revisions.

PROJECT CONCLUSION

When a project is completed, the team should participate in a close-out meeting. This will include an assessment of the success of the project for meeting its deliverables, on time and on budget. Outstanding issues should be identified. A valuable component for the final report is to include lessons learned so that the organization can implement process improvement for subsequent projects. The output of this meeting should be summarized for the project sponsors. Recognition by the project champions and team leader for the team's accomplishments and dedication is an important conclusion to a project.

SUMMARY

A well-executed project provides significant value and opportunity for improvement in the health-care system. Complex, interdisciplinary projects need good project management skills to deliver high-quality projects on time and on budget and achieve the desired results for the organization. It is important for pharmacists to develop these skills for their own professional development and as a key ability to deliver cost-effective, continuous improvements for patient care with superior pharmacy practice in an increasingly complex health-care environment.

BIBLIOGRAPHY

1. Ferraro J. *Project Management for Non-Project Managers*. AMACOM, American Management Association. New York, 2012.
2. Albanese NP, Rouse MJ. Council on Credentialing in Pharmacy. Scope of contemporary pharmacy practice: roles, responsibilities, and functions of pharmacists and pharmacy technicians. *JAPhA* 50:2 e35–69, 2010.
3. Project Management Institute. *A guide to the Project Management Body of Knowledge (PMBOK® guide)*, 5th edition. Project Management Institute, Newtown Square, PA, 2013.

Case Study

An example of a project that would utilize project management process is as follows: "A health care system antibiotic utilization program with a goal to reduce development of resistant organisms in your hospital."

Complete a project charter for this project team.

- Who would be the likely sponsor(s) for this project?
- What are the business needs for your hospital and your recommended project deliverables? Be sure they are specific and measurable. Why is this important? Are there additional deliverables you considered but did not select? Why not?
- What do you recommend for the project scope?
- What hospital personnel should be included as members of this team?
- Do you have other resource needs (budget, space, or equipment) for this project?
- What timeline would you propose to realistically complete this task? Should there be interim checkpoints?
- Are there any constraints or obstacles for the ability for this project team to succeed?

9 Managing People

Gary E. Sloskey

CONTENTS

Learning Objectives: After reading this chapter and working through the case, the reader will be able to:

1. State one strategy for forecasting the staffing needs of a pharmacy
2. Provide three preferred options for recruiting and retaining pharmacy staff
3. List three violations of employment law
4. State three questions you are not allowed to ask prospective employees
5. Explain the importance of orienting new employees and having them read policies and procedures
6. Provide three examples on how to get pharmacy employees to work as a team
7. Explain how to identify what motivates an employee
8. Contrast the goals of employee mentoring versus coaching versus counseling
9. List and describe the steps involved in progressive discipline
10. Explain some effective techniques in managing and rewarding employee performance
11. Provide the preferred techniques for managing conflict
12. Contrast management versus leadership and implications relative to the direction of professional employees

INTRODUCTION

People are the most valuable investments and resources of every organization, business, or clinical practice. It is not surprising, therefore, that the most important responsibility and obligation of every manager is the capable shepherding of the processes described in this chapter, all very important components of the personnel management continuum.

This chapter touches on the major components of this continuum. We cover issues in the planning of appropriate manpower staffing, recruitment, hiring, and orientation of new employees. We discuss federal laws that guide us in our provision of fair treatment and safe environments for our employees and coworkers in the workplace. We discuss the subtleties of interpersonal dynamics such as teamwork, conflict management, and job satisfaction. And finally, we describe appropriate performance management, from planning performance to mentoring and motivation to counseling and discipline.

PLANNING FOR STAFFING NEEDS

The most critical assets of a pharmacy practice or any business are its employees. Hiring a poor candidate can be disastrously costly and can result in long-term, burdensome management challenges and practice inefficiencies. Negligently hiring incompetent, unqualified, or criminal candidates into health-care positions risks lives and threatens legal liability for the employer. On the other hand, denying employment to candidates through intentional, unintentional, or even well-intentioned discrimination is damaging to both potential employees and the organization and must also be actively avoided. It goes without saying, therefore, that effective hiring must be accomplished through a knowledgeable and prospectively planned multistep process (Table 9.1).

TABLE 9.1
Recruitment and Hiring Process Steps

Staffing need analysis	• *New positions*: determine numbers and categories of staff needed based on business plan and productivity benchmarks
	• *Replacement positions*: reevaluate continuing need for position or opportunities for position enhancements
Position description	• Create or revise accurate, up-to-date position descriptions including the education, experience, qualifications, and skill sets required of a qualified candidate
Planning the hiring process	• Determine who will be involved in the interview and hiring decision processes
	• Determine required candidate application materials
	• Letter of intent, CV or resume, references, academic/training transcripts
	• Develop a standardized scoring system to facilitate an objective evaluation of candidates required and desired qualifications and comparative ranking
Recruitment	• Determine a recruitment strategy to nurture the interest of potential candidates on a local, regional, or national scope
	• Choose appropriate recruitment channels
	• Lay or professional association print or web advertising, networking, direct mailing, in-house postings
	• Develop a well-written, comprehensive, and promotional recruitment document
Screening	• Determine an efficient screening methodology
	• Scoring of application materials, brief screening interviews, screening telephone interviews
	• Assess candidate's qualifications regarding suitability for progression to an on-site interview
Interviewing	• Choose interview composition and structure
	• One-on-one versus group interviews; number of interviews
	• Be knowledgeable of and comply with laws prohibiting discrimination; avoid leading and irrelevant questions and bias
	• Develop and administer a standardized interview script preferably utilizing behavioral, relevant, and open-ended questions
Reference checks	• Always check references at an appropriate time prior to offering a position
	• Confirm candidate's education and certification history
	• Additionally many organizations require criminal and child abuse background checks, drug screens, and in some cases lie detector testing

Prior to recruiting, screening, and interviewing potential employees, it is important to do some basic planning regarding anticipated staffing needs. The type of staff planning depends on whether a new practice or new or expanded service is being planned or whether a vacancy of a current position is being refilled. Both situations should be considered opportunities to optimize your organization's resources, productivity, and potential for success. Planning to hire new employees for a startup pharmacy practice or service is obviously a complex task. Important considerations for a new pharmacy practice entity might include how many pharmacists, technicians, and other supportive personnel will be needed. What special skills, specialties, and traits will optimally support a successful practice? This is where a well-developed business plan is crucial. Productivity benchmarks are also available and can potentially be used as a guide in the manpower planning process. It should be noted, however, that caveats to the dependence on productivity benchmarks for pharmacist staffing decisions were offered in an editorial published in the *American Journal of Health-System Pharmacy* (Shane, 2009). The authors questioned the wisdom of some management consultants regarding their misplaced focus on operational "efficiency" versus pharmacy staff "effectiveness."

For established practices, the planning required for the replacement of a current vacancy is less complex but should not be taken lightly. Managers should avoid the simple knee-jerk reaction of a one-on-one replacement without reviewing the practice's current needs. Is this position still required? Has the position, practice, or health-care environment evolved in such a way that this vacancy should be filled with a candidate with different qualifications and more relevant job responsibilities? Although we discuss later in this chapter the costs and difficulties associated with employee turnover, filling a vacant position should always be looked at as a potential opportunity for the improvement of the practice and an enhancement of the staff talent and abilities pool.

EMPLOYEE RECRUITMENT

Effective recruitment is an essential step in the hiring process with the goal of providing the employer with a rich pool of qualified applicants for positions needed to be filled. Prior to the initiation of recruitment efforts, it is vital that a comprehensive and up-to-date position description be prepared. A position (job) description is a legal and functional document describing the role of the employee, the position's essential responsibilities, skill sets necessary to adequately perform the job, educational and training prerequisites, and other qualifications required of a candidate to fill the position. Additionally, position descriptions define Americans with Disabilities Act (ADA) requirements and the employer's expectations related to employee attitudes, values, and behavior. See Appendix A for an example position description.

Recruiting strategies and media are numerous. Selecting the most appropriate recruiting approach depends on a number of issues including the type and specialty of the position being recruited and the availability of desirable candidates on a local, regional, or national level. Recruiting venues include lay newspaper and professional journal print advertisements, lay and professional association electronic job posting boards, networking and employee referral, direct mailing, job fairs, and in-house position postings. Specialized positions and executive senior positions within the hierarchy of an organization usually require more specialized recruitment media outlets and broader geographical coverage. In some such cases, the engagement of a search firm (professional recruiter or headhunter) might be appropriate. Fees associated with the services of search firms vary in structure and amount depending on the position being searched and contractual relationship between the search firm and the hiring organization. In some cases, a simple fee for service is charged and in other cases a significant percentage of the annual salary of the position being recruited. Recruiting for an organization's CEO or for a specialized position such as a pediatric oncology pharmacist or a pharmaceutical outcomes researcher would probably not fare well from a "help wanted" advertisement in a local newspaper. On the other hand, it might not be necessary or cost effective to place a position announcement in a national pharmacy association journal for an entry-level pharmacy technician.

Now that a decision has been made regarding what recruitment media are appropriate for the position, develop a comprehensive, but concise, recruitment document for listing. Keep in mind that a recruitment listing not only serves as a notification of a position's availability and expected candidate qualifications but also serves as a promotional communication selling the positive aspects of being an employee in your organization. Depending on the limitations of the advertising media chosen ("want-ad" listings versus larger block advertisements; printed ads versus web listings, etc.), information frequently found in recruitment listings can be found in Table 9.2.

Recruiting for specific position openings as they occur is an important aspect of the hiring process; however, many established and respected organizations maintain

TABLE 9.2
Recruitment Listing Content

Position description	• Position title
	• Primary job responsibilities
	• Other:
	• Exempt status, work hours, supervisory/budget responsibilities
Compensation information	• Subjective compensation statements
	• Competitive salary commensurate with experience
	• Competitive benefits package/health coverage
Candidate requirements	• Education, certification, licensure, experience requirements
	• Essential skill set requirements
Application requirements	• Letter of intent
	• Resume or curriculum vitae (CV)
	• References or letters of reference
	• Number and types of reference sources
Contact information	• Address application material and references to:
	• name/address/e-mail/telephone
Organization information	• Organization's: name/description/location
	• Visionary or promotional brief statement
	• Hiring practices: Equal Opportunity/Affirmative Action

a philosophy of continuous recruitment through positive public relations and pro-grams resulting in a custom skilled pool of candidates familiar with the organiza-tion. Such programs are commonly company-based internships and residencies as well as pharmacy college collaborative clerkship rotations.

WORKPLACE FEDERAL ANTIDISCRIMINATION LAWS

Pharmacy practices and businesses are highly regulated by a multitude of state and federal laws and regulations. Since this chapter focuses on the topics of employment and personnel management, we limit our discussions to two categories of federal law. First, we discuss a group of laws regulating the practices of hiring, discipline, promotion, and employee compensation, in other words, antidiscrimination legisla-tion. We then discuss a group of laws fostering values such as fairness and safety in the workplace and patient confidentiality.

Eight laws or amendments passed into federal law between 1963 and 2008 were aimed at protecting workers and employment candidates in the United States from discrimination with respect to compensation, terms, conditions, or privileges of employment. In other words, it became unlawful for an employer to discriminate in hiring decisions, work assignments, promotion/discipline, or compensation based on certain employee or job applicant attributes. These statutes are listed in Table 9.3

TABLE 9.3

Federal Antidiscrimination Laws 1963–2008

- The Equal Pay Act of 1963
  - Requires that men and women in the same workplace be given equal pay for equal work
- Title VII of the Civil Rights Act of 1964
  - Protects against hiring and work discrimination based on race, color, religion, sex, and national origin
- Sexual Harassment—section 703 of Title VII of the Civil Rights Act of 1964
  - Recurrent behavior creating a hostile environment of a sexual nature based on gender
- Age Discrimination in Employment Act of 1967
  - Protects individuals who are 40 years of age or older from employment discrimination based on age
- The Pregnancy Discrimination Act 1978 amendment to title VII
  - Protects against discrimination based on pregnancy, childbirth, or related medical conditions
- Americans with Disabilities Act Amendments Act of 1990
  - Protects against discrimination of qualified people with a disability
  - Calls for employer to provide reasonable accommodations if not an undue hardship
- Equal Opportunity Act of 1995
  - Defines discrimination as:
  - Direct and indirect
  - By commission or omission
  - Irrelevant of motive
- The Genetic Information Nondiscrimination Act of 2008
  - Protects against discrimination based on the genetic information of an employee

---

TABLE 9.4
Attributes Federally Prohibited from Workplace Discrimination

Age	Pregnancy
Breast-feeding	Physical features
Religious belief or activity	Political belief or activity
Impairment	Race
Prior employment activity	Gender identity
Parental caregiver status	Sex or sexual orientation
Marital status	Lawful sexual activity

Personal association with a person with the above attributes

and include a brief description of the primary attributes targeted for protection. Collectively, these antidiscriminatory laws are enforced by the Equal Employment Opportunity Commission (EEOC) on a federal level.

Discrimination is not always as clear to those who dispense it compared to those who receive it. Federal law recognizes both direct and indirect discrimination as illegal and prohibited. Discrimination can occur through acts of commission (doing something) as well as omission (failing to do something). Further, one's motives, no matter how well-meaning, are irrelevant when it comes to discriminatory infractions. A manager, who would never otherwise consider discrimination toward any specific individual or group of individuals with a common attribute, might naïvely discriminate with well-meaning albeit poor decisions. Table 9.4 provides a summary of attributes against which discrimination is federally prohibited in the workplace. Let us look at a couple of hypothetical cases demonstrating indirect discrimination.

Mini-Case Study #1

A pharmacy manager has the responsibility of hiring a pharmacy technician for a high-volume store within his chain. Knowing that the technician will be responsible for receiving and processing large wholesale orders on a daily basis, the manager considers only male applicants capable of lifting and carrying 75-pound totes.

Author's Commentary

The pharmacy manager makes two questionable judgments. The first is that only males are sufficiently strong for moderate labor and the second that lifting and carrying 75 pounds is an essential requirement for this position. Appropriate recruiting must be based on realistic and well-thought-out position description requirements and capabilities. Is this lifting requirement a truly realistic and indispensable one or is the ability to process large wholesale deliveries a more accurate expectation? Similar misjudgments are frequently made when dealing with job applicants with disabilities. Applicable to many tasks, there is an old saying, "there's more than one way to skin a cat." Surely there are alternative ways of getting the job done, with or without reasonable accommodations, which do not include heavy lifting.

Mini-Case Study #2

A small drug testing laboratory, primarily dealing with urine samples, is recruiting to replace one of their two sampling observers. The company has traditionally and successfully employed one male and one female observer to accommodate both male and female patients' modesty. The company's manager considers only male applicants in order to retain the one male and one female team.

Both of the above cases illustrate situations in which an organization is excluding one or more segments of the population from an opportunity for employment. Does either or both of these cases demonstrate inappropriate or prohibited discrimination?

Author's Commentary

The exclusion of one gender from consideration might be justified. Respect for the modesty of the laboratory's clients is a basic and realistic concern. It is also likely that the laboratory's contracts, policies, and procedures dictate that observer gender be matched to the gender of the client. Additional considerations might also be in play. For one, fair hiring practices and avoidance of discrimination should always be the goal of all organizations, but this small laboratory might not fall under the jurisdiction of Title VII which regulates organizations with 15 or more employees. Second, blatant disregard for clients' modesty concerns can potentially risk noncompliance with other statutes, such as sexual harassment.

We revisit the implications of these antidiscrimination laws later in this chapter when we specifically discuss appropriate and effective recruiting, interviewing, and hiring practices. At that time, you are directed to review Table 9.5 which provides examples of discriminatory interview questions and their more appropriate counterparts.

WORKPLACE LAWS REGULATING EMPLOYEE RIGHTS, SAFETY, AND PATIENT CONFIDENTIALITY

There are four federal laws that were enacted between 1938 and 1996 about which all employers and employees need to be familiar. The Health Insurance Portability and Accountability Act (HIPAA) statute is especially important to pharmacy practitioners as well as most health-care managers and professionals. These laws are listed in Table 9.6 and include a brief description of their primary provisions.

FAIR LABOR STANDARDS ACT OF 1938

The Fair Labor Standards Act was originally enacted in 1938 with a primary goal of setting standards for the employment of children in the workforce. These standards are intended to protect youthful employees from hazardous work as well as excessive work hours and inappropriate work schedules. This law is better known for its rules regarding minimum wage, payment of overtime, and methods of recording work time and determining compensation relative to hours worked. The standards establish a federal minimum hourly wage and overtime compensation, set at 1½ times the regular hourly rate, for hours worked in excess of 40 hours per week, regardless of full- or part-time employment status. Although most employees are covered by these rules (nonexempt), the act also establishes exemptions to these

TABLE 9.5

Examples of Common Discriminatory Interview Questions and Appropriate Counterparts

Federally Protected Attributes	Inappropriate Interview Question Examples	Appropriate Interview Question Examples
Age	How old are you? In what year did you graduate high school? In what year do you plan to retire? Where were you when JFK was assassinated?	Are you 18 years old or over? Are you old enough to work in the United States or do you have a work permit to do so?
Place of birth, citizenship, national origin, or heritage	In what country were you born? From what country is your family? Are you a citizen of the United States?	Are you eligible to work in the United States?
Marital, family, or children status	Are you married? Do you have children? Do you plan to have children? Do you plan to nurse your children at work?	There is no legitimate or appropriate reason to need to ask about marital, family, children, gender, or gender identity in an employment interview.
Gender, gender identity	Would you consider yourself a dainty or a strong woman? Are you afraid to get your hands dirty? Are you gay?	
Religion	What religion do you follow? Do you follow all 10 Commandments? Which holidays do you observe? Do you eat pork?	Are you able to work on the days and shifts expected of this position? Is there anything in your beliefs that would prevent you from fulfilling the basic functions of this position?
Criminal history	Have you ever been arrested?	Have you ever been convicted of a crime?
Health, disability status, or physical characteristics	Do you have any disabilities requiring special job accommodations? Have you ever had a drug or alcohol problem? Tell me about your medical history.	Can you perform the essential requirements of this position, either with or without reasonable accommodation?

compensation requirements. Certain employees may qualify as exempt and therefore are not entitled to minimum wage or overtime compensation. Determination of exempt versus nonexempt status is not an arbitrary decision. The US Department of Labor provides criteria enabling the appropriate determination of an exempt status for certain employee types. Responsibility criteria are grouped into qualifying tests to determine if a position is justified as being exempt. Exempt status is justified if a position qualifies under one or more tests including an executive, administrative, professional, computer, outside sales, or high compensation exemption test. In general, employees usually classified as exempt are employed in middle to upper

TABLE 9.6
Employee Rights, Safety, and Confidentiality

- Fair Labor Standards Act originally enacted in 1938
  - Defines minimum wage and overtime requirements
  - Defines work hour recording and compensation types
  - Establishes child labor standards
- Occupational Safety and Health Act of 1970
  - Protects against occupational hazards and exposures
- Family and Medical Leave Act of 1993
  - Entitles employees to limited unpaid leave and benefit protection in support of:
  - Birth- and adoption-associated child care
  - Care for serious health conditions of employee or immediate family members
  - Military service activation or active service of immediate family members
- Health Insurance Portability and Accountability Act of 1996
  - Protects personal health information of patients and employees

management, professional, or technical positions, have responsibilities that are considered to be creative and analytical and require decision making, and receive a reasonably high compensation. Exempt employees generally receive a salary independent of hours worked even though many work hours in excess of the standard 40 hours per week. On the other hand, it would be unlawful to dock the pay of an exempt employee who finds the need to leave work a little early one day for personal reasons. Pharmacists frequently fit into the exempt category but by no means universally. Many pharmacists are nonexempt and receive an hourly wage and mandatory overtime pay for hours worked greater than 40 hours per week (or 80 hours per two weeks in the case of overnight schedules requiring 12 hours on and 12 hours off). Others are salaried and are not required to be compensated for extra hours worked or overtime pay, although such compensation is not prohibited. A fact sheet with specific criteria and tests for exempt status can be easily found on the US Department of Labor website.

FAMILY AND MEDICAL LEAVE ACT OF 1993

Life sometimes demands more of us than we can handle in our routine lives. Imagine that your mother, father, mother-in-law, or child became ill and required your full-time care over some period of time. What would you do? Would your employer grant you time off from work to provide this care? The Family and Medical Leave Act (FMLA) guarantees this need. The FMLA entitlement represents an often-needed and humanistic approach to our employees in their special, and often unanticipated, needs. Employees who are critically ill or who have critically ill family members in need of support; employees needing to support the needs of immediate family members who have been called into active military duty; and employees needing to support a newly born, adopted, or foster child are eligible for this accommodation in the workplace. The FMLA provides for unpaid leaves limited to 12 weeks within any 12-month period and benefit protection for the above reasons.

Health Insurance Portability and Accountability Act (HIPAA) of 1996

HIPAA protects patients' and employees' confidentiality regarding their medical conditions and information. With the explosive growth of electronic information system utilization, interprofessional information sharing, and an increased potential for confidentiality breaches, HIPAA was enacted to secure the privacy and confidentiality of patients' health information held by covered entities, among others, pharmacies, physician offices, and hospitals.

In pharmacy practice, maintaining patients' confidentiality is a monumental and sometimes misunderstood task. How should a pharmacist dispose a patient's used prescription vial? How should a community pharmacy manager orient computer monitors in such a way that privileged patient information cannot be viewed by the public? How does a community pharmacist handle a query from an emergency room regarding a patient's medication history? How should a pharmacy technician leave a telephone voicemail message to a patient's home regarding a refill authorization? The following are a couple of situations that might serve as interesting discussion points.

Mini-Case Study #3

You are standing at a community pharmacy counter waiting for your prescription to be filled. During your wait, a pharmacy technician, merely two feet in front of you, is speaking to a patient on the telephone. You cannot help hearing the conversation. It goes something like this: "Is this Mrs. Pollock of 142 Oak St.? Your prescription was ready two days ago and you haven't picked it up yet. What is the prescription? Well, under federal law, I'm not permitted to tell you the actual name of the medication but it is an antibiotic in the cephalosporin class usually used for the treatment of a sexually transmitted disease."

Mini-Case Study #4

A pharmacist was staffing in the medical center emergency room when a patient was admitted with an apparent drug overdosage. It was determined that the pharmacy that the patient faithfully used was the nearby We Care Apothecary. The emergency room pharmacist telephoned the apothecary for information thought critical to the treatment of this patient. In response to the pharmacist request, the apothecary pharmacist refused to share any health-care information on the grounds that it would be a HIPAA violation.

Author Commentaries

Obviously, sharing the medical information of a patient to other parties not involved in the patient's care is a violation of confidentiality. The pharmacy register person who calls out "Mr. Smith, your HIV medications are ready," the clueless pharmacy technician in Case #1 holding confidential conversations in public, the medical residents discussing a patient case in a hospital elevator, a pharmacist discarding a patient's used and labeled prescription vial in an insecure manner, and the medical assistant relaying laboratory results to a patient's husband are all in violation of the confidentiality expected by HIPAA as well as professional ethics. Pharmacy personnel, as with all health-care workers, are entrusted with confidential information about patients and their conditions. This information is to be held in trust on the one hand, but shared with others needing such information within the continuum of care of that patient.

OCCUPATIONAL SAFETY AND HEALTH ACT OF 1970

Safety in the workplace is obviously an important issue. The Occupational Safety and Health Act is administered on a federal level by OSHA (Occupational Safety and Health Administration) within the US Department of Labor. OSHA's primary responsibilities include the promulgation of evolving occupational safety standards and the inspection of workplaces for compliance. Although the administration is concerned with a broad array of industrial and workplace safety issues, such as injuries, environmental hazards, noise hazards, and sanitary conditions, the most commonly recognized hazards in health care, and specifically pharmacy, are related to hazardous chemical exposure and more recently with pharmacist immunization programs, occupational exposure to blood-borne pathogens.

OSHA's Hazard Communication Standard and Material Safety Data Sheets (MSDSs)

The law requires that employers develop and communicate a documented plan to assure that employees are knowledgeable about hazardous chemicals in their workplace, avoid hazardous exposure, and know what to do if an exposure occurs. Pharmacies, laboratories, hospitals, and drug and chemical distributors are required to inventory potentially hazardous chemicals and develop and disseminate Safety Data Sheets (SDSs) formerly known as Material Safety Data Sheets (MSDSs). As of June 1, 2015, OSHA's safety standard will require that new SDSs be developed in a standardized format including at least 12 section headings identifying product information, specific hazards, composition and ingredients, first-aid measures, fire-fighting measures, accidental release measures, handling and storage precautions, exposure control/personal protection, physical/chemical properties, stability/reactivity, toxicological information, and miscellaneous SDS information.

OSHA's Occupational Exposure to Blood-Borne Pathogens Standard

With the growing attention and concern regarding serious viral diseases such as hepatitis B, hepatitis C, and HIV, as well as a potentially increasing risk of occupational exposure to these and other viral and bacterial diseases, OSHA's blood-borne pathogens standard seeks to protect health-care employees who come into contact with and could possibly be infected by potentially infectious body fluids of patients for whom they care. The standard calls for mandatory training of potentially exposed employees regarding the risks and safety precautions associated with patient care including but not limited to compliance with universal precautions, and utilization of gloves, masks, and gowns where appropriate.

WORKPLACE SAFETY REGARDING ROBBERY AND VIOLENCE

It should be noted that a lack of workplace safety represents not only a danger to employees but also a powerful demotivating factor regarding job satisfaction and

employee retention. Regarding the potential danger associated with pharmacy robberies, OSHA recommends that employers establish and maintain a violence prevention program as part of their facility's safety and health program which could include
the following:

- Installing Plexiglass® in the payment window in the pharmacy area
- Providing better visibility and lighting in the pharmacy area
- Providing training for staff in recognizing and managing hostile and assaul-
  tive behavior
- Implementing security devices such as panic buttons, beepers, surveillance
  cameras, alarm systems, two-way mirrors, card-key access systems, and
  security guards

Other issues related to workplace safety and workplace hygiene demotivating factors
are discussed under Employee Retention.

SCREENING, INTERVIEWING, AND HIRING

Candidate recruiting and screening processes differ among organizations and disciplines. Professional recruitment events, such as ASHP's Personnel Placement
Service, offer the opportunity for initial employment screening during national pharmacy association meetings. Such programs generally include an initial screening
interview and are popular forums for facilitating career searches for thousands of
pharmacy practitioners, residents, and fellows on a national level.

A prospectively planned and standardized screening approach is the hallmark of
effective and fair employment practices. When recruitment efforts have successfully
resulted in a sizable pool of candidates, the identification and ranking of applicants
qualified for continued consideration, including onsite final interviews, warrants an
unbiased and objective approach. We discussed the importance of developing an up-
to-date position description in the paragraphs above. A criteria grid or an evaluation
rubric is often used to assess and rank candidates' qualifications against job description requirements and skill sets.

INTERVIEWING

The interview is the most commonly relied upon tool in the hiring selection process.
Interviews are intended to predict future job performance and the fit between candidate and employer based on responses to interview questions.

INTERVIEW TYPES AND APPROACHES

What interview structures, approaches, and styles exist, and do any result in better
validity? A number of approaches can be taken in the employment interview. On
a functional level, interviews are traditionally administered as one-on-one or face-
to-face interactions between the employer and the job candidate. In such cases, it is
common for a candidate to undergo multiple interviews with different members of

the organization involved in the recruiting and hiring process. Alternatively, panel interviews involve several interviewers interacting with one candidate during the interview session. Panel interviews have the potential for reducing the risk of interviewer bias, which can occur in one-on-one interviews. A third type of interview is the group interview. In this case, multiple candidates are interviewed together. The group interview approach allows interviewers additional dimensions of candidate assessment including the interactive communication and leadership skills of the interviewees.

Structured versus Unstructured Interviews

Regardless of the interview delivery method, it is important to appreciate the value of different interview types. Interviews can be either structured or unstructured. The structured interview is preferred and is usually competency based. The hallmarks of a structured interview include interview question standardization and focus on job-related requirements, skills, and competencies defined in the position's updated job description. When utilizing a structured interview style, all candidates being evaluated for the same position receive the same set of thoughtfully planned interview questions. This allows the organization to more objectively score and rank candidates in a uniform and unbiased manner.

The unstructured interview, sometimes referred to as the traditional interview, lacks standardization, may inconsistently focus on the position's competencies and requirements, does not protect against interviewer biases, and is not a recommended approach in the hiring process. Let us explore a hypothetical case. A well-meaning manager conducts an unstructured interview with a candidate who is attractive and well-spoken and also has several personal characteristics and attributes that are similar to those of the interviewer. The first interview question is somewhat general in nature and the candidate "nails" it with an impressive response. The rest of the interview goes smoothly and pleasantly with the manager doing much of the speaking in the way of promoting the organization and recruiting the candidate for the position. This same manager then conducts an interview with a candidate with somewhat less appealing surface qualities and a background and persona that are somewhat different from his. This interview goes reasonably well with the candidate handling tough questions quite adequately. Unstructured interviews offer us little in the way of protection against the many potential biases that our human nature introduces. Were these two candidates exposed to equally probing and meaningful interviews? Were the two candidates fairly handled relative to each other?

A few typical biases to which interviewers can inadvertently fall victim are enumerated here. The "halo effect" may be in play if the interviewer above allowed himself to form an overall favorable impression of the candidate based solely on the candidate's impressive answer to the first interview question. After hearing the interviewee's response to the initial interview question was the interviewer sufficiently impressed to follow up only with easy questions and a recruiting effort? Likewise, is "personal bias," forming a favorable or unfavorable impression based on personal attributes unrelated to job requirements and ability, "attractiveness bias," forming a favorable or unfavorable overall impression based on physical characteristics, "similarity bias," a tendency to value candidates with characteristics similar to one's own more favorably, and "eloquence bias" overly valuing a candidate's qualifications based solely on interviewing skills?

It seems reasonable to assume that structured and competency-based interviews are superior in many ways compared to unstructured interviews. The next question then is "what types of competency-based, structured interview questions are there and which is best?" There are two commonly used types of competency-based interview questions: situational and behavioral.

Situational versus Behavioral Interviews

Situational questions attempt to gain insight into candidates' competencies through hypothetical scenarios. "What would you do if..." or "How would you handle the situation if..." are typical ways situational questions are initiated. Leading questions should always be avoided but especially so when hypothetical questions are used. The situational question, "How would you go about refusing to fill a narcotic prescription for a patient whom you suspect of substance abuse?" leads the interviewee on regarding your expectation that the prescription should be refused. Candidates commonly attempt to answer situational and hypothetical interview questions with what they think the interviewer wants to hear rather than what they would do or should do. Although situational questions have a place in interviews, a good recommendation would be to use them sparingly, if at all.

Although behavioral interviews have been found in studies to result in higher validity than other types of interviews, these findings are not universal and are somewhat controversial. Nevertheless, behavioral interviews are favored by many experienced and successful recruiters and managers. The basic theory behind the behavioral interview is that a person's past behavior or performance is a predictor of that person's future behavior or performance. This is an assumption shared by other industries such as insurance companies. For example, a client's driving record and auto accident history are major indicators of future risk and help determine the insurability of the individual and what premium rate that individual might be asked to pay. The major characteristic of a behavioral interview question is that it evaluates candidates' job-related competencies and requirements through exploring how they specifically demonstrated those competencies in the past. Typical behavioral interview questions frequently start out as "Tell me about a time when you..." or "In your previous employment, what did you do when..." Competency-based behavioral interviews primarily focus on a candidate's fit with the requirements, skills, and values defined in the associated position description. Therefore, it is not surprising that interviews for pharmacists' positions explore skills and values such as leadership, problem solving, caring and empathy, and ability to work in a team environment. When posed with a behavioral question, the expectation is that the interviewee reflects back to an actual situation in which he or she faced a challenge, responsibility, or decision and then relates how he or she handled the situation. The optimal response to a behavioral question should be answered in a CAR or SAR format which includes

- Context or situation: What were the circumstances or context of the situation?
- Action: What did you do? How did you deal with the situation?
- Result: What was the result of your action?

EXAMPLE

Competency-based behavioral question: Tell me about a time when you were faced with a task requiring leadership and teamwork skills.

CAR response: I was a pharmacy extern at the We Care Pharmacy. It was late Christmas Eve just minutes prior to closing time when our wholesale supplier's delivery truck finally arrived at our back door. It had been snowing for the past two days and our country roads had been virtually impassable. The pharmacy order was large and everyone on the staff, including myself, had family commitments and was anxiously waiting for closing time. Knowing that the order had to be verified and stored appropriately, I was able to rally the prescription area staff as well as the store's retail area managers to contribute to the task at hand. I organized the volunteers into an assembly line team offering assistance where necessary and supervising the task. We were successful in checking the entire delivery into our inventory and did so within five minutes after closing time. No one left work that day without a smile, and I sense that they felt proud about their contributions to our organization and ultimately, patient care.

Wow! Wouldn't you seriously consider hiring this person? Maybe, but just be careful for the halo bias.

PLANNING AND PREPARING FOR THE INTERVIEW

How should I prepare and conduct effective employment interviews? Who should participate? Like many management functions, especially those that show leadership, teamwork plays an integral part. When planning for the recruitment interviewing and hiring of a critical position, one should determine who within the organization are the most appropriate to be involved in this process. In many organizations, the human resources (personnel) department plays an integral role in recruiting and hiring. Whether or not you have a human resources department, involving key individuals within your functional area is critical. Think: Who are the critical stakeholders related to this position? The list most likely includes the successful candidate's future coworkers and supervisors, but often interprofessional stakeholders are key individuals in the selection process for health-care professionals such as pharmacists. It would be wise, for example, to include key critical care leaders such as the medical director or head nurse of the critical care unit when interviewing a pharmacist for a critical care position. Likewise, a pharmacist being evaluated for an infectious diseases position should interview with the section chief or other physicians on the infectious diseases team. Including key stakeholders whether they are in or outside of the pharmacy department is important for at least two reasons. They can be critically important to the selection process but also can be valuable recruiting resources for desirable candidates. Making career choices and accepting job offers is almost always a scary thing. Potential employees need to meet and feel comfortable with those with whom they will be working and progressing in their careers. It is important that the interview itself focus on the job applicant who should be doing as much as 80% of the talking. A well-planned interview day should include sufficient time for informal discussion, touring, and addressing the candidate's questions about the organization and the position.

To prepare for the interview, determine and prioritize the key traits and skills required of a successful candidate based on the position description and the work environment. Prospectively develop a standardized set of interview questions and a candidate scoring method. Saying this, it is important to provide the interviewee with a copy of the position description as well as an interview day itinerary. Preferably, this should be done prior to the interview. Review the candidate's resume or CV as well as any screening information in order to identify any needs for clarification or further exploration. Be knowledgeable of the laws and regulations protecting against discrimination in the workplace. Title VII of the Civil Rights Act was discussed previously in this chapter. See Table 9.5 for examples of discriminatory versus appropriate interview questions.

Once a decision has been made regarding interview formats such as the one-on-one or the panel interviews, prepare a respectful interview environment. Interview timing and locations should always be prospectively determined and included in the itinerary. Two key qualities of an interview include making the candidate feel comfortable and creating an environment without interruptions or disorganization. Interviewers must clear their calendar for the planned interview session and select an interview location devoid of potential interruptions such as telephone calls and coworker queries.

Conducting the Interview

Make the candidate feel comfortable. In this regard, start off with an icebreaker such as a general question and orient the candidate on what to expect during the upcoming interview session. For example, you might want to let the candidate know that the majority of the questions in the interview will be of the behavioral type and will call upon a discussion of the candidate's past experiences. Let candidates know that they can take time to think about their answers prior to responding. It is good practice to take notes during the interview so you might inform the candidates that you plan to do so. Utilize the standardized competency-based questions that you prepared but feel free to ask follow-up questions as needed. Use open-ended and behavioral questions whenever possible and avoid the overuse of hypothetical questions. Sticking to competency-based behavioral questions will partially help you avoid potentially discriminatory interview questions, so be constantly thoughtful of the questions you ask. The most important of all interview skills is the art of listening. Give the candidate sufficient time to reflect and formulate responses to your questions. This is especially important when conducting a behavioral interview. Let the candidate do most of the talking. Avoid the temptation to fill in silent periods with your own comments, especially leading statements and hints. Take good notes and keep them on file in the event that unfair hiring practice concerns arise in the future. Close the interview session by encouraging the candidate to ask questions and share information regarding your time frame for hiring decisions and notifications. Take into consideration that additional applicants may still have to be interviewed and that background checks and references sometimes delay the process. Refer to Table 9.7 for a listing of common causes of poor interview validity.

TABLE 9.7
Common Causes of Poor Interviews and Interview Validity

Weakness in:

Interviewer	• Insufficiently prepared
	• Inflated sense of intuitiveness
	• Excessive interviewer chatter/distractions/recruiting
	• Poor communication skills
	• Listening, focus
	• Body language
Questions	• Lack of the job requirement relatedness/irrelevant
	• Insufficiently probing/close ended
	• Leading/hinting at right answer
	• Unstructured (spontaneous versus standardized)
Environment	• Lack of privacy
	• Uncomfortable conditions (temperature, space)
	• Insufficient time
	• Interruptions (telephone/cell phone, background noise)
Evaluation/ interpretation	• Lack of predetermined evaluation/ranking tool
	• Interviewer biases
	• Contrast bias
	• Similarity bias
	• Appearance bias

FINAL STEPS: REFERENCE AND BACKGROUND CHECKS

So, at this point we have accomplished the recruitment, screening, and interviewing of our candidates for the position we wish to fill. In some hiring procedures, such as pharmacy residency matching programs, letters of recommendation are obtained early in the process and serve as an important component of the screening process. In most cases, obtaining references and letters of recommendation is part of the final process of recruitment and hiring. It is important to note that candidate confidentiality might be a concern in some situations. Individuals applying for your vacant position are often currently employed elsewhere and looking for opportunities for career change or advancement with your organization. In such cases, applicants may desire that reference checks with their current employers be accomplished only after a reasonably sure decision has been made to extend an offer of employment.

Reference checks, qualification verification, and background checks are important and more critical in today's society. Similar to the basic hypothesis of behavioral interview questioning, an applicant's prior performance and behavior is an indicator of future performance and behavior.

As mentioned earlier, negligent hiring carries significant risk of liability and expense. It is a special responsibility of a health-care organization to assure the employment of appropriately qualified, competent, and ethical individuals. Risking the welfare of patients or the security of the hiring organization is unacceptable on a personal and legal level. Prior to hiring, the candidate's education, training, licensure, certifications, and past experience must be validated. Additionally, in today's society, conducting background checks including criminal, child abuse, and drug testing is becoming the norm especially for educational, hospital, and child care positions.

ORIENTING NEW EMPLOYEES

So, we have successfully completed our hiring process and hopefully hired our new employee who is highly qualified, ideally suited, and probably excited over a new and possibly scary career phase. Our hiring process is not quite done. New employees must be made to feel comfortable in their new surroundings and given more than simple directions to the men's and women's lavatories. They need to be provided information necessary for quick and efficient integration into a sometimes complex team. Each new employee requires orientation to the facility, aspects of their new position, their new department, and to the organization as a whole. Regardless of the new employees' familiarity with their position descriptions during the hiring process, new employees need to review their position descriptions again and also be oriented to their performance review expectations. New employees need to meet coworkers within and beyond their department and be oriented to job-related necessities such as small equipment, office supplies, and communication capabilities such as telephones and e-mail accounts.

POLICIES AND PROCEDURES

Policies differ from procedures and standard operating procedures; however, orientation to both is critically important to the new employee. A policy is an official document that defines expected and appropriate behaviors and actions. Policy statements serve to ensure expected levels of conduct and are enforceable within the organization's disciplinary process. There are several policy categories including those dealing with human resources policy, financial policy, legal- and statutory-based policy, safety policy, and operational policy. Procedures and standard operating procedures, on the other hand, represent specific steps and instructions defining the accepted methods of completing specific tasks. On an organizational level, the new employee must become familiar with basic policies and procedures dealing with work rules, work hours, compensation, and benefits. Legal policies, such as HIPAA and sexual harassment identification, and safety policies, such as blood-borne pathogens and universal precautions, are frequently covered during orientation as well as periodically as part of a continuing employee training program. Company policies based on the Occupational Safety and Health Act of 1970 (OSH Act) are examples of policies dealing with both legal and safety issues.

EMPLOYEE RETENTION

Now that we discussed the elements of effective employee recruitment, interviewing, selection, and hiring, let us not be lulled into a false sense of security that our manpower challenges have been answered. Now that we have a complement of qualified employees, our next challenges are to invest in, develop, and retain our organization's team of employees. As employers and managers, we have the responsibility to provide our employees with the necessities and opportunities required for growth and continued satisfaction within our organization. So the questions must be asked: What are the needs of my employees? What will motivate my employees to continue with and grow in their employment within my organization?

MOTIVATORS AND DEMOTIVATORS

A.H. Maslow's 1943 theory of human motivation, frequently depicted as a pyramid, describes a hierarchy of human needs ranging from basic physiological and safety necessities to higher-level social and esteem needs, and finally, the highest and most motivational need, self-actualization. Table 9.8 illustrates Maslow's five employee needs and what satisfies these needs, categorized according to Herzberg's dual factor theory.

It is important first that hygiene factor demotivators are not present in the workplace. Employees must be reasonably protected from danger or harm due to workplace environmental hazards, violence associated with robberies, and harassment. Basic life and work necessities must be provided, including reasonable compensation and benefits, acceptable work hours, and reasonable employment security. When such demotivators are present, higher-level motivators will not effectively promote employee retention.

Assuming a reasonably safe and secure workplace, managers have a responsibility for and benefit by providing their employees with job enrichment. Motivation, job satisfaction, and employee retention can be gained on social, esteem-building,

TABLE 9.8
Maslow Meets Herzberg

Employee Needs Satisfiers	Maslow's Hierarchy of Needs	Herzberg's Dual-Factor Theory
Self-fulfillment, accomplishment, growth	Self-actualization	Motivator
• Challenging and valued work, creativeness opportunities, and self-direction		Job enrichment
Appreciation, approval, respect, recognition		
• Promotional opportunity, job title, support, recognition by organization/profession, merit rewards	Esteem	Motivator
		Job enrichment
Belonging, fitting in, being one of the team		
• Communication, transparency, support, collaboration, coaching, development	Social	Motivator
		Job enrichment
Freedom from danger or harm		
• Workplace free from environmental hazards, dangers, violence, emotional trauma	Safety	Hygiene factor
		Demotivator if absent
Basic life/work necessities	Physiological	Hygiene factor
• Compensation, benefits, work hours and employment security sufficient for food, shelter, health care, and a basic lifestyle		Demotivator if absent

and self-actualization levels. Managers need to communicate transparently and continually support, recognize, and empower their employees. Organizations must determine an equitable rate of pay and avoid both internal and external compensation inequities for positions within an organization. Wage and salary surveys for external equity and job evaluation systems are often used to determine internal compensation equities.

COST OF EMPLOYEE TURNOVER

The cost of failure to retain employees and a high employee turnover rate result in both hard and soft dollars, visible and hidden costs. Earlier in this chapter, we discussed the daunting tasks of recruiting and hiring employees. The time and resources involved in these activities are significant. As employee vacancies are produced secondary to employee turnover, the need for increased recruiting and hiring and its associated costs are multiplied. Further, the costs involved in hiring new employees do not stop there. Employees generally go through an early development stage in which their productivity is less than optimal for some period of time. When established employees who have benefited from the organization's investment in their development leave the organization and are eventually replaced with new employees, a poor rate of return is derived from the organization's development investments and repeated development costs will be expended for the new staff. High employee turnover often breeds high employee turnover. When staff shortages are caused between the time of an employee's termination and the hiring and development of replacement staff, workload issues for the remaining staff can be an issue. Additionally, manpower shortages will often translate into missed opportunity costs.

WORKING AS A TEAM

> The best teamwork comes from men who are working independently toward one goal in unison.
>
> **James Cash Penney**

Teamwork is defined as "work done by several associates with each doing a part but all subordinating personal prominence to the efficacy of the whole" (Merriam-Webster.com, 2014). Teamwork has been long recognized as an important part of the working environment of the pharmacist. The traditional medication use process including medication prescribing, dispensing, administration, and monitoring is a multifaceted process requiring the diverse skills of cooperating interprofessional associates to produce consistently favorable health-care outcomes. In contemporary health care, more and more practices depend on teamwork. A few examples of such include medical homes, antimicrobial stewardship, medication reconciliation through the health-care system, and medication safety. In fact, organizations such as the IOM (Institute on Medicine) and the ACPE (American Council on Pharmaceutical Education) have fostered and now require health-care professionals to be educated within interprofessional collaborative communities.

When a group of individuals are simply assigned to work on a task, does this constitute teamwork? A team is not the same thing as a group. Qualities that are inherent in a true team, as opposed to a group, include interdependency, collaboration, trust, intragroup respect, minimized individualism, and the ability to use conflict constructively. Today's contemporary pharmacy manager needs to understand teamwork dynamics and its associated managerial challenges. Larson and LaFasto (1989) identified eight major characteristics of effective teams. An effective team must have (1) a clearly identified goal, (2) be results driven, (3) have competencies sufficient for the task, (4) be committed to reaching unity, (5) be dedicated to collaboration, (6) share clearly understood team values, (7) receive support and encouragement, and (8) be directed through team-oriented leadership. In other words, a team can be effective only when management provides clear direction to an adequately supported team of individuals having the appropriate knowledge and skills for the task, and a collaborative team spirit.

TEAM FORMATION, CONFLICT, AND PERFORMANCE

It is pretty obvious then, that the effectiveness of a team requires a complex interplay of mutual goals, trust, and community. Teams, whether newly formed or long-standing, are not always immediately effective when first challenged with an assignment. Bruce Tuckman described his early model of teamwork development in 1965 which is commonly referred to as the Forming–Storming–Norming–Performing model of group development. The earliest phase during team development sometimes finds that the team's objectives and the members' roles are not sufficiently clear. During this forming stage, leadership must provide a clear objective on which the team can then focus. The next stage is the storming stage in which conflict between team members and individual's approaches and ideas can rear its ugly head. An observation noted in the book, *Difficult Conversations: How to Discuss What Matters Most* (Stone et al., 2000, p. 46), is as follows: "The first mistake: our assumptions about intentions are often wrong." Conflicts can occur because people see the world differently and sometimes interpret other's intentions incorrectly. This frequently happens within teams and can hamper team interaction and productivity. One team member's lack of participation can be interpreted as passive aggression by another or one team member's enthusiasm can be interpreted as dictatorial when the realities are something much more benign.

The norming stage gives evidence to the calming of the storm and a development of the team's ability to work as a group with unity of purpose in the team's desire for success. Finally, the performing stage is one in which the group truly functions as an effective team, able to handle conflict and make decisions in an effective manner.

Teamwork, performed by employees, is not a substitute for good management practice. It is a powerful and complex management tool that involves and empowers employees and often results in benefits that outweigh traditional management approaches. Simply asking a group of employees to get together and solve a problem is often a recipe for failure. Managing teams in the workplace requires preparation, identification, and clear communication of objectives, team support and encouragement, organization, and often, patience.

CONFLICT MANAGEMENT

Imagine a scene that might be depicted in a Tom Clancy novel, the chairman of an unnamed eastern country rages on and on during a Politburo meeting, calling for a dual nuclear attack targeting Moscow as well as several cities in the United States. Although an obviously bad idea, no Politburo minister raises a single objection or argument against the chairman's psychotic proposal, most likely due to fear of reprisal, and almost certain death. Well, let us think about the dynamics of this Politburo meeting. No conflict, no problem? I think far from it. Conflict, disagreement, and constructive criticism are not all bad. In fact, these are what make teamwork valuable. Although few if any of us will be involved in meetings dealing with worldwide catastrophic decisions, we all will be part of committees, teams, or peer groups making very important clinical and managerial decisions. So, what is the take-away? We must agree to disagree with the eventual goal of a collaborative solution. Conflict is necessary: however conflict is bad when it becomes counterproductive or obstructive.

Note that conflict is discussed in the previous section of this chapter under the discussion of teams and teamwork. This section discusses the management of conflict in a broader arena. Whether in meetings or one-on-one interactions among coworkers or between care providers and their patients, conflict must be managed. We discuss "conflict management" rather than "conflict resolution." The actual resolution of management and interpersonal problems crosses many disciplines and management skills and is beyond the scope of this or any other single chapter.

Although conflict can be the result of personality clashes, counterproductive conflict is often a product of misconceptions regarding other's feelings, attitudes, and intentions. Human nature is such that people are different. People think differently than others, and people feel and react differently than others. Stone et al. (2000), suggest three conversations useful for the avoidance and management of conflict. These three conversations must address the three common things that create and sustain a "battle of messages" rather than a learning conversation in our interactions with others:

- Understand the issue at hand.
- Identify and acknowledge feelings.
- Identify personal stakes and potential threats.

Let us take each of the above three failures and consider them in light of the following scenario.

Mini-Case Study #5

During a weekly pharmacy leadership meeting in a mid-sized community hospital, Bob, the new director of pharmacy, proposes a reprioritization of pharmacy department imperatives that would shift resources away from a current intravenous to oral medication administration (IV to PO) program in favor of a newer clinical program addressing transition of care and medication reconciliation. Also present at this meeting were Tom, the pharmacy operations supervisor, Rita, the assistant director of pharmacy, primarily responsible for managing the drug budget, and Mac, the clinical coordinator, who supervises several clinical pharmacist specialists and a number of clinical protocols. With the exception of the clinical coordinator, Mac, Bob's transition of care proposal seems to fall on deaf, if not hostile, ears. With every justification and project step that Bob offers, Rita and Tom roll their eyes and offer curt rejections and negativism. Bob is not the only team member who feels Rita and Tom's obstructive behavior. Mac shows his frustration and confronts Tom with the question, "Why are you so down on clinical pharmacy practice?" Tom then confronts the director, Bob, and asks, "Since when is Mac your favorite in this department?" Bob then quietly ponders ways to replace his entire administrative staff.

Author Commentaries (Issues, Feelings, and Threats)

Understanding the Issue within the Conflict

You might know that the above scenario is not about the director's favoritism toward Mac, and it is not about Tom's bias against clinical pharmacy practice, but it might not be that obvious to the characters above. Intention can be easily misinterpreted even by the best of people involved in complex human interactions. The real issue is the assessment of the relative needs for and the values of two pharmacy programs and the decision on how resources should be allocated between them. A group is effective only when there is a commonality of purpose. In this case, it was Bob's responsibility to facilitate conversation leading to a clear understanding of the issue among the group participants.

Identifying and Acknowledging Feelings

Feelings are real and if they are not identified and acknowledged may continue to be an obstruction toward the charge of vetting the real issue and progressing toward a solution. Bob, the new pharmacy director, may have been familiar with the history of the department but may not have fully appreciated that the IV to PO program is especially dear to Tom who was the person responsible for its inception and successes over the years. It is not unreasonable to appreciate Tom's feeling of being unappreciated and undervalued when his pet project was overprioritized in an apparently offhanded manner. A conversation is needed during which Tom can acknowledge his feelings; Bob can acknowledge Tom's feelings and accomplishments; and all can attempt to deal with the subject at hand in a depersonalized manner.

Identifying Personal Stakes and Potential Threats

Most decisions directly or indirectly affect others, and hidden agendas are more common than we generally realize. The identification and inclusion of potential stakeholders is a critical step in any planning or decision-making process. In our scenario above, rising drug costs and an increasing proportion of intensive care patients requiring more costly medications has been causing Rita to struggle with her charge of controlling the hospital's drug budget. She perceives that the IV to PO program has contributed to controlling drug costs and views a potential reduction in IV to PO activity as a threat to the drug budget's bottom line, a more difficult job for her, and a potential negative reflection on her ability to accomplish her responsibilities. Rita's concern is valid, but only through a conversation of such concerns can solutions and allowances be formulated and ultimately progress made. Internal conversations are often required in which involved individuals internally reflect on what the issue means to them on a personal level, and on the appropriateness of their stance on the issue.

These same principles pertain to conflicts involving one-on-one interactions as well. Let us explore a simple conflict example where identifying the right issue, acknowledging feelings, finding a commonality, depersonalizing the conflict, and suggesting solutions represent the most appropriate plan for managing conflict.

Mini-Case Study #6

You are the pharmacist on duty at Community Pharmacy when a long-time customer, Mr. Smith, comes in to pick up his prescription refill. His prescription was out of refills and although you left multiple messages, the prescriber has not returned your calls with a refill authorization. You also left a telephone message for Mr. Smith alerting him of the situation. Mr. Smith obviously does not check his voicemail and now he is in your pharmacy and he is angry. He begins to yell and scream, saying you are the most incompetent pharmacist he has ever dealt with and that he is going to report you to the Board of Pharmacy. Other customers and patients waiting for their medications are watching the scene in horror.

How would you manage this conflict? What are the steps that could be taken to control the situation and avoid making it worse and allow an acceptable outcome?

Author Commentary

You are not a bad person or an incompetent pharmacist and Mr. Smith probably knows that. The real issue is simply that Mr. Smith is not getting the prescription medications that he wants and probably needs. You might be tempted to shift the blame to the prescriber who has failed to respond to your requests, but this would probably be a bad idea for a number of reasons. For one thing, the public rarely accepts denials of fault or blame shifting when they have a service complaint. "It's not my fault" often serves only to increase the customer's level of frustration and angst.

1. *Acknowledge feelings*: Although you are not at fault, it is still appropriate, and usually well received, to acknowledge that you are sorry for the patient's inconvenience and that you understand his or her feelings and frustration.
2. *Find a commonality*: The commonality between you, the provider, and Mr. Smith, the patient, is that you both are concerned about his health. You need to tell him so and add that you have only his well-being in mind.
3. *Depersonalize the conflict*: Although Mr. Smith acted inappropriately in disparaging your professionalism in a loud manner, you should inform him in a calm and professional manner that you do indeed care for him as a patient and will continue to act in a responsible and professional manner in his behalf.
4. *Suggest solutions*: Although it is beyond the scope of this chapter to discuss conflict resolution, some options for at least temporarily correcting the situation need to be offered, such as dispensing a limited number of doses to hold him over, offering prescription delivery, or simply committing to continue aggressively pursuing his refill authorization.

CONFLICT MODELS

Numerous conflict models have been proposed in an attempt to explain the hows and whys of conflict. They identify a variety of personality types and behavior types as conflict enablers and in some cases provide suggestions on how to deal with such behaviors in a conflict situation.

I am sure that in your dealings with people, you have noticed various behaviors ranging from the excessive accommodation, the sycophant or typical yes-man, to excessive competition, the "it's my way or the highway" person. The Thomas-Kilmann Conflict Mode Instrument defines five interpersonal behavior modes that result from the combination of an individual's level of assertiveness and cooperativeness. These behavior modes include competing mode, accommodating mode, avoiding mode, compromising mode, and collaborating mode. Under this conflict model, it can be seen that individuals demonstrating a low level of cooperativeness and a high level of assertiveness are likely to behave in a competing mode, asserting their ideas at the possible expense of others' contributions. On the other hand, individuals who demonstrate a high level of cooperativeness and a low level of assertiveness are likely to behave in an overly accommodating fashion, in other words noncontributing yes-men. The most productive of these five modes, collaborating mode, occurs with the ideal balance of assertiveness and cooperativeness and is likely to more often result in win-win interpersonal situations and novel solutions.

Brinkman and Kirschner's *Dealing with People You Can't Stand* (2012) is an interesting and amusing book. Originally published in 1994, it defined 10 personality behaviors that are often at the root of conflict situations. Updated in a third edition in 2012, the authors revised and expanded their scope to include 13 conflict personality behaviors in our newer "e-communication" generation (The 10+3 Most Unwanted List): tank, sniper, grenade, know-it-all, think-they-know-it-all, yes-person, maybe-person, nothing-person, no-person, whiner, judge, meddler, and martyr.

You have probably interacted with any number of people who fit into one of these categories. For example, you may have had the occasion of dealing with a "tank," an overly aggressive and "in your face" character, prone to tirades that do not stop. You may have had the misfortune to work with a "sniper," a person likely to take public potshots at his victims, or a "grenade" that explodes only after his tolerability threshold has been reached. People call me a "know-it-all," but I really wish they would tell me something I do not know. Appreciate that these personality behaviors can be demonstrated routinely by some people, but also by any normal person under the right or more accurately, wrong circumstances. There are people who always say "yes" but cannot follow through, and people who always say "no," and some who too often say "maybe," or worse, nothing at all. There are people who are perpetual complainers, a contagious behavior, and others who are overly judgmental. There are people who stick their noses into other's personal business and people who are overly giving with a subtly associated "now you owe me."

Recognizing these behaviors and personalities is the first step in effectively dealing with behavior conflict. Stand up to tanks, and interrupt their tirades with brief comments. Call out snipers and ask for explanations of their potshots. Let grenades know that you care and that you will listen and they do not have to wait until they have had enough to express their issues. Be informed as much as possible, and ask for clarification when dealing with the "know-it-alls" and "think-they-know-it-alls." Hold yes-men accountable with timelines for their accepted responsibilities. Probe the "maybe-sayers," the "say-nothings," and the "naysayers" and encourage them to make informed decisions. Finally, do not fall victim to the contagious condition of complainers and whiners.

PERFORMANCE MANAGEMENT: MANAGING AND REWARDING PERFORMANCE

From the organization's standpoint, performance management programs are critical to the accomplishment of organizational goals as well as the growth and development of the employee. From the employee's standpoint, humans have a basic need to know how they are doing. Employees need to know how much their work is appreciated by the organization and how their productivity is contributing to the organization's goals as well as to their own career advancement. Performance evaluations, specifically for professional employees, are especially necessary as they are especially difficult. Significant contributions made by professionals are frequently innovative, creative, or subjective and therefore difficult to quantitatively measure in a performance review or even within the employee's own reflection and self-evaluation. We see in this section how effective performance management relates to the organization's business plan success and its employees' potential for development, promotion, and job satisfaction.

Performance Management Rules of Engagement

Before we begin the discussion on the topics of performance management and performance evaluation, we need to appreciate expectations and the responsibilities of both supervisor and employee in these processes. Simply stated, evaluating the performance of employees is a standard in management practice. Employees need to know, and have the right to know, how they are faring in the eyes of their employer. It is also an expected responsibility of supervisors to provide ongoing, periodic feedback to employees regarding their performance in addition to annual performance evaluations. If managed appropriately, an employee should never be surprised during a formal annual performance appraisal.

Mentoring, Coaching, and Counseling

We need to define and differentiate a few associated terms that are sometimes used inappropriately and, too often, interchangeably. An important element of performance management includes providing employees with ongoing feedback, support, and sometimes corrective direction. We often use the words *mentoring, coaching,* and *counseling* interchangeably. In fact, these terms connote slightly different meanings depending on the user's professional setting. In a clinical setting, *counseling* of a patient has a slightly different meaning than the counseling a manager might offer to an employee, but not that much different. For the purposes of this chapter, we define mentoring, coaching, and counseling in the following manner.

Mentoring

Mentoring refers to a unique and special relationship between a knowledgeable, experienced teacher and a protégé. The word itself is derived from Mentor, a close friend of Odysseus, of Greek mythology. Mentor agreed to care for Odysseus' household and to serve as a tutor to Telemachus, the son of Odysseus, while Odysseus went off to the Trojan War. The word mentor connotes an ongoing and purposeful relationship based on mutual faithfulness and the sharing of wisdom.

Coaching

Coaching is a term commonly used in sports. A coach's responsibility is to teach and motivate an athlete to go from good performance to hopefully great performance. Similarly, in management, employee coaching generally focuses on employees who are performing at least adequately with the goal of providing them with the motivation and tools to exceed. We discuss coaching and its place in directing and motivating employees a little later in this chapter as we explore the components of performance management.

Counseling

Counseling is a term commonly used in a variety of clinical practices. The Oxford Dictionary defines counseling as "the provision of professional assistance and guidance in resolving personal or psychological problems." A therapist might provide counseling to a patient having a difficult time adjusting to a personal or emotional problem. A pharmacist might provide counseling to a patient who is nonadherent to his medication regimen. Similarly, a manager might provide counseling to an employee who is performing below standard or is behaving inappropriately. Simply put, mentoring and coaching carry positive and favorable connotations, while counseling is associated with the need for corrective action. It should be noted however that counseling could, should, and often does, result in exemplary employee performance. We will re-address the topic of counseling a little later in this chapter and explore counseling in stage, also known as progressive discipline.

Performance: The Good, the Bad, or the Ugly?

What does successful employee performance look like? What constitutes unacceptable, acceptable, and exceptional performance? These are important questions often inadequately answered especially when evaluating the performance of professional employees who often have creative, cutting-edge, or complicated job responsibilities.

Earlier in this chapter, we discussed the challenges that potential employers face when interviewing and evaluating job candidates. We discussed interview biases such as the halo effect, personal bias, and contrast bias as well as the more general issue of the relative validity of interview types including standardized behavioral interviewing. These issues and potential pitfalls are strikingly similar to those facing the responsibility of employee performance evaluation. Similar to methods for interviewing, there are several methods and approaches to defining performance measurement. Some methods rely heavily on objective performance criteria, some on human resource concerns such as attendance and punctuality, and many on management's judgment of the employee's traits such as job knowledge, initiative, problem solving, and many more. Similar to behavioral interviewing in job recruitment, the performance evaluation approach known as behaviorally anchored rating scales (BARS) is thought by many to provide superior performance assessment validity. Comparative studies however are not sufficiently conclusive to justify the intensive efforts of numerous supervisors required to validate and implement the BARS performance evaluation instrument in their organization.

The bottom line is that criteria of performance should follow the employee's position description and reflect the contributions, traits, behaviors, and abilities expected of the employee and mutually understood by the employee and supervisor. These expectations should also be consistent with organization's goals, objectives, and critical initiatives.

Managing Good Performance by Coaching, Motivation, and Development

Performance evaluations have a purpose, in fact, a number of purposes beyond the simple need to just evaluate employees. Evaluation of past and current performance should be considered the basis for future improvement, improvement and advancement of the individual employee, and improvement and advancement in the organization's progress toward its goals. An organization's most valuable resources are its employees and your employees should be made aware of this. They need to know how their responsibilities, goals, and performance fit into the big picture and how they contribute to the organization's success. On a human resources level, the critical need for employee motivation, support, and development can be intelligently addressed with a well-designed performance management program which includes constructive employee coaching.

Wiseman's *Multipliers: How the Best Leaders Make Everyone Smarter* (2010) provides the "multiplier formula" for enabling employees to apply their full capabilities, expand their potential, and allow for greater and more independent productivity. She contrasts the management styles between a micromanager and an "investor." Different from a micromanager, who tightly manages details and unwittingly encourages inappropriate employee dependence, the "investor" manages, or more aptly leads, by empowering, investing, and supporting employees who are then held accountable. She lists three practices of the "investor," which include (1) imparting ownership for the end goal to the employee; (2) investing resources in the employee through coaching, development, and support; and (3) holding the empowered employee accountable for the end goal. When managing the performance of professional personnel, such as pharmacists, the leadership approach exemplified by the "multiplier formula" makes every bit of sense.

Formal (Annual) Performance Evaluation and Ongoing Progress Review and Goal Resetting

The annual performance evaluation is somewhat of a misnomer. There is little about a good performance management program that is strictly annual. Although a formal performance evaluation meeting is generally scheduled annually with each employee, it represents only a brief, but important, part of the performance management continuum which is an ongoing effort. In the beginning, there is an up-to-date job description as well as ongoing discussions of the employee's responsibilities, goals, and behavioral expectations. When preparing the assessment, the supervisor should review the employee's file rather than work solely from recent memory. Some time prior to the formal annual performance assessment meeting, a brief preparatory meeting is commonly scheduled during which the employee receives the written performance appraisal. The formal performance evaluation meeting should offer no surprise to the employee or to the manager. Continuous feedback should have prepared the employee to be well aware of his or her performance, areas of strength, and areas needing improvement. The performance review should be conducted in privacy and free of distractions. The performance review should be a dialogue rather than a top-down managerial monologue. It is not uncommon and actually recommended that the employee be asked to complete and discuss a performance self-evaluation as part of this dialogue. The evaluation includes not only a discussion of the employee's strengths, weaknesses, and goal attainment status but also the initiation of a developmental plan for continued or improved performance for the coming year. As part of this developmental plan, the employee's commitment to improvement is sought, and the identification of needed management support and employee development explored. Employee performance assessments are legal documents, and as such must be documented accurately and filed in the employees' permanent records. Upon completion of the formal performance evaluation meeting, subsequent review of performance progress should never wait until the next annual meeting but should be conducted periodically, often quarterly, throughout the coming year. Figure 9.1 illustrates the continuous cycle of components (goal formation/reformation, performance monitoring, coaching, and evaluation) that defines the performance management process.

PERFORMANCE MANAGEMENT AND THE BUSINESS PLAN

How does the performance management process tie into the bigger picture of the organization's goals and direction? Performance management and business planning share at least one commonality. In their simplest forms, they can be described as ongoing cycles of goal setting, performance, motivation, evaluation, and goal resetting (Figure 9.2). The success of any organization is dependent on the job

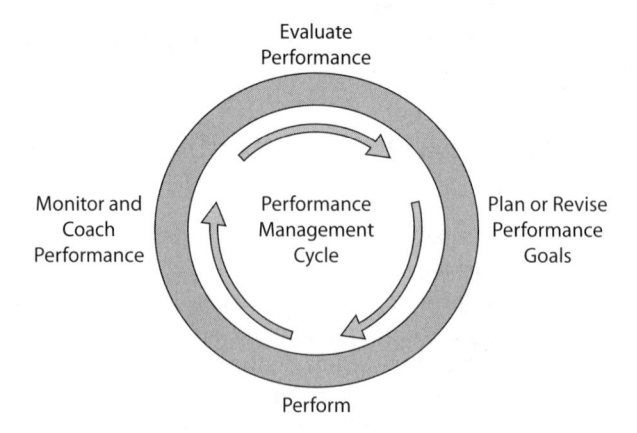

FIGURE 9.1 The performance management cycle. (Adapted from SHRM® / PDI 2000 Performance Management Survey.)

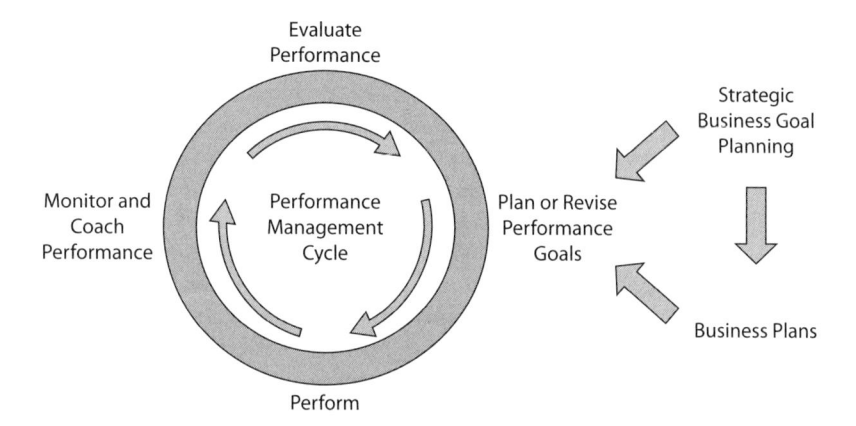

FIGURE 9.2 Linking the business plan and performance management. (Adapted from SHRM® / PDI 2000 Performance Management Survey.)

performance of its employees. In fact, linking the goals of the organization's business plan to the organization's performance management program is essential.

Goal Setting: Assigning Tasks, Responsibilities, and Milestones

"It's about results." In the first chapter of Tim Berry's *Hurdle: The Book on Business Planning* (2002, p. 3), the question is posed: "So what is the value of a business plan?" The incorrect answer "Thousands of dollars, tens of thousands, in some cases" was corrected with a more appropriate and operational view. The value of a business plan is the decisions it influences and only then, ultimate success which might hopefully include money in the bank.

The business plan and its goals should serve to help define the implementation, direction, and organizational milestones of the business, and ultimately, the position descriptions and performance responsibilities of its employees. A well-designed performance management program, synchronized with the organization's goals, can then provide for the meaningful evaluation of operations, its employees, and the potential need for plan refinement and corrective actions. On the level of the employee, performance standards must be clearly understood from the beginning. Employee performance expectations and goals are management prerogatives; however, discussion and negotiation between management and employee are effective tools supporting efficiency, adherence, and job satisfaction. Employee performance goals and behaviors should be both measurable and attainable with the employee held accountable for success which is clearly defined and mutually understood.

DISCIPLINE, SUSPENSION, AND TERMINATION

In the ideal world, all employees would be perfect. All would contribute, meet all goals and expectations, and never break the rules or behave inappropriately. In case you have not noticed, we do not live in an ideal or perfect world. Occasionally employees need to be disciplined. Most people equate the word *discipline* with punishment.

Although this is not entirely untrue, the word *discipline* is derived similarly to the word *disciple*, which refers to a follower of a teacher. Therefore, the intention of disciplining an employee is to teach and hopefully correct unacceptable behavior or inadequate productivity in the workplace. For the purposes of this chapter, we will define employee counseling as the provision of direction or advice regarding a difficulty an employee is having or regarding an employee's loss of a sense of direction and purpose—in other words, intervening when an employee is in trouble. In today's management vernacular, discipline is also referred to as fair punishment, corrective action, or progressive discipline. The most common reasons for progressive discipline include insubordination, failure to meet responsibilities, and failure to comply with policies and procedures. In each of these cases there is an expectation that discipline can correct the unacceptable behavior or lack of performance. Workplace infractions, in which progressive discipline is not warranted, include uncorrectable behavior or behaviors requiring immediate termination, such as theft, violence, and major work rule violations.

When initiating a progressive discipline process with an employee, it is always important to determine the reason for an employee's substandard performance. Is the employee's behavior or productivity deficit due to insufficient ability, resources, or understanding of the situation or job at hand? Is it a lack of desire to perform? The answer to these questions might provide direction regarding which course to follow in the disciplinary and hopefully, corrective process. The solution may be as simple as providing additional training, clarifying instructions, or reassigning responsibilities.

The six key factors in progressive discipline include (1) getting your facts straight, (2) acting in a timely fashion, (3) counseling in privacy, (4) developing an appropriate action plan to correct the deficiency, (5) discussing the consequences of continued infractions, and (6) documenting the entire transaction.

Progressive discipline is generally administered in a step-wise fashion which is illustrated by Figure 9.3. It is critical, and the first law of progressive discipline, to inform the employee of the consequences of failure to improve with each step of the disciplinary process. It generally begins with an informal discussion with the employee regarding expectations and a specific review of the observed shortcomings of the employee, whether they are issues of quantity, quality, and/or timeliness. The next step commonly involves a formal oral warning, which is documented in the employee's personnel file. If improvement is not adequate, a formal written warning is issued which commonly documents an improvement plan or a corrective action plan spelling out specific improvement expectations including when improvement is expected. Subsequent steps may include suspension and ultimately employment termination.

Note the following two issues. Although the manager has the responsibility for helping the employee to solve his or her problems, it is the responsibility of the employee to improve his or her performance or behavior. The laws prohibiting discrimination which were discussed at the beginning of this chapter deal not only with hiring practices but also with managerial decisions related to promotions, demotions, and discipline. Similar to advice offered previously, disciplinary decisions should be made based on job relatedness, objectivity, and uniform fairness.

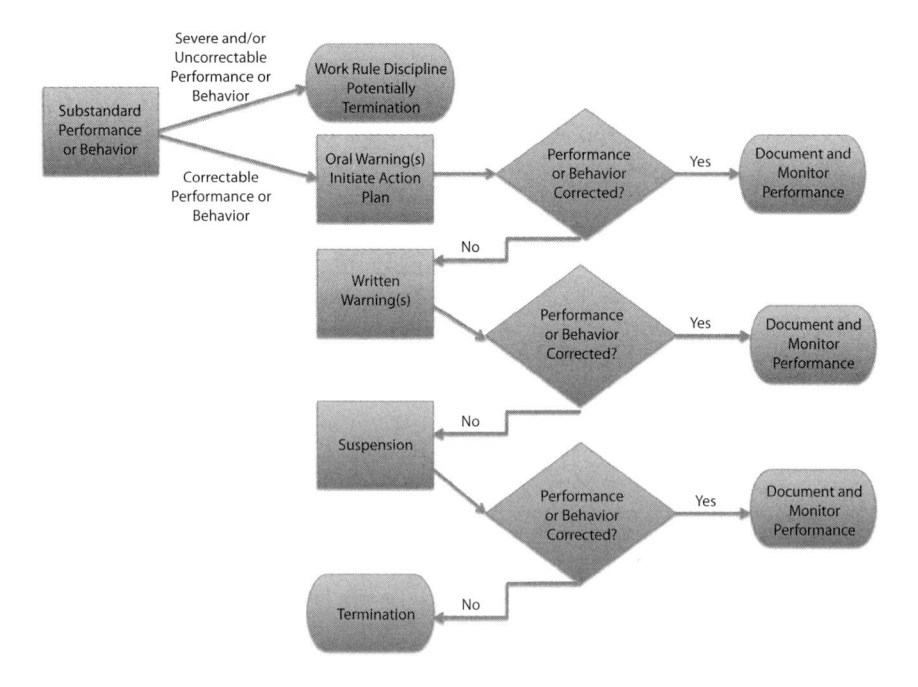

FIGURE 9.3 Progressive discipline.

The Grievance Process

Appeals or grievances are an integral component to a progressive discipline program. When an employee feels that he or she has been treated unfairly or without due process in a disciplinary action, the employee has a right to appeal the disciplinary action. Although different organizations may have a slightly different procedure, the employee's first step in the appeal process is generally to the supervisor initiating the disputed discipline. If this step does not result in an acceptable outcome for the employee, a second appeal step is directed to the employee's department head. Likewise, if this step does not result in an outcome to the employee's satisfaction, a third appeal step can be directed to the organization's human resources department. Grievance processes are routinely available and allow for a guarantee of "due process"; therefore, managers should not get defensive and should be supportive of the employee's rights.

SUMMARY

There is no question that employees are the most valuable resources of every organization, business, or clinical practice. It is not surprising, therefore, that the most important responsibility and obligation of a manager is the capable shepherding of the processes this chapter has described that are components of the personnel management continuum.

This chapter has attempted to touch on the major components of this continuum. We covered issues in the planning of appropriate manpower staffing, recruitment, hiring, and orientation of new employees. We discussed federal laws that guide us in our provision of fair treatment and safe environments for our people resources in the workplace. We discussed the subtleties of interpersonal dynamics such as teamwork, conflict management, and job satisfaction. And finally we described performance management, from mentoring and motivation to counseling and discipline.

We could study hard, read many books, and go to many classes to prepare ourselves to be competent managers. Being knowledgeable, competent, and capable are unquestionably required for this responsibility. But in addition, great managers and great leaders also share a high level of emotional intelligence, listening skills, and a sincere desire for people to succeed.

ACKNOWLEDGMENTS

This author wishes to gratefully acknowledge two authors from the first edition of *Managing Pharmacy Practice: Principles, Strategies, and Systems*. Their original works contributed a wealth of information and insight related to topics covered in this chapter. In the first edition, Ellen Fernberger authored Chapter 6, "Employee Recruitment, Retention, and Compensation" and Chapter 7, "Employee Coaching, Evaluation, and Discipline." Christy-Lee Lucas authored Chapter 8, "Conflict Management." Both Ellen and Christy-Lee are largely responsible for setting the scope and objectives of this chapter's topics and like most of the authors of this book's first edition, have contributed richly to the study of management in pharmacy.

BIBLIOGRAPHY

Berry T. *Hurdle: The Book on Business Planning*. Palo Alto Software Incorporated, Eugene, OR, 2002.
Brainy Quote. James Cash Penney quotes. Available at: http://www.brainyquote.com/quotes/quotes/j/jamescashp226500.html#KDM3Ts0tZoTVLHAV.99.
Brinkman R, Kirschner R. *Dealing with People You Can't Stand* (3rd ed.). McGraw-Hill, New York, 2012.
Gawel JE. Herzberg's theory of motivation and Maslow's hierarchy of needs. *Practical Assessment, Research & Evaluation*, 1997;5(11). Retrieved December 18, 2014, from http://PAREonline.net/getvn.asp?v=5&n=11.
Larson F and LaFasto C, *Teamwork: What Must Go Right/What Can Go Wrong*. Sage Publications, Thousand Oaks, CA, 1989.
Maslow AH. A theory of human motivation. *Psych Rev*. 1943; 50, 370–396. As listed on the Green C.D. Classics in the History of Psychology [online resource]. psychclassics.yorku.ca/Maslow/motivation.htm (accessed December 18, 2014).
Merriam-Webster [online resource]. www.merriam-webster.com/dictionary/teamwork (accessed December18, 2013).
Shane R, Gouveia W. The dilemma of establishing effective pharmacy staffing levels. *Am J Health-Syst Pharm*. 2009 Dec 1;66(23):2103. doi: 10.2146/ajhp090490.
Shapero A. *Managing Professional People: Understanding Creative Performance*. Free Press, London, 1985.
SHRM® / PDI 2000 Performance Management Survey. Accessed December 18, 2014 from www.shrm.org/research/surveyfindings/documents/performance%20management%20survey.pdf

Specter B, Beer M. *Note on Job Evaluations in Human Resource Management: A General Manager's Perspective: Text and Cases.* Free Press, New York, 1985.

Stevens DC (ed). *The Maslow Business Reader: Abraham H. Maslow.* Wiley, New York, 2000.

Stone D, Patton B, Heen S. *Difficult Conversations: How to Discuss What Matters Most.* Penguin Books, New York, 2000.

Thomas KW, Kilmann RH. Thomas-Kilmann Conflict Mode Instrument. Available at www.kilmanndiagnostics.com/overview-thomas-kilmann-conflict-mode-instrument-tki.

Tuckman B. Developmental sequence in small groups. *Psychol Bull.* 1965;63(6):384–399. doi:10.1037/h0022100. PMID 14314073.

US Department of Labor, Wage and Hour Division DOL's Fair Pay Overtime Initiative. www.dol.gov/whd/regs/compliance/fairpay/fs17a_overview.pdf.

Wiseman L, McKeown G. *Multipliers: How the Best Leaders Make Everyone Smarter*, Harper Collins, New York, 2010.

Case Study

The question must be asked, in day-to-day practice, how valid are interviews in predicting employee performance? Here are a few examples of actual interview questions posed to recent pharmacy graduates during employment interview sessions. Comment on these four questions. Do you think that they are effective? Are they valid? Why?

1. If you were a Microsoft Office application, which application would you be? Now, think about this question and answer it carefully.
2. Tell me about yourself.
3. Do you think that you have an adequate database to perform as a clinical pharmacist in our organization?
4. If you observed a coworker stealing company property, how would you go about reporting him to your supervisor?

APPENDIX A: SAMPLE POSITION DESCRIPTION

POSITION DESCRIPTION

Position Title:	Clinical Decentralized Pharmacist	Job Code:	Pharm II
Grade Level:	14	FLSA	Nonexempt
Reports to:	Director of Pharmacy	Department:	Pharmacy
Location:	Acute Care Hospital (in-patient)		

****

Role Statement: Responsible for coordination of medication orders in a clinical practice unit, assuring appropriate use to ensure safety and service to clinical staff and patients.

Job Essentials:

- Review and evaluate medication orders consulting with physicians and caregivers, and identify opportunities for improving drug therapy. Recommend changes to appropriate prescriber.
- Profile and enter medication orders.
- Work closely with other practitioners caring for high-risk patient populations to ensure medications are appropriate upon discharge.
- Work with appropriate caregivers to ensure an efficient and effective medication reconciliation process.
- Participate in multidisciplinary patient rounds.
- Review medication safety and appropriate drug regimes with RNs for specific patient types.
- Counsel patients about medication use and safety as needed.
- Recommend IV to PO conversions authorized by the Pharmacy and Therapeutics Committee.
- Provide education to clinical staff related to pharmaceutical care.
- Manage the medication therapy of specific patient types (e.g., diabetes, chronic heart failure) as authorized by the Pharmacy and Therapeutics Committee.

Skill Set:

- Excellent problem-solving and persuasion skills
- Strong interpersonal skills and empathy for interaction with patients
- Ability to translate pharmaceutical knowledge and provide clinical recommendations for improved patient outcome
- Successfully documented clinical experience to provide clinical counsel to physicians, RNs, or patients

Educational Requirements, Qualifications:

Graduation from an accredited college of pharmacy with a PharmD or BSc Pharm degree and current PA pharmacy licensure are required. Minimum 3 years hospital experience desired. Completion of a PGY-1 pharmacy residency or mentored clinical work in an area of specialty is strongly preferred.

Employees Managed: 0

Employees Supervised: 0

Budgetary/Fiscal Responsibility: N/A

Hospital Requirements:

- Consistently demonstrates values of compassion, professionalism, and team spirit.
- Maintains safe environment and respects hospital facilities and equipment.

ADA Requirements:

- Physical Strength:
- Manual Dexterity:
- Motor Coordination:
- Form Perception:
- Environmental Conditions:
- Environmental Hazards:
- Physical Demands: Talking and hearing, vision, stooping, kneeling, crouching, reaching, handling, feeling, fingering

Machines, Equipment, Work Aids:
(not all inclusive of those commonly associated with this type of work)

Computer (monitor/keyboard/printer), typewriter, calculator, telephone, copy machine, fax machine, and other general office equipment

Revised date: 10/8/13

10 Managing Pharmacy Operations

Steve Gilbert

CONTENTS

Learning Objectives: After reading this chapter and working through the case, the reader will be able to:

1. Describe the medication use process
2. Discuss the impact of technology on the health-system pharmacy operations
3. List medication safety strategies for each step in the medication use process
4. Compare advantages and disadvantages of centralized versus decentralized drug distribution in terms of operational and personnel costs

MEDICATION USE PROCESS

During evolution of the practice of pharmacy during the latter half of the twentieth century, the concept of the medication use process was introduced to provide a conceptual framework to investigate all activities associated with the use of medications in the health system that result in medication errors. The medication use construct allowed the pharmacists to focus staff and activities to take on the enhanced role of advocating for proper use of medications to avoid medication errors and achieve desired outcomes. This framework allowed practitioners to launch quality improvement activities aimed at decreasing the number and severity of medication errors which were identified as a public health problem. Additionally, the framework addressed the expansion of health-system pharmacy services to include outpatient pharmacy and ambulatory clinics along with the traditional inpatient focus. The medication use process forms the organization of this chapter and will use the health system as its primary focus. The medication use process is composed of five activities: prescribing, transcribing, distribution, administration, and monitoring (Figure 10.1).

Prescribing

Prescribing has two parts. First is a decision based on the end result of an assessment of a specific patient issue where a practitioner decides a medication is part of the plan to ameliorate the issue. The next step is the actual act of informing other members of the team of the decision via a legal order, legal being what is defined by the specific state's medical board of what constitutes a legal order. Historically in hospitals, this was accomplished with a handwritten order in a patient chart but includes outpatient prescriptions whether they are traditional paper prescriptions or electronic prescriptions. A copy of the order is transmitted to the pharmacy for further action.

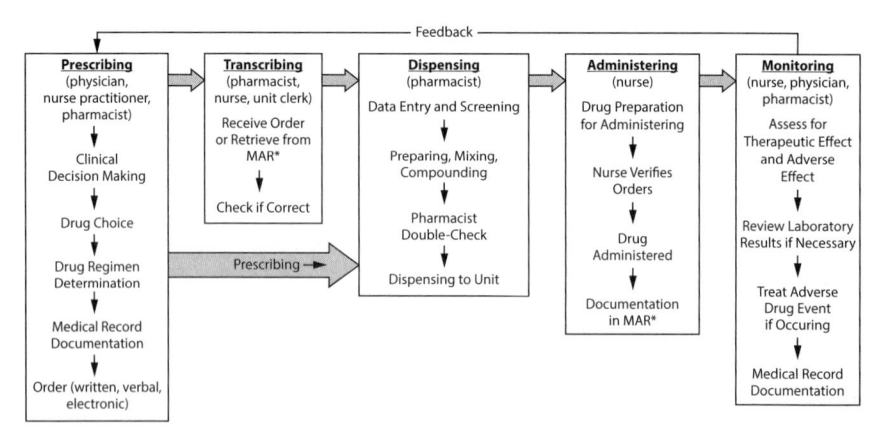

*MAR = Medication Administration Record

FIGURE 10.1   Preventing medication errors.

Handwritten medication orders are fraught with errors such as decimal errors, illegible handwriting, and incorrect patient identification. The classic article on the subject of medication errors estimated 39% occurred at the prescribing step.[1] As a result, many health systems embarked on the acquisition of integrated clinical information systems with computerized prescriber order entry (CPOE) functionality. CPOE has decreased but not eliminated errors at this step. Unintended events occur as a result of CPOE.[2] These unintended consequences include changes in interactions between care providers, overreliance on the infallibility of technology, and increasingly complex working patterns especially at patient-care interfaces.[3]

Health systems work with formularies. The formulary concept is described elsewhere in the text. The hospital's formulary forms the basis of the drug master file with commonly used non-formulary items listed as well. The health-system pharmacy may operate with multiple formularies depending on their systems product lines. Separate formularies may exist for inpatients, clinic patients, and long-term care or hospice patients. Prescribers are presented with lists of medications, dosage forms, available strengths, routes of administration, and frequency of administration. If the prescriber has a knowledge deficit in any one of these factors, unintended medication errors can result.

The same issues described above exist for pharmacy practice in other environments such as community, specialty, long-term care, and infusion services. With the exception of community practice, these environments have an additional challenge of a lack of face-to-face contact with both prescribers and patients missing the context that nonverbal communication provides in assuring understanding. Conversely, the advent of e-prescribing has surmounted some, but not all, issues associated with handwritten prescribing. Prescribers are still provided enough latitude within the e-prescribing applications to free text and make errors especially with directions for use.

TRANSCRIBING

Transcribing is the action of copying the prescriber's order from the original source into another data source/system such as a nursing medication administration or a pharmacy medication profile. It is another area prone to error because the physical act of reading a source document and converting to another document requiring the actions of a person automatically injects a cause for error. CPOE has gone a long way in reducing the error at this point, but error still exists primarily when users adopt work-arounds.

For many years, transcribing occurred within the same physical boundaries defining the work area for the physician, nurse, and pharmacist (i.e., all worked in the same building/contiguous buildings). The pharmacist shortage in rural areas made this traditional process difficult to achieve and meet state and accrediting agency requirements regarding the safe dispensing of medications. One solution is the use of telepharmacy to provide off-site order review.[4] Telepharmacy takes advantage of advances in telecommunications, electronic imaging technologies, and information systems to leverage the skills of remotely located pharmacists. The remote pharmacist views a display of the medication order and reviews its appropriateness against the patient's electronic medical record (eMR). If the pharmacist deems the physical dispensing of the medication to be safe and in accordance with the health-systems policies and state regulations, then the pharmacist authorizes the dispensing from a remote access cabinet. Telepharmacists are also employed to back-load medication information into clinical information systems prior to the launch of a new system. The remote pharmacists can work for the same health system in a different facility or a private firm.

DISTRIBUTION

Health-system pharmacies are the source of medications for their inpatients and sometimes for outpatients whose medication needs are a continuation of care received as inpatient. The pharmacy manager needs to be aware of the board of pharmacy regulations in their respective state regarding the health-system pharmacy's ability to serve other outpatients (i.e., those seen in clinic for care not related to an inpatient stay). This is because the health-system pharmacy has a competitive advantage due to their ability to purchase medications at discounted prices through competitive contractual bidding. Purchasing is discussed elsewhere in the text.

The health system may elect to self-insure its employee prescription drug benefit. The pharmacy leader needs to understand the staffing and purchasing considerations. The need to isolate the outpatient inventory from inpatient is critical for regulatory approval in most states, and this has space considerations for the planning of the outpatient pharmacy. The health-system pharmacy manager needs to be aware of the health system's status as disproportionate share, critical access, sole community, freestanding cancer, or pediatric hospital as well as if it is a rural access center. These designations are covered under the 340b pricing program requiring manufacturers to provide medications at significantly reduced prices to eligible systems.[5]

Inpatient distribution falls under two main types: centralized or decentralized. As the names imply, the method chosen is based on the health system's determination that the patients' needs and those of the organization are best met with pharmacy services in a central location or more proximal to the patient's care areas. Centralized pharmacies realize economies of scale for the pharmacy secondary to smaller staffing contingent and centralized inventory. Additionally, the pharmacy occupies space outside of the direct patient care areas which is at a premium in hospital design. This is contrasted with a decentralized approach that has the pharmacy close by the patient care areas. Order turnaround time is less resulting in better use of nursing time, and the immediate availability of a pharmacist's skills is a positive. Hybrids exist that mix and match factors such as first doses, cart exchanges, small volume parenterals, large volume parenterals, acuity of care, pharmacy budget, and a variety of other factors specific to the system in determining which activities take place where. Based on a recent survey, hospital size is a determinant of what types of services and inpatient distribution philosophies are followed. Generally, larger hospitals tend toward decentralized services, but the overall trend is for hospitals regardless of size to migrate to the decentralized model.[6]

Medication distribution in non-health–system environments includes the use of package delivery services for both local and long-distance dispensing. Most patients covered by a prescription benefit program are virtually required to have their medication filled remotely and for multiple months' supply (usually 90 days). If the patient chooses to have his or her medication filled locally, the price for convenience is a shorter day supply and/or an increased copayment. The insurer uses economic stimuli to encourage the patient to use the insurer's dispensing method of choice.

The ever-increasing availability of effective and expensive regimens for the management of chronic debilitating disorders such as multiple sclerosis and pulmonary hypertension has spawned the growth of the specialty pharmacy practice environment. As the name implies, these practices focus on the processing of only a handful of medications targeted at small patient populations. These medications generally require a level of storage, preparation, dispensing, and counseling outside of the realm of most practitioners. An error at any one step in the medication use process can be quite dangerous and/or excessive. As a result, insurers insist on the dispensing of these products by pharmacies that specialize in all aspects of the medication use process for these medications.

Non-Parenteral Dispensing

Types of non-parenteral dosage forms dispensed by the health-system pharmacy are the same as those found in community practice. Due to the formulary system, the number of line items is usually fewer, but the stock on hand may be larger for some medications. The types and varieties on hand have an impact on storage needs, usually temperature control, and facility planning for the pharmacy manager. The manager must be familiar with the respective state's pharmacy act and attendant square footage and storage requirements specific to the license.

In contrast to community practice, unit-dose dispensing for health-system pharmacies is the norm. Developed in the 1960s as a method of medication error prevention and to decrease waste of increasingly expensive medications, the unit-dose dispensing of oral solids is used by 86% of responding hospitals, according to a national survey.[7] While manufacturer-supplied unit-dose packaging is the primary source, repackaging of oral medications does occur either as a cost-savings measure or if the manufacturer is unable to supply. The pharmacy leader needs to follow the USP 36 standards on repackaging as do commercially contracted repackagers.[7]

Parenteral Dispensing

The quantity and variety of parenteral agents for disease management expanded markedly in the mid-twentieth century and has continued to the present. Two areas that saw the greatest growth and challenge were critical care medicine and oncology. Many of the newly introduced compounds were expensive and potent. Health-system nurses were the primary sterile product compounders, and it became evident this task would need to be reassigned to the pharmacy. In 1963, the first pharmacy-based IV admixture service was started at the Clinical Center of the National Institutes of Health.[8]

More unique individual moieties were released in the following decades along with the demand for increasingly complex admixtures such as parenteral nutrition and cardioplegia solutions. Prior to the publication in 2004 of Chapter 797 in the *United States Pharmacopeia* (USP), standards for the preparation of sterile parenteral products were established by national organizations and a common-sense approach to good practice. The use of laminar flow hoods for preparation and compounding of sterile products was established along with salient policies and procedures. As health-system pharmacies prepared more sterile compounded products such as small-volume parenterals and syringes in batch quantities, the policies and procedures and necessary training for pharmacists and technicians developed likewise.

In 2004, the USP moved key information regarding sterile products to Chapter 797 making the content of those standards legally enforceable and markedly altering the landscape of sterile products. Risk categories were defined. The type of activity performed by risk level delineates the required physical compounding area, sterility standards for the ambient environment, training standards, expiration dating of the compounded sterile products, along with quality control testing.[9]

Adherence to Chapter 797 standards can be expensive especially in regard to facility design and engineering. Based on risk level and other considerations, the health-care system management and/or pharmacy leader may decide to outsource some sterile product compounding to an external company. Weighing the pros and cons of outsourcing sterile products needs to be done deliberately. There are numerous considerations if the decision is to outsource, and all must be thoroughly investigated.[10]

Delivery and Fulfillment Methodologies

The typical method of medication delivery from the pharmacy to the patient's location is via the exchange of medication carts. Depending on the patient's acuity and pharmacy staffing, the exchanges occur from twice a day to once a week. As a patient's medication regimen changes during the day, the patient's medication bin is updated with discontinued medications removed and new medications added. Historically, pharmacy technicians filled the individual patient bins based on a pharmacy-generated medication list. A pharmacist would review the bin contents against the medication list to insure accuracy. Over the last ten years, the use of an alternate process, "tech-check-tech," was developed and matured. In this process, technicians check the work of other technicians. A recent review of the topic demonstrates that concerns about accuracy are unfounded in appropriately structured and implemented tech-check-tech programs.[11] A benefit is enhanced job satisfaction for technicians and the ability to redeploy pharmacists to more clinically focused tasks.

There is increasing use of robotics to fill the individual medication bins. While the use of the term *robotics* may conjure up an image of a human-like automaton, most pharmacy robots are more akin to industrial robots used in the manufacturing industry. They are sessile and contained within cabinets. Essentially, the robot picks the desired medication from a storage site within the cabinet, reads the bar-coded label and compares against the request in the database. The proper drug selection is then placed in a container for delivery to the patient's location. Including large upfront expenditure, these devices require substantial pharmacy manpower to maintain the needed NDC library and bar-coding labeling.

Despite these challenges, there are advantages like long-term cost savings associated with improved personnel efficiency along with decreased product wastage and, most importantly, almost 100% dispensing accuracy for robotically dispensed doses resulting in medication error avoidance. While robotic dispensing is seen primarily with larger hospitals (42% with more than 600 staffed beds) rather than smaller (6% with less than 50 staffed beds), that rate of adoption has risen from 4.5% of all hospitals in 1999 to 7.8% in 2002 showing a steady increase in adoption.

The increase in adoption of robotic dispensing is paralleled by an increase in the use of the automated dispensing cabinet (ADC). In 1999, 49% of surveyed hospitals used ADC and, by 2005 this percentage grew to 72%. Similarly, the prevalence of ADC use, like robotics, was associated with hospital size with a higher percentage of larger institutions using ADC (98% with more than 300 staffed beds) versus smaller (64% with less than 50 staffed beds). ADCs are secured medication storage cabinets located remotely in patient care areas. They are designed to control and track drug distribution. They were originally designed to better manage controlled substance distribution and first-dose as-needed medications but have matured to devices where patient-specific medications can be stored and accessed. Consideration needs to be given to using ADCs as medication carts for routine medications. Queuing of nurses at the device occurs at common medication administration times. The devices limit access to the medications until the medication order is reviewed by a pharmacist who then sends an authorization command to the device. Guidelines are available to assist the pharmacy manager and health system in the safe use of this technology.[12]

Carousel dispensing technology is another form of technology used in unit-dose distribution. Primarily used in pharmacies with centralized distribution and medication carts, they are used to restock ADCs as well.[13] An advantage of carousels is the smaller footprint needed to store the amount of product as traditional shelving. Technician picking time is decreased, improving efficiency.

Hospitalized patients experience frequent changes in their drug regimen. No sooner is a 24-hour supply of medications delivered than the regimen is changed. As medications are changed, discontinued, and added, the medication storage on the patient care area needs to reflect the current medication list as accurately as possible in as timely a manner as possible. Methods of editing the patient-specific medication supplies in the patient care area include pharmacy personnel physically walking the new medication to the patient care area, use of pneumatic tubes to send medications, provision of frequently used medications in ADCs, and the use of mobile robots to deliver.

Controlled Substances

Health-system pharmacies are responsible for the storage of all medications in the system whether the medications are located in the pharmacy or not. Controlled substances are prone to diversion both inside and outside of the pharmacy. The Drug Enforcement Agency and each state publish specific regulations for the ordering, storage, dispensing, and record keeping associated with controlled substances. The pharmacy manager is responsible for the health system's compliance with the regulations.

Health-care workers are not immune to drug addiction. One study demonstrated that nurses were more likely to divert controlled substances if they felt the organization had lax policies and procedures regarding controlled substance security.[14] It is reasonable to assume other professionals with access to controlled substances have the same opinion. It is incumbent on the pharmacy manager to institute controls to limit diversion. Published practice recommendations exist to provide guidance.[15]

MEDICATION DISPOSAL, SHORTAGE, AND COUNTERFEITS

The advent of HIV-AIDS in the late 1970s began to increase the awareness of health systems of the dangers posed to the public and employees by medical waste. Medical waste was no longer limited to tissues removed in surgery and used dressings but now included needles and syringes. In the ensuing years, the definition expanded to include pharmaceutical waste, not limited to just chemotherapy. Numerous national [National Institute for Occupational Safety and Health (NIOSH) and Environmental Protection Agency (EPA)] and state agencies responded to the dangers with regulations requiring the correct disposal of medical waste. Pharmacy managers are faced with what may appear to be a confusing and contradictory array of rules to follow. What is known is that dumping pharmacy-generated medical waste of any type into municipal waste stream or sewage system is not permitted. The pharmacy leader is to be familiar with waste disposal policies and procedures for their organization in addition to NIOSH and Resource Conservation and Recovery (RCRA) defined waste types and methods of disposal. Consultation with those in the health system responsible for waste management is required to develop internal policies and procedures to determine proper end-use disposal methods for injections, infusions, and solids.[16]

A rarity at the end of the twentieth century, medication shortages are a fact of life today for the pharmacy manager. Injectable drug products comprise the bulk of shortages (80%) with oncology drugs being the largest component of that (28%).[17] The causes of shortages are varied, but the end result is the same placing patient care at risk.[18] The pharmacy manager needs to take a lead position in communicating issues in a timely manner to all involved stakeholders. The challenge is one of logistics and ethics potentially involving rationing. As such, the approach is collaborative and transparent. It is suggested the health-care system develop a policy if one does not exist.[19] An excellent resource is available from the American Society of Health-System Pharmacists providing background information on the problem as well as up-to-date information on specific shortages (www.ashp.org/shortages).

Equally alarming and possibly as a result of shortages is the growing problem of counterfeit medications. By law, a counterfeit medication is a drug sold under a product name without proper authorization. While a larger problem outside of the United States, counterfeits are becoming a growing public health issue. It is estimated that less than 1% of prescription medications in the United States are counterfeit. Despite this seemingly low number, medications that are being counterfeited are those in short supply and life-saving such as chemotherapy. The health-system pharmacist manager needs to take the lead role in preventing counterfeits from entering the health system along with communicating strategies to patients served by the system to avoid counterfeits in the home environment. Strategies to maintain the integrity of the medication are published by national pharmacy associations, and the pharmacy leader is encouraged to routinely check the FDA's website for new information and trends.[20]

Administration

Administering medications is the physical administration of the drug to the patient; however, this action is preceded by selection of the medication, identification of the patient, and education of the patient regarding the medication. In 1995, errors at the administration step leading to an adverse event accounted for 38% of the adverse events.[21] Possibly more alarming was the fact that at the time this study was performed, only 2% of the administration errors were detected compared with 48% of the prescribing errors. Since this is the last step in the medication administration process and the only one where a "second set of eyes" is generally not available, preventing errors at this point can yield considerable improvement in the medication use process. Technology plays an important role in mitigating errors at this step, especially the use of bar-code point-of-care (BPOC) solutions.

Administration of medication in a health-care system is generally within the domain of the nursing staff. Classically, nurses are taught the "5 Rs" of medication administration: Right patient, Right drug, Right dose, Right route, and Right time. BPOC technology supports the "5 Rs" of medication administration. On admission, a patient has attached to them a wristband that is bar coded, at the very least, with their demographics. Using this bracelet and scanning equipment, the nurse confirms the patient's identity before administering the medication. If the patient is lucid, the nurse verbally confirms identity as well. The next step is to review the patient's medication administration record (MAR) and select the correct medication from the patient's supply. This is scanned as well providing confirmation that the selected medication is for this patient and matches the MAR for right drug, right dose, right dosage form for prescribed route of administration, and right time. Once all conditions are met, the nurse then administers the medication and documents its administration.

MONITORING

The monitoring step in the medication use process includes the documentation of the previous administration step along with the patient's response to the medication. Similar to administration, the activities associated with this step were, historically, not part of the pharmacist's list of daily tasks; rather, it was one done by the nurses and prescribers. As research documented the value of the pharmacist's contribution to positive medication-related outcomes and the increasing awareness of adverse drug reactions, pharmacists were called upon to take a more active role in this phase of the medication use process. A recent survey reveals 50% of surveyed hospital pharmacies monitor 75% or more of patients.[22] This figure has essentially doubled since the beginning of the twenty-first century reflecting a growing appreciation of what the pharmacist provides in advancing medication therapy. The depth of monitoring is proportional to the hospital size with larger facilities having broader and deeper levels of monitoring. Pharmacists are generally assigned to monitoring patients with abnormal lab results, those who are high risk, or those receiving high-cost medications. A smaller portion is assigned to monitoring on the basis of disease state or drug class. These include infectious diseases, anticoagulants, lipid management, parenteral nutrition, and patients in the emergency room. The latter was based on a Joint Commission standard that initially caused confusion because it was interpreted that a pharmacist needed to provide prospective review. The standard is now modified allowing for retrospective review.[7]

As mentioned earlier, health systems must offer a wide array of inpatient and outpatient services to be competitive. These clinical services can include transplant, chronic lung diseases, heart and cardiovascular, pediatrics, anticoagulation, diabetes, and so on. All are opportunities for the pharmacist leader to investigate as situations where the presence of a pharmacist during the prescribing and subsequent monitoring steps can greatly benefit desired patient outcomes.

The challenge to pharmacists practicing in non-health–system environments is the lack of access to information crucial to appropriate monitoring. There exist restrictions imposed by HIPAA on what information can be shared between caregivers in situations where a business relationship does not exist between the organizations even though employees of the organizations are providing care to the same patient.

RISK AND SAFETY

Health-care systems are risky environments for patients. Patients are exposed to many dangers in an environment where they are dependent on the talents and skills of others to make them well and keep them safe. Health-care systems are akin to other high-reliability organizations like air traffic control and nuclear power plants in that the occurrence of an error can have a devastating impact on an individual. The examples provided obviously affect more individuals with one incident, but they are alike in that all are systems highly dependent on highly skilled individuals working in sometimes unpredictable operating environments. In order to eliminate not just minimize error, high-reliability organizations develop a culture of safety.

The Agency for Healthcare Research and Quality has listed essential attributes defining a safety culture:

- Acknowledgment of the high-risk nature of an organization's activities and the determination to achieve consistently safe operations
- A blame-free environment where individuals are able to report errors or near misses without fear of reprimand or punishment
- Encouragement of collaboration across ranks and disciplines to seek solutions to patient safety problems
- Organizational commitment of resources to address safety concerns

PHARMACIST AS MEDICATION SAFETY LEADER

The pharmacist should take a leadership role in encouraging the safety culture created within the organization. Communicating the value in commitment to patient safety effectively with peers and subordinates is clearly one of the pharmacist leader's primary tasks. Interventions for the establishment of a systemwide safety culture were reviewed and found to be applied with variability in application and level of success.[23] A survey of the safety climate from the perspective of health-system pharmacies demonstrated differences in completion of safety assessments as well as differences between all hospitals, regardless of size, in methods used to create a culture of safety.[7] Based on these results, health systems have much work to be done and the pharmacy leader is in an ideal position to be a champion in this effort.[24] While much effort is focused on inpatient services, outpatient and clinic services provide unique problems requiring extra effort to ensure patient safety.

It is important for the pharmacy leader to have an understanding of human behavior and how it interacts with highly complex environments. Health-care workers are dedicated to the care of their patients. When errors occur, the cause is rarely individual negligence but a culmination of small errors conspiring to create an environment ripe for error. An understanding of how people interface with complex systems is helpful in creating a safety culture.[25]

Health systems are deeply committed to providing a safe environment as are the state regulatory boards that oversee the licensed facilities as well as the individual licensed practitioners themselves. Subsequently, oversight is provided not only by the state regulatory boards but outside independent review organizations subscribed to by the facilities. Among these outside agencies is The Joint Commission (JC). The JC was established 1951 in response to tragic, avoidable deaths of hospitalized patients. Since then, the JC has continually raised the bar to ensure that care provided to patients is safe and effective.

Regardless of practice environment, pharmacist leaders are encouraged to conduct a safety survey in their practice to ensure all that can be done to guarantee patient safety is being done. Activities described in the following section are easily adapted to any type of practice environment.

NATIONAL PATIENT SAFETY GOALS

The JC launched the National Patient Safety Goals (NPSG) in 2003.[26] The NPSG are specific areas of patient safety concern that are global for all organizations surveyed by the JC. Some have been on the list since its inception, whereas others are added/removed based on new information culled from the literature and survey results. The pharmacy manager needs to be knowledgeable about current NPSG, especially those related to medication use, and the health-care systems experience with and strategies to achieve goals. The NPSG for 2013 were as follows:

- Identify patients correctly
- Improve staff communication
- Use medicines safely
- Prevent infection
- Identify patient safety risks
- Prevent mistakes in surgery

Despite all of the best efforts of the health system in preventing medication errors, errors and adverse drug reactions will occur. Health systems need to have in place systems for detection of same along with policies and procedures to report them in a timely manner and without punishment, especially for errors in the medication use process. Errors in the medication use process need to be viewed as system errors and not personnel-based errors (unless the individual involved following remedial action persists in performing the same error). Since the process can be viewed as an engineered system, processes used in engineering are used to prevent errors from occurring in the first place (failure mode and effects analysis) or in reviewing events that have occurred to determine the proximal cause(s) (root cause analysis). The Agency for Healthcare Quality and Research is an excellent resource for patient safety resources on their Patient Safety Network page (http://psnet.ahrq.gov/default.aspx).

RESEARCHING AND PREVENTING ERRORS

Failure mode and effects analysis (FMEA) is a prospective methodology whereby the practitioners involved in a proposed new process or change in an existing process review all steps and identify potential failure points before initiating the new process or change. Each step of the medication use process needs to be investigated and rigorously reviewed for failure at any point. Once identified, the team needs to develop a solution to ensure the error node is designed out of the process.[27] Composition of a FMEA team needs to be broad and to involve all constituencies involved at every step no matter how seemingly unimportant their involvement may appear.

Root cause analysis (RCA) is a retrospective methodology done following an untoward event whether the event resulted in patient harm or not. The JC requires a RCA following all sentinel events. A sentinel event is defined as an unexpected death or serious injury, or the risk of these types of death or injury. The JC provides a template for the sentinel investigation.[28] Care must be taken in doing a RCA because the term itself implies a singular cause for an error. Most RCAs in a health-care system reveal multiple contributors to an adverse event. Alone these "Swiss cheese holes" may not have been enough for the error to occur, but together the "holes" combined to allow the event to occur. Be aware that the imperfect processes may be interdependent on one another.

The pharmacy leader needs to be aware that the medication use process is prone to error and adverse drug events can occur at any step. Using the analysis tools reviewed above, the pharmacist and other key participants in the medication use like administrators, risk managers, prescribers, and nurses as well as others who administer medications need to critically evaluate each step and all processes associated with the same in their organization. An excellent online resource regarding medication safety is the Institute for Safe Medication Practices (http://www.ismp.org).

ADVERSE DRUG EVENTS AND SAFETY STRATEGIES

An initial start would be to define what medication errors are. A medication error is a type of adverse drug event that actually reached the patient whether harm occurred to the patient or not. An adverse drug event is simply harm experienced by a patient due to exposure to a medication. Potential adverse drug events are those intercepted prior to the patient being given the medication. A medication error is to be distinguished from an adverse drug reaction or side effects. In the case of an adverse drug reaction, all steps were successfully performed yet the patient reacted adversely following exposure to the medications.

The health system is required by the Joint Commission to have an active, well-defined system for reporting adverse drug events whether the error reached the patient or not. Organizations with a culture of safety are characterized by voluntary, robust data collection because all involved understand the importance of timely, factual reporting to continually improve the process in question. Table 10.1 points out strategies at primary points in the medication use process to reduce or prevent adverse drug events.

TABLE 10.1

Strategies to Prevent Adverse Drug Events

Stage	Safety Strategy
Prescribing	• Avoid unnecessary medications by adhering to *conservative prescribing* principles
	• Computerized provider order entry, especially when paired with clinical decision support systems
	• Medication reconciliation at times of transitions in care
Transcribing	• *Computerized provider order entry* to eliminate handwriting errors
Dispensing	• Clinical pharmacists to oversee medication dispensing process
	• Use of "tall man" lettering and other strategies to minimize confusion between look-alike, sound-alike medications
Administration	• Adherence to the "*Five Rights*" of medication safety (administering the right medication, in the right dose, at the right time, by the right route, to the right patient)
	• Barcode medication administration to ensure medications are given to the correct patient
	• Minimize interruptions to allow nurses to administer medications safely
	• Smart infusion pumps for intravenous infusions
	• Patient education and revised medication labels to improve patient comprehension of administration instructions

As discussed earlier, the initial step in the medication use process, prescribing, is one of two steps associated most frequently with errors. A patient's orders are often rewritten as their condition improves or does not and when there is a change in level of care usually associated with a change in the patient's location within the facility. Level of care changes include the patient's admission to and discharge from the hospital. Improving processes at this step can yield significant improvement in patient safety. A useful process to improve care at this step is medication reconciliation.

Medication reconciliation is a key activity because of the error potential associated with order writing at care transition points.[29] Medication reconciliation has been shown to reduce adverse drug events on admission[30] and at discharge.[31] A recent review of 26 controlled studies looking at medication reconciliation practices showed that those that use pharmacy staff and are focused on patients at high risk for adverse events are effective. Additionally, the review showed practices were varied and the most effective methodology has yet to be developed.[32]

The use of CPOE, especially with clinical decision support tools used prospectively or concurrently, is viewed with great hope as a strategy of reducing adverse drug events at the prescribing step.[33] Clinical decision support system (CDSS) is functionality within a CPOE module where the prescriber is either alerted by the module or initiates the information request themselves to determine if a planned medication order is safe and/or supported by clinical evidence. A recent review of studies investigating the use and effectiveness of CDSS in CPOE revealed that current CDSS supports medication safety more strongly than appropriate therapy selection. The authors' conclusions point toward a need for pharmacists to continually

TABLE 10.2

Unintended Consequences and Their Frequencies of Occurrence

Unintended Consequence	Frequency (%) $n = 324$
More/new work for clinicians	19.8
Workflow issues	17.6
Never-ending system demands	14.8
Paper persistence	10.8
Changes in communication patterns and practices	10.1
Emotions	7.7
New kinds of errors	7.1
Changes in the power structure	6.8
Overdependence on technology	5.2
Total	100

Source: Campbell EM, Sittig DF, Asj JS, Guappone KP, Dykstra RH. Types of unintended consequences related to computerized provider order entry. *J Am Med Inform Assoc* 2006;13:547–556. Reprinted with permission.

improve their dialogue with prescribers to realize the full benefit of CDSS in therapeutic decision making.[34]

In theory, CPOE looks like the right thing to do; however, there is evidence that CPOE can lead to errors.[35] The pharmacy leader needs to be aware of the potential problems CPOE can cause.[36] There are other additional unintended consequences not related to medication errors that need to be understood to ensure support for CPOE (Table 10.2). While this study looked at prescribers, the same dynamics most likely hold true for other user types.

Medication reconciliation is a key activity because of the error potential associated with order writing at care transition points. Medication reconciliation has been shown to reduce adverse drug events on admission and at discharge. A recent review of 26 controlled studies looking at medication reconciliation practices showed medication reconciliation practices that use pharmacy staff and are focused on patients at high risk for adverse events are effective. Additionally, the review showed practices were varied and the most effective methodology has yet to be developed.

Errors at the transcribing step are eliminated because there is no copying of orders from one system into another as long as all are integrated. CPOE should be integrated into nursing and pharmacy computer systems.

Dispensing is essentially 100% under the pharmacist leader's control. If the pharmacist wishes to spearhead a medication safety effort within the organization, it would be wise to ensure the pharmacy's dispensing is as error-free as possible. The advent of bar coding and robotics as previously described has made this goal within reach. The pharmacy needs to ensure that internal processes do not pass the burden of error into another profession. Tablet splitting is an example. Placing a sticker on a unit-dose package noting that a tablet needs to be split prior to administration places the burden on the nurse. The pharmacy needs to consider doing this prior to dispensing. High-risk populations or medications should have a two-pharmacist check prior to dispensing in areas such as pediatrics or oncology where errors have disastrous consequences. All these steps need to be taken in light of the pharmacy's budget, but every effort needs to be taken for at-risk populations and medications.

Bar-code technology has added an extra set of "eyes" to the administration step. Requiring the nurse to scan the patient's identification bracelet, the medication, and the medication administration record goes a long way to ensure the "5 Rs" of medication administration are satisfied. While not foolproof, significant patient safety gains can be made with bar-code technology. One study reported a relative decrease of 41% in non-timing medication errors comparing nursing units using bar-code technology versus those that did not.[37] Another group reported a decrease in medication errors at the administration step of 54% using bar-code technology integrated with an electronic health record.[38] The pharmacist needs to be aware of types of workarounds employed that will dilute the potential gains.[39]

Technology is also used to support the administration of parenteral medications including infusions given via infusion pumps. Smart infusion devices programmed with libraries of medications, base solutions, and approved infusion rates have the potential to positively impact the administration of parenterally infused medications. In a study of errors reported to the USP Med-Marx program, the analysis of IV administration errors led the authors to conclude that many of the errors could be eliminated by the use of standard concentrations along with the use of smart infusion devices programmed with pre-established doses and upper flow rate limits.[40] While earlier results of medication error prevention using smart infusion devices were equivocal, later studies show a positive impact on error rates.[41,42]

Bar-code–supported medication administration (BCMA) strongly supports the monitoring step. If procedures are followed, BCMA has functionality allowing nurses and others to make determinations as to whether doses were administered or not. Proper evaluation of a patient's clinical response to a medication requires knowledge of if and when a drug was administered. BCMA technology makes a painstaking manual task into a simplified running of a report. Clinicians can then properly interpret a patient's clinical status in regard to medication therapy.

HEALTH INFORMATION SYSTEMS

The American Recovery and Reinvestment Act of 2009 was passed in response to the need to improve the nation's health. Part of the Health Information Technology for Economic and Clinical Health Act requires the adoption of the electronic health record (EHR). It provides resources and dollars to promote the "meaningful use" of the EHR. Health systems and eligible providers, not including pharmacists, are offered financial incentives based on their level of compliance with core objectives. The financial incentives are creating a rush by health systems to become compliant with meaningful use standards.[43,44]

The explosive growth in EHRs, while laudable, is also cause for concern. Technology is a double-edged sword. It allows for repetitive, iterative tasks to be done more quickly; however, it also allows mistakes to be made more quickly, and over a broad patient base. The reporting of issues with EHRs is under the purview of the Food and Drug Administration as they monitor medical devices in the

United States. Reporting to date is anemic, but the low level of reporting may be due to a low level of comprehensive EHR adoption along with a low level of knowledge about reporting of issues with EHRs. As EHR market penetration increases, it is expected that the number of defect reports will climb as well.[45] The pharmacy leader is advised to report all issues associated with any technology, not just the EHR, to the FDA. Since the EHR is touted to improve medication safety, the pharmacy leader needs to ensure all members of the medication safety initiatives in the organization are aware of the dangers associated with the technology that was designed to eliminate danger.

Outside of the potential for risk with the EHR, another danger exists when all of the technology is not integrated or interfaced completely with all the pieces that feed data into a central repository. While technology advances occurred with all steps in the medication use process, the challenge now is to integrate all of these disparate systems into a longitudinal EHR. One organization worked with their information technology vendors to integrate their smart infusion devices, BCMA, and EHR. The end result was a simpler workflow for medication administration of IV infusions and a significant increase in drug library compliance rates and a decrease in the number of edits to infusion variables—all factors leading to a minimization of error potentials within the process.[46] At the time of publication of this text, one single overarching platform to integrate all data feeds is not available. Progress is being made, and until that time, the pharmacy leader is encouraged to work with the health-systems medication safety team and external information technology vendors to develop interfaces that marry the data feeds. It is suggested that EHRs become part of the Joint Commission's National Patient Safety goals.[45]

PERFORMANCE STANDARDS

Just as patients in a health-care system have their general health monitored by the five vital signs, the health-care systems themselves have their general health monitored by vital signs and certainly more than five. The health systems are licensed within their state to operate. The health system may have a variety of facilities within its corporate structure requiring separate and distinct licensure as a hospital, nursing home, ambulatory surgery center, or home health/hospice agency. The pharmacy leader needs to be familiar with these license requirements in regard to pharmacy services if any standard exists.

Licensing

All pharmacies require state licensing. DEA registration is needed to procure and store controlled substances. The pharmacy manager is assumed by organization's upper management to be the resident expert on all matters relating to the practice of pharmacy with that state as well as all DEA rules and regulations. Since the practice of pharmacy interfaces with the practices of medicine and nursing, the pharmacy manager needs to understand those junctures. All pharmacy department policies and procedures need to be in line with the respective state's pharmacy act. Health-care facilities and pharmacy departments undergo routine inspection and surveys to ensure the populace served is cared for safely and effectively.

Health-System Surveys

State inspections of health-care facilities are mandatory. Additional mandatory federal surveys may take place based on the types of services offered by the health-care system. Provision of ambulatory care paid for with federal dollars like home health/hospice requires routine surveys be performed. The pharmacy leader needs to be familiar with what are the expectations of the pharmacy in light of these surveys and prepare the department for successful completion of the surveys.

The health system will undergo surveys by nongovernmental agencies like the JC or American Osteopathic Healthcare Facilities Accreditation Program and, most recently, Det Norske Veritas Healthcare to determine whether the health system meets Centers for Medicare and Medicaid Services (CMS) requirements. In order to qualify for reimbursement of care provided to Medicare or Medicaid recipients, the health system needs to satisfactorily pass one of the surveys. This is vital to the financial well-being of the health system considering that CMS is the biggest payor.

The health-care system uses the standards from their surveying body to assist in setting goals and priorities for the organization considering the dependency of the system's financial health on successfully passing a survey. However, organizations in search of continually improving go beyond basic survey compliance. The development and communication of an organization-wide strategic plan to all personnel helps senior organization management ensure all departments' activities are aligned and there is no confusion about priorities.

The pharmacy leader must coordinate department activities to be in concert with the overall plan and certainly not launch a competing agenda that would waste time and money. Many times strategic plans consist of goals aimed at survey compliance, increased revenue, decreased costs, improved patient and employee satisfactions scores, and improved quality and effectiveness of services. The pharmacy leader needs to critically evaluate all departmental activities and determine if the department is supporting them.

Pharmacy Metrics

The determination of whether or not a pharmacy is supporting organizational goals is best done by the pharmacy manager. If not, an outside firm may be brought in to do the job which is to be avoided. The determination is best done using metrics (the pharmacy department's vital signs) to ascertain if the department is contributing or not to organizational success. While it would be advantageous to see how you are doing compared with a peer group, otherwise known as external benchmarking, these comparisons are fraught with challenge. Valid comparisons need to be made between similar structures. The more alike the structures are to each other the more valid the comparison. External benchmarking is difficult in hospital pharmacy practice because no valid set of metrics exists. Pharmacies in two different hospitals of similar size can have widely varying levels and types of service making comparison invalid.[47]

In the absence of a valid set of published pharmacy productivity benchmarks, a pharmacy manager should be collecting internal benchmark metrics so at least a comparison can be made comparing self with self. The internal benchmarks provide

TABLE 10.3
Examples of Metrics Used in Internal Benchmarking and a Departmental Dashboard

Process	Measurement
Product procurement, storage, retrieval, and preparation	Orders placed, line items ordered, purchases, percentage on contract, product stock-out rate, shorted items necessitating development of a substitution process, total parenteral nutrient solutions mixed, complex admixtures
Drug distribution actions	ADC stock-out rate, ADC override rate, ADC performed for pharmacy (refills/loads/unloads)
Order management	Orders reviewed (entered) per period, order review (entry) turnaround time
Clinical practice	Clinical documentation rate (interventions per adjusted discharge)
Other quality indicators	Clinical opportunities identified versus performed
Financial outcomes	Drug expenses per statistic
Workload	Workforce hours per worked unit of service, ratio of staffed versus filled positions, total 100 workload units

Source: Rough S, McDaniel M, Rinehart JR. Effective use of workload and productivity monitoring tools in health-system pharmacy, part 2. *Am J Health-Syst Pharm.* 2010;67:380–8. With permission.

[a] Any significant component is fair game for measurement. It is often useful to measure something that you are unsure is working well.

[b] These data are readily available from the automated dispensing cabinet (ADC) archive process.

[c] These data should be available from your pharmacy information system.

[d] Indicators that can be positively influenced by the pharmacy department.

the pharmacy manager with insight into the overall health of the department. Table 10.3 provides examples of possible internal data points to track departmental performance. Again, the internal benchmarks at the very least need to capture those directly related to organizational strategic goals. The internal benchmarks need to capture data documenting regularly occurring primary processes of the department. Included are those related to drug distribution and clinical activities.

These metrics and others can be part of a dashboard where the pharmacy leader can see at a glance the overall status of the department compared to itself at a previous time. Some should be viewed daily, weekly, monthly, quarterly, and/or annually depending on factors that can skew the data regardless of the overall performance of the pharmacy. The design of the dashboard is in the hands of the pharmacist and his or her individual creativity and expertise with computer applications.

The pharmacy leader needs to determine with his or her superior which metrics the superior wishes to see at what interval. Included are those that demonstrate the pharmacy's contribution to the organization's strategic plan. This approach to data utilization is referred to as the *balanced scorecard*. The balanced scored is a strategy management tool described by Robert Kaplan and David P. Norton in the book, *The Balanced Scorecard.*[48] Many organizations have found utility in its use because managers at all levels can see how their area of responsibility is performing. Its use encourages responsibility and accountability of actions from top to bottom within an organization. If implemented correctly with continuous communication and updating, it is a powerful tool in creating staff buy-in and ownership to how their daily activities contribute to the success of the organization. The pharmacy leader uses the dashboard results to assess current departmental performance and as a tool to gauge the impact of new programs launched as a result of performance improvement activities. Dashboard metrics can uncover processes that are underperforming.

Performance Improvement

Once uncovered, a quality improvement effort can be launched to address the performance gap. A variety of tools exist that provide a framework for quality improvement projects. Previously, root cause analysis and failure mode and effects analysis (FMEA) were discussed as retrospective and prospective tools employed to improve medication safety. Additional tools are plan, do, check, and act (PDCA); Six Sigma; and lean processes.

PDCA are the steps in the continuous cycle. Simply, a problem is identified and a plan is developed by a team answering the how, what, when, where, and why of the solution. The solution is then launched (do) with data being collected, usually the data point that noted the issue in the first place. The check step is when the impact of the plan is evaluated and compared against anticipated results affecting both the original data element and any other coincident processes. Based on the results of the check step, changes to the original plan may be needed to reach the goal. Those changes are implemented (do) and the process repeats until the goal is attained.

Six Sigma emerged out of PDCA and both were originally used in manufacturing industries but have migrated to health care. Six Sigma uses similar methodology but is more data driven with a focus on limiting the number of defects (variance in process) to a very low number (six standard deviations of the mean, hence the label *Six Sigma*). A critique of Six Sigma is that it is taking a tool developed for a human-machine interface and placing it in an environment of human-human interface. Despite the criticism, it has found value in health care.

Lean process–improvement techniques focus on the elimination of wasted steps and activity in the performance of a process. Like the PDCA and Six Sigma, it is continuous and data driven, but it is focused on getting rid of any activity that is without return. Much of its work is looking at the physical surroundings where the work is performed and removing all impediments and distracters. It may be more adaptable to health care because it more deeply embraces the notion of human-to-human interfaces as a source of error. It is used successfully both within and outside the pharmacy to improve medication safety.[49,50]

FUTURE OF HEALTH-SYSTEM PHARMACY PRACTICE

All health-care system leaders repeat the same mantra: "more with less." The pharmacy leader is not immune to repeating the same mantra. The pharmacy leader in the twenty-first century is expected to involve pharmacists more deeply in direct patient care with an increased responsibility for outcomes while, at the very worst, being cost neutral, and, preferentially, decreasing costs. The pharmacy department is unique among other departments in a health-care system in that a bulk of its budget is medication costs which are contrasted with other departments where personnel costs are the predominant budget driver. The predicament of the pharmacy leader is one where control of medication costs relies on better deployment of pharmacists on the pointy end of treatment decisions rather than retrospective involvement. To do this usually requires more staff, pharmacists or technicians, and technology.

Deciding how to do more with less requires a plan that is regularly monitored and updated but one the pharmacy leader develops with others in the department to create a shared vision. Each plan needs to be unique to reflect the needs of the organization and its patients. Pharmacy is moving along a continuum from drug-distribution centered to patient centered and, possibly for larger organizations, clinical specialist centered. The pharmacy leader must look at where the department is, where it needs to go, what are the organization's priorities, and how feasible all of this is in light of available funds. An excellent resource is a published list of desired elements for the creation of the high-performance pharmacy in the coming years. It is organized in broad performance categories with subheadings attended by a scoring system based on three criteria: feasibility, financial return, and quality and safety return.[51]

How well a pharmacy leader uses the personnel and materials provided to run the department as planned and within budget are a measure of efficiency. More sophisticated decision support tools are needed in the future to assist the pharmacy manager in planning the application of resources to support and meet strategic goals set by the organization. Recent research is now providing the pharmacy leader with methodologies to aid in determining the allocation of pharmacists to clinical services as well as assessing overall departmental efficiency.[52,53]

The use of technology to surmount challenges in medication safety and improve pharmacy efficiency is a common thread throughout this chapter. It is no surprise that technology continues to play a major role in the advancement of health-system pharmacy. The maturation of workflow software and robotics could result in a major shift in pharmacy manpower if state boards of pharmacy permit advanced technicians with appropriate training and credentialing to perform a bulk of the medication distribution tasks, provided there is pharmacist oversight and in-process output sampling. As a result, pharmacists would be reassigned to clinical tasks, thereby enhancing the role and job satisfaction of both groups. Additional health information technology needs for the future have been published.[54]

Sterile product preparation and compounding have used technology to support activities but not to the extent of the distribution of non-sterile products. Recently, robotics was introduced into the sterile compounding area.[55] The extent of deployment will be cost based and is expected to be limited initially to the preparation of antineoplastic agents. As experienced is gained and equipment costs begin to drop, robotics could find their way into other aspects of sterile preparation and compounding.

All pharmacists are encouraged to read outside of the pharmacy professional literature to be aware of changes in the world around them. Paramount are legislative changes that reflect changing societal needs. If pharmacists do not support and take an active role in their respective professional associations that represent them at the legislative table, changes will be forced upon them without their input.

REFERENCES

1. Bates DW, Boyle DL, Vander Vliet MB, Schneider J, Leape L. Relationship between medication errors and adverse drug events. *J Gen Intern Med.* 1995;10:199–205.
2. Strom BL, Schinnar R, Aberra F, Bilker W, Hennessy S, Leonard CE, Pifer E. Unintended effects of a computerized physician order entry nearly hard-stop alert to prevent a drug interaction: a randomized controlled trial. *Arch Intern Med.* 2010 Sep 27;170(17):1578–1583.
3. Campbell EM, Sittig DF, Ash JS, Guappone KP, Dykstra RH. Types of unintended consequences related to computerized provider order entry. *J Am Med Inform Assoc.* 2006;13:547–556.
4. Caeay MM, Sorensen TD, Elias W, Knudson A, Gregg W. Current Practices and state regulations regarding telepharmacy in rural hospitals. *Am J Health-Syst Phar.* 2010;67:1085–1092.
5. 340B Drug Pricing Program, www.hrsa.gov/opa/index.html (accessed July 24, 2013).
6. Pedersen CA, Schneider PJ, Scheckelhoff DJ. ASHP National Survey of Pharmacy Practice in hospital settings: dispensing and administration–2008. *Am J Health-Syst Pharm.* 2009;66:926–946.
7. HMC/USP. https://hmc.usp.org/sites/default/files/documents/HMC/GCs-Pdfs/c1178 percent20USP36.pdf (accessed July 25, 2013).
8. Myers CE. History of sterile compounding in U.S. hospitals: learning from the tragic lessons of the past. *Am J Health-Syst Pharm.* 2013;70:e41–54.
9. ASHP. The ASHP Discussion Guide for Compounding Sterile Preparations. www.ashp. org/s_ashp/docs/files/HACC_797guide.pdf (accessed July 24, 2013).
10. American Society of Health-System Pharmacists. ASHP guidelines on outsourcing sterile compounding services. *AM J Health-Syst Pharm.* 2010:67:757–765.
11. Adams AJ, Martin SJ, Stople SF. "Tech-check-tech": a review of the evidence on its safety and benefits. *Am J Health Syst Pharm.* 2011;68:1824–1833.
12. ISMP Guidance on the Interdisciplinary Safe Use of Automated Dispensing Cabinets. www.ismp.org/tools/guidelines/ADC_Guidelines_final.pdf (accessed July 28, 2013).
13. Temple J, Ludwig B. Implementation and evaluation of carousel dispensing technology in a university medical center pharmacy. *Am J Health-Syst Pharm.* 2010;67:821–829.
14. Trinkoff AM, Storr CL, Wall MP. Prescription-type drug misuse and workplace access among nurses. *J Addict Dis.* 1999;18(1):9–17.
15. McClure SR, O'Neal BC, Grauer D, Couldrey RJ, King AR. Compliance with recommendations for prevention and detection of controlled-substance diversion in hospitals. *Am J Health-Syst Pharm.* 2011;68:689–694.
16. Sherer JT. Pharmaceuticals in the environment. *Am J Health-Syst Pharm.* 2006;63:174–178.
17. FDA. A Review of FDA's Medical Product Shortages. www.fda.gov/downloads/AboutFDA/ReportsManualsForms/Reports/UCM277755.pdf (accessed July 27, 2013).
18. Wittmer DR, Deffenbaugh J. The pharmaceutical supply chain: a perfect storm is brewing. *Am J Health-Syst Pharm.* 2004;61:143.
19. Rosoff PM, Patel KR, Scates A, et al. Coping with critical drug shortages—an ethical approach for allocating scarce resources in hospitals. *Arch Intern Med.* 2012;172(19):1494–1499.
20. Chambliss WG, Carroll WA, Kennedy, D, et al. Role of the pharmacists in preventing distribution of counterfeit medications. *J Am Pharm Assoc.* 2012;52:195–199.
21. Bates DW, Cullen DJ, Laird N, et al. Incidence of adverse drug events and potential adverse drug events. Implications for prevention. *JAMA.* 1995;274:29–34.

22. Pedersen CA, Schneider PJ, Scheckelhoff DJ. ASHP National survey of pharmacy practice in hospital settings: monitoring and patient education–2012. *Am J Health-Syst Pharm*. 2013;70:787–803.
23. Weaver SJ, Lubomski LH, Wilson RF, et al. Promoting a culture of safety as a patient safety strategy. *Ann Int Med*. 2013;158:369–374.
24. American Society of Health-System Pharmacists. ASHP statement on the role of the medication safety leader. *Am J Health-Syst Pharm*. 2013;70:448–452.
25. Grasha AF. Into the abyss: seven principles for identifying the causes of and preventing human error in complex systems. *Am J Health-Syst Pharm*. 2000;57:554–564.
26. The Joint Commission's National Patient Safety Goals. www.jointcommission.org/standards_information/npsgs.aspx (accessed July 21, 2013).
27. ISMP Example of Failure Mode and Effects Analysis for IV PCA. www.ismp.org/Tools/FMEAofPCA.pdf (accessed August 1, 2013).
28. The Joint Commission Framework for Conducting a Root Cause Analysis and Action Plan. www.jointcommission.org/Framework_for_Conducting_a_Root_Cause_Analysis_and_Action_Plan/ (accessed August 1, 2013).
29. Lee JY, Leblanc K, Fernandes OA, et al. Medication reconciliation during internal hospital transfer and impact of computerized prescriber order entry. *Ann Pharmacother*. 2010;44:1887–1895.
30. Boockvar KS, Blum S, Kugler A, et al. Effect of admission medication reconciliation on adverse drug events from admission medication changes. *Arch Intern Med*. 2011;171:860–861.
31. Walker PC, Bernstein SJ, Tucker Jones JN, et al. Impact of a pharmacist-facilitated hospital discharge program: a quasi-experimental study. *Arch Intern Med*. 2009;169:2003–2010.
32. Mueller SK, Sponsler KC, Kriplani S, Schnipper JL. Hospital-based medication reconciliation practices. *Arch Intern Med*. 2012;172:1057–1069.
33. Kaushal R, Shiojania KG, Bates DW. Effects of computerized physician order entry and clinical decision support systems on medication safety: a systematic review. *Arch Intern Med*. 2003;163:1409–1416.
34. Robertson J, Walkom E, Pearson S, et al. The impact of pharmacy computerized clinical decision support on prescribing, clinical and patient outcomes: a systematic review of the literature. *Int J Pharm Prac*. 2010;18:69–87.
35. Zhan C, Hicks RW, Blanchette CM, Keyes MA, Cousins DD. Potential benefits and problems with computerized prescriber order entry: analysis of a voluntary medication-error reporting database. *Am J Health Syst Pharm*. 2006;63:353–358.
36. Campbell EM, Sittig DF, Ash JS. Types of unintended consequences related to computerized provider order entry. *J Am Med Inform Assoc*. 2006;13:547–556.
37. Poon EG, Keohane CA, Yoon CS, et al. Effect of bar code technology on the safety of medication administration. *N Engl J Med*. 2010;362:1698–1707.
38. Paoletti RD, Suess TM, Lesko MG, et al. Using bar-code technology and medication observation methodology for safer medication administration. *Am J Health-Syst Pharm*. 2007;64:536–543.
39. Koppel R, Wetterneck T, Telles JL, Ben-Tzion K. Workarounds to barcode medication administration systems: their occurrences, causes and threats to patient safety. *J Am Med Inform Assoc*. 2008;15:408–423.
40. Hicks RW, Becker SC. An overview of intravenous-related medication administration errors as reported to MEDMARX, a national medication-error reporting program. *J Infus Nursing*. 2006;29:20–27.
41. Rothschild JM, Keohane CA, Cook EF, et al. A controlled trial of smart infusion pumps to improve medication safety in critically ill patients. *Crit Care Med*. 2005;33:533–540.
42. Danello SH, Maddox RR, Schaack GJ. Intravenous infusion safety technology: return on investment. *Hosp Pharm*. 2009;44:680–687.

43. Anderegg SV, Gumpper KF. What *meaningful use* means for pharmacy. *Am J Health-Syst Pharm*. 2012;69:890–894.

44. Sittig DF, Singh H. Electronic health records and the national patient-safety goals. *NEJM*. 2012;367:1854–1860.

45. Myers RB, Jones SL, Sittig DF. Review of reported clinical information system adverse events in the US Food and Drug Administration databases. *Appl Clin Inf*. 2011;2:63–74.

46. Prusch AE, Suess TM, Paoletti RD, et al. Integrating technology to improve medication administration. *Am J Health-Syst Pharm*. 2011;68:835–842.

47. Rough S, McDaniel M, Rinehart JR. Effective use of workload and productivity monitoring tools in health-system pharmacy, part 1. *Am J Health-Syst Pharm*. 2010;67:300–311.

48. Kaplan RS, Norton DP. *The balanced scorecard: translating strategy into action*. Boston, MA: Harvard Business Review Press.

49. Hintzen BL, Knoer SJ, Van Dyke CJ, Milavitz BS. Effect of lean process improvement techniques on a university hospital inpatient pharmacy. *Am J Health-Syst Pharm*. 2009; 66:2042–2047.

50. Ching JM, Long C, Williams BL, Blackmore CC. Using lean to improve medication administration safety: in search of the "perfect dose." *Jt Comm J Qual Patient Saf*. 2013;39:195–204.

51. Vermuelen LC, Rough SS, Thielke TT, et al. Strategic approach for improving the medication-use process in health systems: the high-performance pharmacy practice framework. *Am J Health-Syst Pharm*. 2007; 64:1699–1710.

52. Grank RP, Poppe LB, Savage SW, et al. Method to determine the allocation of clinical pharmacist resources. *Am J Health-Syst Pharm*. 2012;69:1398–1404.

53. Barnum DT, Walton SM, Shields KL, Schumock GT. Improving the efficiency of distributive and clinical services in hospital pharmacy. *J Med Syst*. 2011;35:59–70.

54. Siska MH, Tribble DA. Opportunities and challenges related to technology in supporting optimal pharmacy practice modes in hospitals and health-systems. *Am J Health-Syst Pharm*. 2011;68:1116–1126.

55. Seger AC, Churchill WW, Keohane CA, et al. Impact of robotic antineoplastic preparation on safety, workflow, and costs. *J Onc Prac*. 2012;8:344–350.

Case Study

Grace was hired as the director of pharmacy (DOP) for Chamberfest Regional Hospital (CRH). CRH is a 250-bed acute-care hospital serving the Chamberfest area with general medical/surgical services specializing in maternity, nursery, invasive cardiology, and orthopedics with an associated assisted living facility. Grace was most recently an assistant director at a large teaching facility in the closest major metropolitan area to Chamberfest. The previous director at CRH was the DOP for 20 years. CRH has new ownership and a number of other service line and department heads with long tenure were replaced with a new management team.

At her first department head meeting, Grace received news that CRH was installing a new, state-of-the-art, integrated clinical information system (CIS) highlighted by an EHR combined with CPOE over the next six months. At an individual follow-up meeting with her manager, Grace understood the next six months were focused on the design and configuration of the system's functionality plus testing followed by a rollout to the institution. Grace was excited by the system's capabilities, but her enthusiasm was tempered by her manager's suspicion that the system would not deliver on the proposed return on investment. Her manager requested that Grace report back in 30 days with what she believed were the functional priorities of the new CIS based on CRH's most recent Joint Commission survey where CRH received negative comments concerning medication safety requiring CRH's response in the next 60 days. Additionally, the manager wanted to know what metrics were going to be followed to determine whether the advertised cost savings and improvements in clinical outcomes were realized or not.

The hospital's current order entry system is paper based, but the pharmacy uses a computerized system for order entry and filling is centralized with a 24-hour cart exchange seven days a week. Grace decided the best approach was to assemble a multidisciplinary team in addressing the JC survey's concerns.

1. Using the medication use process described in the chapter, what are potential problem areas known to be associated with a handwritten order entry system?
2. How could a CPOE solve those issues? Include limitations and unanticipated issues in your response.
3. What tools are available to Grace's team to pinpoint specific deficiencies?

Using the team's output as a guide, CRH's information technology department configured the new CIS to address the identified problems. Rollout is scheduled in three months following CIS testing and staff training. Grace believes this is a good time to gather performance data to respond to her manager's concerns about whether or not the CIS is a good investment. What types of data points could Grace collect now and compare to the same set collected later to determine if, from a pharmacy perspective, the CIS investment is worthwhile?

11 Managing Clinical Services

Gene A. Gibson

CONTENTS

Learning Objectives: After reading this chapter and working through the case the reader will be able to:

1. Explain the term *evidence-based formulary* and describe its importance
2. Explain the function of the pharmacy and therapeutics committee and list its required membership
3. Define the terms *patient-centered care, pharmaceutical care, medication therapy management, accountable care*, and the *medical home.*
4. Provide at least three types of pharmacy practice plans and explain the pros and cons of each
5. Explain the importance of having a plan to develop clinical pharmacy services and achieve safe, effective, and evidence-based medication therapy, and how the plan should be developed

6. Explain the importance of drug use evaluation and how it should be implemented and used
7. Explain the keys and pitfalls of leading and managing clinical practitioners

INTRODUCTION

The practice of pharmacy consists of two domains, drug product and cognitive services, called *clinical services*. Clinical services are the activities and processes employed by pharmacists to assure optimal therapeutic outcomes and minimize adverse drug events in a cost-efficient manner. Clinical services can be provided in all health settings where pharmacists practice. The purpose of this chapter is to introduce the reader to a set of activities and processes used by pharmacists to optimize a patient's drug therapy, improve patient outcomes, and avoid adverse drug events. A discussion will also be provided on how to manage these activities and processes to assure optimum drug therapy outcomes.

GETTING THE DRUGS RIGHT: EVIDENCE-BASED FORMULARY

FORMULARY

Achieving rational drug therapy is the goal of the pharmacy department. The basis of this goal starts with the organization's formulary. The formulary first started as a basic drug list of approved medications that can be prescribed within the organization. This list of drugs represents the clinical judgment of physicians, pharmacists, and other experts within the organization. The Joint Commission on Accreditation of Health Organizations (JCAHO) in their accreditation guidelines states, "The hospital develops and approves criteria for selecting medications which at a minimum include the following" (Anonymous, 2012a):

Indication for use
Effectiveness
Drug interactions
Potential for errors and abuse
Adverse drug events
Sentinel event advisories
Population served (e.g., pediatrics)
Other risks
Costs

Furthermore, JCAHO states, "The formulary should be a resource for prescribers and staff to know which products, strengths and dosage forms are available within the organization" and "Before you add a medication to your formulary list, staff and practitioners are trained on the effects of the medication and monitoring requirements. In addition the organization must have access to appropriate lab and diagnostic testing which may be required to monitor effectiveness." (Anonymous, 2013b)

All organizations have a defined process to review drugs for addition to the formulary. Drugs are reviewed in one of two ways: retrospectively via a request by a member of the medical staff after the medication is approved by the Food and Drug Administration (FDA); or prospectively, by the pharmacy department at the time the medication is approved by the FDA.

Formularies are categorized as closed, open, or mixed (Pederson, 2004). Closed formularies are strictly monitored and controlled. They are based on the premise that the formulary achieves rational therapeutics by providing a selection of drugs of choice at reduced inventory burden and minimizing duplication and emphasizing the use of generic medications.

Open formularies have little control and offer all available medications to be prescribed to any patient. Mixed formularies attempt to provide a combination of closed and open and are most commonly used by hospitals and health systems and allow for flexibility. There may be three types of drug classes within a mixed formulary: an open drug list, restricted drugs, or targeted drugs. An open list allows any drug within the list to be prescribed for any patient. The restricted drug list can be prescribed for only specific patient populations and/or by specific physician specialists. Chemotherapy is usually restricted to prescribing by oncologists, with the exception of chemotherapy agents that have been shown to be safe and efficacious in other disease states such as methotrexate for rheumatoid arthritis. Targeted drugs are restricted to prior approval before they can be prescribed. These are targeted to assure they are used in accordance with approved guidelines and protocols. Expensive and high-cost antibiotics are usually targeted to prior approval by infectious disease physicians or pharmacists who are trained in antibiotic therapy to assure they are appropriate for the indication and dose so as not to fail or cause antimicrobial resistance.

A medication is reviewed for formulary addition via a drug monograph that utilizes evidence-based review of the medical literature and is usually performed by the pharmacy department. In Table 11.1 the American Society of Health-System Pharmacy (ASHP), in a published guideline on the formulary system, provides a listing of components for a formulary monograph (ASHP, 2008).

In addition, within the drug monograph one of the following recommendations is proposed: add the medication to formulary without restrictions, reject the medication or add to formulary with restrictions to patient types, or require approval by a physician specialist. Criteria for formulary approval include new medication with unique properties (better pharmacokinetic properties, equal efficacy, side effect profile, and lower cost), unique patient population, and is not a duplicate of other medications on formulary.

FORMULARY SYSTEM

Along with the drug list, the formulary also includes a formulary system, a set of policies and procedures related to the optimization of the medication use process. ASHP in 2008 calls the formulary system, "The multidisciplinary, evidence based process employed by an organization to select and use medications that offer the best therapeutic outcomes while minimizing potential risks and costs for patients" (American Society of Hospital Pharmacists, 2008). The medication use process as

TABLE 11.1

Components of a Formulary Monograph

- Brand and generic names and synonyms
- FDA approval information, including data and FDA rating
- Pharmacology and mechanism of action
- FDA-approved indications
- Potential non-FDA-approved indications
- Dosage forms and storage
- Pharmacokinetic considerations
- Use in special populations—pediatric, geriatric, patients with renal and liver dysfunction
- Pregnancy category and use in breastfeeding
- Comparison of drug efficacy, safety, convenience, and cost with therapeutic alternatives
- Comparison of efficacy versus placebo
- Clinical trials and critique
- Medication safety assessment and recommendations (adverse drug reaction, drug-drug and drug-food interactions; specific monitoring recommendations; stability issues and potential for medication errors such as look-alike and sound-alike issues
- Financial analysis

described by the JCAHO consists of selection and procurement, storage, ordering and transcribing, preparing and dispensing, administration, and monitoring. The development and implementation of policy and procedures should be evidence based and assure safe and effective use of medications within the organization.

ASHP has provided examples of policies and procedures within the formulary system and they include the following:

Process for adding and reviewing or deleting a drug from formulary
Process for reviewing a drug for formulary addition or deletion
Process for developing, implementing, and monitoring drug use guidelines
Methods for assuring safe prescribing, distribution, administration, and monitoring of medications (e.g., accepted abbreviations, adverse drug reaction reporting, automatic stop orders, controlled substances, drug shortages, generic and therapeutic interchange, use of investigational drugs, patients use of own medications, medications stored in automatic dispensing devices, use of drug samples, process for non-formulary medications, therapeutic interchange—IV to PO pharmacist process)
Rules of pharmaceutical representatives
Process for drug use evaluations

JCAHO requires policies and procedures to be reviewed periodically by expert panels or subcommittees of pharmacy and therapeutics (P&T) (American Society of Hospital Pharmacists, 2008). Another component of a functioning formulary system is a series of special information to aid the prescriber in special situations, and they are listed in Table 11.2. The formulary and the formulary system are valuable tools for ensuring rational drug therapy and optimizing medication outcomes. It is

---

TABLE 11.2
Information for Prescriber for Special Situations

- Drugs that cannot be crushed
- List of sugar-free products
- Sodium content of medications
- Analgesic equivalence
- Equivalent doses of similar drugs (corticosteroids)
- Dosing guidelines and nomograms
- Contents of emergency carts
- Apothecary/metric equivalents
- Medications to avoid with patients with latex allergy
- Tyramine-containing foods
- Desensitization protocols

---

a dynamic process that changes with new information and is viewed as vital to the support of the medication use process.

PHARMACY AND THERAPEUTICS COMMITTEE

Every health organization has physicians, and they are organized to have officers, bylaws, and a governing board. They are organized into departments and have several committees to help manage the care that is provided by the organization. The P&T committee is established to oversee the use of medications as well as develop policies and procedures that ensure the safe and effective use of medication within the organization. The committee reports to the medical staff, and all recommendations are subject to approval of the entire medical staff or representatives of the medical staff called a medical executive committee or medical board (American Society of Health-System Pharmacists, 2008).

Composition

The P&T committee is composed of physicians, nurses, pharmacists, administrators, and any other support staff involved with medications and the medication use process, such as nutrition, respiratory therapy, radiology, laboratory medicine, as well as risk managers and legal affairs. Frequently, the director of pharmacy serves as the secretary and therefore develops the agenda. The committee meets as often as necessary, but usually monthly.

Generally, P&T committees have subcommittees to provide recommendations for specific groups of drugs that require expert advice or the development and monitoring of processes to assure the medication use process is optimized. Examples of committees with experts include antibiotic subcommittee, oncologic therapy, pain management, and radiology. Some examples of subcommittees involved with the medication use process include medication safety, adverse reaction monitoring, and drug use evaluation.

When a new medication enters the marketplace, there may be considerable interest in having the medication available on the formulary. The desire to have the medication on the formulary may be due to interests besides rational drug therapy. These other interests may include stock investments with the pharmaceutical company manufacturing the medication, research support from the company, or a participant in the company's speakers bureau. The P&T committee has developed a methodology to deal with these conflicts of interest. Annually, all members are asked to disclose any financial or other interests they may have with pharmaceutical companies that may be involved with the addition of medications to the formulary. Additionally, at the beginning of the P&T meeting in which medications are to be reviewed for formulary addition, all members are asked to review the list of medications and verbally affirm any conflict of interest the members may have with the discussion of the medications.

The P&T committee is vital to the development of rational, cost-effective therapy with an institution. A well-organized, functioning committee can provide leadership necessary for fulfilling the development of optimum drug therapy. Pharmacists play an essential role in the functioning and implementation of the committee's recommendations.

Drug Use Evaluation

A valuable tool in the formulary process is the review of the quality of medication prescribing. Historically, the following terms have been used to describe this process: drug-use review (DUR), drug use evaluation (DUE), and medication use evaluation (MUE).

In the 1980s, the JCAHO required the review of appropriate antibiotic prescribing and called it antibiotic use review. The process involved medical staff review through the oversight of the P&T committee.

In the 1990s, JCAHO adopted the term *medication use review* to emphasize evaluation of the medication use through all stages to the medication use process. The medication use process consists of procurement and storage, prescribing, preparation, dispensing, administration, and monitoring, and if any one of these steps is compromised there could be a breakdown in the medication use process (American Society of Hospital Pharmacists, 2008).

In the Omnibus Reconciliation Act of 1990 (OBRA 90) retail pharmacists were required to resolve drug-related problems for Medicaid patients prior to receiving their prescription. More recently, the National Committee for Quality Assurance (NCQA) has incorporated the elements of DUE within their standards of utilization management. In its recent accreditation manual, JCAHO has become less prescriptive toward DUE and describes the process as evaluating the effectiveness of the medication management system as follows (Joint Commission, 2012).

Collect data and analyze the performance of its medication management system: Compare data over time to identify risk points, levels of performance, patterns, trends, and variations of its medication management system.

Review literature and other external sources for new technologies and best practices: Based on the data, the literature, review of new technologies and best practices, opportunities for improvement are identified in the medication management system.

After implementation, the system changes are reevaluated to confirm they have resulted in improvements in the medication management system. Additional action is taken when the planned improvements are either not achieved or not sustained.

Regardless, drug use evaluation is a structured, quality improvement program, designed to promote appropriate, safe, and effective drug use within the health system. Drug use evaluation is performed as a proactive, criteria-based, ongoing, planned, and systematic process designed to monitor and evaluate the prophylactic, therapeutic, and empiric use of drugs within the health-care system. It is a collaborative effort between prescribers, pharmacists, nurses, and administrators. The process is designed to analyze a drug's actual use and identify problems or potential problems. The DUE process also includes resolution of problems as they have been identified and the documentation and reporting of findings, recommendations, actions taken, and results. The action may be regulatory or educational based on the results, circumstances, and policies of the health-care system.

DUE Process

Table 11.3 is a general outline for conducting a drug use evaluation as presented by ASHP (American Society of Health-System Pharmacists, 1996).

Gain Organizational Authority and Assign Responsibility

At the very least, the drug use evaluation process should be based on established policy and procedures within the P&T committee structure or designated subcommittees.

Identify Areas of Opportunity: Problems, Adverse Events, Interventions, Guidelines

Generally, high-volume, high-risk, or problem-prone drugs are selected for evaluation. Specifically, the drug may be selected for one or more of the reasons as listed in Table 11.4.

Develop Criteria and Indicators for Optimal Use Based on Prescribing Information, Guidelines, Indications, or Evidence from the Literature

Objective criteria and accepted thresholds will be established for every DUE. The objective criteria will reflect current knowledge, clinical experience, and relevant medical literature. Pharmacy departments are usually responsible for the initial development of the background material, criteria, and thresholds.

TABLE 11.3
Outline for Conducting a Drug Use Evaluation

- Gain organizational authority and assign responsibility
- Identify areas of opportunity—problems, adverse events, interventions, guidelines
- Develop criteria for optimal use based on guidelines, indications, etc.
- Involve practitioners who practice in the setting to be evaluated
- Initiate criteria
- Collect data and evaluate care
- Develop and implement plans for improvement
- Assess effectiveness of actions and document improvements
- Repeat cycle of plan, evaluate, and take action
- Regularly assess effectiveness

TABLE 11.4
Reasons for Selecting a Drug for a Drug Use Evaluation

- The drug is known or suspected to cause adverse reactions or interact with another drug, food, or diagnostic procedure in a manner that presents a significant health risk.
- The drug is known to be highly toxic if prescribed incorrectly or inappropriately or not optimally monitored.
- The drug requires specific criteria for administration either restricting the use or requiring specific monitoring parameters.
- The drug is used in the treatment of patients who may be at high risk for adverse reactions.
- The drug is potentially toxic or causes discomfort at normal therapeutic doses.
- The drug is most effective and safest when used in a specific manner.
- The drug is one of the most frequently prescribed or is expensive.
- The drug is more expensive than comparable drugs without demonstrable clinical advantages.
- The drug is newly added to the formulary or is undergoing formulary evaluation for deletion or retention.
- The drug had been identified through infection control as causing changes in sensitivity patterns of microorganisms.
- The drug has been identified by routine quality assurance, pharmacokinetics, or adverse reaction monitoring as being inappropriately or incorrectly prescribed or associated with serious adverse reactions.
- There are patient populations or clinical situations in which the drug has absolute contraindications.
- There are guidelines targeting, limiting, or restricting the use of the drug in specific populations.

Involve Practitioners Who Practice in the Setting

For every DUE, it is important to solicit comments from major prescribers or interested prescribers in the establishment of the finalized criteria and thresholds. It is important to have their buy-in to the DUE process, and when the results are presented they will accept the results and are prepared to make changes in the medication use process to optimize medication prescribing.

Collect Data and Evaluate Care

Data collection is usually coordinated through the pharmacy department. The personnel responsible for the DUE depend on the scope, sample size, and duration of the DUE. Sample size and frequency of data collection depend on the scope and focus (number of criteria and processes evaluated per patient). Generally, infrequent failure (less than 5%) to meet criteria will require a large population sample (more than 200 patients) and frequent failure (25 to 50%) to meet criteria will require a small population (50 patients).

Methods of Collecting Data   DUEs can be performed prospectively, concurrently, or retrospectively (AMCP, 2009). Prospective DUEs involve review of a planned therapy prior to dispensing the medication. This DUE requires the involvement of pharmacists to identify issues prior to dispensing the medication and resolution of a problem prior to dispensing the medication. Prospective DUEs require access and review of patient records, and a set of agreed-to interventions to resolve the problem. Another disadvantage is the requirement of the reviewer to be present at the time of the prescription and thus does not allow for review after the prescription has been received. Problems useful for prospective DUEs include drug-drug, drug-disease, and drug allergy interactions, therapeutic and generic interchange, and incorrect dosage and duration of therapy.

In concurrent DUEs, the review involves the assessment and identification of problems with therapy and involves the identification of problems and the ongoing monitoring of drug therapy to ensure positive outcomes. The process allows the review to intervene and modify a patient's treatment plan. The concurrent process requires access to patient records and direct access to the prescriber. It allows for collection of data upon review and discussion and is not limited to information documented in the patient chart. This process requires a lot of man hours and requires the presence of the pharmacist at the time the medication is prescribed. Problems useful for concurrent DUEs include drug-drug and drug-disease interactions, drug-age and drug-pregnancy precautions, excessive or low doses, duplicate therapy, over- and underutilization of medications, and dose adjustment and laboratory monitoring.

Retrospective DUEs are the simplest to perform since drug therapy is reviewed after the patient has received the medication. The process involves the review of patient records and screens the records to determine if the drug therapy meets criteria. These evaluations are not time dependent, can be scheduled when resources are available, and require limited resources. Unfortunately, the results are dependent on the information recorded in the patient record. Retrospective DUEs can detect patterns in prescribing, dispensing, administration, and monitoring. Retrospective DUEs are useful for identifying problems in appropriateness and misuse of therapy, over- and underutilization, appropriate generic and therapeutic duplication, drug-drug and drug-disease interaction, and incorrect dose and duration of therapy.

Develop and Implement Plans for Improvement

Data should be displayed to demonstrate trends and patterns of use and percentage of patients whose therapies met predetermined criteria. Attention should be paid to evidence of specific problems (e.g., improper prescribing versus improper monitoring of therapy, improper dosing versus use for wrong indication). Problem identification should be followed by determining the possible causes of deviation from criteria. Possible interventions include contact with prescribers, information and education (newsletters, guidelines), changes to the medication use system, changes in medication monitoring process of medications, and order sets. Optimally, the conclusion and recommendations should be submitted to the P&T committee. Following comments by original contributors, corrective action in the form of regulatory or educational interventions should be developed and approved by the P&T committee.

Assess Effectiveness and Actions and Document Improvements

After implementation there should be a follow-up plan to evaluate what has been implemented. This should include the content of the intervention and who was involved in the process. The assessment should include a report to P&T summarizing when the interventions were completed.

Repeat Cycle of Plan, Evaluate, and Take Action

A one-time DUE may not achieve desired results. In order to assure success, the initial action plan needs to be assessed and if needed, the action plan may need to change. Corrective actions should be reevaluated at regular intervals. The purpose of the reevaluation is to see if the corrective actions implemented were successful, to determine if established standards are still pertinent to quality patient care as drug therapies change, and to ascertain if further interventions are necessary Consequently, the initial DUE should be reassessed at a later time to monitor for successful implementation.

Regularly Assess Effectiveness

Every year there should be an assessment of the current DUE process. Issues to evaluate include the scope and scale of DUEs, as well as the source of data. If needed the information systems and the methods used to collect information may be upgraded or changed.

Keys to a Successful DUE Process

The biggest key to success is to include the major prescribers at the onset of a DUE. Without their support, the results will not be heard and there will be reluctance to change. Another key is to keep the DUE simple (limited criteria) and drug process based. If you involved outcomes the number of patients needed to show significance would be very time consuming. Focus on the essential steps in the drug use process that assure optimal therapy. The most important key to assuring improvement after a drug use evaluation is to close the loop and have proper and complete follow-up with prescribers and changes in the drug use process.

By developing and completing the steps involved with assuring a successful DUE, improvement in the drug use process will be assured.

PRACTICE MODEL OPTIONS

Since the economic turmoil of 2007 and the changes in the health-care laws, there has been considerable discussion regarding pharmacy practice models. The pharmacy practice model describes how a pharmacy department's resources are deployed to provide patient care services and includes pharmacists and how they practice and provide care, utilization, and involvement of technicians, and use of automation and technology.

In 2007, Breland suggested pharmacy practice models must meet the following seven basic principles:

1. Each patient should have a pharmacist
2. Patients should receive consistent care
3. Drug therapy should be for all patients, 24 hours a day, 7 days a week
4. Pharmacy work should be prioritized by patient severity
5. Pharmacy time should not be driven by tasks
6. Pharmacists should be working in areas to advance their skills to a higher level
7. Pharmacists are responsible first to the patient

In 2010, the UHC Task Force on Practice Models identified and developed a list of patient care services that should be provided by pharmacists in academic medical centers (Bush, 2010). Two categories of services were developed: services for all patients and services for high-risk patients.

Services recommended for all patients included:

- Reconcile medications on admission and during changes in level of care as well as discharge
- Review all nonemergent orders prior to first dose administration
- Develop individualized treatment and monitoring plans for patients
- Conduct daily monitoring of medication profiles
- Participate in daily care rounds
- Educate patients about new medications
- Communicate a patient's discharge information to the patient's pharmacy and physician

Special services currently recommended for specific clinical situations included:

- Anticoagulation management
- Resuscitation teams
- Parenteral nutrition
- Streamline medication orders (e.g., IV to oral)
- Antimicrobial stewardship
- Pharmacokinetic evaluation, dosing, and monitoring
- Medication dose adjustments based on renal function
- Collaborative drug therapy management
- Patient education on preventing disease and improving health

In November 2010, the American Society of Health-System Pharmacists sponsored the Pharmacy Practice Model Initiative Summit. After several presentations and breakout sessions the group agreed that practice leaders need to commit to serving high-order needs in helping patients make the best use of medications, move from pharmacy-centric to patient-centric thinking about the mission of the pharmacy enterprise, and assume responsibility for medication-related outcomes while collaborating with patient care teams (Shane, 2011).

There was substantial discussion with regard to the development and implementation of new, innovative pharmacy practice models, and successful implementation of advance practice models has been published (Pickett, 2010; Knoer, 2010).

Pharmacist practice has been categorized into three models: drug distribution centered, clinical specialist centered, and patient centered integrated practice model (Strand, 1990; Woods, 2011; Kelly, 2007). As shown in Table 11.5, there are several differences between the models. Drug distribution is medication order focused, has no direct patient care, is focused on timely delivery of medications to the patients' bedside, is not involved in patient outcomes, requires only a pharmacy license, usually takes place away from the patient care area, and has roles that could be performed by technicians.

TABLE 11.5

Description of Pharmacy Practice Models

Comparison of Hospital Pharmacy Practice Models

Pharmaceutical Care	Clinical Pharmacy	Drug Distribution
More of a primary care model	More of a specialty, consultant model	General model
Patient focused	Physician focused	Medication order focused
Provided directly to patients	Usually provided indirectly to patients	No direct patient care
Outcome directed	Process directed	Focus on timely delivery of medications
Focuses on a variety of outcomes	Mostly focuses on clinical outcomes	No need for credentials
Based primarily on caring	Based primarily on competency	Physician responsible for patient outcome
Pharmacist responsible for patient outcome	Physician responsible for patient outcome	
Quality-of-life role	Quality-of-care role	Quality of drug distribution
Practice in all settings	Practice mostly in acute-care settings	Practice in a centralized site
All pharmacists can provide	Some pharmacists provide	Roles could be provided by technicians

Source: Adapted from WN Kelly, *Pharmacy: What It Is and How It Works,* 2nd Ed., Boca Raton, FL: CRC Press, 2007.

The clinical specialist model involves rounding up a team of providers and usually does not involve any responsibility for drug distribution. There are two types of pharmacists in this model: pharmacists for distribution and clinical pharmacist specialists for special groups of patients. The clinical specialist acts as a consultant, is physician focused, and consequently indirectly affects patients. Their interactions are based on improving processes in the medication use system, require the physician to be responsible for care, and focus on quality of care, and only very competent pharmacists can provide this care. These pharmacists provide care to special groups of patients such as patients in the intensive care units, those requiring antibiotic stewardship, oncology patients, organ transplant patients, or pediatrics.

The patient-centered integrated practice model has also been called unit-based and involves participation as members of interdisciplinary teams, assisting with evidence-based medicine and developing therapeutic plans. This model should include the majority of pharmacists on staff, and is patient focused, following more of a primary-care model where care is provided directly to the patient and is outcome focused. It is based on caring for a patient, and the pharmacist is responsible for the patient outcome. In this model the patient's quality of life is the goal.

In 2009, in an ASHP survey on monitoring and patient education, 24.4% of respondents stated they had a drug-distribution practice mode, 10.9% had a clinical specialist with drug-distribution pharmacists, and 64.7% stated they had a patient-centered integrated model with clinical generalists with distributive and clinical responsibilities (Pederson, 2010).

In a letter to the editor, a fourth model was presented that included clinical specialists and patient-centered integrated pharmacists working together (Weant, 2011). This is the case for most academic medical centers.

The type of model developed at an institution is dependent on a host of factors including logistic issues (number of units and number of buildings), utilization and deployment of technicians, automation and technology, pharmacist training, and the scope of pharmacy practice. To date only the components of a pharmacy practice model have been discussed. Unfortunately a transferable, standardized model has not been developed. However, there is agreement to the following: involving pharmacists directly in patient-centered care avoids and reduces medication errors; getting pharmacists involved in patient-centered care helps physicians see the value of pharmacists, establishes credibility, and physicians are more likely to trust a pharmacist and their recommendations; and pharmaceutical costs are best managed when drug distribution, automation, and information systems are fully developed and allow pharmacists to reallocate to direct patient care.

PATIENT-CENTERED CARE/PHARMACEUTICAL CARE

In 1990, Hepler and Strand defined new responsibilities and a role for pharmacists to practice pharmacy. Previously, pharmacy practice was centered on dispensing the correct drug, with correct dose, to the correct patient. This new practice was called pharmaceutical care and requires "responsible provision of drug therapy for the purpose of achieving definite outcomes that improve a patient's quality of life" (Hepler, 1970). The outcomes are:

- Cure of disease
- Elimination or reduction of a patient's symptoms
- Arresting or slowing of a disease process
- Preventing a disease or symptom

Later, in 1993, ASHP refined the definition for pharmaceutical care: "Pharmaceutical care is defined as the functions performed by a pharmacist in ensuring the optimal use of medications to achieve specific outcomes that improve a patient's quality of life; further, the pharmacist accepts responsibility for outcomes that ensue from his or her actions, which occur in collaboration with patients and other health-care colleagues" (American Society of Health-System Pharmacists, 1993).

In 1997, Strand provided a revised definition of pharmaceutical care as a practice in which a practitioner takes responsibility for a patient's drug-related need and is held accountable for this commitment (Strand, 1997).

Additionally, Hepler and Strand describe pharmaceutical care as a process that involves pharmacists cooperating with patients and other professionals to develop, implement, and monitor medication treatment plans. Initially they described the process to involve three functions:

Identifying potential and actual drug-related problems
Resolving or slowing a disease process
Preventing potential drug-related problems

Later in 1993 ASHP (American Society of Health-System Pharmacists, 1996) has expanded the functions to include:

- Collecting and organizing patient information
- Determining the presence of drug-related problems
- Summarizing patient health-care needs
- Specifying medication therapy goals
- Designing a therapeutic regimen
- Designing a monitoring plan
- Developing a therapeutic regimen and monitoring plan in collaboration with the patient and other health professionals
- Initiating a therapeutic regimen
- Monitoring the effects for the therapeutic plan
- Redesigning the therapeutic regimen and monitoring plan

The essential element of the pharmaceutical care plan is determination of the presence of drug-related problems. Originally, Hepler and Strand identified eight drug-related problems; ASHP has added another five (Table 11.6).

The key elements to the success of pharmaceutical care are shown in Table 11.7 (Kelly, 2007)—the importance of talking to the patient and establishment of a pharmacist-patient relationship. The table identifies medication-related problems and four methods that may be used to identify the problems: review dispensed

---

TABLE 11.6
Drug-Related Problems

- Medications with no medical indication
- Medical conditions not treated
- Inappropriate medications prescribed for a medical condition
- Inappropriate dose, dosage form, schedule, route of administration, or method of administration
- Therapeutic duplication of medications
- Patient is allergic to prescribed medication
- Actual or potential adverse drug events
- Actual or potential drug-drug, drug-disease, drug-nutrient, and drug-laboratory test interactions
- Interference of drug therapy through social or recreational drug use[a]
- Failure to receive full benefit of prescribed medication therapy[a]
- Problems due to financial impact of medication therapy on patient[a]
- Patient's lack of understanding of medication therapy[a]
- Failure of patient to adhere to prescribed medication therapy[a]

[a] Added by American Society of Health-System Pharmacists, 1996.

TABLE 11.7
Identification of Medication-Related Problems (MRP)

MRP	Rx or Drug	Patient's Computer Profile	Patient's Medical Record	Talk with the Patient
An untreated problem		X	X	X
Wrong drug prescribed			X	X
Taking too little drug	X	X	X	X
Taking too much drug	X	X	X	X
Not taking the drug	X	X	X	X
Taking an unneeded drug				X
Experiencing a drug interaction	X	X		X
Experiencing an adverse drug reaction			X	X

Source: Adapted from WN Kelly, *Pharmacy: What It Is and How It Works,* 2nd Ed., Boca Raton, FL: CRC Press, 2007.

medication, complete the patient's medication profile, consult the patient's medical record, and talk with the patient. The most efficient and comprehensive review of medication-related problems is obtained when talking with the patient.

Since the introduction of pharmaceutical care, the expansion of roles and responsibilities has been readily accepted by professional organizations, colleges of pharmacy in the form of curriculum changes, and acceptance of the Doctor of Pharmacy (PharmD) as the entry-level degree. Many pharmacy faculties have incorporated the process into their practice but barriers remain. The barriers include (1) the time the pharmacist takes to perform the review; (2) the location of the interview (at the pharmacy checkout stand, at the patient's bedside, or in a patient counseling room); (3) background and training of the pharmacist; (4) lack of acceptance by other health professionals; and (5) lack of reimbursement for this cognitive service on top of payment for dispensing a medication.

A variety of articles documenting the importance of medication-related problems on health care have been published since pharmaceutical care was first introduced. The Institute of Medicine has published two reports noting that annual deaths and illness from medication systems and medication errors contribute to 44,000 deaths a year and 1.5 million preventable adverse events a year (Kohn, 2000; Aspden, 2006). Adverse drug events and patient noncompliance with medications have been associated with up to 10% and 5.3% of all hospitalizations, respectively (Manasse, 1989; Sullivan, 1990). The annual costs for medication-related mortality and morbidity have been estimated to be $76.6 billion (Johnson, 1995). Later it was estimated that at least $56.6 billion is associated with avoidable drug-related problems (Johnson, 1997). Clearly, by providing patient-specific pharmaceutical care there is a potential to improve outcomes and reduce health-care costs.

Pharmaceutical care as described previously is important because it provides a philosophy of practice and describes a process for the practice of pharmacy that optimizes patient care.

MEDICATION THERAPY MANAGEMENT

As a result of the Omnibus Budget Reconciliation Act 1990 (OBRA 1990), pharmacists are expected to offer patient counseling at the time of dispensing a prescription (McGiveney, 2007). The counseling consists of providing to Medicare patients the following: the purpose of the medication prescription, proper administration, length of therapy, special directions for use, proper storage, refill instructions, information on adverse effects, potential interactions, contraindications, and steps to take when an adverse effect is identified. The service is voluntary and the patient has the option to refuse the discussion. Consequently, the service is not routinely performed.

There are several issues with patient counseling. First, the counseling is based upon the dispensing of a medication prescription to a patient and the cost of counseling is embedded with the prescription costs. There is no payment of services associated with the counseling. Second, the transmission of information is one way, pharmacist to patient, and there is no further discussion regarding the patient's disease states or other medications. Last, there is no documentation of the counseling and assessment of the patient's understanding of the instructions.

In 2003, the Medicare Modernization Act established the Medicare Prescription Medication Benefit (Part D) and required providers of the benefit to provide medication therapy management services (MTMSs) and receive reimbursement for MTMSs. The Medicare Modernization Act describes MTMS as "the evaluation of medication therapy to improve continuity of care and health care outcomes" (American Pharmacists Association, National Association of Chain Drug Stores Foundation, 2005). The goals are to improve outcomes, decrease adverse events, and control costs.

Later, national pharmacy organizations joined to further define MTMS. They defined MTMS as "a distinct service or group of services that optimize therapeutic outcomes for individual patients. Medication therapy management services are independent of, but can occur in conjunction with, the provision of a medication product." (Bluml, 2005, p. 571). In other words, MTMS can occur in any outpatient venue where patients may be seen by a pharmacist, ambulatory clinics, private pharmacies, or chain pharmacies, just as long as the process is completed.

Subsequently, the American Pharmacists Association and the National Association of Chain Drug Stores established a model framework of core elements for the implementation of MTMS. These elements are to be offered to all patients in need of MTMS and include medication therapy review, personal medication record, medication-related action plan, intervention and/or referral, and documentation and follow-up. The structure is remarkably similar to the pharmaceutical care process discussed previously (American Pharmacists Association and the National Association of Chain Drug Stores Foundation, 2008). In fact, MTMS has been described as a strategy to incorporate pharmaceutical care into pharmacy practice (McGiveney, 2007).

With the passage of the Medicare Part D program, reimbursement for a service not associated with a prescription was established. Current Procedural Terminology

(CPT) codes are used for billing for health-care services. The American Medical Association develops and maintains the codes. In 2006, three temporary codes were developed for pharmacy services: 99605, initial visit with new patient (15 minutes); 99606, follow-up visit with established patient (15 minutes); and 99607, each additional 15 minutes. In 2008 these codes were made permanent and can be used by pharmacists to bill third parties for MTM services. Unfortunately each insurer determines the CPT codes it will pay for. Currently, the average rate for MTMS is $1 to $3 per minute (Flowers, 2013).

Initially, the Centers for Medicare and Medicaid Services (CMS) required all Part D programs to offer MTMS for targeted enrollees who have the following: multiple chronic disease states: receiving multiple Part D medications and are likely to have at least $4000 in usage of Part D medications (Flowers, 2013). Later, the eligibility of patients expanded to include history of non-adherence and frequent hospitalizations and emergency room visits (Flowers, 2013). In 2010, CMS changed the criteria for eligibility. If the plan targets specific diseases, it must target a minimum of the four diseases from the CMS core chronic diseases of: hypertension, heart failure, diabetes, dyslipidemia, respiratory disease, bone disease/arthritis, and mental health diseases. Also, each plan must develop eligibility criteria based on a patient taking a set minimum number of medications (two to five medications). The plan can choose all Part D medications, chronic medications, or drugs for specific disease states. Additionally, the minimum drug expense per patient eligible for MTMS decreased from $4000 to $3000. Finally, all plans must provide documentation quarterly and annually for all MTMS encounters per patient (Flowers, 2013). The addition of the required documentation increases the opportunity for pharmacists to perform MTMS.

Originally, MTMS was a part of plans providing coverage for Part D Medicare Prescription Plans. In 2010, the scope of patients eligible to receive MTMS increased to include patients with private insurance, state Medicaid programs, employer benefit groups, health maintenance organizations, managed care organizations, and preferred provider organizations. The provision of MTMS is viewed as a valuable service that improves patient outcomes and lowers health-care costs.

A variety of methods are used to implement MTMS. Many plans used in-house or contracted pharmacists while others used nurses of physicians. A novel methodology utilizes a MTMS administrative services company that trains pharmacists, and provides an infrastructure for documentation, billing, quality assurance procedures, claim payments processing, and data reporting (Flowers, 2013).

Finally, in 2010, the Patient Protection and Affordable Care Act and the Health Care and Education Reconciliation Act were signed into law and are known as the Affordable Care Act (ACA). This focuses on quality, safety, and reducing health-care costs and affects pharmacy in many ways including with MTMS (Flowers, 2013). Starting in 2013, all Medicare Part D plans must offer MTMS to increase adherence and improve patient outcomes. The programs must offer encounters either face to face or via telehealth technologies. The programs must provide documentation of an annual comprehensive medication review which includes a printed summary of the review as well as follow-up interventions. Also the plan must have a process to review quarterly the medication use of all patients enrolled in the plan but not eligible for MTMS.

There are also provisions to expand MTMS beyond Medicare Part D. There are opportunities to obtain grants to evaluate the provision of MTMS by pharmacists who are part of multidisciplinary teams. The grant programs should target patients who take four or more prescribed drugs, including over-the-counter drugs and dietary supplements, patients on high-risk medications, patients with two or more chronic diseases, and patients who have undergone a transition of care (discharged from a hospital or long-term care facility).

By including the expansion and opportunities for development and implementation of expanded MTMS, the passage of the ACA validates and supports the use of MTMS by pharmacists. The future of a patient-focused practice of pharmacy appears to be achievable and ready for pharmacists to begin the transformation to patient-centered care.

AFFORDABLE CARE AND FITTING INTO THE MEDICAL HOME

A major component of the ACA is the development of accountable care organizations (ACOs). An ACO is to have providers, physicians and hospitals, voluntarily develop a health system to improve patient health, improve quality of care, and reduce healthcare costs. The ACO concept has been compared to the integrated delivery networks of the 1990s (Burns, 2012). No framework has been developed but the expectation is for ACOs to use a variety of methods such as implementing disease management programs; improving coordination of care between physicians, physician specialists, and hospitals; aligning physician and hospital incentives for savings; using non-physician providers; and forming patient-centered medical homes to achieve the goal.

Each ACO must care for at least 5000 Medicare patients for three years and agree to quality and cost targets. The idea was to attract large health systems with a large number of primary-care physicians. As of December 2013 there are 360 ACOs registered with CMS (Hoban, 2013). The foundation of ACO care relies on the patient-centered medical homes with interdisciplinary teams under the leadership of a primary-care physician. The home must improve patient health and quality of care, and reduce costs by reducing utilization. Unfortunately, a patient's access to care is not restricted to the ACO and the patient has the option of seeking care from a provider or specialist outside of the ACO at any time. The goal of the primary provider is to persuade the patient to avoid care outside of the ACO. Payment systems for ACOs do not rely on fee-for-service but may utilize a variety of methodologies such as risk contracting, capitation (fee per patient per year), bundled payments, shared savings from pay for performance for providers, and direct employment of physicians. The expectation is the ACOs will save the federal government $940 million over four years.

Patient-Centered Medical Home

The concept of the patient-centered medical home (PCMH) was first introduced by the American Academy of Pediatrics in 1967 (Bates, 2009).

The American Academy of Family Physicians describes a patient centered medical home provides access to comprehensive integrated healthcare, focusing on quality and safety through ongoing relationships with medical professionals (Kahn, 2004).

The Agency for Healthcare Research and Quality (AHRQ) defines a medical home as a model that delivers five core care functions that are comprehensive, patient centered, coordinated, readily accessible, and committed to quality and safety (Anonymous, 2011).

Typically a PCMH has a fixed patient population based on a predetermined patient-to-physician ratio and includes the following personnel: physicians, physician assistants, nurse practitioners, nurses, medical assistants, and pharmacists. In some instances a physician specialist may be included such as internal medicine or cardiology. The role of the pharmacist includes assessment of medication needs, development of a comprehensive MTM, identification of medication-related problems, development of a care plan, and provision of follow-up recommendations. Patients identified for pharmacist interaction follow the MTMS criteria as stated previously or may include the following: patients on anticoagulation or insulin; patients who require post-discharge medication reconciliation; patients who need vaccination; or patients who need refill prescription authorization (Erickson, 2011).

The Patient-Centered Primary Care Collaborative summarized evidence from 33 PCMHs demonstrating improved quality and reduced health resource utilization for patients managed by a specific PCMH. The results include the following: hospital admission reduced from 3% to 40%; emergency room visits reduced from 12.4% to 50%; cost reductions varied from 5.5% to 34% or $640 per patient; and total savings amounted to $530 to $1364 per patient or $3.7 million in 2 years, a 9% savings (Nelson, 2014).

In the ACA of 2010, resources have been committed to the development of initiatives utilizing the PCMH concept. Step one was the awarding of state planning grants to develop strategies to coordinate patient-centered care between primary, acute, behavioral, and long-term care as well as test models to improve transitions of care for Medicare and Medicaid patients. Finally, grant money has been set aside to implement medication management services provided by licensed pharmacists as part of a collaborative, interdisciplinary, interprofessional approach to the treatment of chronic diseases for targeted patients. Since there are currently several sites where pharmacists are already practicing in a PCMH, the stage is set for there to be a transformation in pharmacy practice to provide patient-centered care.

Affordable Care Act and Value-Based Purchasing and Hospital Readmission Reduction Program

The ACA had two additional sections, Value-Based Purchasing (VBP) and Hospital Readmission Reduction Program (HRRP), that impact hospitals and pharmacy departments (Anonymous, 2012b) (Anonymous, 2013a). VBP rewards acute-care hospitals with incentive payments for quality of care provided to Medicare patients. Quality of care was defined initially with two domains—clinical process and patient experience of care—and adds two more domains by 2015—outcome and efficiency. Clinical processes include measures associated with acute myocardial infarction (timeliness of fibrinolytic therapy), heart failure (discharge instructions), pneumonia (timeliness of blood cultures), and surgical care improvement (timeliness of surgical prophylactic antibiotics). Patient experience includes patient satisfaction survey of the following: nurse communication, physician communication, hospital staff responsiveness, pain management, communication regarding medications, hospital cleanliness and quietness, discharge information, and overall hospital rating.

Outcome measures are associated with acute myocardial infarction, heart failure, pneumonia, patient complications, and central line bloodstream infections. The efficiency domain is based on expenditures per Medicare patient.

The HRRP reduces payments to hospitals with excessive 30-day readmissions in the following diseases: acute myocardial infarction, heart failure, and pneumonia. Future diseases include the addition of chronic obstructive pulmonary disease, elective total hip arthroplasty, and total knee arthroplasty.

The amount of payments earned or reduced is based on the hospital's baseline data and how well the hospital improves over the baseline data. In the beginning, as much as 2% of CMS payments to hospitals are at risk but will increase to as much as 6%.

The proposed changes in reimbursement to hospitals provide a wide variety of opportunities for hospital pharmacy practice. The clinical processes are involved with the appropriate use of medications and therefore involve pharmacy. Members of the pharmacy department should be involved with the assurance of achieving the process outcomes; collection and analysis of the data: and participation on interdisciplinary teams for the development of performance improvement activities related to improving the clinical processes.

The patient experience involves the patient answering a series of questions related to their hospital stay. At least one set of questions is associated with pharmacy practice. The communication regarding medications involves the education of patients regarding the indication for starting a new medication and the side effects. The hospital pharmacist can help with the education of patients either directly through patient counseling or providing teaching aids for nurses so they are able to communicate with the patient regarding their medication.

In reviewing the literature regarding reasons for 30-day hospital readmissions, at least 9% of the readmissions are related to medications, either due to side effects or poor adherence (Macantonio, 1999). Patients admitted with side effects were more likely to have not received patient or family education regarding medications and did not have a discharge medication list (Macantonio, 1999). Literature also states as many as 70% of all patients discharged have an error in their medication discharge list (Wong, 2008). Based on the literature, by changing hospital pharmacy practice to include patient education, and review of medication list on discharge, a reduction in 30-day readmissions may be achieved.

The ACA has the potential to improve patient outcomes and reduce Medicare expenditures. Additionally, the ACA has the potential to provide opportunities for changing pharmacy practice to include patient education and review of the medication discharge document. These activities move the pharmacist to the patient's bedside and form the foundation for providing pharmaceutical care.

HAVING AND FOLLOWING A PLAN FOR CLINICAL SERVICES: ACHIEVING EVIDENCE-BASED MEDICATION THERAPY AND SAFE THERAPY

In today's financial environment, the development of patient-centered clinical services is imperative. With the implementation of the ACA there will be changes in reimbursement and increased expectations in patient outcomes. The hospital environment will be changing and pharmacy must be ready to change in order to survive. The best way for a pharmacy department to survive is to develop a strategic plan that synergizes with the health system and meets the needs of the patients, physicians, and nurses. This plan should include the development and implementation of clinical services that address financial issues and patient-centered outcomes.

There are four stages involved with the development of a plan for clinical service: assessment of current clinical services, review of literature supporting clinical services, development of clinical services, and implementation of services.

The first step in developing a plan for clinical services is to make a complete assessment of the clinical services within the environment of the hospital. Initially, the current pharmacy practice model needs to be characterized as either centralized, specialized, or decentralized, or a mixture. Next, the performance of the pharmacists within the model needs to be assessed by reviewing the number and types of interventions as well as what type of direct patient care is currently being provided. Along with interventions, the overall productivity of the pharmacists needs to be evaluated. The productivity analysis should include all of the activities performed by the pharmacist, such as medication orders reviewed and processed, interventions, technician activities (dispensing cabinet stocking, delivery of medications, and medication cart checks), as well as listing of all daily activities completed by pharmacists during their work hours.

The next step is to evaluate the use of technology within the department and hospital that assists with the medication process. The final step is to evaluate the culture of the department and the culture of the physicians and nurses toward pharmacy. The following are a list of issues that need to be assessed within the department: are pharmacists engaged, do they talk to patients, is there a process for the growth and development of pharmacists? The list of issues that need to be assessed in understanding the external culture toward pharmacy includes the support of pharmacists by physicians and nurses, the function of the P&T committee, and the formulary process.

The next stage is to compile the evidence published in the literature and within the health system regarding clinical pharmacy services. A summary of the literature regarding clinical services should be compiled and include the impact of pharmacist interventions on avoidance of medication errors and adverse drug events as well as medication reconciliation on admission and discharge. Additionally, health system data regarding targeted patient outcomes such as most frequent diseases associated with readmission rates and readmission rates or patient outcomes associated with reductions in payments from payers should be assessed. Finally, net profits, capital expenditures, and the debt rating of the hospital need to be reviewed to assess the financial climate of the hospital or health system.

The third stage involves the development of clinical services. This stage must have a vision and clear description of activities and expectations. The most crucial element is to develop a mission statement and job descriptions with clear expectations for proposed clinical activities. The ideal process should include the pharmacists. There needs to be a clear understanding of the role, the work processes, and expectations. Additionally, metrics need to be developed to demonstrate the effectiveness of the clinical services. Unfortunately, there is no clear standardization of metrics for clinical services. Regardless, the department will need to develop metrics associated with the mission and expectations of the hospital. Some examples of possible metrics include number and type of pharmacist interventions (pharmacokinetic notes, renal dose adjustments, adverse drug reactions avoided, etc.), number of patients educated by pharmacists, number of medication reconciliations reviewed and modified, medication orders modified, drug costs avoided, time to verify medication orders, and turnaround time for medication deliveries.

The implementation stage may be the most difficult and depends on the scope of the clinical services. Implementation should include orientation and training of personnel involved in clinical services as well as time lines for implementation. In some cases a pilot may need to be developed and deployed. Regardless of the scope of the services, orientation includes learning about the hospital and pharmacy department, training pharmacists in the skills necessary to perform the clinical services, and deploying the infrastructure to support the clinical services. The orientation process may include knowledge of hospital and pharmacy policies and procedures, knowledge of hospital-wide technologies—tube delivery systems, physician order entry, paging and phone systems; knowledge of pharmacy practice within specific populations—oncology and chemotherapy ordering, transplant patients, intensive care patients, and operating room processes, and how the pharmacy department is organized and how it works.

Training of pharmacists may include how to talk to patients using the "teach-back method." It could also include training in pharmacokinetics, codes, processing of orders, pain management, preparation of sterile products, management of pharmacy technologies (medication dispensing cabinets, robot dispensing, computer order entry), and how to enter and record pharmacist interventions.

Deployment of infrastructure includes how technicians are integrated within the department to help facilitate clinical services. Working as a team, the department will need to break down the processes and activities and develop work plans for pharmacists and technicians. There will need to be clear expectations of roles and responsibilities.

After implementation, there needs to be ongoing monitoring and feedback to the pharmacists with regard to the clinical services. At least monthly, a list of interventions by pharmacists should be available, with a summary of type (pharmacokinetic dosing, adverse drug event avoided, drug-drug interaction avoided, and renal dose adjustments). Additionally, there needs to be ongoing shadowing and coaching by supervisors to assess the performance of the pharmacist.

MANAGING CLINICAL PRACTITIONERS

The management of clinical practitioners requires the combination of leadership and management skills and an understanding of their roles and abilities. As a leader and manager of clinical services you must be informed about your profession and connected to your employees and the work environment. As a leader you need to know what is going on in clinical pharmacy practice, healthcare, and management of pharmacy systems and personnel. This will involve reading articles, attending national, state, and local pharmacy association meetings, and constantly discussing the latest issues. You will need to constantly assess where your clinical services are in relation to the world of pharmacy. You will need to self-reflect on your services, to assure the performance of your personnel constantly improves.

As a manager, you need to have an understanding and inventory of the current status of your clinical services—from clinical data to patient issues and performance of the services to the relationship with nursing, physicians, and providers. You must understand the culture of the workforce and of the pharmacy department. There needs to be a clear understanding of performance expectations for clinicians and managers. Consequently, job descriptions need to have clear expectations and performance standards. You need to constantly monitor and provide feedback to personnel as well as discuss what they need on a daily basis to do their job. You will need to provide direction for professional development and encourage personnel to grow and develop through the department's career ladder.

The more involved you are with clinical practitioners, the more they will favorably respond. You will discover that the relationship is symbiotic—the more you depend on them, the more they depend on you. Consequently, the development and maintenance of clinical services is dependent on good leadership and management.

BIBLIOGRAPHY

Academy of Managed Care Pharmacy (AMCP). (2009, November). Drug Utilization Review. Retrieved November 26, 2013 from www.amcp.org: www.amcp.org/WorkArea/DownloadAsset.aspx?id=9296http://www.amcp.org/WorkArea/DownloadAsset.aspx?id=9296.

American Pharmacists Association and the National Association of Chain Drug Stores Foundation. (2008). Medication therapy managment in pharamcy practice: core elements of an MTM service model (version 2.0). *J Am Pharm Assoc,* 48(3): 341–353.

American Pharmacists Association, National Association of Chain Drug Stores Foundation. (2005). Medication therapy management in community pharmacy practice: core elements of an MTM service. Version 1. *J Am Pharm Assoc,* 45(5): 573–579.

American Society of Health-System Pharmacists. (1996). ASHP guidelines on a standardized method for pharmaceutical care. *Am J Health-Syst Pharm,* 53(14): 1713–1716.

American Society of Health-System Pharmacists. (1996). ASHP Guidelines on medication-use evaluation. *Am J Health-Syst Pharm,* 53(16): 1953–1955.

American Society of Health-System Pharmacists. (1993). ASHP Statement in pharmaceutical care. *Am J Hosp Pharm,* 50: 1720–1723.

American Society of Health-System Pharmacists. (2008). ASHP Statement on the pharmacy and therapeutics committee and the formulary system. *Am J Health-Syst Pharm,* 65(13): 1272–1283.

American Society of Health-System Pharmacists. (1996). ASHP guidelines on standardized method for pharmaceutical care. *Am J Health-Syst Pharm,* 53(14): 1713–1716.

Anonymous. (2012a, January). Approved: Updated Medication Selection Criteria for Hospitals. *Joint Commission Perspectives,* p. 9.

Anonymous. (2012b, August 1). Fact sheet: CMS makes changes to improve quality of care during hospital inpatient stays. Retrieved December 15, 2013, from www.cms.gov/apps/media/press/factsheet.asp?Counter=4422.

Anonymous. (2013a, August 2). Readmissions Reduction Program. Retrieved December 15, 2013, from www.cms.gov/Medicare/Medicare-Fee-for-Service-Payment/AcuteInpatientPPS/Readmissions-Reduction-Program.html.

Anonymous. (2011, October). Patient-Centered Medical Home Decisionmaker Brief. Ensuring that patient-centered medical homes effectively serve patients with complex health needs. Retrieved November 13, 2013, from http://pcmh.ahrq.gov/sites/default/files/attachments/Ensuring%20PCMHs%20Serve%20Pts%20with%20Complex%20Health%20Needs.pdf.

Anonymous. (2013b). Standards FAQ Details/Joint Commission. Retrieved August 21, 2013, from www.jointcommission.org/standards_information/jcfaqdetails.aspx?StandardsFAQId.

Aspden P. (2007). *Preventing medication errors: quality chasm series.* Washington DC: National Academies Press.

Bates D. (2009). Role of the pharmacist in the medical home. *Am J Health Syst Pharm*, 66(12): 1116–1118.

Bluml B. (2005). Definition of medication therapy management: development of profession-wide consensus. *J Am Pharm Assoc*, 45(5): 566–572.

Breland B. (2007). Believing what we know: pharmacy provides value. *Am J Health-Syst Pharm*, 64(12): 1284–1291.

Burns LR. (2012). Accountable care organizations may difficulty avoiding the failures of integrated care networks of the 1990s. *Health Affairs*, 31(11): 2407–2416.

Bush PW. (2010). Pharmacy practice model for academic medical centers. *Am J Health-Syst Pharm*, 67(21): 1856–1861.

Erickson S. (2011). A pharmacy's journey toward patient-centered medical home. *J Am Pharm Assoc*, 51(2): 156–160.

Flowers SK. (2013). Medication therapy management. In A.C. Pharmacy, *Updates in Therapeutics: The Ambulatory Care Pharmacy Preparatory Review and Recertification Course* (pp. 2-557-68). Chicago: ACCP.

Hepler CD. (1990). Opportunities and reponsibilities in pharmaceutical care. *Am J Hosp Pharm*, 47(3): 533–543.

Hoban R. (2013, December 24). North Carolina Health News. CMS announces six new N.C. accountable care organizations. Retrieved December 31, 2013, from www.northcarolina-healthnews.org/2013/12/24/cms-announces-six-new-n-c-accountable-care-organizations/.

Johnson JA. (1997). Drug related morbidity and mortality and the economic impact of pharmaceutical care. *Am J Health-Syst Pharm*, 54(5): 554–558.

Johnson JA. (1995). Drug-related morbidity and mortality: a cost-of-illness model. *Arch Intern Med*, 155(18): 1949–1956.

Joint Commission. (2012). The Joint Commission Edition. Retrieved March 16, 2012, from Joint Commission Resources: https://e-dition.jcinc/Chapters.aspx?C = 22.

Kahn N. (2004). The future of family medicine: a collaborative project of the family medicine community. *Ann Fam Med*, 2(suppl 1): S3-S32.

Kelly W. (2007). Pharmaceutical Care. In W. Kelly, *Pharmacy: what it is and how it works* (pp. 155–190). Boca Raton, FL: CRC Press.

Knoer SJ. (2010). Lessons learned from a pharmacy practice model change at an academic medical center. *Am J Health-Syst Pharm*, 67(21): 1862–1869.

Kohn LT. (2000). *To err is human: building a safer health system.* Washington, DC: National Academy Press.

Manasse H. (1989). Medication use in an imperfect world: drug misadventuring as an issue of public policy, Part 1. *Am J Hosp Pharm*, 46(5): 929–944.

Marcantonio ER. (1999). Factors associated with unplanned readmission among patients 65 years of age and older in a medicare managed care plan. *Am J Med*, 107(1): 13–17.

McGiveney MS. (2007). Medication therapy management: its relationship to patient counseling, disease management, and pharmaceutical care. *J Am Pharm Assoc*, 47(5): 620–628.

Nelson M. (2014, January). Patient-Centered Primary Care Collaborative. The patient-centered medical home's impact on cost and quality: an annual update of evidence, 2012–2013. Retrieved January 19, 2014, from www.pcpcc.org/sites/default/files/resources/4%20-%20Executive%20Summary%20and%20Evidence.pdf.

Pederson A. (2004). Pharmacy and Therapeutics Committee and Formulary Management. In Pederson AM, *Managing Pharmacy Practice: Principles, Strategies, and Systems* (pp. 183–192). Boca Raton, FL: CRC Press.

Pederson CS. (2010). ASHP national survey of pharmacy practice in hospital settings: monitoring and patient education—2009. *Am J Health-Syst Pharm*, 67(7): 542–558.

Pickett SG. (2010). Implementation of a standard pharmacy clinical practice model in a multihospital system. *Am J Health-Syst Pharm*, 67(9): 751–756.

Shane R. (2011). Critical requirements for health-system pharmacy practice models that achieve optimal use of medications. *Am J Health-Syst Pharm*, 68(3): 1101–1111.

Strand LM. (1990). Integrated patient-specific model of pharmacy practice. *Am J Health-Syst Pharm*, 47(3): 550–554.

Strand L. (1997). Pharmaceutical care: the Minnesota model. *Pharm J*, 258(6): 899–904.

Sullivan SD. (1990). Noncompliance with medication regimens and subsequent hospitalization: a literature analysis and cost of hospitalization estimate. *J Res Pharm Econ*, 2(1): 19–33.

Weant KA. (2011). Alternative pharmacy practice model. *Am J Health-Syst Pharm*, 68(15): 1395–1396.

Wong JD. (2008). Medication reconciliation at hospital discharge: evaluating discrepancies. *Ann Pharmacother*, 42(10): 1373–1379.

Woods TM. (2011). Making a case for a patient-centered integrated pharmacy practice model. *Am J Health-Syst Pharm*, 68(3): 259–263.

12 Marketing the Pharmacy

Melanie Oates

CONTENTS

Learning Objectives: After reading this chapter and working through the case, the reader will be able to:

1. Describe the role and importance of marketing in a twenty-first-century retail pharmacy
2. Analyze the environmental factors impacting the market for a pharmacy

3. Describe the elements of the marketing mix
4. Develop a marketing strategy for a retail store

INTRODUCTION TO PHARMACY MARKETING

In the twenty-first century, pharmacy customers enjoy the choice to shop in a traditional community pharmacy, a national or local chain pharmacy, a supermarket pharmacy, a mail-order pharmacy, an online pharmacy, or even an outpatient pharmacy associated with a hospital. For many consumers, the convenience of the corner store is giving way to the greater convenience of the lounge chair and the iPad. The loyalty of customers and patients cannot be taken for granted in an ever-more sophisticated retail environment. For pharmacy managers, this means that marketing is growing in importance. If a pharmacy is to succeed, potential customers must know that the store will meet their needs better than the other retail options available to them. This chapter introduces the basic concepts of marketing and offers pragmatic examples of marketing in a pharmacy environment. Examples refer to retail pharmacy as well as to the pharmaceutical industry.

IMS data analyzed by the Drug Channels Institute indicate that in 2012, chain drugstores and mass merchants with pharmacy departments accounted for more than half of all the prescriptions distributed in the United States, while mail-order pharmacies filled over 18% of prescriptions.[1] The diversity of the retail pharmacy market can be seen in Figure 12.1. The Drug Channels Institute also analyzed the market share of the largest US pharmacies by prescription revenue.[2]

In the diverse and competitive environment of the twenty-first-century retail pharmacy, the techniques of marketing are vital elements of any leader's management tool kit. Modern marketing aims to provide the right product to the right consumer for the right price at the right time and in the right place. Marketing is often misunderstood as merely advertising, or as sales pitches reminiscent of the days of the "traveling medicine show." This hard-sell approach, known as the *sales concept*, was prominent in early twentieth-century retailing. Sellers positioned themselves in opposition to customers, who were to be convinced to buy whatever the seller had to offer. As the market environment became more competitive in the middle of the twentieth century, a new approach, the *marketing concept*, evolved. According to the marketing concept, the marketer and the customer are partners in creating an exchange of value. Marketers seek guidance from consumers to design and provide products that meet the expressed needs and wants of customers. Marketing transactions involve an *exchange* between two or more parties. Each party gives up something and expects to receive something of value in return. The purpose of marketing is to facilitate a voluntary exchange that benefits both the seller and the customer.

The American Marketing Association defines *marketing* as "the activity, set of institutions, and processes for creating, communicating, delivering, and executing offerings that have value for customers, clients, partners, and society at large."[3]

The concept of value is central to marketing. People do not buy products; they buy benefits. Purchasers attempt to maximize the value of the benefit that they receive

Number of Prescriptions by Dispensing Format, 2011 vs. 2012

	Prescriptions (millions)			Share of Prescriptions		
Dispensing Format	2011	2012	% Change	2011	2012	Change
Chain Stores[1]	2,213	2,230	+0.8%	52.4%	52.2%	−23 b.p.
Independent Drugstores	741	739	−0.3%	17.6%	17.3%	−26 b.p.
Supermarkets with Pharmacies	484	514	+6.2%	11.5%	12.0%	+57 b.p.
Mail Pharmacies[2]	783	789	+0.8%	18.6%	18.5%	−8 b.p.
Total	4,221	4,272	+1.2%	100.0%	100.0%	

1. Chain stores includes chain drugstores and mass merchants with pharmacies.
2. Prescription data for mail pharmacies show Equivalent Scripts (Actual Scripts x 3)
Totals may not sum due to rounding.
b.p. = Basis Point (one hundredth of one percent; 0.01%)
Source: IMS Health, May 2013.

Published on Drug Channels (http:/www.DrugChannels.net) on May 14, 2013

DRUG CHANNELS
INSTITUTE

FIGURE 12.1 Diversity of the retail pharmacy market.

relative to the value of whatever they must trade in order to obtain the benefit. Value is personal, however. The value of a benefit or the cost of an exchange to one consumer may be more or less than the value of the same benefit or exchange to a different consumer. For example, a socially conscious teenager may place more value on a brand that displays a conspicuous status symbol than would a more secure adult. A very busy professional may place more value on the time required to negotiate a purchase than would a retired person.

Marketing is best understood as *communication*. Today's marketer attempts to convey the features and benefits of the product to a carefully targeted audience of potential consumers. The tools of successful communication, such as social media, face-to-face customer counseling, special events, and press releases are integrated with advertising and sales promotion to create a cohesive product message. The heart of the message should be the benefit that the product will offer to the customer. Good marketing communication should be two-way communication, seeking feedback from the customer. Feedback allows collaboration between the seller and the customer.

MARKETING MIX AND THE 4 PS

Since it was introduced by Harvard Business School Professor Neil H. Borden in the 1960s,[4] managers have used the *4 Ps model* to organize marketing campaigns. Product, Price, Place, and Promotion, "the 4 Ps" are known as the marketing mix. The marketing mix is the basis for planning the strategies and tactics that marketers use to promote retail establishments, products, services, and ideas.

PRODUCT

Product is the first, and perhaps the most important, element of the marketing mix. Without a product, no exchange is possible. *Product offerings* include actual physical products, as well as services and ideas. Physical products are the items that the retail store stocks or offers, such as drug products, medical devices, and sundries. Blood pressure screening, diabetes monitoring, and weight loss counseling are examples of services that could be marketed as products. The retail establishment, whether it is a brick-and-mortar store, an Internet retailer ("e-tailer") or an outpatient pharmacy inside a hospital, is also a product. The drug products marketed by a pharmaceutical manufacturing company are product offerings. Ideas can also be marketed. The national campaign to encourage young people to avoid smoking is an example of the marketing of an idea.

Total Product Offering

Total product offering includes all of the aspects of the product that the customer may consider when he or she makes a purchase decision. Consumers and sellers may have different perspectives about what constitutes a "product." Sellers tend to focus on the *actual product*, the observable features such as size, shape, color, dosage, side effects, taste, and so on.

However, the *actual product* is only one aspect of the total product offering. Consumers and patients look for the value of the product, which mainly comes from the outcomes and benefits derived from the purchase. Benefits constitute the *core product*.

Some product benefits that may interest customers are as discussed below.

Outcomes: Does the Product Meet the Customer's Perceived Need?

From the perspective of the consumer, a product is purchased in order to meet needs. If no need is perceived, the customer is not motivated to purchase or consume a product. For example, a head cold can cause inconvenience or discomfort to the patient, who is motivated to find a product to relieve symptoms. In contrast, essential hypertension may be asymptomatic, and the patient may be less likely to comply with medication regimens. The underlying need for the hypertension patient, therefore, will not be symptom relief. Clinical parameters may not motivate that patient. The product must fill a need that the patient will understand as a *benefit*. Since blood pressure control may promote survival, the marketer might associate the medication with a benefit that the target consumer values (such as living to see one's children marry). A key marketing principle is to promote the product benefits from the customer's perspective, rather than simply to describe the product features. Any feature should always be paired with a customer benefit. For example, "The Greenville Pharmacy offers a refill reminder service, which means that you will never have to worry about forgetting your prescription."

Compatibility: Does the Product Fit with the Consumer's Lifestyle?

A recent public TV lecture by a popular nutritionist suggested that her viewers eliminate all sugar, corn, milk, eggs, and grains from their diet. A collective gasp could be heard from the audience, who winced at a diet that forbids most of their usual foods. It would be difficult for most persons to sustain a diet that radically alters their customary behaviors. Similarly, a drug product that interferes with a person's usual activities (such as an antibiotic that interacts with a patient's preferred breakfast juice) will not be well accepted. A business establishment that is not open at the hours when customers prefer to shop will be less attractive than an establishment that caters to customer time constraints.

Convenience: Is the Product Easy to Use? Is the Product/Business Easy to Access?

Patients sometimes complain that childproof containers are also often "adult proof," particularly if the adult suffers from arthritis or other disabilities. Some major over-the-counter (OTC) analgesic brands have addressed this problem by creating easy-to-open containers intended for homes with older adults. Ease of use can include clear directions, easy-to-read labels, and well-written patient package inserts. As the large Baby Boom generation ages, the need for packaging designed for aging eyes and stiff hands will grow.

A retail business is a product that customers will evaluate for ease of access. If the store is a "brick-and-mortar" establishment, proximity to public transportation and/or convenient parking may be a benefit that attracts business. An online business with a difficult-to-navigate website is likely to lose customers before orders are placed. Payment options that include the customer's preferred credit cards and accept the customer's insurance provider are also convenience benefits.

Social Impact: Does the Product Offer Prestige to the Customer Or Does the Product Embarrass the Customer?

Customers will sometimes purchase a product for the social benefit of the product, rather than for the physical features of the product. Consumers sometimes purchase fashionable but uncomfortable shoes, expensive name-brand jackets that are no warmer than an off-brand substitute, or a "real" ruby rather than a man-made synthetic that is identical in chemical composition and superior in appearance. These purchases offer benefits that are not directly linked to the basic physical features of the product. Patients are sometimes noncompliant with medications because of embarrassment. For example, a young person may be reluctant to use an asthma inhaler in public.

Emotional Impact: Does the Product Have an Emotional Attraction to the buyer?

Breck shampoo recently ran a marketing campaign targeting Baby Boomers who might feel nostalgia for a brand they used as young children. Television advertisements seeking donations to animal rescue operations routinely play upon the emotions of animal lovers.

In addition to the *actual product* (observable features) and the *core product* (benefits), the *total product offering* includes any added services or incentives that accompany the purchase. For example, an inhaled steroid prescription might add a free extender for the patient's inhaler, or the package for a hair-care product might include a link to an Internet site for styling tips. A retail pharmacy might offer free delivery for prescriptions. These additions constitute the *augmented product*. To offer the best value to customers in a highly competitive retail environment, product designers must consider all three levels of the total product offering and focus on benefits that fill the expressed needs of the targeted consumer audience.

PRICE

Price, the second "P" of the classic marketing mix, is arguably the most misunderstood element. A purchase involves the exchange of more than simply currency. Anything that the customer must give up, or that the customer must invest, is a cost. In addition to the currency price of the product, costs to the customer include the time needed to buy the product, the effort required to access the product, the effort required to understand the product, any inconvenience in the purchase process, any embarrassment in the purchase process or in the use of the product, and any other time or effort "exchange" required for the purchase. As the popularity of processed food and prepackaged food demonstrates, customers are sometimes willing to pay a higher monetary price to avoid the costs of inconvenience.

Cost-Based Pricing

Retailers often set monetary prices using simple formulae based upon profit goals. This is particularly likely when the retailer offers many products, such as sundries in a pharmacy. Cost-based pricing is appropriate when there is little or no competition, or when competitors' prices for competing products are similar. The most common form of cost-based pricing used by retailers is markup pricing.[5] The formula for markup pricing is:

$$Price = (Cost\ of\ product\ to\ retailer)*(1\text{-}desired\ markup\ percentage)$$

The markup percentage is determined by local competitive practices, target profit margins, and the desired rate of inventory turnover. Third-party payer agreements and government regulations may also dictate price decisions.

Demand-Based Pricing

Cost-based pricing, however, may be naïve in highly competitive markets. If a marketer is attempting to penetrate a category dominated by another seller, or if a marketer is trying to establish a market leadership position, demand-based pricing strategies are appropriate. Demand-based pricing strategies consider the customers' reactions to the price, and the impact of price on purchase volume.

PLACE

Place, also called distribution, is the third "P" of the marketing mix. Place decisions impact the customers' access to the product. Place decisions involve the selection of the location for a retail outlet as well as the design of the physical layout of the store.

Market-related factors influencing store location decisions include population size and trends (Can the population support another pharmacy outlet?); proximity to other similar retail outlets (How successful are the other local outlets?); travel logistics that influence customers' likelihood to patronize the retail facility (Is the location near a highway? Will the facility be easy for customers to locate?); perceived safety of the location (Will customers be afraid to shop here?); proximity to health-care institutions and clinics; and proximity to other shopping outlets (Will it be convenient for customers to shop at the pharmacy when they are doing other errands?). Store layout should make it easy for customers to locate familiar brands such as cough and cold products and to access the prescription area. A private area for customer counseling is desirable. Pharmaceutical companies must decide which type of retail outlet will carry their products. For example, the brand manager may decide that health food stores may not be appropriate outlets for the OTC products of that company.

PROMOTION

The fourth "P" of the classic marketing mix is *promotion*. Promotion is a broad term for a number of marketing communication tools including advertising, sales promotion, personal selling, and publicity.

Advertising

Advertising is marketer-sponsored, non-personal communication. Promotional messages are conveyed to selected target audiences using mass media such as television, radio, newspapers, magazines and journals, billboards, smartphone text messages, Internet pop-up ads, and other mass media techniques. The timing and media for an advertising message are controlled by the marketer, who pays for exposure in target venues. Advertising tends to have a lag effect; that is, it may take several months before the sales impact of advertising is measurable. Similarly, it may take several months before the negative impact of ceasing to advertise is felt.

Sales Promotion

Sales *promotion* includes promotional items such as free goods and special incentives (such as coffee mugs), as well as couponing, contests and sweepstakes, price-off deals, event marketing, sampling, and trade show exhibits. Sales promotion is usually intended to stimulate an immediate buyer response, and leads to a short-term increase in sales.

Personal Selling

Personal selling traditionally involves face-to-face contact between the sales representative and the potential customer. The scope of sales activities has grown with the Internet. Customer service representatives may handle buyer inquiries online using text chat or VOIP (Voice Over Internet Protocol) with programs such as Skype. Webcams can allow the representative to offer a "face-to-face" sales presentation despite differences in location or time zone. Personal selling enhances the marketing program by focusing on the immediate and long-term needs of buyers.

Publicity

Publicity is non-marketer-sponsored, non-personal communication. Publicity may be either positive or negative as news items (and even rumors) are published in mass media. The marketer cannot control the timing, media, message, or audience for news reports. However, businesses may influence the news cycle by proactively releasing their own data and publicizing their perspectives on important news developments. Many businesses employ public relations firms or use internal public relations departments as a way to manage publicity. Tools used in public relations include press releases and press packets, video news releases, special events, and press conferences.

UNDERSTANDING THE MARKETING ENVIRONMENT

A business that follows the *marketing concept* is customer centered. In order to serve the needs of customers, marketers must understand their customers. In addition, marketers must understand the environment in which they and their customers operate. Marketing in the twenty-first century is data driven. Thorough research into market dynamics is needed before any promotional strategies or tactics can be implemented.

MARKETING RESEARCH

The American Marketing Association defines marketing research as "the function that links the consumer, customer, and public to the marketer through information—information used to identify and define marketing opportunities and problems; generate, refine and evaluate marketing actions; monitor marketing performance; and improve understanding of marketing as a process. Marketing research specifies the information required to address these issues, designs the method for collecting information, manages and implements the data collection process, analyzes the results, and communicates the findings and their implications."[3]

Many of the same research methods that inform clinical decisions are also applicable to marketing decisions. Marketing research methods may be divided into two broad categories: secondary market research and primary market research.

Secondary Market Research

Secondary market research uses data that were gathered and recorded for some other purpose, and analyzes that data to answer new questions. Secondary research is growing in importance as the Internet offers increasing access to corporate data, sales data, and customer analyses. In today's data-rich environment, many marketing questions can be answered with the use of secondary data. For example, a retail pharmacist may wish to know more about the local competitive landscape. A search of the Internet can reveal lists of competing stores, links to advertising and websites from those stores, and news articles relating to the local pharmacy market. This type of information is usually available at no cost. Extensive reports on major markets are also available for purchase at the websites of commercial marketing research firms. Pharmaceutical manufacturing companies make extensive use of secondary data available from sources such as IMS.

Secondary sources available online include press releases, annual reports from companies (typically available on the organizations' websites), government websites (useful for updates on regulatory issues), trade and professional websites such as NACDS (www.nacds.org), and expert or academic websites and blogs. One of the most helpful expert blogs is *Drug Channels* (www.drugchannels.net), written by economics professional Adam J. Fein, president of Pembroke Consulting.

Primary Market Research

Primary market research uses data gathered from original sources with studies specifically designed to answer the marketer's questions. Primary research may be qualitative or quantitative.

Qualitative Research

Qualitative research uses small sample sizes (less than 30) that do not provide statistically significant results. The techniques of qualitative research include *depth interviews* (one-on-one structured conversations that explore the issues and uncover the terminology used by the customer) and *focus groups* (guided group discussions with 6 to 10 respondents). Qualitative studies are usually less time consuming and less expensive than quantitative research. Although qualitative research does not offer generalizable results, it can give insight into market directions and identify the issues that are important to customers. Most marketing research projects begin with a qualitative phase to clarify issues and to understand the terminology used by the target audience.

Quantitative Research

Quantitative research uses larger sample sizes (more than 30) that can provide generalizable, statistically significant results. A major tool of quantitative research is the survey. Surveys today are often administered in person, via the mail, online through e-mail or a website, through a text message or smartphone application, or as an inclusion in a product package. In the past, fax transmission was used to administer surveys. Good survey design involves careful attention to the structure of questions to avoid bias, ambiguity, and false information. Ideally, a random sample design should be fielded. In practice, however, convenience samples are often used by retailers and smaller marketers. A convenience sample is collected from respondents who are easily accessed by the researcher. For example, a retailer might distribute a survey to customers who visit the store on a given Monday. Although convenience samples are not strictly generalizable, a well-designed convenience sample may be adequate to address the retailer's questions. The design and administration of a valid survey instrument require expertise in the discipline of marketing research. Pharmacy managers who do not wish to incur the expense of a marketing research consultant might consider seeking assistance from a local college or university. Consulting teams of marketing students are often available for experiential projects in the field.

Test marketing is a quantitative marketing research technique used by larger marketers prior to the launch of a new product or a new marketing campaign for an existing product. Test marketing employs an experimental research design to forecast the sales potential for a new product or to evaluate the relative sales impact of different promotional tactics. A test market should reflect the actual level of promotional activity that will be undertaken nationally.

For example, a large chain drugstore company may wish to evaluate the market potential for in-store primary-care clinics prior to instituting a national rollout. Good test market locations should be relatively self-contained SMSAs (standard metropolitan statistical areas) with populations similar to national demographics. The chain drugstore company, therefore, might choose to test the in-store clinic idea in Indianapolis and Pittsburgh (Midwest cities with relatively self-contained economic environments). The chain might evaluate the effectiveness of TV advertising in one city compared to radio or newspaper insert advertising in the other city. Product design options, such as hours/days of operation, might be compared between the two cities. Results of the test market can be used to help the chain make cost-effective marketing decisions for the new product.

ENVIRONMENTAL ANALYSIS

Marketing research results provide the data for customer analysis and environmental analysis. The marketing environment consists of the macroenvironment (external factors) and the microenvironment (internal business factors).

Macroenvironmental Factors

The external environment incorporates economic factors, legal and regulatory factors, social and cultural factors, technological factors, and competitive factors.[6] Depending upon the scope of the business, these factors may be analyzed at the local, regional, national, or global level. A community pharmacy may be most impacted by events at the local level, whereas a national chain pharmacy will monitor environmental changes at the national level. In today's mass communication environment, however, national or even global events may impact local retailers. For example, a 2012 news report of contaminated injectable steroids from a New England compounding pharmacy made national headlines and was featured on network television evening news. This means that consumers all over the nation were made aware of the problem. Awareness of the risk of contamination could impact the business of any compounding pharmacy.

Economic Factors

Economic factors of interest to pharmacy managers include unemployment trends, income trends, and trends in third-party reimbursement for health care. Before the 2014 implementation of the Affordable Care Act, unemployment leading to loss of health insurance could lead to noncompliance with expensive health-care regimens. In addition, unemployment reduces disposable income and may impact sales of non-essential retail sundries.

Changes in the *legal and regulatory environment* may impact the cost of doing business as a pharmacy. Additional personnel or additional hours of work may be needed to comply with required paperwork. The enactment of the Affordable Care Act will impact pharmacy at all levels and may be particularly relevant to the pharmaceutical manufacturing sector. Demand for prescription drugs may increase as the customer base of insured patients expands.

Social and Cultural Factors

Social and cultural factors can influence the choice of products and services offered by a pharmacy. For example, a pharmacy manager may have to consider cultural and religious factors when deciding to carry or promote contraceptive products or tobacco products. In addition, cultural factors can influence the decision of store hours and days of operation.

Technological Factors

Technological factors such as the growth of social media and the prevalence of smartphones among the pharmacy customers will influence the manager's choice of marketing communication media.

Competitive Factors

Competitive factors include the proximity of other retail pharmacy outlets as well as the availability of mail-order and online pharmacy sources. Pharmacy managers should analyze any changes in customer purchase patterns. Is the pharmacy gaining or losing business to other local pharmacy outlets or to mail-order or Internet sources? What is the prescription market share for the business? What are the local competitors' strengths and weaknesses?

Microenvironmental Factors

Pharmacy managers must also conduct an objective assessment of the capabilities of their own pharmacy. An otherwise outstanding marketing plan will fail if the business does not have the financial strength or the organizational capability to implement the plan. For example, a $3 million Superbowl advertisement would reach millions of potential customers for an online pharmacy but would be financially impossible for many small businesses. The revenues from a growth strategy that would increase daily prescription volume must be compared to the costs of hiring additional pharmacists to fill those prescriptions.

SWOT Analysis

The last step in environmental analysis is to summarize the data in the form of a *SWOT table* (strengths, weaknesses, opportunities, and threats).

Strengths

Positive factors, internal to the business, can contribute to the success of the marketing campaign. Examples are: Greenstreet Pharmacy is a well-respected community institution with a strong base of local support. Galant Pharmaceuticals Company, Inc. has a strong management team with a CEO who has 25 years of experience in pharmaceutical manufacturing.

Weaknesses

Negative factors, internal to the business, may hinder the success of the marketing campaign. Examples are: Greenstreet Pharmacy does not provide parking for patrons. Galant Pharmaceuticals Company, Inc. does not own a manufacturing facility.

TABLE 12.1

Strengths, Weaknesses, Opportunities, and Threats (SWOT)

Internal	External
Strengths	**Opportunities**
Respected in community	New pediatric clinic may bring patients
Strong customer loyalty	Lower unemployment may bring business
Good relationships with physicians	
Weaknesses	**Threats**
Poor parking discourages business	CVS is opening an outlet within one block
No pharmacist coverage on Sundays	

Opportunities

Developments or factors in the external environment may have a positive impact on the success of the business. For example: A new pediatric clinic will open one block from Greenstreet Pharmacy in September 2014; additional prescriptions from newly insured patients under the Affordable Care Act may increase demand for drug products marketed by Galant Pharmaceuticals.

Threats

Developments or factors in the external environment may have a negative impact on the business. Examples are: CVS plans to open a pharmacy next door to the new pediatric clinic; Galant Pharmaceuticals' leading brand may be challenged by a new market entry from competitor AstraZeneca.

Firms seek to capitalize on strengths, minimize weaknesses, exploit opportunities, and avoid or negate threats. An example of a SWOT table for a retail community pharmacy is shown in Table 12.1.

CUSTOMER RELATIONSHIP MANAGEMENT

The popularity of the Internet, the increasing power and affordability of small computers, and the development of user-friendly database programs have allowed the marketing concept to enter a new phase known as relationship marketing or customer relationship management (CRM). CRM relies upon sophisticated databases to collect, store, and organize customer data. Unlike statistical programs that summarize and aggregate data, CRM programs report customer information at a granular, individual level. This allows the marketer to design product offerings, create promotions, and target marketing messages to the specific needs and preferences of individual customers. Large mass marketers such as Amazon.com can now offer individualized service that rivals the personalized attention of an old-fashioned neighborhood shop. Increasingly sophisticated customer service enhances customer satisfaction and promotes customer loyalty and retention.

Ideally, a marketer should know "everything" about the customer. The better a marketer knows a customer, the more likely it is that the marketer can meet the needs of the customer. Companies with active CRM programs will often share customer data throughout the company in order to facilitate customer relationship building by all employees. In a health care market, however, privacy needs must also be respected. In general, no health information should be collected, retained, or shared without a specific health care related need for the data. Nevertheless, customer data not protected by the laws governing medical privacy (Health Insurance Portability and Affordability Act, HIPAA) can and should be collected and shared within a retail business that practices CRM. For example, knowing the customer's favorite brand of shampoo, favorite color, and children's names can help retail clerks build relationships with customers leading to loyalty and repeat purchasing behavior. Pharmaceutical manufacturing companies develop extensive databases on prescribing physicians.

DEVELOPING A MARKETING STRATEGY

MARKET SEGMENTATION

Analysis of environmental data and customer information allows a marketer to develop effective strategies to reach company goals. The first step in strategic market planning is market segmentation. Market segmentation is the process of dividing the heterogeneous mass market into subsets (segments) of homogeneous consumers who share similar characteristics, wants, needs, and media preferences. Market segmentation can improve the efficiency and cost-effectiveness of the marketing effort. Companies or retailers can match their product offerings to the particular needs and wants of selected market segments, thereby increasing customer satisfaction. Marketing communication is more cost effective when customers' preferred media are employed. For example, a late-night television advertisement, while inexpensive, would be ineffective if the target patient audience preferred to view streaming videos on their computers.

The *segmentation bases* used to divide markets into identifiable homogeneous segments include the following:

Demographic: Consumers and patients may be grouped based upon age, gender, education, occupation, race, or ethnicity. For example, a health-care provider may choose to create marketing and product development efforts targeting to women's health care.

Geographic: Segments may be created according to the location of customers.

Behavioristic: Customers may be grouped according to their buying habits. A business may choose to target large volume purchasers, such as with a "frequent buyer" program.

Psychographic: Consumers may be grouped according to social class, personality, lifestyle, activities, and interests. For example, a retail pharmacy chain could target working mothers, who need ready access to children's products and who require evening and weekend hours of operation.

MARKET SEGMENT TARGET SELECTION

After the consumer market has been divided into segments, marketers must select which segment or segments to target. It may be financially and operationally undesirable to attempt to reach all consumers in a mass market. An attractive customer segment should be

1. Large enough to meet the revenue goals of the business
2. Identifiable—can be differentiated clearly from other consumer groups
3. Accessible—the business is able to communicate with the segment and the segment is able to locate and interact with the business
4. Operational—the business has the capacity to sell to this segment, to compete effectively for the segment business, and to offer the products that appeal to this segment

Most retailers pursue a *multisegment strategy*; that is, they target two or more segments that are attractive and profitable. Some marketers choose to focus on only one segment for a *single-segment strategy*. A subset of the single-segment strategy is the *niche segment strategy*, in which a marketer focuses efforts on a small subsegment of consumers. For example, a health-care provider might choose to serve patients with an orphan disease such as scleroderma. A newer strategic option, the *mass-customization strategy*, has become viable due to Internet marketing and CRM database development. Marketers using mass-customization treat each customer as an individual "niche" by designing product offerings and marketing communication tactics tailored to that customer. For example, Amazon.com creates customer-centric home pages for each consumer, highlighting that customer's favorite authors and suggesting products that match the customer's profile of preferences.

MARKETING PLAN

A *marketing plan* should be written for the retail establishment as well as for any major products/services that the retailer expects to promote. A marketing plan is a written document that guides the implementation of marketing programs and resource allocations for a product, service, or retail establishment during a specified planning period.

Formal planning is important for several reasons:

A plan facilitates systematic thinking by management.

A formal plan helps management anticipate future events.

A written plan allows managers to coordinate the activities of all parties involved in the marketing and sales of the product.

A written plan facilitates objective evaluation of the success or failure of marketing tactics, allowing better performance control.

Marketing plans are usually updated annually, in contrast to *strategic planning* (producing a business plan for the enterprise as a whole), which is usually undertaken on a three- to five-year basis. The marketing plan describes the market environment, provides the data needed to make effective promotional decisions, sets goals and objectives for the sales efforts of the business, and specifies the strategies and tactics intended to meet those objectives.

The marketing plan acts as a road map. It helps managers plan for resource allocation and stimulates thinking, leading to better use of resources. The marketing plan also assigns responsibilities for task completion, thereby facilitating performance evaluation. Finally, the marketing plan enhances managers' awareness of problems, opportunities, and threats in the market environment. Table 12.2 offers a commonly used format for a marketing plan.

The standard planning framework addresses a series of questions:

1. Where are we now? (situation analysis)
2. Where do we want to be? (goals and objectives)
3. What is the best route to our desired goal? (strategies)
4. What are the specific actions that we need to take? (tactics)
5. How do we know if we are succeeding? (monitors and controls)
6. What do we do if something changes? (contingency plans)

The *executive summary* is an abstract of the entire marketing plan. It is usually one to five pages in length. It should contain summaries of all relevant environmental data, marketing objectives, strategies, tactics, and financial projections.

The *situation analysis* contains the relevant results of the environmental analysis, category analysis, competitor analysis, and customer analysis. The components of the environmental analysis were discussed earlier in this chapter. The category analysis reveals the growth or decline of the category as a whole. In the pharmacy market, the relative market share for independent pharmacies, chain pharmacies, and other pharmacy

---

TABLE 12.2
Outline of a Marketing Plan

1. Executive summary
2. Situation analysis
   a. Environmental analysis
      i. Macroenvironment
      ii. Microenvironment
   b. Category/competitor analysis
      i. Category analysis
      ii. Competitor analysis
   c. Customer analysis
   d. Planning assumptions
3. Objectives
4. Product/brand strategies
5. Tactics and marketing programs
6. Financial documents
7. Monitors and controls
8. Contingency plans

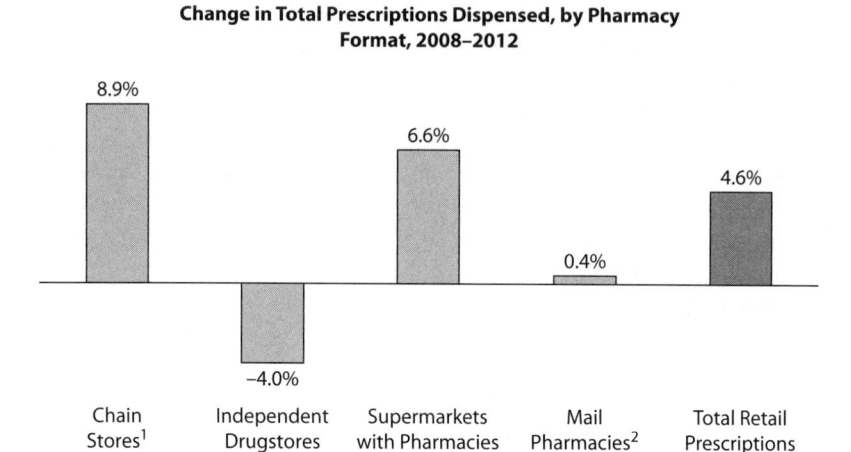

FIGURE 12.2   Changes in dispensed prescriptions by pharmacy format.

outlets should be covered. Marketers should examine the growth or decline of their own businesses within the context of the category as a whole. The Drug Channels Institute published data (Figure 12.2) showing that total prescriptions dispensed by chain pharmacies grew by 8.9% from 2008 to 2012, whereas total prescriptions dispensed by independent pharmacies fell by 4.0% during the same period.[1] These data suggest that an independent retail pharmacy that has shown a prescription decline of less than 4% since 2008 is actually performing better than the category as a whole.

The situation analysis also examines the target customers for the business. The analysis should include a review of the customer:

Demographics (age, gender, ethnicity)
Sociocultural factors (religion, social class, language)
Income and economic factors (employment, insurance coverage)
Geographic factors (distance from the business, neighborhood characteristics)

The third main section of the marketing plan details the marketing *goals and objectives* for the product. Goals are general outcomes such as "become the most respected pharmacy in town." Objectives describe the specific, measurable outcomes that will lead to the achievement of the goals. From a business perspective, a good objective is "SMART":

S: specific (not abstract)
M: measurable (the planner measures if it is met)
A: actionable (the planner can influence the outcome)

R: realistic (the objective is possible to achieve)
T: time bound (a time frame for completion)

An example of a pharmacy business objective is as follows: "Achieve a volume of 200 filled prescriptions per day by May 1, 2014." SMART objectives become the basis for outcome evaluation of the marketing plan.

The fourth and fifth sections of the plan describe the *strategies and tactics* that the marketer will use to promote the product. Strategies are the broad approaches designed to lead to a realization of the objectives in the previous section. Therefore every strategy must be referred to an identified objective that it supports. Tactics are the marketing activities that the marketer plans to pursue. Each tactic must be described in detail: when it will be enacted, where it will be enacted (such as the media selected for an advertising program), and what it will cost.

PHARMACIST AS HEALTH LEADER: SOCIAL MARKETING

The concerns of the pharmacy profession extend beyond filling prescriptions. As health-care professionals, pharmacists embrace the concept of *pharmaceutical care*, taking responsibility for treatment outcomes and not merely for the provision of drug products. Positive treatment outcomes require compliance with recommendations for healthy behaviors. Pharmacists may take leadership in promoting the healthy behaviors that lead to positive outcomes and to improved quality of life. This is the realm of *social marketing*, a practice that employs traditional marketing tools to influence behaviors for the good of the community.

Philip Kotler, a leader in marketing education, has defined social marketing as "the use of marketing principles and techniques to influence a target audience to voluntarily accept, reject, modify, or abandon a behavior for the benefit of individuals, groups, or society as a whole."[7]

Social marketing employs all of the tools of commercial marketing but with the intention of changing behavior for the good of society rather than making monetary profit. Social marketing for health-related behavior does not focus on whether a clinically undesirable behavior is "good" or "bad." Instead, a social marketer tries to discover what perceived benefits motivate the behavior. If patients or consumers change their behavior, they are losing whatever benefit motivates them to perform the undesirable behavior. For example, an overweight patient who gives up carbohydrates may lose the emotional comfort of eating her favorite foods. A smoker who enjoyed a social break with "smoking buddies" will not only suffer the effects of nicotine withdrawal if he quits smoking, but may also find himself isolated from his friends. The social marketer facilitates an exchange in which the target consumer receives a perceived benefit that outweighs the perceived benefit of the clinically undesirable behavior. It is important to recognize that consumers may value an immediate non-health benefit more than they value a health benefit in the future.

To offer a desirable benefit to the target consumer or patient, the social marketer must understand what it is that the target values. For example, teenagers may not value the increased chance of avoiding cancer in 50 years if they quit smoking today. However, an adolescent may be motivated by social attractiveness. Positioning nonsmoking as socially attractive (improved breath, better athletic performance) may be more motivating than positioning smoking as "bad" or "unhealthy."

The marketer should target a patient segment who will respond to the social marketing effort. Ideally, this means that the target segment should be:

Vulnerable to the health effects of the behavior
Unserved or underserved by other efforts aimed at changing the undesirable behavior
Ready to change their behavior
Able to change their behavior

An important aspect of social marketing is funding. Projects that do not generate profit may suffer from lack of financial support. A retail pharmacy marketer may justify a social marketing program for a number of reasons: Compliance is a health-related behavior that can impact the success or failure of a treatment regimen. A social marketing program aimed at compliance behavior may improve outcomes, thereby leading to patient satisfaction and repeat business.

Health-related services such as cancer screening and blood pressure monitoring can attract patients to the pharmacy and increase traffic, leading to a growth in sales. Social marketing programs to encourage regular health screenings will facilitate the use of pharmacy services.

Social marketing efforts aimed at health promotion offer the retailer opportunities to gain positive publicity. Good publicity increases public awareness of the business. Increased public awareness may drive consumer business to the retailer, thereby improving sales.

ACKNOWLEDGMENTS

The author gratefully acknowledges Chatham University MBA (Health Care Administration) graduates Hang-Li, Rebecca Shoop, and Michelle Sullivan, who collected the data for this case and developed marketing recommendations for the outpatient pharmacy.

REFERENCES

1. How the Pharmacy Industry Ch-ch-ch-changed in 2012. Available at: www.drugchannels. net/2013/05/how-pharmacy-industry-ch-ch-changed-in.html#more (accessed August 1, 2013).
2. 2012 Market Share of Top Pharmacies. Available at: www.drugchannels. net/2013/01/2012-market-share-of-top-pharmacies.html (accessed August 1, 2013).
3. Definition of Marketing. Available at: www.marketingpower.com/AboutAMA/Pages/ DefinitionofMarketing.aspx (accessed August 1, 2013).
4. Borden NH. The Concept of the Marketing Mix. *The Journal of Advertising Research.* Classics, Volume II, September 1984 (originally published in 1964).
5. Sandhusen RL. *Marketing.* 3rd Ed. Hauppauge, NY. Barron's Educational Series. 2000, pp. 412–417.

6. Sandhusen RL. *Marketing*. 3rd Ed. Hauppauge, NY. Barron's Educational Series. 2000, pp. 79–100.
7. Kotler P, Roberto N, and Lee N. *Social Marketing: Improving the Quality of Life.* 2nd Ed. Thousand Oaks, CA. Sage. 2002.
8. Magee Women's Hospital. Available at: www.brooklineconnection.com/history/Facts/MaGee.html (accessed July 30, 2013).
9. Magee-Women's Hospital of UPMC. Pittsburgh, PA. Available at: www.upmc.com/locations/hospitals/Magee/Pages/default.aspx (accessed July 30, 2013).

Case Study: Magee-Women's Hospital of UPMC Outpatient Pharmacy

Magee-Women's Hospital (Magee) of UPMC, located in Pittsburgh, Pennsylvania, is a 360-bed inpatient facility affiliated with the University of Pittsburgh Medical Center Health System (UPMC). Opened in 1911, Magee originally served Pittsburgh's women. In the 1960s, the hospital expanded its offerings to include some health services of interest to men.[8] Today, Magee is one of the nation's top hospitals specializing in women's health, and continues its traditional focus on gynecologic and obstetric services. Nevertheless, Magee is a full-service hospital caring for both men and women, with services including cardiology, geriatrics, urology, and bariatrics.[9]

In January 2013, a team of graduate students from Chatham University was asked to develop a marketing plan for expanding the business of the outpatient pharmacy at Magee. As a service to the patient population of the outpatient Women's Health Clinic, Magee currently provides an outpatient pharmacy to ensure that clinic patients can fill their prescriptions at the time of leaving the clinic visit. In addition, as a service to Magee employees the outpatient pharmacy fills employee prescriptions. The outpatient pharmacy is a 340B eligible pharmacy. This is a government program that provides the opportunity for medications to be purchased at a better price than hospital contract pricing.

The consulting team and Magee agreed on the following parameters for the project:

Develop a plan to overcome customer barriers to obtaining outpatient prescriptions in an inpatient facility.

Develop a process for medication education by the pharmacist for inpatients.

Create a marketing plan for expansion of the outpatient pharmacy business.

Evaluate the physical space of the outpatient pharmacy and recommend changes to support the marketing plan.

OUTPATIENT PHARMACY DATA*

Provides prescription services to Women's Health Clinic patients and Magee employees

Volume averages 100 prescriptions per day

---

* Source: Rosella Hoffman RPh, Director of the Magee-Women's Hospital Outpatient Pharmacy.

Employs one full-time pharmacist, with minimum technician support

Budget $2 million

Currently operates financially at a breakeven level

Located in the basement (zero level) of the hospital, adjacent to the Women's Health clinic

Hours of operation: 10 a.m. to 4 p.m., Monday through Friday

Magee administrators expressed interest in targeting patients being discharged from the inpatient internal medicine unit for prescription fulfillment through the outpatient pharmacy. Administrators also expressed concern that the existing facility in the basement of the hospital would not be attractive to patients or adequate for storing and dispensing a larger volume of prescriptions.

INTERNAL MEDICINE UNIT DATA*

Below are discharge data provided by Magee from the Internal Medicine Unit from November 1, 2012, through January 31, 2013. The total number of discharges was 599 with 92 of these patients discharged on a weekend. According to Magee reimbursement records, 54.5% of the patients in the Internal Medicine Unit are covered by Medicare, a payment source which is not currently accepted by the outpatient pharmacy.

Day of the Week	Number of Discharges Nov 2012	Average Number of Discharges	Number of Discharges Dec 2012	Average Number of Discharges	Number of Discharges Jan 2013	Average Number of Discharges
Sunday	14	3.50	10	2.00	7	1.75
Monday	25	6.25	37	7.40	27	6.75
Tuesday	30	7.50	21	7.00	31	6.20
Wednesday	46	11.50	29	7.25	44	8.80
Thursday	24	6.00	41	10.25	40	8.00
Friday	38	7.60	40	10.00	34	8.50
Saturday	17	4.25	23	4.60	21	5.25
Total	194	46.60	201	48.50	204	45.25

Month	Average Number of Discharges Monday–Friday	Average Number of Discharges Per Week Day	Number of Prescriptions Per Day*
November	38.85	7.77	15.54
December	41.90	8.38	16.76
January	36.75	7.35	14.70
3-Month Average	39.17	7.83	15.67

* Estimate of two prescriptions per discharge.

* Source: John Silipingi, Director of Health Services, Magee-Womens' Hospital of UPMC.

DECISION POINT 1

Should the Magee-Women's Hospital of UPMC target patients being discharged from the internal medicine unit for expansion of the pharmacy prescription business? Why or why not? What are the pros and cons of targeting these patients?

DECISION POINT 2

If Magee targets selected inpatients for marketing the hospital's outpatient pharmacy services, how can the pharmacy be made more convenient and attractive to the patient? Should the outpatient pharmacy be enlarged in its current location across from its main customers at the Women's Health Clinic, or should the outpatient pharmacy be moved to the main lobby of Magee-Women's Hospital? What are the marketing factors that support your recommendation? What are the financial factors that should be investigated?

13 Budgeting and Accounting

Robert J. Votta and Andrew M. Peterson

CONTENTS

Learning Objectives: After reading this chapter and working through the case, the reader will be able to:

1. Define basic accounting terms
2. Explain an income statement
3. Explain a balance sheet
4. Explain how to budget and to manage a budget successfully
5. Explain the pharmacy revenue cycle, how it works, and where it can go wrong

INTRODUCTION

Budgeting and accounting are related fiscal processes that help an organization plan, allocate, and disburse money throughout its components. This interrelationship requires coordination, and it is incumbent on pharmacy managers to understand how these processes operate within their organization. Generally speaking, budgeting is related to the planning and enacting of a financial plan, whereas accounting focuses on analyzing, classifying, recording, summarizing, and interpreting financial transactions. Budgets are built upon prior- and current-year financial reports generated through the accounting cycle. This chapter provides a general overview for each of these financial functions and how the pharmacy manager needs to understand their intricate relationship.

BUDGETING

The budget is an essential tool for any pharmacy to help translate general plans into specific, action-oriented goals and objectives. All pharmacy organizations have complex moving parts, and these parts need to be coordinated to work together in a cohesive fashion. Budgets are key tools that communicate the expected outcome and provide a detailed outline for assuring that all parts work in harmony. As such, the budget is the tool that provides a mechanism for identifying departures from the plan. A well-designed budget provides benchmarks against which success or failure is measured and facilitates timely corrective measures.

MASTER BUDGET

A *master budget* is a summary of the organization's financial and operating plans. The master budget is a comprehensive picture of the organization's plans for the future and how the plans will be accomplished. The master budget, which varies with different organizations, may include a revenue budget, an expense budget, a sales budget, a personnel budget, a drug budget, and/or a capital budget.

The *financial plan* includes financial and accounting data that are shared with outside parties and may consist of the typical accounting statements (balance sheet, income statement, statement of owners' equity and cash flow statement) along with a business plan. Banks, government agencies, and investors typically require a financial plan when examining the value of a business opportunity. In contrast, the *operating plan* is typically an internal document used to help managers forecast how much profit or losses are anticipated, and how much money they have to spend on expenses.

Budgets cover a specific period of time, most commonly one year, which is referred to as the fiscal year. For some organizations, the fiscal year follows the calendar year, beginning January 1 and ending December 31. In other organizations, such as academic institutions, it may cover a one-year period starting July 1 and ending June 30 of the following year.

BUDGETING IN PHARMACY

Developing a budgeting process that helps manage drug spending and overall pharmacy expenditures is crucial for the success of any pharmacy. As noted earlier, budgets help to guide decision making, provide insights into the success or failure of a program, and determine if an organization is meeting its goals.

OPERATING BUDGET AND THE BUDGET CYCLE

The operating budget, the primary budget for an organization, is a detailed projection of all estimated income and expenses based on forecasted revenue during a given period. Since an operating budget is a short-term budget (usually one year), capital expenditures such as equipment purchases are budgeted separately because they are long-term costs. There are four phases to a typical budget cycle: preparation, approval, execution, and evaluation. These are graphically represented in Figure 13.1.

Preparing the Budget

The first step of the budget process is to actually create a budget. Preparation for the new budget begins at the end of last year's budget cycle. For pharmacies, this may include finding estimates for drug price increases and changes in drug utilization, determining new program needs, estimating salary changes, and other factors that may significantly impact the budget (e.g., accreditation costs).

Changes in salary need to be discussed with the human resources (HR) department. These changes may include merit raises, cost-of-living raises, promotions/demotions, health benefits, or even changes in the responsibilities of pharmacists and technicians. HR can help identify these changes; link them to the economic health

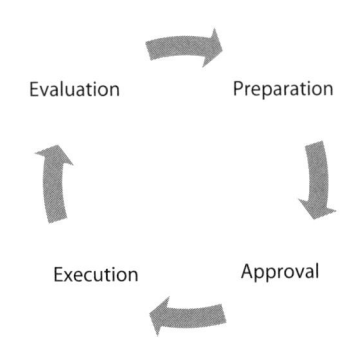

FIGURE 13.1   The budget cycle.

of the organization; and identify factors on a local, state, and national level that may affect salaries. Maintaining a close working relationship with HR is key to developing the personnel aspect of the budget.

Drug cost estimates are created from researching pharmacy resources, such as professional literature and organizational meetings, purchasing organization data, considering past utilization trends, and assessing trends in the health-care arena that could affect drug use. For example, even with the increase in the number of generic medications becoming available, the increase in use of high-cost biotechnology drugs targeted at specific conditions could drive up the cost of medications dramatically. Estimating drug costs must take into consideration the strategic goals of the organization and how pharmacy fits within those goals. For example, if the institution is planning to open a cancer center, the pharmacy needs to be involved in the budgeting for the high-cost drugs associated with treating those patients. Therefore, leadership and vision from the C-suite is critical in this aspect of the budgeting cycle.

Approving the Budget

The next phase of the budget cycle is the approval of the budget. Depending on the nature of the organization, budget approval may occur easily, with perhaps just one or two layers of managers reviewing and approving the budget. In other organizations, upper-level managers may have to justify the budget to committees or other stakeholders and wait for final approval from a board of trustees. While the politics of a budget approval may seem unnecessary, the value of the process lies in the C-suite member's commitment to the final budget and a statement of the direction an organization is taking.

Executing the Budget

The approved budget goes into effect at the beginning of the fiscal year. Most of the time, the money is spent according to plan. However, as the fiscal year rolls out, the budget officer can reallocate funds to another priority depending on the needs of the department and the organization. Similarly, the C-suite officer responsible for the pharmacy can appropriate funds from a budget to prevent wasteful spending or to fund a different initiative.

The performance benchmarked against the budget is typically reviewed monthly by the pharmacy director, the director's C-suite leader, and a representative from the finance department. Example financial metrics that can be used in many pharmacies are shown in Table 13.1. Trending these metrics over the course of the year and

TABLE 13.1
Example Financial Metrics

- Orders processed (departmental driver statistics)
- Total hours paid
- Drug expense
- Total revenue over expenses
- Total expense per unit (per order)

comparing them to budgeted projects will help the manager understand the actual performance of the organization compared to the expected performance. Deviations from the budget are often scrutinized and action plans for improvement are developed with steps designed to improve the issue within a pre-specified timeline and measurable goals to demonstrate success. The success of this plan may impact a pharmacy manager's annual performance review.

Evaluating the Budget

While the audit and evaluation process was once focused on ensuring that funds were being spent in accordance with the law and in a non-corrupt fashion, this phase of the budget has grown in scope. Now, auditing and evaluating also focus on how effectively the funds are being spent. It is not enough to see who used their money and who did not. What really matters in government and in business is if the money generated a return.

CAPITAL BUDGET

Costly purchases, such as dispensing devices, robots, IV hoods, and other high-end equipment expenses are usually *capitalized* over several years. Capitalizing expenses over time allows a company to spread out the cost over several years, thereby minimizing the negative impact on revenues. Capital budgets are separate from operating budgets because they not only allocate the expenditures over the long term, they represent an investment in the organization's fixed assets. A long-term investment, such as a purchasing or leasing a robotic system or constructing a new counseling area, represents decisions that cannot be reversed without significant financial loss. Therefore, capital purchases need to be made considering the value added to the future of the organization and are distinct from the year-to-year decisions made in an operating budget.

As such, capital purchases require a multilevel approval process. Depending on the purchase, various other constituents need to be involved in the decisions, such as information technology (IT), facilities (for construction needs), finance, and even human resources. Of course, the pharmacy manager must include the appropriate C-suite stakeholder(s) as well.

The capital budgeting process is not unlike the operating budget, following a similar budget cycle. The timing may be different, but typically a capital budget will follow the same fiscal year as the operating budget. Funding for capital projects may come from anticipated revenue excess, unspent funds from prior fiscal years, or investment realizations. Regardless of the source of funding, the pharmacy manager needs to realize that there is a finite pool of funds available.

INTRODUCTION TO ACCOUNTING

Accounting is the essence of any business organization as it provides a useful tool for creditors, employees, investors, managers, owners, and all interested parties to make well-informed business decisions. Accounting is basically an artificial business language. Some basic accounting and financial terms include accruals, payables and receivables, yields, and evaluations. It is essential that this artificial language be comprehended for effective financial decision making. The more accounting knowledge a pharmaceutical professional acquires, the better armed this person will be to enter the business marketplace. The pharmaceutical professional will not only have a better understanding of accounting information but will also know how to compile it, use it, and recognize the limitations of accounting.

DEFINITION OF ACCOUNTING

Accounting is the process of analyzing, classifying, recording, summarizing, and interpreting business information into understandable financial terms to facilitate effective business decision making. The first part of the definition refers to the following:

- *Analyzing* entails examining business transactions that involve basic ongoing activities, such as investing personal cash or equipment into the business, purchasing supplies with cash or credit, and so on.
- *Classifying* refers to the activity of providing a name for each specific account analyzed in the transactions, such as assets, liabilities, and owner's equity.
- *Recording* is the process of writing the accounting transactions in journals, ledgers, and financial statements to provide a permanent record of the accounting activities.
- *Summarizing* is the totaling of the ledgers and statements in order to acquire final figures to be used in the next step.
- *Interpreting* involves the various interested parties analyzing the final totals to facilitate comprehensive and effective business decisions.

NEED FOR ACCOUNTING AND THE ACCOUNTING ENTITY CONCEPT

There are vital reasons for using accounting concepts. First, annually compiling and presenting the firm's financial data can provide a picture of the financial history of the organization. The financial history of a firm is not always available without accounting statements, and the financial history of a pharmacy is important in many investment decisions. Second, an immediate snapshot of a pharmacy's financial condition is provided via financial statements such as a balance sheet, income statement, or statement of owner's equity. Investors, company managers, creditors, governmental agencies, and the general public can analyze and interpret this accounting data for effective business decision making.

While there are many other advantages to accounting, one interesting use revolves around a situation referred to as the accounting or separate entity concept. An accounting entity is any organizational unit for which financial data are gathered and interpreted for decision-making purposes. For example, in addition to personal items, a single entrepreneur, Amy Harris, owns a pharmacy, a restaurant, a bakery, and a delivery service. Each business owned by Harris must keep separate and distinct accounting records because all activities combined would be useless for decision making within any single unit. Therefore, she cannot pay a purchasing order for the restaurant with cash receipts from the bakery or pharmacy. A set of accounting records is developed for *each* of her individual businesses to facilitate planning and controlling decisions, and her accountants must focus on each individual business as a separate and distinct business unit. This is just one of the many accounting rules and requirements included under the generally accepted accounting principles.

GENERALLY ACCEPTED ACCOUNTING PRINCIPLES

Consistency is an essential aspect of accounting, and because it is vital for everyone who acquires accounting reports to be able to interpret them, a set of guidelines has been developed. These guidelines describing how the accounting process should be completed are called the generally accepted accounting principles (GAAPs).

The GAAPs, developed and agreed upon by accountants, provide the rules that cover financial accounting rather than other types of accounting such as tax accounting. In relation to a pharmacy, financial accounting develops financial statements that report the pharmacy's overall performance to internal and external users.

FINANCIAL STATEMENTS

A financial statement is a report developed by the accounting department for both internal and external users. Numerous statements are developed by way of journal and ledger entries. However, a firm uses four major financial statements to report its financial condition:

1. Income statement
2. Statement of owner's equity
3. Balance sheet
4. Statement of cash flows

These statements provide a snapshot of the business in relation to profit and losses, increases and decreases in capital, status of assets and debts, and the efficient or inefficient use of cash by the firm.

Income Statement

The most popular statement is the income statement, also referred to as the profit and loss statement. This statement reflects the results of all business transactions over a period of time and is a summary of all the firm's earned revenue (i.e., income from sales and services less all expenses incurred, i.e., costs associated with the earning process). The income statement usually covers a specific period of time selected by the firm, generally called a fiscal period, as previously indicated.

Income statements are generally completed on a monthly basis, especially in a pharmacy, because it is essential to keep track of the company's profitability in a timely manner in order to institute corrective actions when necessary. When total revenue exceeds total expenses over the period selected, the remaining positive amount reflects a net income (profit). When the opposite occurs and total expenses exceed total revenue, the result is a net loss. Table 13.2 shows the income statement for Harris Pharmacy.

TABLE 13.2

Sample of an Income Statement

Harris Pharmacy

Income Statement

For the month ended May 31, 20–

Revenues		
Net sales[a]		$15,500
Expenses		
Salaries and wages expense	$8,200	
Rent expense	$750	
Advertising expense	$125	
Utilities expense	$230	
Miscellaneous expense	$45	
Total expenses		$9,350
Net income		$6,150

[a] Net sales represents the dollar amount of annual sales less sales tax and any sales returns and allowances.

Statement of Owner's Equity

This statement reflects the changes that occurred in owner's equity during the period included on the income statement. The accountant uses the net income or net loss compiled on the income statement, including withdrawals, to show how owner's equity has changed over time, resulting in a (new) beginning balance for the next accounting period. This statement for pharmaceutical corporations such as Pfizer and Glaxo is also referred to as a statement of stockholder equity, since the owners are the shareholders of the corporation. The equity of a corporation also includes Retained Earnings, which is the total for the income amounts less dividends (declared earnings attributed to stockholders on a periodic basis) paid annually.

Balance Sheet

This statement is a picture of a firm's financial position as of one day in time. The balance sheet includes distinct balances under the following classifications:

- Assets (e.g., cash, furniture, or land)
- Liabilities (e.g., notes or wages payable)
- Owner's equity (e.g., capital or retained earnings)

The balance sheet changes with every transaction based on the accounting equation:

$$Assets = Liabilities + Owner's\ equity$$

Assets are things of value that the business owns such as equipment. Liabilities are amounts that the firm owes to others such as suppliers. For example, the amount owed on

TABLE 13.3
Sample of a Balance Sheet

Harris Pharmacy

Balance Sheet

May 31, 20–

Assets		Liabilities and Owner's Equity	
Current Assets		**Current Liabilities**	
Cash	$24,800	Accounts payable	$1,350
Accounts receivable	$8,425	Total current liabilities	$1,350
Merchandise inventory	$12,200	**Long-Term Liabilities**	
Prepaid insurance	$1,460	Notes payable (due after one year)	$2,000
Total current assets	$46,885	Total long-term liabilities	$2,000
Fixed Assets		Total liabilities	$3,350
Equipment	$5,215	**Owner's Equity**	
Furniture and fixtures	$3,400	A. Harris, capital[a]	$52,150
Total fixed assets	$8,615		
Total Assets	$55,500	**Total Liabilities and Owner's Equity**	$55,500

[a] The new capital amount is from the May 31 statement of owner's equity.

the purchase of a computer is a liability. Finally, owner's equity represents claims of the owner, wherein claims can increase by personal investments from outside the business and by earning revenue; however, claims may also decrease from withdrawals by the owner and/or incurring losses as the result of conducting business. Equity that is accumulated from a successful business and kept by the firm is included in the capital and/ or retained earnings account. Table 13.3 shows the balance sheet for Harris Pharmacy.

Statement of Cash Flows

An essential consideration of financial management is liquidity: the ability to turn assets into cash quickly. Assets included on the balance sheet are categorized as current and long term (plant assets), with current assets representing assets that can be readily turned into cash within one year, such as cash, accounts receivable, supplies, inventory, and prepaid expenses. Plant assets, such as equipment, buildings, and land, take longer than one year to turn into cash and are therefore not as liquid. Note that assets are always presented in their order of liquidity. Because cash is the most liquid asset, it is vital to any organization to keep track of the inflows and outflows of this asset. The statement of cash flows outlines how cash balance and cash equivalents have changed from the beginning to the end of the fiscal year. This statement has also been referred to as the sources and uses of cash statement. In addition to determining the liquidity of the firm, this statement can aid managers in determining the company's dividend policy and evaluating potential investment opportunities and ability to borrow and make cash payments on time. To determine whether there is a positive or negative cash flow, the statement of cash flows divides cash receipts and payment into three areas: cash flows from (used by) operating activities, investing activities, and financing activities.

INTERPRETATION OF FINANCIAL STATEMENTS

COMPARATIVE FINANCIAL STATEMENT ANALYSIS

Management, investors, creditors, and various other business professionals depend on accounting data to facilitate effective business decision making. To evaluate accounting information, businesspeople evaluate financial statements in three broad areas: (1) horizontal analysis, (2) vertical analysis, and (3) ratio analysis.

Horizontal Analysis

Numerous business decisions depend on how the figures for sales, income, and expenses fluctuate during the period of operations. How have sales changed within the last five years? Are expenses increasing at a faster rate than income? Although very interesting, the answers to these questions may not be useful for decision making unless the percentage change is analyzed in any account classification (e.g., sales over time). The study of percentage changes among years in comparative statements is called *horizontal analysis*. The procedure to compute the percentage change in horizontal analysis requires computing the dollar amount of the change from the base (earlier) period to the latter period by dividing the dollar amount of change by the base period amount (Table 13.4).

Vertical Analysis

Vertical analysis is another strategy employed by accountants to analyze financial statements. When an income statement is used for vertical analysis, each account in the statement is expressed as a percentage of net sales (i.e., dividing the total amount of any item by the total of net sales). A firm would raise a red flag if it normally experiences gross profit at a rate of 40% of net sales and then suddenly records a drop in gross profit to 25%.

In a balance sheet, total assets and total liabilities should be used as denominators to determine the percentage of specific assets, liabilities, and owner's equity, respectively. All financial statement users, including shareholders, will exhibit concern because this drop in gross profit may make the firm report a net loss on the

TABLE 13.4
Horizontal Analysis

	2013	2012	Increase or Decrease	Amount (%)
Sales	$42,430	$36,864	$5,566	15.1[a]
Net income	$17,800	$16,560	$1,240	7.5

[a] The firm has a percentage increase in sales that is approximately twice the percentage increase as net income between 2012 and 2013.

TABLE 13.5
Vertical Analysis

Current Assets	December 31, 2013	Vertical Analysis (%)
Cash	$32,000	17.2
Accounts receivable	$14,400	7.7
Inventory	$23,720	12.7
Total current assets	$70,120	37.6
Fixed Assets		
Land	$8,000	4.3
Building	$96,000	51.5
Store equipment	$12,210	6.6
Total fixed assets	$116,210	62.4
Total Assets	$186,330	100.0

Note: The vertical analysis of the balance sheet reflects any account selected as the numerator and the amount of total assets as the base or denominator (e.g., cash account $32,000/$186,330). Each liability or owner equity account is divided by the total of liabilities and owner's equity.

current income statement. Table 13.5 illustrates a sample of vertical analysis for a balance sheet.

Ratio Analysis

In addition to using financial statements for comparative horizontal and vertical analysis, ratios are another available tool. Developing relationships among financial statement items is the crux of ratio analysis. In this type of analysis, it is extremely important for the evaluators, such as creditors or management, to select the ratio applicable to their immediate area of concern. Then, the relevant ratio can be calculated for analysis, and finally, more research might be necessary as ratio analysis is limited.

SOLVENCY (LIQUIDITY)

Solvency refers to an enterprise's ability to meet its long-term debt obligations on a continuing basis. All financial statement users are interested in the liquidity of a firm in addition to the obvious liquidity concerns of creditors and management. Will the firm be able to pay its short-term debts as they become due? Can the firm cover its current liabilities with its current assets? Does the firm have an efficient mix of current assets (e.g., cash and inventory)? Do owners and management properly use the current assets? To effectively answer these and other financial questions, it is necessary to use various financial tools which include horizontal, vertical, and ratio analyses.

AUDITING (ACCOUNTING ACCURACY)

Auditing involves the independent review of a firm's accounting records and supporting financial statements. The auditor analyzes and provides a fair opinion of the accounting records under the guidelines of the GAAPs. Many companies have their own internal auditors who also adhere to the firms' managerial policies and procedures. Usually, independent certified public accountants (CPAs) act as public auditors by preparing tax returns and occasionally designing accounting systems for these firms. The task of determining the GAAPs is a primary function performed by the Financial Accounting Standards Board (FASB), an independent group of accountants whose philosophy of accounting principles is recognized by the accounting profession, industry, and government. In addition, the FASB has been designed to be independent of the users of accounting principles.

Tax Liability

Accurate tax records are essential to satisfy a firm's tax obligations because an excellent accounting system is required to document all revenues and expenses for not only the long-term success of the organization but also income tax purposes. The IRS requires proper documentation in the event of a tax audit.

CONCLUSION

Budgeting and accounting do not solve problems, but they do provide the tools necessary for the pharmacist to see the fiscal health of an organization. The accounting process, budget cycle, and associated financial tools not only increase the supply of timely financial information but also help the pharmaceutical professional acquire the financial expertise to make more informed decisions. However, they are not crystal balls that predict the future.

A basic understanding of accounting concepts is therefore essential for the operation of all pharmaceutical organizations, from neighborhood pharmacies to chain pharmacies and international pharmaceutical corporations. In essence, the knowledge of accounting contributes to the overall success of business ventures in the dynamic environment of pharmaceutical management.

BIBLIOGRAPHY

Manson BJ. *Downsizing Issues: The Impact of Employee Morale and Productivity (Studies on Industrial Productivity)*. New York: Garland; 2000.

Nobles TL, Scott CJ, McQuaig DJ, Bille PA. *College Accounting*. 11th ed., Southwestern and Cengage Learning: Mason, OH; 2013.

Shane R. Critical requirements for health system pharmacy practice models that achieve optimal use of medicines. *Am J Health-Syst Pharm*. 2011;68(12):1101–1111.

Tootelian DH, Mikhailitchenko A, Wertheimer AI. *Essentials of Pharmacy Management*. 2nd ed. Pharmaceutical Press: London, UK; 2012.

Case Study

Develop a two-year budget for the expansion of a clinical service from a single person, 9 a.m. to 5 p.m., Monday through Friday service to multiple persons, 9 a.m. to 9 p.m., Monday through Friday and 9 a.m. to 5 p.m. on Saturday and

Sunday. Include personnel costs (salary/wages) and supply costs. Use the following questions to guide your budget development:

1. What is the staffing pattern for the service?
2. What is the current salary in your area for a pharmacist? How does that change if the pharmacist is just entering practice or has been in practice for more than 7 to 10 years?
3. How much do benefits cost?
4. How do you account for recruiting costs?

DISCUSSION QUESTIONS

1. How do the supply needs differ from a clinical service focused on diabetes versus one focused on immunizations? How would that differ for a hypertensive clinic?
2. What ratio analyses would you perform to see if the service is cost effective?

14 Purchasing and Inventory Management

James M. Hoffman and Andrew M. Peterson

CONTENTS

Learning Objectives: After reading this chapter and working through the case, the reader will be able to:

1. Generally discuss the pharmaceutical purchasing process
2. Differentiate between prime and secondary vendors
3. Explain three discount strategies employed by wholesalers
4. Explain inventory costs such as procurement cost, carrying cost, and opportunity cost
5. Calculate inventory turnover rates, calculate economic order quantities, and determine reorder points for pharmaceuticals
6. Describe three methods for valuing inventory

PURCHASING

On the surface, the purchase of pharmaceuticals might appear to be one of the most mundane tasks encountered in the management of a pharmacy. Although there is little glamour associated with the purchasing process, efficient purchasing practices are essential to the operation of any pharmacy (McAllister, 1985). Pharmaceuticals represent the largest operating expense for any pharmacy, and therefore their purchase requires careful management. Depending on the pharmacy, drug purchases account for 60 to 80% of a pharmacy's expenses (Bickett and Gagnon, 1987). A sufficient quantity of pharmaceuticals must be available at all times to allow for quality patient care, but the quantity of pharmaceuticals stocked cannot be in excess so that it wastes the pharmacy's money through unnecessary inventory.

Many of the technical functions required to purchase pharmaceuticals can be delegated to nonpharmacist staff. For example, duties such as placing an order, receiving stock, and managing inventory levels can be performed by properly trained technical staff. However, the oversight and guidance of a pharmacist are required throughout the purchasing process (Vidal, 1998). Nonpharmacist personnel may not have the drug knowledge to order substitutes when a certain drug is unavailable or to determine reasonable stock quantities for drugs, especially expensive items that are not routinely used. The management of these challenges is improved when a pharmacist takes responsibility for the purchasing process, and this is especially important when drug shortages exist and alternative medications must be identified.

Purchasing pharmaceuticals is a complex process that requires the pharmacy staff to interface with a variety of other parties. In this chapter we review the sources of pharmaceuticals and the purchasing process. Purchasing continues to grow in complexity, and this chapter describes the contemporary difficulties, such as restricted distribution programs and drug shortages, that face pharmacists today. Table 14.1 explains the purchasing terms used throughout the chapter.

SOURCES OF PHARMACEUTICALS

In general, pharmacies use two methods to obtain drugs. Pharmaceuticals are purchased directly from the product manufacturer (direct purchases) or indirectly (indirect purchases) through a pharmaceutical wholesaler (Allen, 1992). Purchasing directly from manufacturers may reduce handling fees or other additional costs charged by wholesalers. However, direct purchases require additional staff time, because multiple orders must be placed, received, and processed. Because wholesalers allow pharmacies to order multiple products from a single source, pharmaceutical wholesalers are clearly the most common source of pharmaceuticals. Consolidated ordering through a wholesaler improves purchasing efficiency by reducing personnel time spent on purchasing and improving order turnaround time. The primary disadvantage of purchasing through a wholesaler is the additional cost the wholesaler might charge for some products. There is some concern about the growth of the "gray" market for distributing pharmaceuticals. This will be further discussed in the "Drug Shortages" section.

TABLE 14.1
Key Purchasing Terms Used in the Chapter

Direct purchasing	Purchasing pharmaceuticals directly from the manufacturer
Indirect purchasing	Purchasing pharmaceuticals from an intermediary such as a wholesaler
Group purchasing organization (GPO)	Organization that negotiates and maintains contracts with drug manufacturers on behalf of member organizations
Prime vendor relationship	Agreement with a wholesaler that states the pharmacy will purchase a set quantity or dollar amount of pharmaceuticals; in exchange for guaranteed sales, wholesaler provides discounts to pharmacy
Wholesalers	Companies that purchase pharmaceuticals from manufacturers and resell them to pharmacies
Restricted distribution program	Program wherein pharmaceuticals can be purchased only from the manufacturer or a designated pharmacy; usually developed for drugs that require extensive monitoring or patient education due to safety concerns
Reverse distributor	Companies that organize and manage the return and appropriate destruction of expired pharmaceuticals
Purchase order	Document that lists all the items to be purchased in a given order; used to track items that have been ordered

Despite the common use of wholesalers, drug manufacturers remain important sources of drugs in some situations. An example of a pharmaceutical commonly purchased directly from the manufacturer is the influenza vaccine. The vaccine must be purchased each season because its formulation changes. Each year it is adjusted to protect patients against the strains that are expected to be most prevalent during the next flu season. In early fall, pharmacies purchase a large quantity of influenza vaccine directly from the manufacturer which will be used throughout the coming months. Because organizations purchase a single large quantity of the influenza vaccine and the product changes each year, buying from the manufacturer can result in efficiencies and savings.

Other common direct purchase (or "drop shipment") scenarios include orphan drugs, drug shortages, and limited distribution systems. Orphan drugs are drugs used to treat rare diseases, and they can usually only be obtained directly from the manufacturer. When a drug is in short supply, manufacturers may develop a program in which the product is available only from the manufacturer. Patients must meet criteria to obtain the drug, and the product is allocated to pharmacies based on patient need. The program may require health care practitioners to contact the manufacturer with patient-specific information (e.g., patient diagnosis or previous therapies that have failed on the patient). The intent of these programs is to ensure that drugs in short supply are used appropriately. Limited distribution programs are systems in which manufacturers or their designees (often specialty mail-order pharmacies) are the only sources for a pharmaceutical. Although these programs add complexity to the drug-purchasing process, they are usually instituted for safety reasons. Further discussion of drug shortages and limited distribution programs is provided in the sections on special situations in pharmaceutical purchasing and drug shortages.

The majority of pharmacies' drug purchases are indirect purchases through a pharmaceutical wholesaler who purchases drugs from manufacturers and sells them to pharmacies (Carroll, 1997). Wholesalers do not sell products directly to patients; instead they act as middlemen between drug manufacturers and pharmacies. In 2012, the largest pharmaceutical wholesalers included McKesson Corporation, AmerisourceBergen, and Cardinal Health (MDM, 2013). These wholesalers provide a full range of pharmaceuticals to all types of pharmacies, but other smaller wholesalers also exist who specialize in selling specific products such as biologicals, parenterals, or oncology drugs (Allen, 1992). In recent years, pharmaceutical wholesalers have become diversified businesses that provide a variety of products and services besides drugs. Examples of these products include pharmacy automation and dispensing technology, pharmacy information systems, drug-repackaging services, and pharmacy management services.

Prime and Secondary Vendors

Pharmacies often choose one pharmaceutical wholesaler and establish a prime vendor relationship. The prime vendor relationship is an agreement that stipulates that the pharmacy will purchase a set amount of drugs from the wholesaler. In return for guaranteed purchases, wholesalers provide a discount to the pharmacy. As part of the agreement, wholesalers may provide further discounts based on purchase volume. Some pharmacies might also retain a secondary wholesaler to use as an alternative source of pharmaceuticals. However, purchases from the secondary wholesaler are usually kept to a minimum so as not to jeopardize quantity discounts from the primary wholesaler.

Discounts and purchase terms from wholesalers or other suppliers may be structured several different ways. Examples of discounts include quantity, cash, and bundled discounts (Tootelian and Gaedake, 1993). Quantity or volume discounts are arranged based on the number of units or dollars of a product purchased. The discounts may be fixed and paid after a set quantity is purchased, or discounts often increase as the quantity purchased increases. Quantity discounts are usually based on multiple purchases over a set period such as a year, and a rebate is paid to the pharmacy at the end of the period. Discounts provided by manufacturers, via either direct purchases or contracts negotiated by group purchasing organizations (GPOs), are often based on purchase volume of a product or group of products. When discounts are based on purchases of a group, or a bundle of a company's products, these agreements are called *bundled contracts*. Quantity discounts may provide significant savings, but these contracts may encourage pharmacies to purchase more products than necessary. In the case of bundled contracts, pharmacies may purchase products they might not normally carry so that they receive the discount.

Purchase terms between pharmacies and suppliers usually provide flexibility and potential discounts. Typically, the supplier allows the pharmacy 30 or more days to pay for an order, but discounts, called *cash discounts*, are paid if bills are paid immediately. For example, the terms of the agreement could allow suppliers to provide a 1 to 3% discount if purchases are paid within 10 days. If pharmacies consistently take advantage of these discounts, they can result in annual savings of 15 to 30%, depending on the purchase terms. However, quick payment of drug purchases may reduce cash flow and drain the pharmacy's cash reserves.

ROLE OF GROUP PURCHASING ORGANIZATIONS

The services of GPOs are used extensively in most pharmacy settings, especially in hospitals and health systems. Because they may never actually purchase drugs, the term *purchasing* does not accurately describe the activities of most GPOs (Wetrich, 1987). Instead, GPOs negotiate contracts with drug manufacturers and other vendors on behalf of their member hospitals or pharmacies. In hospitals, GPOs establish and maintain contracts for nearly every product a hospital might need to purchase. Contracts may exist for simple and inexpensive items, such as latex gloves, or complex and expensive items, such as cardiovascular stents, pacemakers, or orthopedic implants.

Because GPOs negotiate on behalf of hundreds or even thousands of organizations, they are able to combine the purchases of all members during contract negotiations. By pooling resources for purchases, the contracts GPOs negotiate are larger than any single pharmacy might negotiate, and they are able to demand more favorable pricing for the drugs and other products under those contracts. Drug manufacturers and other companies that enter into GPO contracts are assured significant purchases for the item under contract. Some GPOs may only contract for a limited number of drugs within a therapeutic class. These contracts are designed to help manufacturers increase market share over competing products. Although controversial (Young, 2002a), these contracts allow the pharmacy to receive the best possible price for a given drug and the cost of drugs is reduced.

GPOs have evolved to provide services to pharmacies beyond contract negotiation. Purchasing organizations often provide newsletters, drug information, formulary resources, and other benefits to GPO members. Formulary resources and drug information may provide an additional benefit of converting a member hospitals' drug use to the preferred agent under the GPO's contracts.

In addition to the obvious benefit of potentially reducing drug costs, purchasing organizations may provide other advantages to member organizations (Carroll, 1997). Purchasing organizations can provide valuable information to member hospitals. For example, they often provide reports on purchasing trends and drug costs. By contracting with only a limited number of vendors, GPOs help pharmacies standardize their inventory, which can reduce costs. Because the GPO handles contract negotiation and maintenance, labor costs for this time-consuming and complex task are reduced. Drug cost savings and other advantages do not come without a cost. Pharmacies that use the services of a GPO have less control over the purchasing process. Pharmacies may also be required to institute formulary or other changes in the drug use process in order to use the product preferred by the GPO.

PHARMACEUTICAL PURCHASING PROCESS

The pharmaceutical purchasing process is continuous (Figure 14.1). Drugs are ordered and received, drug inventory is managed, and the purchasing cycle is complete when pharmaceuticals are returned or destroyed.

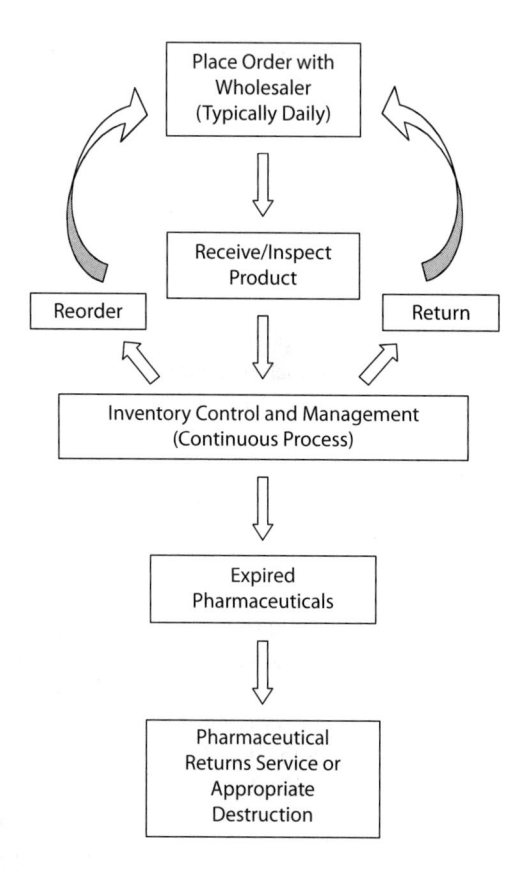

FIGURE 14.1   The pharmaceutical purchasing process.

Computer systems are the primary method for placing drug orders. A purchase order, a document with all the items to be purchased, is generated. The purchase order allows the pharmacy to track the items ordered. The order is then placed via a dedicated computer terminal typically provided by the wholesaler. The computer has the necessary software and connections needed to place the order with the wholesaler.

Most pharmacies place an order with their wholesaler each weekday or several times each week, and the order is usually received the next day. Frequent ordering allows pharmacies to purchase drugs using a just-in-time approach. The goal of this purchasing method is to reduce inventory costs by purchasing only the minimum amount of product needed until the next order is placed. Clear procedures for receiving a drug shipment should be established and maintained (Allen, 1992). Once an order is received, care must be taken to be sure that the correct items were received (correct product, dose, quantity, and strength). The products received must be inspected for evidence of tampering or damage during shipping. Damaged products must be returned to the wholesaler, and products not received must be reordered. Before an item is added to inventory, the expiration date of the product should be verified. Items with short expiration dates should be returned to the wholesaler.

To allow for double checks within the ordering system, the personnel receiving and inspecting the order should be different from the personnel who placed the order.

A systematic process should be developed and maintained to check drug expiration dates and remove expired drugs from the pharmacy inventory. For example, a system could be developed in which technical staff is assigned to perform monthly inspections in areas of the inventory for expired drugs. The types of expired drugs should be evaluated, because they might yield useful information that can be used to improve the inventory system. If the same expired product is found on a consistent basis, inventory levels of the product should be reduced.

Expired drugs are not simply discarded within the pharmacy, because they retain some value. Most manufacturers provide credit for returned expired drugs. The returns process can be complicated, and multiple Drug Enforcement Administration (DEA), Environmental Protection Agency (EPA), and individual state board of pharmacy regulations must be followed. Consequently, most pharmacies outsource this function to a reverse distributor, a firm that organizes and manages the return of expired drugs to manufacturers. In exchange for these services, pharmacies pay reverse distributors a percentage of the credit value of the expired drugs. If a manufacturer does not provide credit for a certain product, reverse distributors appropriately dispose of the expired drugs.

As the final step of the purchasing cycle, proper destruction of pharmaceuticals cannot be ignored. The EPA classifies many drugs, including epinephrine, nitroglycerin, warfarin, choral hydrate, and chemotherapy agents, as hazardous waste (Smith, 2002). When discarded improperly, these and other pharmaceuticals are harmful to the environment. Although the majority of pharmaceutical waste is managed through a reverse distributor who must be registered with the EPA, pharmacies must properly manage the disposal of incidental waste such as partial containers, compounded IVs, and broken or spilled products (EPA, 2013). Hazardous, nonhazardous, and chemotherapy pharmaceutical waste should be separated. Some waste such as intravenous fluids can be disposed of through sewer systems, but all other types of pharmaceutical waste should be incinerated by a regulated medical waste disposal firm (FDA, 2013).

SPECIAL SITUATIONS IN PHARMACEUTICAL PURCHASING

Several situations increase the complexity of the purchasing process and may demand greater attention from the pharmacist managing the purchasing process. Examples of these situations include controlled substances, investigational drugs, restricted distribution programs, and drug shortages.

Different processes and additional record keeping are required to order controlled substances and investigational drugs. A DEA 222 form must be used to order and document the receipt of Schedule II controlled substances. These forms must be kept on file in the pharmacy, and a perpetual inventory of Schedule II substances must be maintained. Automated dispensing cabinets and other technology can be useful to maintain such an inventory. Investigational drugs, agents undergoing clinical trials but not yet approved by the Food and Drug Administration (FDA), can be ordered only under institutional review board approved studies or for compassionate use in

individual patients. These drugs often have special handling and storage requirements, and study sponsors require strict accountability for investigational drugs.
Pharmacists should develop specific procedures for handling investigational drugs
and physically separate them from other pharmaceutical inventory.

Restricted distribution programs are common for drugs used in small populations
or drugs with significant safety concerns. Restricted distribution programs establish
special systems for ordering and dispensing drugs, usually through a single pharmacy.
Patient information, such as diagnosis, laboratory test results, or documentation of
patient education, may be required to comply with the terms of the program. In many
cases, these programs are developed in cooperation with the FDA as a condition
of drug approval. Examples of drugs available only through restricted distribution
programs include dofetilide, sodium oxybate, mifepristone, isotretinoin, bosentan,
epoprostenol, and thalidomide. As these programs have become more common,
pharmacists and pharmacy organizations have criticized them for their complexity,
interference with the pharmacist-patient relationship, and exclusive relationship with
a single pharmacy (Glaser, 2001). However, this type of distribution system keeps
important products on the market and allows patients safe and routine access to
them. An example of a restricted distribution program is the System for Thalidomide
Education and Prescribing Safety (STEPS) (Young, 2002b). Thalidomide, a terato-
gen that caused over 10,000 birth defects worldwide in the 1950s and 1960s, was
recently approved for use in the United States. Although thalidomide is indicated
for the treatment of leprosy, it has become widely used for a variety of cancers,
especially multiple myeloma. The program includes multiple elements to reduce the
risk of birth defects in patients taking thalidomide. Prescribers are required to counsel patients on the risks of thalidomide and provide pregnancy testing to women
with childbearing potential on a monthly basis. To use thalidomide, patients must
use two reliable forms of contraception, and pharmacists can dispense only a single
28-day supply. The entire program is monitored by telephone surveys that prescribers, patients, and pharmacists must complete on a monthly basis.

Drug Shortages

Drug shortages represent a growing challenge to the pharmacist responsible for purchasing pharmaceuticals. Within the last few years, drug shortages have become
more common and severe (ASHP, 2009). Drug shortages have always existed, and
national organizations like ASHP have been providing guidance on how pharmacists
can manage them since at least 2001. Drug shortages occur for a variety of reasons,
such as raw and bulk material unavailability, manufacturing difficulties, recalls,
regulatory issues, manufacturer decisions to reduce or stop production, unexpected
increases in demand, and even natural disasters. One survey found that raw material shortages and regulatory issues were the most common reasons for shortage
(Wellman, 2001). In another analysis, manufacturing problems and product discon-
tinuation by the manufacturer were the most common reasons for drug shortages.
And yet another suggests that low quality and increased oversight by the FDA caused
shortages (Fox and Tyler, 2013). Depending on the reason for shortage, they may last
several weeks or continue for several years.

Besides disrupting normal purchasing operations in a pharmacy, drug shortages may have a negative impact on patient care. In some cases, no other alternative therapy is available, and patients go without optimal drug therapy. This is acutely apparent in cancer patients, where shortages of long duration can have a dramatic impact on relapse rates and possibly survival (Metzger et al., 2012). During many shortages, a similar drug is available, but health-care practitioners and patients may not be familiar with the alternative therapy. During a drug shortage, pharmacists must take an active role in selecting alternative agents, determining equivalent dosages, and educating practitioners and patients on the use of the new agent.

Concerns exist with the growth of the "gray" market, or "parallel" market. Gray markets are those markets in which a commodity is distributed through unauthorized or unofficial channels. Companies that operate in this market take advantage of drug shortages and charge inflated prices to make a profit, thereby further contributing to the existing drug shortage (Staff Report, 2012).

INVENTORY

The drug-purchasing process does not end once drugs are ordered and received. Managing a drug inventory can be viewed as a component of the purchasing process. Because the drug inventory represents a substantial investment for any pharmacy, the goal of inventory management is to maintain the minimum amount of necessary inventory to control drug costs. Excess inventory can substantially harm the financial performance of a pharmacy. Whereas inventory should be kept to a minimum, a sufficient quantity of medications must be maintained to allow immediate access to drugs needed for patient care. The pharmacy manager should develop purchasing and inventory control systems that balance product availability and cost concerns.

Inventory is probably the largest single investment a pharmacy can make. Regardless of whether the pharmacy is retail, hospital, or another type that serves patients, inventory investment is significant and needs to be managed well consistently. There are a variety of reasons for managing inventory, including the need to keep costs at a minimum and to have a sufficient supply of products for good customer service. Too much inventory results in loss of profits because products remain on the shelf and do not generate cash flow. Too little inventory can result in customer dissatisfaction and employee frustration because needed products are not available.

Costs are also associated with managing inventory. The obvious cost is the purchase price, also called the acquisition cost. It also costs money to procure and carry a product. Procurement costs, such as shipping and handling, can vary depending on the product. Similarly, carrying costs vary depending on the product and include overhead costs such as electricity and heating.

There are various ways of managing inventory, ranging from visual inspection of stocked items to computerized accounting of items entered and removed from inventory at the time of stocking and the time of purchase. Each of these strategies has advantages and disadvantages and is discussed in detail in the chapter. Last, because inventory comprises a significant investment, there are many ways to value it. These too are discussed further.

INVENTORY COSTS

The most obvious cost associated with an inventory is the acquisition cost. This is the cost the pharmacy pays to the supplier, be it the manufacturer, the wholesaler, or other sources. The cost associated with the acquisition cost includes the markup the wholesaler may impose, discounts offered (e.g., cash or quantity discounts), and cost of the product.

PROCUREMENT COSTS

Procurement costs include the cost of shipping, receiving, stocking, and bookkeeping of the inventory. Shipping costs depend largely on the product and the quantity of product purchased. Clearly, larger, heavier products cost more money to ship. But when items are purchased in large quantities, the per-item shipping costs are typically less. The costs to receive an item include the personnel time spent receiving the item on the loading dock and checking in the inventory (i.e., to review it against the purchase order to make sure the shipment is complete). Stocking costs include the time it takes to move the items to the storeroom and then from the storeroom to the shelf. Bookkeeping costs include payment to the supplier.

CARRYING COSTS

Carrying costs are costs inherent in the product and might be difficult to quantify for individual items. The first carrying cost is the cost of storage. Also, because medications must be kept at appropriate temperatures to maintain their shelf lives, the conditions of storage must be maintained. For example, the storage cost of refrigerated items includes the purchase of a refrigerator, the electricity to run the refrigerator, and the cost of maintaining the refrigerator. Further, the pharmacist must be aware that the items have expiration dates, and if the drugs are past the expiration dates, they cannot be sold. This is also a carrying cost: if the items do not sell and expire, the money used to purchase them cannot be regained through a sale. Another hidden carrying cost is the cost of insuring the pharmacy against fire, theft, or other disasters. Typically, the higher the inventory value, the higher are the insurance costs.

OPPORTUNITY COSTS

The opportunity cost of purchasing an item must also be considered. The opportunity cost is the cost of something in terms of something else that could be purchased and sold instead. If the pharmacy has a certain monthly budget for purchases, there is often a tradeoff between purchasing large quantities of one item at a steep discount versus purchasing a wide variety of other items. For example, if the pharmacy uses its entire monthly budget to purchase acetaminophen at a discounted price, it loses the opportunity to purchase all other medications, therefore losing the opportunity to sell other items. The cost associated with this decision is the opportunity cost.

Customer dissatisfaction is one of the hardest costs to determine, but is the most easily observable. Customers expect that products typically held by a pharmacy are readily available for purchase during normal business hours. Stockouts—when there is insufficient inventory on hand at the time of purchase—often produce frustration and dissatisfaction among customers, but if infrequent, may be forgiven. However, frequent stockouts can result in a loss of business. In hospitals, frequent stockouts of commonly used products can result in a decline in the quality of patient care, create frustration among the medical and nursing staffs, and promote dissension between the pharmacy and other staff.

MECHANICS OF INVENTORY CONTROL

The primary goal of inventory control is balance between having sufficient amounts of a product on hand when needed and minimizing costs associated with the inventory. Fundamentally, inventory control is assuring this balance—when to order the product and how much to order. As such, the pharmacy manager must be aware of the total cost of the inventory, which is the sum of all the costs associated with inventory:

$$\text{Total cost (TC)} = \text{Acquisition costs (AC)} + \text{Procurement costs (PC)}$$
$$+ \text{Carrying costs (CC)}$$

ORDERING INVENTORY

The first concern is how much the pharmacy manager should order considering all the costs. Many pharmacy managers use their intuition and decide how much to order based on prior knowledge of usage patterns and current costs. There is a more scientific method of ordering, called the *economic order quantity* (EOQ). The EOQ is essentially a formula that determines the point at which the ordering and carrying costs for a product are the lowest. The EOQ should be considered whenever there is a repetitive buying pattern for a product, as it will help minimize the costs associated with the inventory costs of the product.

The EOQ formula is as follows:

$$\text{EOQ} = \sqrt{[(2 \times \text{Annual usage}) \times (\text{Ordering costs})/(\text{Carrying costs\%} \times \text{Unit cost})]}$$

This formula considers the annual usage, per-order ordering costs, cost of the item, and carrying costs. As the order quantity increases, ordering costs decrease. However, as the order quantity increases, the carrying costs also increase. Therefore, the total cost decreases at first, until the carrying costs exceed the ordering costs. The point at which the carrying costs equal the ordering costs is the lowest total cost. This quantity, the EOQ, will produce the minimum total cost. The concept of the EOQ is best expressed graphically (Figure 14.2).

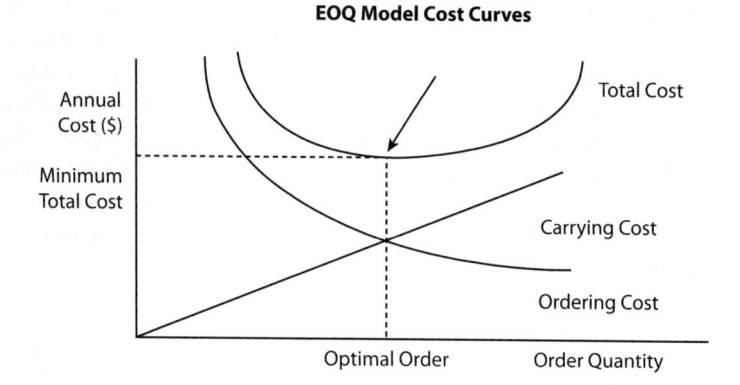

FIGURE 14.2   Economic order quantity cost curves.

Consider the following example. A pharmacy uses 1200 bottles of aspirin annually, and each order costs $5.00. Further, a single bottle of aspirin costs $0.50, with a carrying cost of 10% of the cost. The EOQ equation would be as follows:

$$EOQ = \sqrt{\left[(2 \times annual\,usage) \times \frac{Ordering\,Costs}{Carrying\,Costs\,(\%) \times Unit\,Cost} \right]}$$

$$EOQ = \sqrt{\left[(2 \times 1200) \times \left[\frac{\$5.00}{\$0.50 \times 0.1} \right] \right]}$$

EOQ = 490 bottles per order

Therefore, the pharmacy should order 490 bottles of aspirin.

When to Reorder

If, according to the EOQ model, aspirin should be ordered every 20 weeks, the idea of when to order seems inherent in the model. However, this model assumes that the usage pattern is consistent throughout the ordering period and that when the stock reaches zero, there is immediate replenishment to the EOQ. Because buying patterns vary over time and it takes time to order, receive, and stock items, the pharmacy manager needs to have an idea of the reorder point. The reorder point is that point at which the manager needs to reorder inventory to assure adequate supply for the customer. The formula for reorder point is

Reorder point (ROP) = Demand rate (DR) × Lead time (LT) + Safety stock (SS)

The demand rate (DR) is the amount of product used or sold within a given period of time. It is expressed as the number of units per unit of time. The lead time (LT) is the amount of time it takes to order and receive a product from a supplier. In pharmacies the LT is often one day, it but can be upward of one to two weeks, depending on the product and the supplier. The safety stock (SS) is the buffer of product kept on hand to accommodate increases in demand or longer than expected LTs.

In the aspirin example, we can consider a two-day LT, a daily usage rate of three bottles (1200 per year/365 days per year), and a safety stock of a two-day supply.

Therefore, the formula would become

$$ROP = 3 \text{ bottles/day} \times 2 \text{ days LT} + 2 \text{ days SS}$$
$$ROP = 12 \text{ bottles}$$

The pharmacy manager should reorder the EOQ of 490 bottles of aspirin when there are twelve bottles left in the pharmacy.

CONTROLLING INVENTORY

Inventory measurement is part and parcel of controlling inventory. One of the most common measures of inventory control is the inventory turnover rate (ITR). The ITR measures how fast inventory moves (i.e., how frequently inventory is sold and repurchased for stocking). A high ITR indicates frequent usage, which in turn indicates continued sales and profits. Therefore, typically, it is best to have a high ITR—up to a point. Recall from the EOQ model that ordering costs can influence overall costs. Ordering too frequently can increase overall inventory costs. The optimal ITR for items varies based on the total inventory costs of the product and should be individualized. Each item should have its own ITR calculated. This will allow the manager to determine specific situations in which the inventory is not turning over sufficiently. If the ITR needs to increase, purchasing a lower quantity more often should be considered. For items with a typical 20 to 30% average gross margin (GM%), the ITR is usually five to six times per year; for items with a lower average GM%, the ITR should be higher.

VALUING INVENTORY

There are at least three different methods for valuing inventory: (1) first-in–first-out (FIFO), (2) last-in–first-out (LIFO), and (3) weighted average cost (WAC).

The FIFO method considers that the first items brought into the pharmacy are the first ones sold. This creates an inventory of newer items. The value of the inventory is calculated by multiplying the number of units remaining in the inventory by the cost per item. If the cost of the items has risen (i.e., the items in inventory are more expensive than those already sold), the value of the inventory can be inflated using the FIFO method; conversely, if the cost of the items has declined, the value of the inventory can be underestimated.

The LIFO method assumes that the inventory on hand is the oldest inventory, and the value is calculated based on those items. In times of increasing costs, the LIFO method might underestimate the inventory value, and vice versa.

The WAC method determines the weighted average of the inventory, considering the cost of the older and the newer items, thus trying to avoid the impact of increasing or decreasing prices.

TABLE 14.2

Background Information for Valuing Inventory

Month	Number of Units Purchased	Cost Per Unit ($)	Total Cost ($)
January	20	60	1200
February	10	70	700
March	30	75	2250
April	10	65	650
Total	70		4800
Average			4800/70 = 68.58

TABLE 14.3

Valuation Methods

Method	Ending Inventory Value
FIFO	$2150 (10 × $65 + 20 × 75)
LIFO	$1900 (10 × $70 + 20 × 60)
WAC	$2057 (30 × $68.58)

Let us discuss the methods briefly. Refer to Table 14.2 for the background information and Table 14.3 for the resulting calculations. In the FIFO method, it is assumed that the 30 remaining bottles were purchased in April (10) and March (20). Therefore, the value of the inventory is 10 × $65 + 20 × $75 = $2150. The LIFO method assumes that the remaining bottles were purchased in February (10) and January (20) for a total value of $1900. The WAC method averages the cost of the bottles at $68.58 each for a total cost of $2057.

To calculate the annual value of the inventory, total the value of each product in the inventory (quantity on hand times cost) at the same time each year. Use the following equation to get the company's inventory value:

Ending inventory = Beginning inventory + Net purchases − Cost of goods sold

Therefore, take what you have in the beginning, add what you have purchased, subtract what you have sold, and the result—ending inventory—is what remains. You can also determine the annual average inventory value by calculating the monthly inventory values, adding these monthly inventory values, and dividing by 12. Regardless of the method chosen, the pharmacy manager must consistently use the same method from year to year.

METHODS OF INVENTORY CONTROL

The most commonly employed method of inventory control is the visual inspection method. This method requires the pharmacist, or other designated personnel, to visually inspect the number of items remaining on a shelf. From this number, the person then determines whether there is adequate inventory or whether an order should be placed. The person may use the ROP and EOQ to help determine whether an order should be placed and the quantity of the order. This is a fixed-quantity reorder system, in which the date of reordering varies but the quantity remains the same.

Often, the manager sets up a periodic inspection schedule to aid in inventory control. In this modified visual inspection, the inventory manager routinely inspects designated inventory levels (e.g., on a daily or weekly basis) to determine whether an order should be placed. This routine examination of inventory minimizes the potential for stockouts and can potentially improve inventory control. This is a fixed-time reorder system, in which the quantity ordered might vary but the date of ordering remains the same. This is ideal for small to medium businesses for which a prime vendor is the main supply source and the true volume of activity can be determined easily.

However, because a pharmacy contains hundreds or even thousands of items, it is difficult to use either method reliably, particularly if there are multiple vendors. In such cases, there is an added method to the periodic inspection called the ABC method of control (Figure 14.3). The ABC method of control prioritizes the items into three levels based on the theory that a small percentage of all the merchandise accounts for a large percentage of the dollar investment. "A" items typically comprise only 20% of the inventory items but account for nearly 80% of the cost. Because one of the main objectives of inventory control is to minimize the inventory investment, it is only logical to focus on the items that involve the most cost. "B" items typically compose about 30% of the items in the inventory and about 10% of the total costs. "C" items account for the remaining 50% of the items and the remaining 10% of the costs.

Therefore, "A" items are typically inspected and reordered daily, or near daily; "B" items are ordered less frequently; and "C" items are ordered even less frequently. This method allows the pharmacy to focus on those items that have a higher ITR and can be managed more efficiently.

With the advent of computers and the introduction of automated dispensing devices, the idea of a perpetual inventory is within the grasp of today's pharmacy. Further, the routine use of bar coding allows integration of point-of-care inventory management systems. In such systems, the inventory is constantly inspected and ordering and restocking take place much faster.

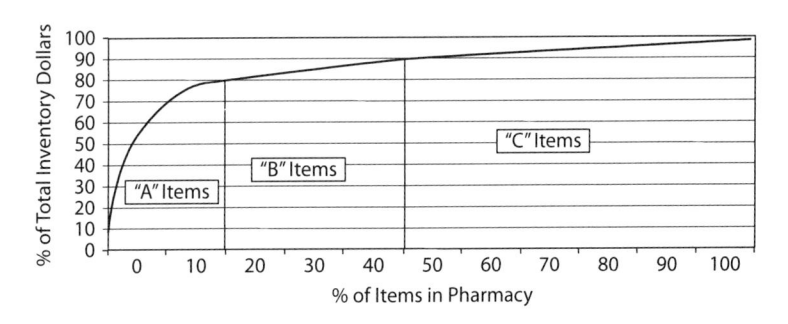

FIGURE 14.3 ABC method of inventory control.

CONCLUSION

Efficient pharmaceutical purchasing and inventory management are prerequisites for operating a successful pharmacy. Careful attention to the purchasing process and inventory management will result in a positive impact on the pharmacy's financial performance. The drug-purchasing process is complicated, and it has become more complex with the growth of restricted distribution programs and drug shortages. Pharmacy managers must develop clear drug-purchasing and inventory control systems and work proactively to eliminate inefficiencies within these systems.

BIBLIOGRAPHY

Allen SJ. Purchasing and inventory management. In: Brown TR, Ed. *Handbook of Institutional Pharmacy Practice*. Bethesda, MD: American Society of Health-System Pharmacists, 1992; 73–79.

American Society of Health-System Pharmacists. ASHP guidelines on managing drug product shortages in hospitals and health systems. *Am J Health-Syst Pharm*. 2009; 66:1399–1406.

Bickett WJ, Gagnon JP. Purchasing and inventory control for hospital pharmacies. *Top Hosp Pharm Manage*. 1987;7:59–74.

Carroll NV. Changes in channels of distribution: wholesalers and pharmacies in organized health-care settings. *Hosp Pharm Rep*. February 1997; 11:48–57.

Carroll NV. *Financial Management for Pharmacists: A Decision-Making Approach*, 2nd ed. Philadelphia: Lippincott Williams & Wilkins; 1998.

Environmental Protection Agency (EPA). Management of Hazardous Waste Pharmaceuticals. www.epa.gov/waste/hazard/generation/pharmaceuticals.htm (accessed February 3, 2014).

Food and Drug Administration (FDA). How to Dispose of Unused Medications. www.fda.gov/forconsumers/consumerupdates/ucm101653.htm (accessed February 3, 2014).

Fox ER, Tyler LS. Call to action: finding solutions for the drug shortage crisis in the United States. *Clin Pharmacol Ther*. 2013;93:145–147.

Glaser M. Off limits: the growth of pharmaceuticals bearing restrictions has the profession and pharmacists worried. *Drug Top*. 2001;5:57.

Huffman DC. Purchasing and inventory control. In *Effective Pharmacy Management*, 8th ed. Alexandria, VA: NARD, 1996, chap. 11.

IPC and ServAll Combine Strengths for Community Pharmacists. IPC/ServAll website. Available at www.ipcrx.com/announcements/pressrelease/final/press.htm (accessed June 11, 2003).

McAllister JC. Challenges in purchasing and inventory control. *Am J Hosp Pharm*. 1985;42:1370–1373.

Metzger ML, Billett A, Link MP. The impact of drug shortages on children with cancer—the example of mechlorethamine. *NEJM*. 2012;367;2461–2463.

Modern Distribution Management 2013. www.mdm.com/2013_pharmaceuticals_mdm-market-leaders (accessed February 3, 2014).

Smith CA. Managing pharmaceutical waste: what pharmacists should know. *J Pharm Soc Wisc*. November/December 2002:17–21.

Staff Report. Shining light on the "gray market." An examination of why hospitals are forced to pay exorbitant prices for prescription drugs facing critical shortages. July 2012. http://democrats.oversight.house.gov/uploads/7.25.12%20Staff%20Report%20Shining%20Light%20on%20the%20Gray%20Market.pdf (accessed March 10, 2014).

Tootelian DH, Gaedeke RM. Purchasing and inventory control. In: *Essentials of Pharmacy Management*. St. Louis, MO: Mosby, 1993; 357–377.

Vidal BA. Drug procurement responsibilities [Letter], *Hosp Pharm.* 1998;33:918.

Wellman GS. National supply-chain survey of drug manufacturer back orders. *Am J Hlth-Syst Pharm.* 2001;58:1224–1228.

Wetrich JG. Group purchasing: an overview. *Am J Hosp Pharm.* 1987;44:1581–1592.

Young D. Investigation of GPOs yields mixed opinions. *Am J Hlth-Syst Pharm.* 2002a; 1004:10,14.

Young D. Thalidomide prescribers cannot assign survey responsibility to pharmacists. *Am J Hlth-Syst Pharm.* 2002b; 1 : 1700, 1702, 1704.

Case Study

Andrew's Apothecary (AA) uses 10,000 bottles of 30 tablets of Cholnix (Hoffstatin) annually. Hoffstatin has an AWP of $120 per bottle of 30 tablets. The usual prescription is for 30 tablets per month (once-daily dosing). Hoffstatin is also available in bottles of 100 for $350. AA's procurement costs are $15 per order, with a carrying cost rate of 20% and a lead time of two days. It would cost $0.16 per prescription to transfer 30 tablets from the large bottle.

1. If AA was to order the bottles of 30 tables, how many should AA order at a time and how many orders per year would AA have to make? What are the annual total inventory costs for this method of purchasing?

2. If AA were to use only the 100 tablet bottles, how many should AA order at a time and how many orders per year would AA have to make? What are the annual total inventory costs of this method of purchasing?

3. Which method would you recommend AA use to minimize inventory costs?

4. What would happen to the number of orders per year if the carrying costs decreased to $5 per order?

15 Managing Pharmacy Automation and Informatics

Dennis A. Tribble and Mei-Jen Ho

CONTENTS

Learning Objectives: After reading this chapter and working through the cases, the reader will be able to:

1. Define three tenets of a general framework for approaching automation
2. Define computerized prescriber order entry (CPOE) and its relationships to pharmacy practice
3. Describe two uses for bar codes in pharmacy practice
4. Describe at least one limitation to the use of bar coding in pharmacy practice
5. Describe bar code medication administration (BCMA) and its relationships to pharmacy practice
6. Describe two key differences between CPOE and electronic prescribing (eRx)
7. Define three key requirements of the privacy and security regulations under the Health Information Portability and Accountability Act of 1996 (HIPAA)
8. Define changes to the HIPAA regulations arising from the HITECH Act
9. Define at least one additional requirement for automation that may arise as a result of that automation being classified as a medical device by the FDA
10. Define a request for proposal (RFP) and key elements of an RFP
11. Describe three considerations for deploying "smart" IV pumps

FRAMEWORK FOR HEALTH-SYSTEM PHARMACY AUTOMATION

The application of automation to pharmacy spans a wide variety of systems and applications which have in common their potential ability to improve both patient safety and staff productivity. The pharmacist who wishes to implement technology must ensure that the technology to be adopted is consistent with the goals and capabilities of the pharmacy being automated. To that end, it is important to develop and apply a conceptual framework within which technology is to be evaluated.

While each pharmacy should construct its own framework, the following sections highlight points of consideration that can be applied to constructing that framework.

Technology is a Tool[1]

The acquisition of technology should not be an end in itself, but should become the acquisition of a set of tools intended to address specific needs of the pharmacy in accomplishing its mission or missions within a health system. As such, when acquiring technology, the pharmacy must identify the job (or jobs) in which the technology will be applied, and determine whether or not the technology is capable of performing those jobs. For example,

1. What portion of the workload is the technology expected to carry? Will the technology be able to meet the demands implicit in carrying that workload? This is a function of both workload (the total amount of work the technology is expected to perform) and timing (the period of time within which that workload must be performed).
2. What kind of staffing will be required to install, maintain, and operate the technology?
3. Do the current pharmacy personnel have the requisite skills to operate the technology? If not how will the requisite skills be acquired and maintained?
4. Can the pharmacy provide the physical space and facilities required by the technology?
5. How will the pharmacy know that the technology has been successfully installed and is meeting its intended purpose?

Be Careful: Technology Will Change the Way the Work is Performed

Technology is not only a tool; it is a *power* tool. If it does not change the way work is performed, it is unlikely to be worth the time and expense necessary to acquire and install it. The adoption of technology requires *change management* skills and planning. Pharmacy staff will have become accustomed to an established, and probably manual, method of performing the tasks the technology is intended to perform. They will have to unlearn old work habits and practices and acquire a new set of habits and practices around the technology. The management of this change will require planning and will likely require temporary additional staffing.

One of the most common mistakes made when adopting technology is insisting on inserting the technology into a current manual set of work processes. Manual processes are more often evolved than planned, and are often incompletely understood. When applying technology to work processes, it is worthwhile to spend the time to map the current workflow, to consider how work should be performed in the presence of the new technology, and to construct new work processes that appropriately leverage the capabilities the technology has to offer. The exercise of mapping current workflow will expose workflow issues that need to be accommodated (or discontinued) and will provide the insights about what is truly required to be included in the new workflow around the technology to be adopted.

Technology Requires Infrastructure

It is increasingly rare that technology can be implemented within a pharmacy without both physical and procedural changes to the pharmacy.

Physical changes may include additional physical support to bear additional weight, additional electrical service, compressed air, local area network connections, or space to accommodate the technology.

Implementation of the technology also requires a carefully considered infrastructure of operating procedures, training, quality assurance, and maintenance to ensure that the technology is used properly and safely, both for the benefits of the patients whose medication is managed, and for the operators who interact regularly with the technology.

The Adoption of Pharmacy Technology Requires the Involvement of Stakeholders Outside of the Pharmacy

There are few occasions in which the implementation of technology in the pharmacy affects only those people working in the pharmacy. Other people likely to be affected include:

- Information technology (IT) workers, who may have to set up and enable the use of the technology within the IT infrastructure of the larger environment in which the pharmacy operates and perform maintenance and upgrade functions on the technology at regular intervals
- Patient care providers, who will likely be affected by the way the technology facilitates medication dispensing or manages documentation around the medication use process
- Finance managers, who must fund both the purchase and ongoing maintenance expenses of the technology
- Infectious disease professionals, who may have to consider whether or not the technology adequately mitigates risk (if it involves the production of sterile doses)
- Risk management professionals, who need to consider how the adoption of the technology may affect the health system's risk
- Contracting and purchasing managers, who will likely have to manage both the purchase and the ongoing maintenance contracting

The pharmacy manager who attempts to deploy technology without involving the proper stakeholders does so at considerable professional peril.

TECHNOLOGY PLATFORMS ARE LESS IMPORTANT THAN WHAT THE TECHNOLOGY CAN DO

The functions a technology can perform are more important than the platform on which it runs. This is especially true of computer software. While the pharmacy environment may place constraints on what kinds of hardware can be connected to a network, technology must first be evaluated in terms of its suitability to perform specific tasks, and only secondarily on the computer hardware it requires. While some consumer electronics seem compelling, such items should not be presumed to be useful in automating pharmacy practice. Much time and effort has been wasted trying to force-fit attractive consumer electronics solutions into practice models, where they may lack the display capability, performance, or processing power to meet the proposed needs for which they were suggested.

Therefore it is imperative for a pharmacy manager to be involved in developing, building, implementing, and ongoing maintenance of each technology employed by the pharmacy. Continuous evaluations of the focused technology should be employed to ensure the said technology continues to improve patient safety and streamline workflow. A manager should identify problems and assist both clinical and nonclinical members of the IT team to resolve the issue.

Technology Systems Should Operate from a Single, Reliable Source of Truth on All Data

Not all of the data used by any given technology will come from that technology. For example, patient information in a hospital pharmacy will likely come from a health-system computer system (increasingly, an *electronic medical record*) that is considered to be the sole authoritative source of information about patients. It is better for a technology to *interoperate* with such systems and to acquire the information from those systems directly rather than require users to manually transcribe that information into a stand-alone technology. An adopted technology should not be the single source of truth for any data unless it is the undisputed source of that truth.

For example, a pharmacy information system cannot be the source of the current patient location, the name of the patient, or the patient's primary identifiers. It is a consumer of that information, but not the source. Where there is a conflict between the pharmacy system and the electronic medical record (EMR), the EMR should be presumed to be correct.

Interoperability is the Key to Success

One of the hallmarks of early automation (and, sadly, much current automation) was the tendency of each automation product to think of itself as the center of the universe. The natural extension of the notion of a "single source of truth," however, is that other systems are the source of key data a piece of automation may require, and it can only acquire that information if either: (a) a user keys the data from other systems into it, or (b) the technology interoperates with other systems available on the hospital network to acquire the data that it needs. Since the early days of unit-dose drug distribution, transcription (option a) has been known to be a significant source of error. Therefore, the best option is to have any particular technology able to converse with other technologies to acquire data that it needs.

A common form of interoperability is *interfacing*, in which two technologies mutually agree to exchange data in either one or both directions using an agreed-upon message structure (the *syntax* of the exchange) under agreed-upon conditions and vocabulary (the *semantics* of the exchange). Experience has shown that the vocabulary requires particular attention to avoid using the same words to mean something entirely different.

Going into detail about interfacing technologies is beyond the scope of this chapter. It is worth noting, however, that even the best designed and planned interfaces require a significant amount of management to ensure that they operate properly on an ongoing basis. Since dissimilar technologies often approach the work of the pharmacy from very different conceptual frameworks, getting the semantics right represents a significant portion of the interfacing work. Interfaces often represent significant additional purchase cost, as well as ongoing costs in support and manpower to keep running.

Interfaces grew out of a concept entitled *best-of-breed* in which each functional area of a health system would acquire the technology that seemed best from its point of view, and then would work to have those technologies exchange information.

An increasingly popular form of interoperability is *integration,* in which technology systems all operate from a common data store, using a common core of processes. Quite often, this means that the technologies all come from the same supplier. The advantage of this method is that both syntactic and semantic issues are addressed from the beginning, and there is excellent clarity on how the various systems interoperate.

The kinds of system requirements that have grown out of recent strategies that are looking to truly eliminate paper in the provision of health care seem to favor integration over interfacing. This may well be the result of the need to agree on a common semantic before what has been the patient medical record can be properly automated. As a pharmacy informatics manager, he/she is responsible for providing resource expertise for pharmacy and relay technical needs to software developers to bridge technology to clinical needs.

REGULATION OF TECHNOLOGY AND MEDICAL DEVICES

Some but not all of the technology used in health care, including some of the technology used in pharmacy practice is regulated by the US Food and Drug Administration (FDA) as medical devices. Medical devices fell under the jurisdiction of the FDA starting in 1976; prior to that time, there was no control over devices intended to be used in the treatment of human disease. Table 15.1 contains lists of technology items that are and are not considered medical devices. The list is not exhaustive, but it conveys the general landscape of what technology generally falls under FDA control.

TABLE 15.1

Examples of Technology That Is and Is Not Regulated by the FDA

Not a Medical Device	Medical Device
Pharmacy information system	Blood bank system
Pharmacy workflow software	Laboratory information system
Bar code medication administration system	TPN compounder
Inventory management systems	IV robotics
EMR/CPOE systems	Computerized decision support systems[a]
Pharmacokinetic dosing software	TPN order entry software[b]
Automated dispensing cabinets	IV infusion pump

[a] The FDA has recently identified CDSS as potentially considered a medical device but is not currently enforcing registration or governance.

[b] TPN order entry software contained in pharmacy information systems or EMR/CPOE systems is generally not regulated. TPN order entry software sold as part of a TPN compounding system is regulated as an accessory.

Technology becomes a medical device principally because the FDA chooses to regulate it. The process by which a device is governed is analogous to the process by which a drug is introduced into the marketplace:

- A manufacturer registers with the FDA.
- The manufacturer designs, manufactures, sells, installs, and services the device as defined in the Quality System Regulations (21FCR820 and following).
- The manufacturer submits its device to the FDA for clearance/approval.
  - If the device is substantially equivalent to an already marketed device, the manufacturer submits a 510(k). The FDA response is clearance to market, not approval.
  - If the device is wholly new, then the manufacturer submits a premarket approval (PMA) and must demonstrate both safety and efficacy. The FDA response is clearance to market, not approval.
- Upon receipt of clearance, the manufacturer may then sell the device in the US marketplace. Ongoing development, as well as all sales and marketing literature, continue to be subject to the Quality System Regulations.
- At regular intervals, the FDA will visit the manufacturer's facility (or facilities) to ensure that the manufacturer continues to conform to the Quality System Regulations. If such a visit determines nonconformances, the FDA may take disciplinary action up to recall of the devices from the marketplace and punitive legal action on the manufacturer.
- If upgrades to a device significantly impact the safety and efficacy of the device, the FDA may demand that the manufacturer resubmit the upgraded device as if it were a new device.

Software that would ordinarily not be considered a medical device may be regulated as a medical device if it is sold as an accessory to a regulated device or controls the operation of a regulated device. This means that a software product may be a medical device while identical software provided in a different context may not be regulated as a medical device.

Until recently, hospitals could write software that controlled medical devices, such as programming IV infusion devices, or managing alerts from patient monitoring systems. The FDA now considers such hospital-created software as *Medical Device Data Systems* and has begun requiring hospitals that create these systems to register under and develop under the Quality System Regulations.[2]

Medical devices are classified into Class I, Class II, or Class III medical devices that represent increasing opportunity for patient harm. Class I technology devices are generally diagnostic devices connected to a laboratory information management system (LIMS) which is also regulated as a Class I device. Pharmacy pumps that simply transfer fluid from one container to another tend also to be classified as Class I devices. If and when regulated, Computerized Decision Support System (CDSS) components of CPOE systems will also be considered Class I devices. Class I devices do not require premarket approval but are subject to the Quality System Regulations.

Class III medical devices are implantable devices that operate independently while implanted within human beings. Pharmacies do not generally employ devices in this class but may be involved in inventorying and dispensing them (such as intra-ocular lenses, or implantable infusion devices).

Most devices, especially computer-controlled devices, fall into the intervening Class II devices, which include TPN compounders and IV infusion devices.

In March 2001, the FDA created a special class of devices called *Pharmacy Compounding Systems*, which are Class II devices that are exempted from the pre-market approval process. As such, these devices may be placed on the market without requiring premarket approval but are required to comply with the Quality System Regulations and will eventually be inspected under those regulations. Note that this exemption applies only to the device itself, and not to any disposable components that actually handle sterile fluids.[3]

Compliance with the Quality System Regulations includes:

- Having a defined quality system as described within a quality manual
- Maintaining complete design history for each device designed, including requirement, design, verification and validation, and release to the field
- Maintaining a complete record of all changes to each device manufactured (a device history record)
- Providing a mechanism for receiving, handling, and resolving customer complaints
- Including information in the device labeling (which includes all promotional material, including verbal sales material) only when it can be conclusively demonstrated

Software compliance becomes especially involved, because medical device software can only operate in the software environment in which it was validated. This may mean that a medical device that needs to be connected to a hospital's network cannot receive the ordinary operating system upgrades and antivirus signature upgrades that network administrators otherwise push to all networked devices. It is important to clarify these issues with the device manufacturer.

Pharmacists who use technology need to maintain awareness of which of their technology is registered with the FDA, and which is not, and understand what that distinction may mean in terms what is required to communicate with such devices, especially across a hospital network.

OTHER REGULATORY CONSIDERATIONS

Regulations around medical devices are only one instance of the regulatory environment within which technology must exist. Careful consideration of other federal requirements (such as requirements by the Drug Enforcement Agency), patient privacy requirements (HIPAA), and state pharmacy laws regarding the implementation of technology must also be considered.

State Laws

State laws often dictate requirements for notification, inspection, or even approval for the implementation of specific types of technology. For example, the State of

Ohio has specific requirements for irrefutable identification of pharmacist identity whenever a pharmacist check is documented online.

Drug Enforcement Agency (DEA) Regulations

Technology that must manage the storage and distribution of controlled substances may need to conform to specific security requirements to comply with DEA regulations.

Privacy and Security of Patient Information

The Health Insurance Portability and Accountability Act of 1996 (HIPAA) was enacted to encourage the use of electronic systems in health-care claims adjudication. Because the requirements of this act place patient health-care information into electronic transactions, and because placing them there makes it theoretically possible to inappropriately acquire and disclose that information on a broader scale, a key feature of HIPAA and its regulations involves ensuring that patient privacy is appropriately maintained. There is therefore significant federal regulation that governs what patient information must be protected, how that information is to be protected, and what the consequences are for inappropriate disclosure of that protected health information.

The Health Information Technology for Economic and Clinical Health (HITECH) act further clarifies both requirements for protection and consequences for inappropriate disclosure.

A complete discussion of HIPAA and its regulations is beyond the scope of this chapter. A pharmacy manager who deploys technology needs to be aware of HIPAA and HITECH (and their related regulations in the Code of Federal Regulations) and needs to carefully consider how well any technology enables compliance with these legal responsibilities to protect patient information.

PURCHASING TECHNOLOGY

The process of purchasing technology should be formal and planned. Routinely, the process starts by the preparation of a Request for Proposal (RFP) in which the buyer (the pharmacy) details the requirements for the technology they intend to purchase and requests the various vendors who might supply the technology to describe which of the requirements they can meet and how they meet them. The RFP may also ask the vendor to describe their service offerings, information about their current user base, and other information that the pharmacy may deem important. If the RFP is for a very large purchase and/or is very complex, the pharmacy may conduct a bidder's conference, in which they present the RFP in detail, and field questions from the vendors who will propose their systems for purchase.

One of the important issues to consider when issuing an RFP is that there may be vendors who can meet the pharmacy's requirements but who may do so in ways the pharmacy had not previously considered. It is for this reason that it is important for the RFP to state their requirements in terms that are agnostic to how those requirements are met. For example, if requesting proposals for a syringe-filling technology that will fill, cap, and label syringes, it is better to specify the information that must be on the label than to attempt to stipulate a specific label format. Pharmacy informatics managers oversee the technical requirements to fulfill the clinical needs for the successful implementation of the technology, while the financial responsibilities may fall on other personnel in the department.

Appendix A at the end of this chapter contains an example of an RFP for an IV robot.

BAR CODE APPLICATIONS

Bar coding is a type of machine-readable encoding that permits rapid and consistent input of data into a computer system. The data to be machine-read into a software package are encoded into a sequence of bars or squares that represent individual characters. The advantage of bar coding over other machine-readable technologies, such as optical character recognition, is that it is very reliable, very fast, relatively inexpensive, and relatively insensitive to physical orientation of the code to be scanned.

In general, the scanning process involves identifying the beginning and ending of the bar code, determining the sequence and width of the individual bars, and then converting the sequence of bars into a corresponding series of characters that represent the data that the bar code was intended to deliver.

In order to perform the last step, the scanner must either be told, or must be able to detect the *symbology* used in the bar code, which is the language that translates bars into characters. Symbology may dictate the following:

- The characters that can be encoded (e.g., some symbologies encode only numbers)
- The length of the data that can be encoded (some symbologies require that the data be of a certain length [number of characters])
- How the beginning and end of the code are recognized
- Additional characters (check digits) that may help validate that the entire code was correctly scanned
- The type of code displayed (one-dimensional versus two-dimensional)

In order to read a bar code, a user must employ a *bar code scanner* that performs the reading and interpretation function, and computer software that knows how to receive the decoded data from the scan and use it. Scanners exist in two varieties: linear scanners that can read only one-dimensional bar codes and imagers that can read both one-dimensional and two-dimensional bar codes. Most scanners available today can perform *autodetection*—that is, they can determine the symbology used for the bar code during scanning, and then use that symbology to decode the data from the bar code. When a scanner autodetects symbologies, it can also be programmed to ignore symbologies it would otherwise successfully read, and can be programmed to recognize symbologies it does not automatically recognize.

One-dimension bar codes represent their data as a linear sequence of variable-width black bars on a white background. If a one-dimensional scanner is used to read them, then the scan must pass over the entire linear sequence to successfully read the code. If the scanner is an imager, the entire bar code image must be captured by the imager. The data such bar codes can contain are limited either by the symbology or by the physical length of a code that can be printed.

FIGURE 15.1 An example of a 1D bar code.

FIGURE 15.2 An Aztec Barcode, an example of a 2D bar code.

Examples of one-dimensional symbologies are Universal Product Code (UPC, Figure 15.1), Interleaved 2 of 5, Code 39, and Code 128.

Two-dimension bar codes represent their data as a two-dimensional sequence of black squares on a white background. Two-dimension bar codes can be read only by imagers, which must be able to capture an image of the entire two-dimensional structure. These codes typically can contain larger amounts of data than one-dimensional codes, and multiple codes can be linked to store even larger amounts of data. Examples of two-dimensional symbologies include Datamatrix, QR Code, Aztec (Figure 15.2), and PDF417.

In the United States, all commercially available medication containers are required to contain a bar code that contains the National Drug Code (NDC) of the medication. The NDC describes a particular manufacturer's instance of a product in a particular package size. This means (for instance) that the NDC within the bar code for one manufacturer's vial of ampicillin 1 g powder for injection is different from another manufacturer's vial of ampicillin 1 g powder for injection, and it also means that the NDC for a box of 10 such vials is different than the NDC for the individual vial.

The NDC is a three-part number containing a labeler code (the manufacturer selling the product), a drug code (a number representing the description of the product [e.g., ampicillin 1 g powder for injection vial], and a package code (a number representing the level of packaging [e.g., individual unit, box of 10, case of 100, etc.]. Only the labeler code is assigned by the FDA; the remainder of the NDC is assigned by the manufacturer. This means, for example, that the drug code portion of the NDC for an ampicillin 1 g powder for injection vial *is different for every manufacturer* (USFDA, Guidance for Industry: Bar Code Label Requirements Questions and Answers, 2011).

Maintaining a current list of NDC numbers represents a significant challenge for bar-coding systems because new NDCs tend to enter the supply stream much faster than most system's updates. Pharmacies must often manage this problem by scanning each item as it is received to ensure that the item will be recognized and produce the correct results when scanned for filling a prescription.

The data within a bar code may be further encoded to permit the software receiving the scanned data to locate and use the data within the scan. The two most common encoding schemes are defined by GS1 (www.GS1.org) and HIBCC (www.hibcc.org).

These encoding schemes define methods by which a single code can contain a variety of data including data type, identifier, lot, expiration, and serial number.[5]

As currently defined by US law and regulation, the bar code need only contain the 10-digit, unformatted NDC and must be presented in a one-dimension (linear) symbology.[6] Current initiatives include permitting two-dimensional representation, inclusion of lot number and expiration date, and inclusion of a serial number to facilitate maintaining a pedigree for each encoded item. Note that, as currently encoded, a bar code scanning system cannot distinguish between scanning ten identical items and scanning the same item ten times.

Bar coding in pharmacy practice is used primarily for product identification and/ or patient identification. *In these applications, the bar code is reliable only if the bar code is physically attached to the item its encoded data describes.* This means that the bar code is on the patient's wristband (or otherwise attached to the patient) for patient identification, and physically included in the label or otherwise attached to the product for product identification.

BAR CODE MEDICATION ADMINISTRATION

Also known as *bar code point of care* (BPOC) and *bar code medication verification* (BMV), bar code medication administration (BCMA) represents the most extensive use of bar coding in the medication use process. In this process, a nurse administering medication first scans the patient's wristband (to ensure the correct patient) and then scans each medication package *prior to administration* in order to ensure that the medications intended to be given to this patient are correct. In this case, correct means that the medication is currently ordered to be given to this patient and is intended to be given on or about the current date and time.

If the doses are fulfilled by commercially packaged medication products, then the bar code scanned is the NDC bar code on the commercial package, which is then compared to the current patient's medication orders.

In cases where the pharmacy compounds the dose, such as a compounded IV, the bar code contains a numeric code that represents the medication order, or a specific dispensing against that medication order for that patient. If the encoded number references a current medication order for which medication administration is currently required, then the BCMA system permits it to be administered.

Note that, in this case, the BCMA system presumes that the dose contains the correct label solely on the basis of the label referencing the correct medication order. The pharmacy must employ appropriate systems in order to ensure that the dose actually contains the medication referenced in the encoded order. Note further that the same value may be encoded on several doses, which permits the BCMA system to verify that a given dose is appropriate for the patient at the current time, but does not permit the BCMA system to distinguish exactly which of potentially several doses for that order is currently being administered.

If the medication scanned represents medication that is ordered for this patient and is due to be administered on or about the current time, then the system permits medication administration to proceed. If the scanned medication is incorrect, or if it is not recognized by the system, then the system halts medication administration until the correct medication is presented. If the caregiver believes that the medication is correct (especially in cases where the medication is not recognized by the BCMA system), they may be authorized to *override* the BCMA system and administer the medication anyway.

The effectiveness of BCMA systems has been controversial, although they are gaining in popularity. Studies have shown that incomplete or improper implementations can result in their being ineffective, and known workarounds are plentiful. Completeness of the underlying bar code database, hardware reliability, and ongoing monitoring for compliance seem to be significant in ensuring success of such systems.

Bar Code Medication Preparation

Bar codes can be used within the pharmacy to ensure that compounded doses contain the correct ingredients in a manner similar to BCMA. Although not as widely used, BCMP provides the same values and suffers from the same issues as BCMA. BCMP tends to be included in larger workflow management systems that include bar code verification of source ingredients as one of many in-process verification steps to ensure that compounded doses are properly made and labeled.

Dose Tracking

Bar codes can also be used to track doses throughout their delivery process, either within stand-alone systems or within the context of larger systems, including automated dispensing cabinet (ADC) systems, medication carousel systems, and workflow management systems. The bar codes used for tracking may or may not be the same as bar codes used for BCMA. If they are different, careful delineation of what bar codes are to be used for what purposes is required to avoid confusion.

Employee Identification

Bar codes may also be used to identify employees for automated timekeeping devices. This application is less common than other machine-readable encoding since it is easier to falsify.

As a pharmacy manager, bar coding enables pharmacy to deliver the core functions of any pharmacy with improved efficiency and fulfills HIPAA compliance. Bar coding enables pharmacy management to track and manage inventory and dispensing of the correct medication. In addition, it eliminates the need for pharmacists to remember and keep up with the ever-changing and strict requirements. This in turn improves the workflow and leads to greater customer satisfaction.

ROBOTICS

The definition of *robotics* has been the subject of some debate. Early definitions included the notion that the technology employed one or more robotic "arms" that mimic human arm/hand movements. While this is true of several of the devices ordinarily included in lists of robotic systems, there are others to be described in this chapter that are considered robotic that do not use robotic arms. There are different kinds of robotic devices that are aimed at the preparation of specific kinds of doses. There is a robotic device that fills unit-dose cassettes (and some first doses). There are devices that fill some (but not all) IV admixtures. There are robotic devices that perform delivery from the pharmacy to patient care units.

Technology can generally be asserted to be robotic when:

1. The technology performs tasks that pharmacists or pharmacy technicians would ordinarily perform by hand, requiring minimal human input while performing those tasks.
2. The technology receives orders for items to be prepared or packaged electronically from another system, queues those orders for preparation according to internal rules of priority, and proceeds from one preparation to the next with little or no human input.
3. The technology performs delivery according to a preprogrammed route without requiring human attendance.

The majority of robotic applications are aimed at preparing doses for distribution to patients, performing tasks associated with product acquisition/selection, product manipulation and preparation (e.g., reconstitution), product counting and/ or measurement, and where required, the printing and application of appropriate labeling.

Currently, all robotic devices tend to be expensive, require changes to facilities to permit them to operate, and require an operator to resupply them and deal with occasional interruptions in operation.

With the exception of delivery robotics, robotic devices operate with their own internal computer systems that may include a formulary that must be maintained in synchronization with other systems with which they interoperate.

Current robotic devices therefore require operators who are trained in their proper operation and who perform regular maintenance. Those trained operators need to understand both the clinical necessities of the robotic operation, and the downstream implications of decisions they make when placing information into drug databases.

For dose preparation robotics, there are no known robotic devices that completely remove the requirement for human preparation. It is therefore important when considering the purchase of a robotic device to ensure that the device will prepare enough doses to reasonably off-load human workers and will prepare them fast enough to meet operational needs. While not explicitly demonstrated through experimentation, it is generally accepted that speed and flexibility (the ability to handle multiple different kinds of dose preparations) are mutually exclusive.

Prescription-Filling Robots

Larger ambulatory pharmacies may use prescription-filling robots to automate the filling and labeling of prescriptions for oral solid medication. These devices maintain canisters of medication attached to pill-counting technologies. When supplied with a prescription for oral solids to be filled (usually from an ambulatory pharmacy information system), the robot performs the following functions:

- Selects a correctly sized prescription vial
- Presents the vial to the canister/counter
- Counts the tablets or capsules out into the vial
- Places a lid on the vial
- Prints and applies the label to the vial
- Delivers the filled and labeled prescription for pharmacist inspection

In some cases, the prescription-filling robot is part of a larger workflow system that actually manages the entire process of receiving, evaluating, pricing, filling, and checking the prescription.

UNIT-DOSE CART-FILLING ROBOTICS

The first robotic device on the market was a robotic device to fill unit-dose cassettes. This robotic device uses a robotic arm mounted to a track that can move back and forth along a wall on which are mounted solid medications in packaging that includes a bar code that the robot can use to identify the medication and select it.

This robot can receive a list of patients and the medications that each patient needs to have dispensed, locate a unit-dose cart bin for each patient, pick the medications to be placed in that bin, and deliver the filled bin for pharmacist checking. In many states, pharmacist checking can be statistical; that is, pharmacists are obliged to check only a small sample of the total number of filled bins as long as the error rate in the checked bins does not exceed a specified threshold.

This robot can also receive a group of returned doses, evaluate them for appropriate shelf life, and place the doses with suitable shelf life back into its supply for subsequent use.

This robotic device requires that all medications to be distributed be packaged in bags that are marked with appropriate bar coding and designed to be hung on pegs along its wall. Typically this packaging is done by an external third party, rather than being done by the hospital.

This robotic device supports a limited number of drug products. It can pick; it must therefore inform the user if there are additional products that need to be acquired and supplied by hand.

IV ADMIXTURE-PREPARING ROBOTICS

There are a few robotic devices that are intended to fill doses with sterile contents. These devices all have in common that they receive a list of doses to be prepared from an external system, select from that list the doses that they can prepare, acquire the medications needed to fulfill those doses, prepare those source containers as needed (e.g., reconstitute them), measure out the dose of drug needed, supply the measured quantity to the dose container, cap the container (if needed), and print and apply a label.

One of these devices is a syringe-filling robot that prepares doses from vials or from pre-prepared "reservoirs." This device fills only one size syringe (a 12-mL syringe), but is capable of filling both stock and patient-specific doses into those syringes in volumes from 0.5 to 11.5 mL at rates up to 600 doses per hour. It requires both compressed air and electrical supply and has been validated for use outside of a clean room.

Other devices have been designed to fill both IV bags and a variety of sizes of syringes. These doses offer the ability to address a wider variety of dose sizes and packaging, but at the cost of slower rates of speed. Published rates of speed for these devices vary between 20 and 65 doses per hour. These devices require that they be loaded with the drug containers, syringes, and IV solutions needed to supply the preparations they will compound.

To date, none of these devices can prepare a dose that has more than one active ingredient. Doses prepared by these devices may all contain a single active drug and (optionally) a single carrier/diluent ingredient. As a result, these devices cannot completely replace the preparation of sterile doses by hand.

Since these devices compound doses that are intended to have sterile contents, they are subject to Chapter <797> of the United States Pharmacopoeia (USP). One of the advantages of these robotic devices is that they remove the most common source of microbial contamination (human touch). Nonetheless, it is important to both establish and maintain the aseptic environment within the robotic device to ensure that it can consistently produce doses whose contents are reliably sterile.

These devices are considered to be medical devices under the purview of the US Food and Drug Administration. This places significant controls on their design, manufacture, installation, and service, as well as their behavior on hospital information system networks.

These devices maintain formularies of drug products that contain the information these devices need to manipulate containers in three-dimensional space. This means that the information they require extends beyond the kinds of information available in commercial drug databases and can include such information as reconstitution volumes, container dimensions, and specific speeds and other operating parameters for each known container. Many of these parameters need to be experimentally derived. It is important to understand the processes involved in adding a new and different product to the device formulary, both in terms of the tasks involved, and where those tasks may need to be performed.

CYTOTOXIC-PREPARING ROBOTICS

Cytotoxic-preparing robotic devices are a distinct subset of the IV admixture-preparing robotic devices in that they must both prepare the various doses and must take appropriate steps to contain aerosols and vapors from cytotoxic drugs, which are considered hazardous materials. This makes these devices subject to specific portions of USP <797> that relate to sterile doses prepared from hazardous materials.

The ability to protect pharmacists and pharmacy technicians from exposure to these hazardous materials is considered a benefit of these devices, especially in jurisdictions where the occupational safety laws make staffing for manual preparation of these doses difficult.

Since the insides of these devices are regularly exposed to hazardous materials, special considerations are required for normal and exceptional maintenance of the devices, especially if the direct compounding area of the device must be exposed to the external environment, both to keep the compounding area suitably clean, and to prevent exposure of the external environment to hazardous materials.

DELIVERY ROBOTICS

A relatively recent addition to the panoply of robotic pharmacy devices are delivery robots. These devices have secured storage spaces within which the pharmacy places medication for delivery along with the destination needed for each medication supply. These robots are preprogrammed with routes that take them to the location(s) where they need to drop off medication supplies, including programming to call, enter, and exit an elevator. When the robot is sent on its way, it knows what it is carrying, and where each item it is carrying needs to go. It then navigates the hallways and elevator systems until it arrives at its first stop. Personnel at that stop interact with the robot, removing the material for them and (optionally) placing things for return to the pharmacy in their bin, and then send the robot on its way to its next stop. When the robot has completed its rounds, it returns to the pharmacy to await its next trip.

TPN COMPOUNDING SYSTEMS

Although not strictly robotic, devices that can maintain an inventory of several different admixture ingredients and mix them to create a total parenteral nutrition (TPN) dose were among the first automated products for preparing compounded sterile doses. These devices may be macro compounders (designed to deliver only large-volume ingredients), micro compounders (designed to deliver small-volume ingredients), or combination micro-macro devices.

The process these devices automate tends to be cumbersome and error-prone when performed by hand, and these devices have generally been shown to improve both the speed and the quality of the process (Figure 15.3).

WORKFLOW SYSTEMS

A relatively recent addition to the pharmacy automation armamentarium is a group of software products referred to as workflow systems. Workflow systems got their start in paper-intensive industries (such as insurance application and claims processing) where they were able to demonstrate value by standardizing the processing of submitted paper documents, providing exceptional visibility to the state of any submitted document at any time, reducing lost work, speeding processing, and enforcing appropriate review steps.

Workflow systems provide value by guiding and standardizing manual processes, maintaining detailed records about the dispensing process, providing visibility into the current state of work within the pharmacy, and providing reporting on that work.

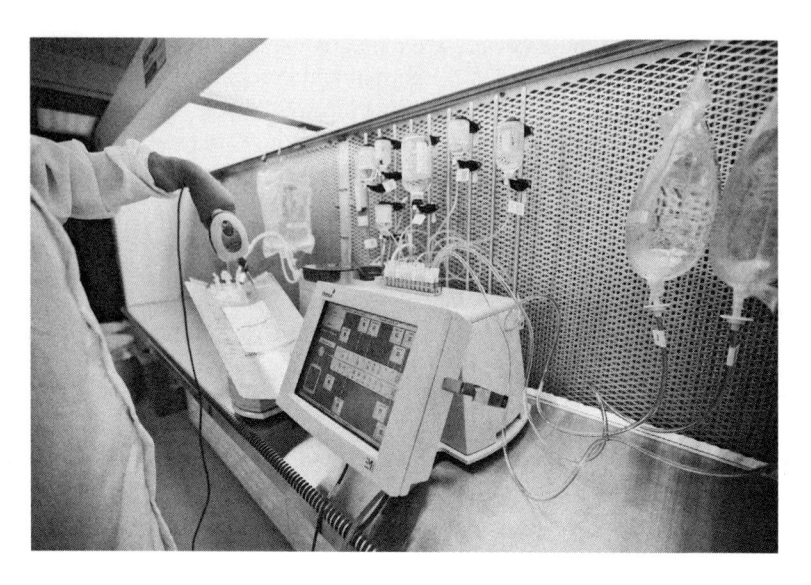

FIGURE 15.3   Baxter ExactaMix 2400 TPN Compounder. (Courtesy of Baxter Corporation, Englewood, CA.)

Workflow was first introduced to pharmacy practice in outpatient prescription processing, where standardizing and automating a number of the processes associated with prescription filling demonstrated a reduction in overall processing time, better handoffs between pharmacists, and more reliable documentation. One pharmacy demonstrated the ability to double work volume without adding staff.[7]

More recently, vendors of automated inventory/storage (e.g., carousel) systems have built workflow for using those devices in the dispensing of non-IV doses, significantly reducing steps involved in the dispensing process, and dramatically improving the amount of inventory control.

Most recently workflow software has been applied to the compounding of IV solutions, using camera technology, bar code scanning, customized procedures, weighing on an electronic balance, and other tools to route and prioritize work for the compounding technician or pharmacist, track the compounding process in detail, use bar code scanning to validate use of correct compounding ingredients, automate routing of the completed doses for checking, permitting remote checking, enforcing in-process checking where appropriate, tracking dose delivery to patient care areas, and providing both summary and detailed reporting to the pharmacy for managing the process.

AUTOMATED DISPENSING CABINETS

Automated dispensing cabinets (ADCs) represent one of the more successful forms of pharmacy automation and represent truly disruptive technology. Pharmacy dispensing in health systems had worked hard since the 1970s to centralize medication processing to the pharmacy only to have this technology force the primary delivery system back to a decentralized (patient-care-unit–based) delivery model. In the process of so doing, these devices have leveraged the best features of both the ward stock and unit-dose drug distribution models.

Automated dispensing cabinets place the most commonly used medications in any patient care area on that patient care area, with the result that the delays in medication availability associated with centralized drug distribution are effectively eliminated. This reduces conflict between the pharmacy and the staff in patient care areas, and reduces the amount of pharmacist time spent in purely dispensing activities. Figures 15.4 and 15.5 show two types of general purpose dispensing cabinets that can be seen in a patient care area. In all implementations, access to the medications is limited to appropriately authorized patient care personnel, and documentation of the use of the medication occurs automatically as a by-product of acquiring the medication.

Levels of control may vary widely, even within a specified cabinet. Cabinets may be completely open (control is limited to who may open the door of the cabinet), may present drawers whose access is individually controlled, or may control what subdivisions of drawers may be accessed. Some cabinets store the individual medication profiles of the patients they serve and only permit access to the medications needed by specified patients within a reasonable time of when those medications are due to be administered.

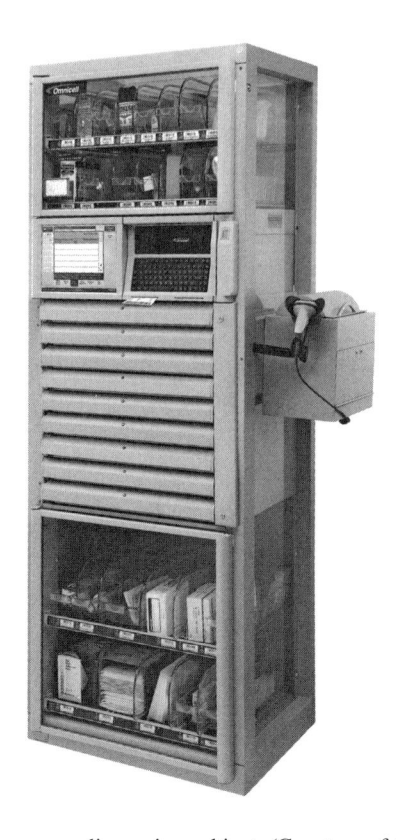

FIGURE 15.4 General purpose dispensing cabinet. (Courtesy of Omnicell, Inc.)

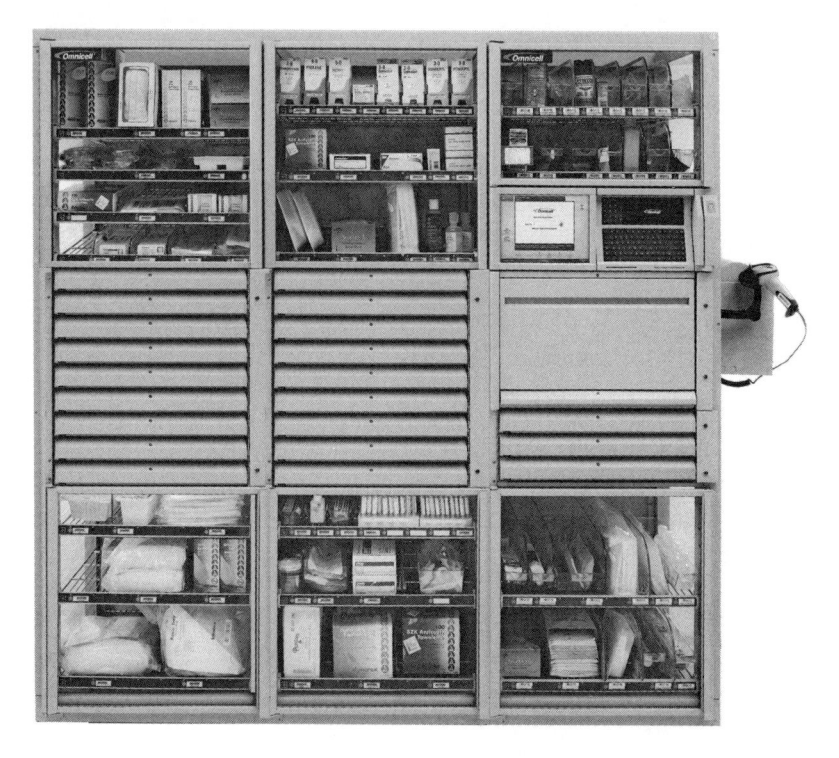

FIGURE 15.5 Arrangement of three cabinets configured for general dispensing. (Courtesy of Omnicell, Inc.)

These cabinet systems may include apparatus that can be applied to a refrigerator or other already available storage to control access to that device.

All of these options result in significant improvements in the available documentation of medication access. One of the first benefits of the implementation of these cabinets was to significantly reduce the nursing time required for controlled drug inventory accounting, and to reduce the frequency of missed charges associated with ward-stock use.

ADC systems find use in both the pharmacy and in patient care areas. In the pharmacy, carousel units minimize floor space and walking required by pharmacy personnel to acquire medications, essentially bringing the shelves to the user rather than making the user go to the shelves. Figure 15.6 is one type of carousel unit that can be found on patient floors.

Current ADC systems use the hospital's network to permit centralized server computers to interact with the cabinets and communicate with other systems. In some cases, the number of cabinets that a given server can support is limited, and large implementations may require the replication of several of these servers in order to support all the required cabinets. In these cases, the pharmacy may be required to replicate formulary management and interface strategies for each of the server systems.

FIGURE 15.6 Carousel unit. (Courtesy of Omnicell, Inc.)

More recent analyses of operations on these cabinets have shown some concern about the actual level of control that is possible, and managing workaround behavior, as well as ensuring that the cabinet remains adequately stocked can represent significant amounts of work for the pharmacy. Caregivers may resent having to come to the unit to acquire medication and may remove more than they document taking in order to reduce trips to the cabinet. In some cases this behavior has resulted in medication errors.[8]

It is therefore important that pharmacies using these devices make regular and careful use of the information gathered by these devices in order to identify and address workaround or diversionary behavior. There are commercial add-on software systems that monitor ADC transactions and report possible diversionary behavior.

It is also important to remember that ADC systems that maintain patient profiles and control drugs on a patient-specific level must be interfaced with hospital pharmacy systems so they can maintain profiles on the individual patients and report utilization/charge data back to the pharmacy systems or health-system billing systems.

In general, the benefits of ADC technology appear to have outweighed the risks, and these devices have become a staple of health-system pharmacy drug distribution.

IV ADMINISTRATION DEVICES

One of the oldest groups of devices that automate medication delivery are IV administration or *infusion* devices. IV administration devices were originally designed to ensure the infusion of medication intravenously at the prescribed rate over a period of time. As such, these devices were given a rate of administration, typically in drops per minute or in mL per hour, and would then govern the flow of fluid from the dose container.

IV administration devices have evolved over time to have additional capabilities such as the following:

- *Loading Dosing*—The ability to deliver a somewhat larger initial dose to establish a blood level and then retreat to an ordered infusion rate
- *Bolus Dosing*—The ability on command to deliver a large dose of the infused drug over a short period of time and then return to an ordered infusion rate
- *Secondary Dosing*—The ability to interrupt the infusion of a continuous infusion dose for the delivery of an intermittent IV dose, and then return to the primary infusion
- *Patient-Controlled Analgesia*—The ability to permit the patient to command the delivery of an intravenous dose of an analgesic medication subject to restrictions over the amount of the dose and the frequency with which that dose can be administered
- *Smart Libraries*—The ability of the pump to be programmed with sets of infusion limits that permit the pump to challenge or prevent the overadministration of infused drug therapy, including:
  - The ability to compute dose based on standard infusion concentrations and patient weight or body surface area
  - The ability to titrate doses to patient response
  - The ability to alert if the dose exceeds a dose limit in absolute amounts (e.g., mg/hour or mL/hour), in amounts per kg of patient body weight, or in amounts per square meter of body surface area
  - The ability to provide different infusion warning limits for different care areas of a hospital
  - The ability to push new libraries of warning limits and controls to pumps over wireless connections
- The ability to log and record pump data in a dedicated computer system and to report against that accumulated pump data to permit ongoing surveillance of drug infusion in great detail

Modern infusion devices are networked devices that communicate on a regular basis with other networked systems through a computer often referred to as a *gateway*. In some instances, this connection permits an infusion pump to query an EMR and retrieve pump programming instructions directly from the patient's EMR. Figure 15.7 shows examples of modern infusion devices.

Modern infusion devices are medical devices governed by the Food and Drug Administration under the Quality System Regulations. See the section on Medical Devices for the implications for deployment and programming.

While the hospital pharmacy may be involved in the management of infusion devices, more frequently the primary responsibility falls to a clinical engineering department. Where the pharmacy contributes most significantly to these devices is the building and maintaining of the master drug library, the list of infusions known to the infusion device, and for each such infusion, the controls and warning limits applied to that infusion.

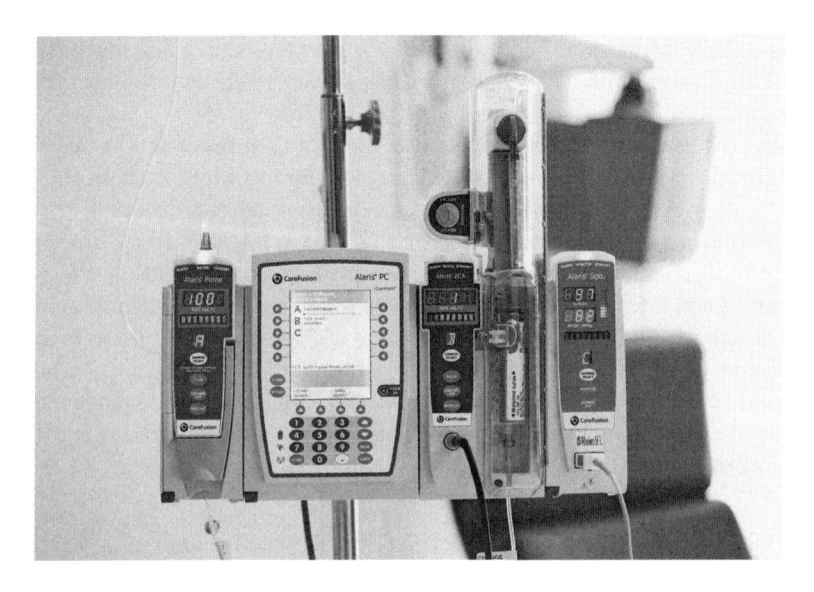

FIGURE 15.7   Alaris infusion pump.

The master drug library is often organized around specific areas of use, the infusions used within those areas, the permitted concentrations of each of those infusions, the manner in which the pump is programmed for each of those concentrations, and the limits within which the pump is permitted to deliver those medications. The implementation of a new or different infusion device at a hospital therefore represents a significant investment of time and effort by the pharmacy to get those devices ready for use.

The library is considered a primary safety net for patients receiving infusion therapy. Its primary intent is to ensure that the pump does not harm patients by over- or underdelivering infused medications.

As defined in the library, the pump may require different information of the caregiver depending on the area of use, the drug being infused, and the concentration of that drug being infused. Standardization of these infusions is considered to be beneficial, if not required, for a successful smart pump implementation.

Most, if not all, of these smart devices permit their libraries to be overridden by the caregiver and used as a "dumb" device that is programmed to deliver fluid at a specified rate in mL per hour. Depending on the device, the user starts with the drug library disabled and opts in to use the library, or starts with the drug library enabled, and must choose to disable it, or opt out of its use. In either case, it is important to use the accumulated pump data, if available, to monitor the frequency and reasons for overrides. Overriding has been reported to be associated with medication errors. (ISMP, 2007). The data from this monitoring guide modifications to the library to make it more useful and to identify caregivers who may be putting their patients at risk by disabling the checking performed by the library.

Ongoing maintenance of the drug library is also typically a pharmacy responsibility. This responsibility is often managed by a team at least one member of which is dedicated to this task.

Infusion devices may be designed to use standard IV infusion sets or may require the use of special IV administration sets designed for use with the pump.

For pediatric and neonatal use, there are infusion devices that deliver infused drug solutions from a syringe. It is not unusual for the infusion device used in these areas to be different from the infusion device used for adult patients.

The decision to implement these devices or to replace a current device with a different device or from a different manufacturer is a complex, multidisciplinary project that can occupy a hospital staff for weeks or months. The pharmacy informatics manager needs to work with pharmacy leadership to ensure that the implementation is planned and executed and that ongoing use of the infusion devices is appropriately governed.

ELECTRONIC MEDICAL RECORDS/COMPUTERIZED PRESCRIBER ORDER ENTRY/ELECTRONIC MEDICATION ADMINISTRATION RECORD

MEDICAL RECORD

A discussion of the *electronic medical record* (EMR) requires a brief overview of the general concepts around the medical record.

The traditional medical record, sometimes called the "patient chart" has until recently been a collection of paper documents intended to contain a legal record of the care rendered to a patient. Medical records occur in virtually all patient care venues and are intended to be continuous and cumulative records of care rendered to a patient. Payers and other external agencies rely on the medical record as the authoritative record of care given, especially when considering whether or not to pay for that care.

Each institution defines for itself what information is contained in the patient record and who may record what information within that record. While there may be slight variations from health system to health system, a typical medical record contains the following:

- Current patient demographic information
- A clinical summary or list of known problems and conditions
- A record of the administrative details of the patient's current encounter
- A record of all care ordered to be rendered on behalf of the patient (including medication orders)
- A record of medications administered to the patient (medication administration record)
- A record of diagnostic testing performed on the patient and results
- A record of the nursing care provided to the patient, including vital signs and assessments
- Physician's notes—a record of observations and thoughts by physicians
- Nursing notes—a record of observations and thoughts by nurses

- Notes and reports from other caregivers

Because the medical record is a legal record, it contains only those records stipulated by the care location to be contained by it; there may be other records of care within a care location that may not be included in the patient's medical record. Pharmacy dispensing records have long been among those not included in the medical record, and the recording of clinical pharmacy encounters in the medical record remains controversial. In practice, a paper chart might accumulate a number of unofficial documents during a patient health-care encounter, but those documents are removed before the medical record is finalized for that encounter.

The paper chart imposes significant limitations on the pace of health care, simply because it must be located to be able to be used, and may only be used by one person at one time. One pundit described what he characterized as "the law of charts" which, simply stated, was "Wherever the chart is, you are not."[10]

An EMR, therefore, is a medical record that has been transformed from its paper predicate to an electronic form, using a database and supportive software. The impetus to move from a paper-based system to an electronic system is based on three primary drivers: patient safety, cost reduction, and improvements in operational efficiency:

- *Patient Safety*—In its 1999 report ("To Err is Human"), the Institute of Medicine (IOM) cites electronic records (more specifically, automated medication order entry systems) and bemoans the failure of health care to adopt such systems to address medication error.[11]
- *Cost Reduction*—The Healthcare Information and Management Systems Society (HiMSS) Electronic Health Records Association documents EMRs are believed to significantly reduce cost of care by eliminating the need for some services (e.g., transcription services, physical records retention), reducing undesirable physician behavior, reducing medication errors, improved efficiency of services (e.g., improved medication order fulfillment turnaround times), and improved ability to document compliance with incentive programs yielding improved revenue.[12]
- *Improved Efficiency*—The same document describes reported instances in which the adoption of electronic medical records produced a 22% improvement in the patient discharge process, a 54% reduction in the time between specimen collection and laboratory results being available, a 62% reduction in time between radiology exam and results being available, an 83% reduction in time between medication order and administration, and 11% improvement in both physician and patient satisfaction scores.

EMRs are not without risks. Weiner et al. warned the health-care community of the risk of unintended consequences of automation, and coined the term *e-iatrogenesis* to describe errors associated with those unintended consequences. Design and implementation of EMRs are critical to their success.[13]

The HITECH Act of 2009,[14] part of the American Recovery and Reinvestment Act (ARRA) of 2009, provides incentives for the adoption of EMR systems. Incentives are predicated on the demonstration of "meaningful use" of those systems through a series of three stages of evaluation. At the end of each stage, organizations (hospitals, physicians' offices, and other health-care systems) that can demonstrate meaningful use of EMR systems are eligible for incentive payments; those that do not demonstrate meaningful use are subsequently penalized by reduced reimbursement. The criteria by which meaningful use is judged vary with each stage and are established by the Centers for Medicare and Medicaid Services (CMS) and the Office of the National Coordinator for HealthIT.[14–16]

Creating EMR systems has raised significant questions around who should have access to the information contained within them. Administrative provisions are provided in the Health Information Portability and Accountability Act (HIPAA) of 1996 and its related security regulations (45 CFR Part 142, 160, 164a, c) and privacy regulations (45 CFR Part 160, 164 a, e). The HITECH Act has strengthened the enforcement of these regulations.[17,18] Pharmacists need to be aware of these regulations and the impact they may have in managing clinical information.

An EMR must provide all the features and functions of the original paper record. From a medication use standpoint, the primary features of the EMR involve electronic signature, computerized prescriber order entry (CPOE), and an electronic medication administration record (eMAR).

Physical signature is an implicit feature of the paper chart that must be transferred to an electronic chart. Conceptually, the physical signature provides proof that an entry in the legal patient record was authorized by an appropriate caregiver at a specific date and time and has not since been undetectably altered. *Electronic signature* is the functional equivalent of a physical signature, which means that it must irrefutably bind the signer to the signed contents.

The Electronic Signatures in Global and National Commerce (ESIGN) Act of 2000 defined the general circumstances under which an electronic signature could be considered the equivalent of a physical signature for commercial documents.[19] Electronic signature requirements for health care are enabled in HIPAA and defined in its related privacy and security regulations in the Code of Federal Regulations (45 CFR Part 142). Electronic signature provisions for the pharmaceutical and medical device industries are defined by the FDA in Title 21 Code of Federal Regulations Electronic Records; Electronic Signatures (21 CFR Part 11).

Home Health News provides a clear discussion of electronic signature which can be summarized as an electronic symbol affixed to an unalterable record, irrefutably attributed to a person who affixed this mark to the document with intent.[20]

Practically, electronic signatures are a combination of procedures and technology that permit an individual to electronically sign a document in such a way that it is clear they intended to sign the document, that they are who they say they are, and that the document so signed has not been subsequently modified.

COMPUTERIZED PRESCRIBER ORDER ENTRY

Computerized provider order entry (CPOE) provides the electronic equivalent of written patient care orders in the paper chart. The organization and presentation of medications for physician order entry have been the subject of much debate, and it is clear that the simple transfer of order entry paradigms from departmental systems (such as laboratory or pharmacy systems, which depend on the knowledge and experience of departmental personnel) do not transfer easily or well to physicians. A great deal of effort typically goes into CPOE implementations to build predefined order sets to facilitate physician ordering, and these order sets typically require significant pharmacy resources to both develop and maintain.

A significant feature of CPOE systems is an underlying decision-support system intended to warn physicians when a newly entered order may duplicate existing therapy, may conflict with patient allergies or cause drug-drug interactions, or may be out of appropriate dosing range. The proper design and implementation of such systems is crucial to the success of CPOE and represents a delicate balancing act between thoroughness and what has been characterized as "alert fatigue," in which the provider experiences an overwhelming number of alerts and responds by ignoring them.[21]

As a result, Bates et al. have described what they call the "ten commandments of clinical decision support" in an effort to identify the kinds of implementations that can overcome alert fatigue and ensure meaningful alerts and messages.[22] Pharmacists have also published reports that customization of CDSS systems is the key to CPOE success[23] and consistent monitoring of CPOE implementations has also been called for as a measure of ongoing success.[24]

Kravet et al. have offered what they describe as ten lessons from CPOE implementation that provide guidance in approaching the project of developing a CPOE system.[25]

CPOE definitely changes the way pharmacy dispensing practice operates; it significantly reduces transcription error and cycle time for medication order processing.[26] Some have bemoaned, however, that the cost of this efficiency has been the loss of context, claiming that review of handwritten orders permits the reviewing pharmacist more context for the orders being reviewed.

The companion to CPOE in the EMR is the electronic medication administration record (eMAR). In the paper record, MARs are printed documents where nurses hand-record administration of medication to patients. This document also serves as the document from which a nurse will schedule the administration of medications to the patients under their care.

The eMAR is an online document that provides prompts to the nurse to prepare medications and receives documentation (sometimes from a BCMA system). The eMAR is intended to document administration in real time and can help enforce more timely medication administration. Because the eMAR is updated automatically as a function of CPOE and pharmacy dispensing, it tends to be more current and complete. A study from Brigham and Women's Hospital demonstrated that implementation of a bar code system with an eMAR resulted in significant error reductions.[27]

Many hospitals have also shifted from billing medication at dispensing to billing at the time of medication administration. While this usually results in a reduction in reported revenue, it also reduces the number of billing challenges the organization must manage.

Challenges remain for EMR systems, primarily in the area of interoperability, and the ability to transfer information from one EMR to another remains elusive.

ELECTRONIC PRESCRIBING

Electronic prescribing, also known as e-prescribing, is an electronic generation of medical prescriptions to eliminate the use of paper-based prescribing (USDHHS). Ideally, this would improve patient safety by eliminating errors associated with interpreting illegible handwritings, encouraging the use of a clinical decision support system for appropriate evidence-based selection, and incorporating formulary considerations for cost-effective therapy. This will improve safety and efficiency in prescribing and delivery of prescriptions.

CASE SCENARIO

A patient complains of frequent urination accompanied by a burning sensation. The physician suspects a urinary tract infection and prescribes amoxicillin after urine confirmation. The patient agrees to the therapy after a brief explanation of the condition and then leaves.

This is a common case scenario that occurs in an outpatient setting, and normally this would be a simple prescription that the patient obtains and the patient is cured of the infection a week later. However, this patient may have just been recently discharged from the hospital with methicillin-resistant *Staphylococcus aureus* (MRSA) infection.

How can technology assist the prescriber in this situation to minimize the potential for ineffective drug therapy?

CPOE VERSUS E-PRESCRIBING

Similar to CPOE, e-prescribing enables prescribers to electronically transmit medical care instructions for their patients. Both systems include functions for ordering, decision support, regulatory compliance and security, and billing, but they differ in practice and scope. A CPOE system allows prescribers to enter orders for a wide array of services such as medications, diagnostic studies, imaging studies, therapeutic services, and nutrition and food services. This bridges the communication between multiple medical services, pharmacy department, nursing care, and other ancillary services within a hospital or long-term–care facility. On the other hand, e-prescribing is limited to ordering medications that can be transmitted to retail pharmacies. Both systems may be linked to decision support systems, but decision support in stand-alone systems may be limited due to limited patient data available. In addition, e-prescribing requires constant formulary updates from different health plans in the community settings, whereas CPOE only requires update from the hospital formulary. In our case scenario, this patient's previous hospital visit would be documented in the CPOE system with the medication list, but a manual update would be necessary for the clinic e-prescribing system to include the treatment course during the hospital visit. As a pharmacy manager, it is imperative to understand the culture that exists within the organization to determine which system is appropriate. Table 15.2 describes the similarities and differences of both systems.

TABLE 15.2

Similarities and Differences between CPOE and e-Prescribing

Parameter	CPOE	e-Prescribing
Setting	Hospital or long-term care facility	Physician groups, clinics
Prescribers	Physicians Nurses (charting) Technicians (meals)	Physicians Allied health care with prescribing privileges
Decision Support	*Guidelines*	*Guidelines*
Regulatory Compliance/ Security	Secure connection within the hospital system	Secure routing to retail pharmacies and insurance adjusters
Billing	Hospital formulary	All insurance companies formulary

E-Prescribing History

The changes in the pharmacist's role from a primarily dispensing role to pharmaceutical care as part of the changes implemented with Omnibus Budget Reconciliation Act of 1990 (OBRA 90) became the impetus driver for increasing technology into a pharmacist's workflow. Pharmacies incorporated automation to relieve pharmacists from the manual tasks of count and pour. Technology was also presented as the key solution to reduce the documented medication errors IOM report, *To Err Is Human*.[29] The report identified avoiding reliance on memory and avoiding reliance on vigilance as two concepts to decrease medication errors.[28] Electronic prescribing became the solution to incorporate clinical support to eliminate reliance for prescribers to remember all the doses while eliminating the potential for incorrect medication dispensing due to handwriting.

The Medicare Modernization Act (MMA) of 2003 created a voluntary prescription drug benefit under Medicare Part D to foster e-prescribing among prescribers. The American Recovery and Reinvestment Act (ARRA) of 2009 and Health Information Technology for Economic and Clinical Healthy (HITECH) Act provided financial subsidies for those using health information technology (HIT) and required providers who wish to participate in Medicare to obtain HIT by a specified date or pay a penalty. As part of Medicare Part D, pharmacies were required to accept e-prescriptions by 2009. The Electronic Prescribing (eRx) Incentive Program uses a combination of incentive payments and penalties to encourage e-prescribing by eligible prescribers beginning in 2009. Starting from 2012, financial penalties were made for those who did not meet the e-prescribing requirements and incentives were graded down until finally removed by 2014. A 2% payment adjustment will be placed on physicians who do not meet the requirements thereafter. In 2012, 93% of community pharmacies accepted e-prescriptions (98% chain pharmacies and 85% independent pharmacies). However, only 38% of the prescriptions were electronically submitted.[30]

PHYSICIAN'S ROLE OF E-PRESCRIBING

A study by MGMA's Group Practice Research Network estimated the time spent managing unnecessary administrative complexity related to prescriptions can be valued at approximately $15,700 a year for each full-time physician (2004 *MGMA*, Analyzing cost of administrative complexity in group practice). This includes time associated with manually processing refills, resolving issues related to formulary, and resolving issues relating to dosage and legibility. e-Prescribing can reduce the amount of time for each of these issues and improve efficiency use of the staff.

In an ideal setting, prescribers can prescribe via their computer terminal during their patient's visit. This usually requires the same sign-on during the patient visit. The prescriber will sign into the patient record to chart and enter a prescription when necessary. Electronic charting and writing prescriptions can reduce or eliminate errors associated with handwriting. This also allows the prescriber the opportunity to review the patient's medication history and other clinical information while prescribing. In addition, a clinical decision support system can be embedded into the system to conduct real-time drug-drug and drug-allergy interactions. Prescribers can select formulation and dosage forms while placing the order.

Once the prescription order is ready, the prescriber can verify the pharmacy with the patient. The prescription will be transferred to the transaction hub to determine eligibility and prescription coverage. Not only will this allow patients to receive the correct medication in a timely manner, it will also reduce the potential of fraudulent or tampered prescriptions to be filled.

This process will reduce administrative support that is typically related to the manual process. The ability to access the patient's prescription benefit up front will reduce unnecessary phone calls from pharmacy staff to make a therapeutic substitution due to drug coverage. The ability to conduct prospective drug utilization review during prescribing enables prescribers to evaluate medication adherence, potential drug interactions, and misuse.

Finally, the prescription may be sent to the patient's pharmacy to encourage compliance and reduce clerical errors. This in turn will save time for the pharmacy staff to retype the prescription. A report from 2012 showed an internist has the highest adoption rate with 93%. Figure 15.8 shows the flow of the prescription via e-prescribing.

PHARMACIST'S ROLE OF E-PRESCRIBING

The American Society of Health-System Pharmacy states that pharmacists are the experts to effectively translate and communicate medication use across the continuum of care.[31] Although electronic prescribing improves pharmacy workflow efficiencies by reducing interruptions to pharmacies due to fewer verbal and faxed orders and time savings from not having to manually enter the prescription,[32–35] pharmacists will be presented with different challenges.

The key difference between interpreting hardcopy and electronic prescriptions is more focus will be needed to determine the feasibility of each prescription.

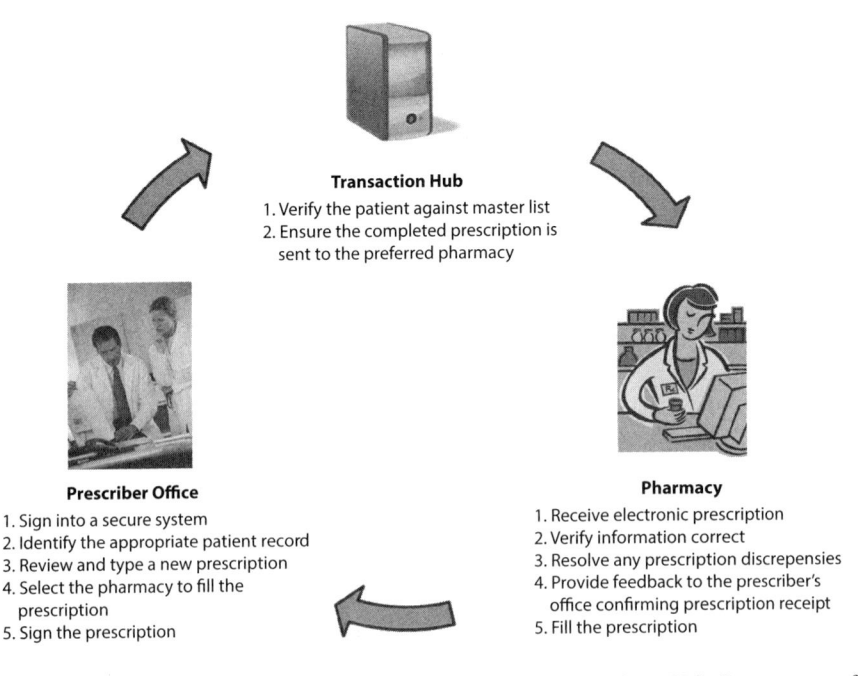

Transaction Hub
1. Verify the patient against master list
2. Ensure the completed prescription is sent to the preferred pharmacy

Prescriber Office
1. Sign into a secure system
2. Identify the appropriate patient record
3. Review and type a new prescription
4. Select the pharmacy to fill the prescription
5. Sign the prescription

Pharmacy
1. Receive electronic prescription
2. Verify information correct
3. Resolve any prescription discrepensies
4. Provide feedback to the prescriber's office confirming prescription receipt
5. Fill the prescription

FIGURE 15.8   Flow of prescription via e-prescribing. (Adapted from U.S. Department of Health and Human Services. What is ePrescribing? http://www.hrsa.gov/healthit/toolbox/ HealthITAdoptiontoolbox/EvaluatingOptimizingandSustaining/aboutepresribe.html)

Pharmacists are trained on the job how to select the prescribed product based on availability on hand, product packaging, and cost. An e-prescription may also be stopped when a physician selects a medication with a different FDA National Drug Code (NDC) than what is in the pharmacy system. The pharmacist would have to manually select the appropriate medication from what is available and consequently lose its autopopulation function of the e-prescription.

The system also puts the physician in the position to pick specific packaging, drug form, or other features that would normally be up to the discretion of the pharmacist at the pharmacy based on the product availability and cost. Sometimes it is difficult for physicians to know the cost differences and availability (i.e., dosage form, generic brands) without actually contacting the pharmacy. In addition, physicians are usually not aware of the container or packaging for multiuse medications such as inhalers or creams. Although handwriting interpretation errors will be minimized, pharmacists will continue to translate the instructions to be "patient friendly" (e.g., "tid" to "three times a day"). Table 15.3 shows some examples of potential causes for pharmacists to scrutinize the e-prescriptions more closely than handwritten prescriptions.

e-Prescribing not for Every Drug

In order to maximize the benefits of e-prescribing, both physician offices and pharmacies need to use the available HIT effectively. In addition to financial incentives,

TABLE 15.3

Examples of Potential Prescription Problems

Type of Problem	Problem Description	Examples
Availability	Mismatched NDC for generics with multiple suppliers	Amoxicillin 500 mg
	Product packaging selection	Bactroban 2% cream 15 g when only 30 g tube is available at the pharmacy
Packaging size	Inhalers	1 albuterol inhaler instead of 17 g
	Biologics	1 Enbrel syringe instead of 3.92 mL
Autopopulated most common dose	Pediatric population	Amoxicillin 500 mg every 12 h instead of calculating based on weight
	Renal impairment	20 mg once a day instead of dose reduction for patients with Clcr <30 mL/min to 10 mg once a day

Key: Clcr = creatinine clearance

new laws have been created to eliminate the potential of workarounds. The Drug Enforcement Administration (DEA) approved electronic prescriptions for controlled substances (EPCS) effective June 1, 2010.[36] This enables pharmacies to receive, dispense, and archive electronic prescriptions without a handwritten copy to file.

Each state has the ability to determine if EPCS is appropriate for their state. Currently 37 states and District of Columbia allow EPCS. In the states in which EPCS is illegal, an e-prescribing system can remind, alert, and generate a printed prescription to reduce legibility errors; however, this still leaves room for manual errors. It has been estimated that approximately 15% of all prescriptions written in the United States for controlled substances need a workaround.

In addition to laws and regulations, physicians may choose not to use e-prescribing when patients request hard copy due to preference, save for a future date, or are unsure of their preferred pharmacy due to moving or insurance preference. One cross-sectional study estimated more than 50% of the community pharmacies received less than 15% of prescriptions electronically. Some of the reasons why workarounds exist are to provide customer satisfaction such as obtaining a verbal order when patients arrive to pick up prescriptions before the e-prescription is ready.

In other cases, pharmacies try to avoid additional fees by requesting refills verbally or via fax for electronic renewal authorization requests.[10] However, when multiple processes are in place, confusion may occur due to patients and pharmacies calling for refills on the same prescriptions.[37] Because there are several methods to request for refills, the pharmacies may reenter the prescription as if they were "new" to avoid delays to provide the prescriptions to the patient. Consequently, these prescriptions would not benefit from the autopopulation from e-prescribing, and the manual updates and continuous checks are needed to ensure complete patient medication history both from the pharmacies and physician offices. This becomes a vicious cycle and reinforces inconsistent response from providers' offices.

Mail-order pharmacies also present a difficult challenge for physician offices. Some practices find a "lost" e-prescription to mail-order pharmacies may be lost for four to five days before anyone realizes, so many physician offices elect to fax prescriptions instead of electronically transmitting. Due to technical difficulties, some transaction hubs convert e-prescriptions to be delivered by fax and process them as paper prescriptions.[36]

Pharmacies also have workaround procedures for saving time as a means to provide better customer service to their customers. Pharmacies may bypass e-prescription application when a partial order is being filled. This is used to prevent pharmacies from inputting the prescription again when the complete order can be filled. This then leads to batch processing for all the partial orders. In addition, pharmacists may sign on to all the machines in the morning and allow technicians to process batch orders because it is faster. This would circumvent all the security measures and double-checking functions that are built into e-prescribing.

REFERENCES

1. ASHP Section of Pharmacy Informatics Technology Executive Committee. Technology-enabled practice: a vision statement by the ASHP Section of Pharmacy Informatics and Technology. *American Journal of Health-System Pharmacy.* September 1 2009;66(17):1573–1577.
2. US Food and Drug Administration. Medical Device Data Systems. 2011; www.fda.gov/MedicalDevices/ProductsandMedicalProcedures/GeneralHospitalDevicesandSupplies/MedicalDeviceDataSystems/default.htm (accessed September 16, 2013).
3. US Food and Drug Administration. Class II Special Controls Guidance Document: Pharmacy Compounding Systems; Final Guidance for Industry and FDA. *Medical Devices* 2001; www.fda.gov/medicaldevices/deviceregulationandguidance/guidance-documents/ucm073576.htm (accessed September 15, 2013).
4. US Department of Health and Human Services. Guidance for Industry: Bar Code Label Requirements Questions and Answers. 2011; www.fda.gov/downloads/biologics-bloodvaccines/guidancecomplianceregulatoryinformation/guidances/ucm267392.pdf (accessed September 15, 2013).
5. GS1 US. GS1 Barcode Chart. 2012; www.gs1us.org/DesktopModules/Bring2mind/DMX/Download.aspx?PortalId=0&TabId=56&EntryId=365 (accessed September 15, 2013).
6. Bar Code Label Requirements, Title 21 Code of Federal Regulations, Pt. 201.25. 2012 ed.
7. Richard Paoletti from Lancaster Memorial Hospital, personal communication, 2007.
8. Institute for Safe Medication Practices. Institute for Safe Medication Practices (ISMP): Guidance on the Interdisciplinary Safe Use of Automated Dispensing Cabinets. 2008; www.ismp.org/tools/guidelines/ADC_Guidelines_final.pdf (accessed September 15, 2013).
9. Institute for Safe Medication Practices. Smart Pumps are not Smart on Their Own. *ISMP Medication Safety Alert* 2007; www.ismp.org/newsletters/acutecare/articles/20070419.asp (accessed September 15, 2013).
10. Ralph Korpman, MD, President and CEO of Health Data Sciences Corporation, personal communication, August 1986.
11. *To Err Is Human: Building a Safer Health System.* Washington, DC: National Academy Press; 1999.
12. HiMSS Electronic Health Record Association. The Value of Electronic Health Records. 2009; www.himssehra.org/docs/ValueEHRs.pdf (accessed September 15, 2013).

13. Weiner JP, Kfuri T, Chan K, Fowles JB. "e-Iatrogenesis": the most critical unintended consequence of CPOE and other HIT. *Journal of the American Medical Informatics Association.* May–June 2007;14(3):387–388; discussion 389.

14. HealthIT.gov. Certification and EHR Incentives. *HITECH Act;* www.healthit.gov/policy-researchers-implementers/hitech-act (accessed September 15, 2013).

15. HealthIT.gov. EHR Incentives and Certification. Meaningful Use Definition and Objectives; www.healthit.gov/providers-professionals/meaningful-use-definition-objectives (accessed September 15, 2013).

16. HealthIT.gov. Health IT Regulations. Meaningful Use Regulations; www.healthit.gov/policy-researchers-implementers/meaningful-use-regulations (accessed September 15, 2013).

17. Tribble DA. The Health Insurance Portability and Accountability Act: security and privacy requirements. *American Journal of Health-System Pharmacy.* May 1 2001;58(9):763–770.

18. Public Law 106-229: Electronic Signature in Global and National Commerce Act. (114 Stat. 465; Date: 9/15/00). Text from: United States Public Laws. Available from: www.gpo.gov/fdsys/pkg/PLAW-106publ229/pdf/PLAW-106publ229.pdf (accessed September 15, 2013).

19. Kinsella A. A Review of Electronic Signature Regulations. 2012; www.homehealthnews.org/2012/06/a-review-of-electronic-signature-regulations/ (accessed September 15, 2013).

20. Appold K. Alert Fatigue: When Too Many Alerts Lose Physicians' Attention. 2010; www.aacc.org/publications/cln/2010/july/pages/PSF_AlertFatigue.aspx (accessed September 15, 2013).

21. Bates DW, Kuperman GJ, Wang S, et al. Ten commandments for effective clinical decision support: making the practice of evidence-based medicine a reality. *Journal of the American Medical Informatics Association.* November–December 2003;10(6):523–530.

22. Traynor K. Customization key to successful CPOE. *American Journal of Health-System Pharmacy.* June 1 2004;61(11):1087, 1092, 1094.

23. Thompson CA. Leapfrog Group wants hospitals to monitor, not just implement, CPOE systems. *American Journal of Health-System Pharmacy,* August 15, 2010;67(16):1310–1311.

24. Kravet S, Knight A, Wright S. Ten lessons from Implementing a computerized provider order entry system. *J Clin Outcomes Manage.* 2007;14(2):105–109.

25. Young D. CPOE reduces number of steps in medication-use process. *American Journal of Health-System Pharmacy.* July 1, 2001;58(13):1170, 1173.

26. Poon EG, Keohane CA, Yoon CS, et al. Effect of bar code technology on the safety of medication administration. *New England Journal of Medicine.* May 6, 2010;362(18):1698–1707.

27. US Department of Health and Human Services. What is ePrescribing? www.hrsa.gov/healthit/toolbox/HealthITAdoptiontoolbox/EvaluatingOptimizingandSustaining/aboutepresribe.html (accessed May 22, 2013).

28. Surescripts. The National Progress Report on E-Prescribing and Safe-Rx Rankings Year 2012. 2013; www.surescripts.com/downloads/npr/National Progress Report on E Prescribing Year 2012.pdf (accessed May 22, 2013).

29. American Society of Health-System Pharmacists. ASHP statement on the pharmacist's role in informatics. *American Journal of Health-System Pharmacy.* 2007;64:200–203.

30. Goldman RE, Dube C, Lapane KL. Beyond the basics: refills by electronic prescribing. *International Journal of Medical Informatics.* July 2010;79(7):507–514.

31. Lapane KL, Rosen RK, Dube C. Perceptions of e-prescribing efficiencies and inefficiencies in ambulatory care. *International Journal of Medical Informatics.* January 2011; 80(1):39–46.

32. Hollingworth W, Devine EB, Hansen RN, et al. The impact of e-prescribing on prescriber and staff time in ambulatory care clinics: a time motion study. *Journal of the American Medical Informatics Association.* November–December 2007;14(6):722–730.

33. Rupp MT, Warholak TL. Evaluation of e-prescribing in chain community pharmacy: best-practice recommendations. *Journal of the American Pharmacists Association.* May–June 2008;48(3):364–370.

34. Electronic Prescriptions for Controlled Substances, 73 *Federal Register* 125 (27 June 2008), 36722–36782.

35. Grossman JM, Cross DA, Boukus ER, Cohen GR. Transmitting and processing electronic prescriptions: experiences of physician practices and pharmacies. *Journal of the American Medical Informatics Association.* May–June 2012;19(3):353–359.

Case Study

You have been asked to implement a pharmacy in a new hospital and are planning to use automated dispensing technology heavily in the practice. You also know that the hospital is planning to start out using Barcode Medication Administration that will drive both charting and billing, and plans to use IV pumps for all infusions. The hospital will serve a neonatal intensive care unit (NICU) population, but not pediatrics. Biomedical engineering will manage the fleet of IV pumps, but pharmacy must maintain the pump libraries. The hospital will start out with an EMR which has an e-prescribing module.

1. Who are the stakeholders that need to be involved in the decision making around these technologies? For each technology mentioned, identify each and the role that they may play in the decisions.
2. Will you use different IV pumps in the NICU than in the rest of the hospital? Why or why not?
3. What does the presence of the e-prescribing module mean for your pharmacy?
4. In addition to normal pharmacy clinical and dispensing functions, what other staffing do you think you will need to support this automation plan?

APPENDIX A: REQUEST FOR PURCHASE FOR A ROBOTIC IV SYSTEM

Saint Judicious Hospital is a 360-bed community hospital located in Anytown, IA. The hospital averages 90% occupancy (approximately 120,000 patient days of care). Bed capacity breaks down as:

Bed Type	Capacity	Occupancy
General Medical/Surgery	300	320
Adult Med/Surg ICU	10	10
OB/Gyn	30	11
Oncology	20	10

The hospital pharmacy operates from a centralized pharmacy located in the basement that operates on a 24/7/365 staffing. The pharmacy occupies 2,000 square feet and services only the inpatient population. The IV room occupies 400 square feet divided into an anteroom (100 square feet), a negative pressure chemotherapy room (100 square feet) that contains one 6-foot biological safety cabinet, and a 200 square foot positive-pressure IV preparation area that contains two 6-foot horizontal laminar air flow hoods.

The IV room prepares an average of 350 doses per day of which 280 are batch doses received in three batches per day and 70 represent stat and first dose requests. The dose breakdown by type is:

Type	Daily Volume
Small Volume Parenterals	250
Frozen Premix	100
Compounded	150
Large Volume Parenterals	80
Cancer Chemotherapy	20

Batch scheduling occurs on the following schedule:

Batch Starts	First Dose	Last Dose
07:00	10:00	17:59
15:00	18:00	01:59
23:00	02:00	09:59

Saint Judicious Hospital desires to place an IV robot into service that will automate the production of as many of the 230 doses prepared daily in the IV room as can be automated on a single device. The hospital therefore offers this Request for Proposal to vendors of IV Admixture robotic systems and requests interested vendors to submit answers to the following questions:

A. Dose types supported   Yes   No
  1. Large-volume parenterals
     i. One additive   ☐   ☐
     ii. Two additives   ☐   ☐
     iii. Three additives   ☐   ☐
     iv. More than three additives   ☐   ☐
  2. Small-volume parenterals
     i. Syringes   ☐   ☐
     ii. IVPB   ☐   ☐
  3. Chemotherapy
     i. Syringes   ☐   ☐
     ii. Small-volume parenterals   ☐   ☐
     iii. Large-volume parenterals   ☐   ☐
     iv. Elastomeric infusers   ☐   ☐

4. If syringes are supported, please identify the smallest syringe and largest syringe supported

   Smallest: 0.5 mL ☐   1 mL ☐   2 mL ☐   5 mL ☐   10 mL ☐
   Largest: 10 mL ☐   20 mL ☐   30 mL ☐   50 mL ☐

5. If syringes are supported, please identify the smallest dose volume and largest dose volume supported.

   Smallest: _____ mL   Largest: _____ mL

6. What is the accuracy specification for the device?
7. Please indicate if one device will support preparation of both hazardous and non-hazardous doses. If so, how is cross-contamination managed?

B. Space and facilities
   1. Does the robotic device require placement in an ISO Class 7 or ISO Class 8 environment?
      Yes ☐   No ☐
   2. What amount of floor space is required for the device? Please provide a drawing of the space required.
   3. What electrical service is required?
   4. What compressed air service is required?
   5. Is the device required to connect to the hospital network?
      Yes ☐   No ☐
   6. If network connectivity is required, is the device an FDA-registered medical device?
      Yes ☐   No ☐
   7. If network connectivity is required, how is the device protected against malware?
   8. Will the device require file storage on the network on a network share?
   9. Will the device support remote service?
      Yes ☐   No ☐
   10. If yes, how will that service be delivered?
   11. What Information Technology (IT) support will be required for installation?
   12. What IT support will be required for ongoing support?
   13. What does the device weigh? _____ lb
   14. Is special anchoring required?
       Yes ☐   No ☐

C. Throughput – please describe the throughput (in doses per hour or minutes per dose) that we can expect for each of the dose types supported.
D. Installation and Training – please describe the installation and training process.
E. Product Support
   1. Please describe the printed and/or electronic user documentation available for this device.

2. Please describe routine maintenance the pharmacy staff is required to perform.
3. Please describe when technical support is available
4. If technical support is available after normal business hours, please describe how that support is accessed.
5. What preventive maintenance is provided for the device?
6. Is field service available?
   Yes ☐   No ☐
7. If field service is available, what response time can we expect when it is required?
8. Will a field service engineer be stationed in our geographic area?

F. Labeling
   1. Does the device print and apply a label to each dose?
      Yes ☐   No ☐
   2. Are all labels the same size?
      Yes ☐   No ☐
   3. Can label formats be customized?
      Yes ☐   No ☐
   4. If yes, can the hospital modify label formatting?
      Yes ☐   No ☐

G. Quality Assurance
   1. What types of sterility validation has been performed on the device? Is there a known contamination rate?
   2. What routine cleaning is required and what materials does that cleaning require?
   3. Does your company provide a validated process for ongoing microbial surveillance?
   4. Please describe how the device complies with Chapter <797> of the United States Pharmacopoeia.

H. Currently deployed systems
   1. How many systems are currently in use in the United States?
   2. How many systems are currently in use in hospitals of the size and scope of Saint Judicious?
   3. Is there a hospital similar to Saint Judicious within driving distance (200 miles)? If so, will they entertain a site visit?
   4. If not, where is the nearest hospital where we could see the device in use?

APPENDIX B: EXERCISE ANSWERS AND DISCUSSIONS

EXERCISE #1

You have been asked to lead the installation of an IV robotic device in your hospital pharmacy.

1. You decide to build an oversight team. Which of the following stakeholders should be represented on that team?
   a. IV room supervisor
   b. IV room technician
   c. Nursing manager
   d. IT manager
   e. Infection control physician
   f. Risk manager
   g. All of the above
2. What additional policies and procedures may be required?
   a. Who may operate the device
   b. Quality assurance
   c. Daily operation
   d. Maintenance and technical support
   e. Label creation and approval
   f. All of the above

EXERCISE #2

Your pharmacy is interested in acquiring a TPN compounding system with a network-distributed order entry system in which TPN orders are directly sent to the TPN compounder. The network administrator at your hospital indicates that all machines connected to the network be made available to him to push out antivirus updates and operating system upgrades. Your response is:

1. This is fine; every device should have up-to-date antivirus and operating system patches
2. This is impossible; all medical devices are prohibited from operating under conditions for which they have not been tested
3. You need to consult with the manufacturer of the compounding system to determine if it needs to be exempted from such a policy

EXERCISE #3

1. A bar code scanning process was added to the filling of an automated dispensing cabinet (ADC) to ensure that the correct product was placed in each section of the ADC. There have been recent reports that the wrong drug product has been showing up in the ADC sections. Which of the following explanations are possible?
   a. The technician filling the section is scanning the same vial over and over to log the containers into the section.
   b. The technician is scanning the correct section and then throwing the product into the wrong section.
   c. Both of the above.

2. A medication error occurred in which the patient received the wrong IV infusion. The infusion administered is labeled for the patient to whom it was given. According to the BCMA system, the correct bar code was scanned when the infusion was administered. What is the likely explanation?
   a. The nurse scanned a different container than s(he) administered.
   b. The pharmacy applied the wrong label to an IV bag that was compounded.
   c. There was an error in the bar code scanner that transposed some numbers.

Exercise #4

You have been asked to implement a pharmacy in a new hospital and are planning to use automated dispensing technology heavily in the practice. You also know that the hospital is planning to start out using Barcode Medication Administration that will drive both charting and billing, and plans to use IV Pumps for all infusions. The hospital will serve a Neonatal Intensive Care Unit population, but not pediatrics. Biomedical engineering will manage the fleet of IV pumps, but Pharmacy must maintain the pump libraries. The hospital will start out with an EMR which has an e-prescribing module.

1. Who are the stakeholders that need to be involved in the decision-making around these technologies? For each technology mentioned, identify each and the role that they may play in the decisions.

   The different types of technologies will include a Pharmacy Information System (PIS), an Automated Dispensing Cabinet system (ADC), probably some automated inventory management systems in the pharmacy, and software to implement and manage pump libraries. Pharmacy will likely not actually drive the BCMA system in use (nursing will) but Pharmacy will have to maintain the databases that drive the BCMA system, including ensuring that each item properly scans.

   The NICU population creates an interesting wrinkle in that the doses will be quite small, and the pharmacy will likely need to prepare and use dilutions of injections and oral liquids that are not commercially available. The PIS will have to be configured to handle these products and support their preparation. It is likely that some standardization of the list of dilutions will be needed to ensure reliability and safety.

   Labeling for IV preparations will have to support both BCMA and IV pump use. Configuration of the PIS labels will be a significant feature.

   It is likely that interfaces will be needed to at least some of these systems. The list of stakeholders at minimum would be:
   Pharmacy personnel (pharmacists and technicians)
   Nursing personnel (nurses, aides and unit secretaries)
   Physicians (both for standardizing inpatient prescribing patterns and for managing e-prescribing relationships).

> IT will be needed to manage the various interfaces and assist in vendor relationships
>
> PIS vendor
>
> BCMA vendor
>
> Medication Safety Officer/Risk Manager – to review and approve labeling

2. Will you use different IV pumps in the NICU than in the rest of the hospital? Why or why not?

This can actually be a thorny question. Some pump vendors produce either a syringe pump (most NICU doses are delivered in syringes, even what we would think of as large-volume infusions) or an infusion pump designed to deliver from bags. Many hospitals have let the NICU (and sometimes PICU – Pediatric ICU) choose their own infusion equipment. The problem this creates is that users familiar with one of the devices are not likely to be familiar with the other, and the user interfaces on the pumps can be very different.

Ideally, you would want the same pump to be used in all locations to simplify training and reduce opportunity for error. Depending on the required feature set, that may not be practical. The next best option is to have all the pumps come from the same vendor with the same user interface so that, even if the pumps operate slightly differently, the prompts to which the users respond look the same so programming is relatively similar.

3. What does the presence of the e-Prescribing module mean for your pharmacy?

e-Prescribing should mean that physicians can prescribe discharge medications for patients in your hospital directly from the CPOE system, and send them to your outpatient pharmacy. This means that your outpatient pharmacy system will likely need to be tied into the e-Prescribing network.

In addition to normal pharmacy clinical and dispensing functions, what other staffing do you think you will need to support this automation plan?

The presence of a BCMA system likely means that the pharmacy will be required to ensure that all commercial products delivered to the patient care areas for use have bar codes, and that the contents of those bar codes are known to the BCMA system so that it will work properly. The most effective way to discharge this responsibility is to scan everything on the way into the hospital to be certain it is properly recognized by the system. This may require a full-time person.

Exercise #5

As an extension of exercise #4, your pharmacy has decided to purchase a robotic IV filling system to support the preparation of IV admixtures. Please prepare a Request for Proposal for vendors of IV admixture robotics.

16 Managing Compliance, Performance, and Outcomes

William N. Kelly and Sarah J. Steinhardt

CONTENTS

Learning Objectives: After reading this chapter and working through the case, the reader will be able to:

1. Define the term *compliance* and explain why it is important to pharmacy
2. Compare and contrast the terms *law* and *regulation*
3. Compare and contrast the terms *standard* and *guideline*
4. Define the term *star rating* and explain why it is important to pharmacy
5. Develop performance criteria and a procedure for measuring performance of an important pharmacy activity

6. Define the term *HEDIS,* and explain why it is important
7. Compare and contrast the terms *process indicator* and *outcome*
8. Name four types of healthcare outcomes
9. Define the terms *metric, adherence, baseline,* and *process indicator*
10. Explain why there should be someone responsible for compliance and medication safety in every pharmacy

INTRODUCTION

This chapter is about managing compliance, performance, and outcomes. *Compliance* is making sure that policies, procedures, and activities are consistent with laws, rules, regulations, standards, and guidelines. *Performance* is about how well a certain activity is accomplished, and *outcomes* are the result of performance.

Healthcare is loaded with compliance issues—more than most other industries—because it deals with the quality of life. Thus for a pharmacy manager, compliance is a way of life, and special attention needs to be given to this high priority area.[1,2]

Pharmacy is a highly regulated profession. The four areas concerning pharmacy compliance are (1) federal and state pharmacy and healthcare laws, rules, and regulations; (2) professional standards and guidelines for treatment and care; (3) performance of important functions; and (4) managing patient outcomes (clinical and economic).

Each pharmacy practice site must meet these requirements or risk penalties or restrictions, which can be severe. The accountability for meeting compliance with requirements rests squarely on the Chief Pharmacy Officer (CPO), Director of Pharmacy, or Pharmacy Manager, although duties and responsibilities can be delegated to others.

The main skill needed by pharmacy leaders and managers to have a fully compliant program is first, to recognize its importance, and second, to assign responsibility for this critical function.[3] Once this is accomplished, there must be routine assessments and reporting of results to the pharmacy leader/manager.

LAWS, RULES, AND REGULATIONS

As shown in Table 16.1, there are two sets of laws, rules, and regulations affecting pharmacy practice: (1) federal and state healthcare laws, and (2) federal and state laws concerning drugs and the practice of pharmacy. Laws are passed by the US Congress and state legislatures. Regulatory agencies, such as the Food and Drug Administration (FDA), the Center for Medicare and Medicaid Services (CMS), and state boards of pharmacy and departments of health write regulations or rules on how healthcare law is to be carried out under statutory authority.

FEDERAL LAWS

There are many federal laws, rules, and regulations that cover practice and activities in pharmacies. The major ones are as follows.

The *Food, Drug, and Cosmetic Act of 1938* is the primary statute affecting applications for new drugs; the manufacture, preparation, distribution, and use of drugs in

TABLE 16.1
Laws, Rules, and Regulations Affecting Pharmacy Practice

Healthcare Laws, Rules, and Regulations		Drug and Pharmacy Laws, Rules, and Regulations	
Statute	**Enforcement**	**Statute**	**Enforcement**
Health Insurance Portability and Accountability Act (HIPAA)	Health and Human Services (Federal)	Food, Drug, and Cosmetic Act	Food and Drug Administration (FDA) (Federal)
Care of Patients	Health Department (State)	Omnibus Budget Reconciliation Act (OBRA 90)	US Department of Labor
Medicare Modernization Act	Center for Medicare and Medicaid Services (CMS)	Controlled Substance Act	Drug Enforcement Agency (Federal)
Affordable Care Act	Health and Human Services (Federal)	Practice of Pharmacy	Boards of Pharmacy (State)
Long-Term Care, Hospice, and Home Care (OBRA 87)	CMS	Practice of Pharmacy	Department of Health (State)
Employment			
Americans with Disabilities Act	The U.S. Equal Employment Opportunity Commission	Prescription Drug Marketing Act	FDA
Amendments Act		Medicare Prescription Drug Improvement and Modernization Act	CMS
Age Discrimination in Employment Acts	Civil Rights Center Equal Employment Opportunity Commission		
Fair Labor Standards Act		The 340B Federal Drug Discount Program	CMS
Family and Medical Leave Act	U.S. Department of Labor	Patient Safety and Quality Improvement Act	AHRQ
	U.S. Department of Labor	State agencies concerned with controlled substances	State dependent: most commonly the State Board of Pharmacy or Health Department

the United States; and what empowers the Food and Drug Administration. However, the proper testing and labeling requirements for drugs are the domain of the United States Pharmacopeia (USP)—a nongovernmental, not-for-profit organization.[4]

The *Food and Drug Administration Modernization Act of 1987* provides for the fast-tracking review of certain *new drug application* submissions; clarification of permissions for the pharmaceutical compounding of prescriptions; allows for the use

TABLE 16.2
Example of Performance Measurement in Pharmacy Practice

Measurable Baseline Performance Indicator	Who and How Measurement Will Be Done	How Often Measured	National or Local Benchmark	Audit Result	Action Needed
Allergy information is entered in every patient's medication profile. If the patient has no known allergies, the term "NKA" should be used and counted as "in compliance."	Thirty-five patient medication profiles will be randomly selected from the prior 30-day period for review by an assigned technician and a report generated for the quality assurance (QA) pharmacist.	Monthly	85%[1]	75%	All pharmacy personnel need to be reminded of the importance of recording this information.

TABLE 16.3
Accountable Care Measures Concerning Opportunities for Medication Management

Number	Measurement
12	Medication reconciliation after discharge from an inpatient facility
14	Prevention—Influenza immunization
15	Prevention—Pneumococcal immunization
17	Prevention—Screening for tobacco use
18	Prevention—Screening for depression
21	Prevention—Screening for blood pressure
22	Diabetes—Hemoglobin A1c control <8%
23	Diabetes—LDL <100
24	Diabetes—Blood pressure <140/90
26	Diabetes—Daily aspirin use
27	Diabetes—Hemoglobin A1c poor control
28	Hypertension—Controlling high blood pressure
29	Ischemic vascular disease—Drug therapy for LDL lowering
30	Ischemic vascular disease—Aspirin or another antithrombotic
31	Heart failure—Beta-blocker
32	Coronary artery disease—Lipid control
33	Coronary artery disease—ACE or ARB

of the symbol "Rx Only" in place of the prescription drug legend "Caution: Federal law prohibits the dispensing without a prescription"; and supported research of unapproved uses of drugs.[5]

The *Controlled Substances Act* controls the manufacture, distribution, labeling, storage, record keeping, and dispensing of controlled substances.[6]

TABLE 16.4
HEDIS Measures Concerning Medication Management

Number	Metric
1	Childhood immunization status
2	Immunization of adolescents
3	Human papillomavirus for adolescents
4	Appropriate treatment of children with pharyngitis
5	Appropriate treatment of children with upper respiratory infection
6	Avoidance of antibiotic treatment of adults with acute bronchitis
7	Pharmacotherapy management of chronic obstructive pulmonary disease (COPD) exacerbation
8	Use of appropriate medications for people with asthma
9	Medication management for people with asthma
10	Asthma medication ratio
11	Cholesterol management for patients with cardiovascular conditions
12	Controlling high blood pressure
13	Persistence of beta-blocker treatment after heart attack
14	Disease-modifying anti-rheumatic drug therapy for rheumatoid arthritis
15	Osteoporosis management in women who had a fracture
16	Antidepressant medication management
17	Follow-up care for children prescribed attention deficit-hyperactivity disorder (ADHD) medication
18	Adherence to antipsychotic medications for individuals with schizophrenia
19	Annual monitoring for patients with persistent medications
20	Medication reconciliation post-discharge
21	Potentially harmful drug-disease interactions in the elderly
22	Use of high-risk medications in the elderly
23	Management of urinary incontinence in older adults
24	Aspirin use and discussion
25	Flu vaccinations for adults ages 18 to 64
26	Flu vaccinations for adults age 65 and older
27	Medical assistance with smoking and tobacco use cessation
28	Pneumococcal vaccination status for older adults
29	Antibiotic utilization

The *Prescription Drug Marketing Act of 1987* was enacted to correct the problem of drug diversion from normal distribution channels. The act covers drug reimportation; shipping and storing of drugs; proper recordkeeping; drug samples and starter packs; receipt of prescription drugs; reselling of drugs; sales representative activity; and penalties.[7]

The *Omnibus Budget Reconciliation Act (OBRA 90)* is a large piece of legislation, portions of which concern dispensing and medication counseling for patients. Major portions include requirements for a prospective drug use review and extending a verbal offer by the pharmacist or pharmacy intern to the patient or a patient's caregiver to discuss matters that will improve therapy.[8]

The *Health Insurance Portability and Accountability Act (HIPAA)* assures the security and privacy of patients' medical records while allowing the flow of health information needed to provide quality health care.[9]

The *Patient Protection and Affordable Care Act* is commonly called the Affordable Care Act (ACA). This new legislation and the Health Care and Education Reconciliation Act represent the most significant regulatory overhaul of the US healthcare system since the passage of Medicare and Medicaid in 1965. The act was enacted with the goals of increasing the quality and affordability of health insurance, lowering the uninsured rate by expanding public and private insurance coverage, and reducing the costs of health care for individuals and the government.[10]

The *Long-Term Care, Hospice, and Home Care (OBRA 87)* legislation enhanced regulating nursing homes and included new requirements on quality of care, resident assessment, care planning, and the use of neuroleptic drugs and physical restraints. Some of the key provisions of this act were that all nursing facilities must have a medical director, each resident should have an attending physician who visits the resident at specified intervals, and a drug regimen review (DRR) must be conducted monthly by a consultant pharmacist.[11]

The *Medicare Modernization Act* created the Part D component of Medicare that pays for outpatient prescriptions.[12]

The *Public Law 102-585 of the Veterans Health Care Act* created the 340B Federal Drug Discount Program that expanded access to affordable medications to low-income populations by supporting the operations of healthcare safety net providers.[13]

The *Patient Safety and Quality Improvement Act* established a voluntary reporting system to enhance the data available to assess and resolve patient safety and healthcare quality issues, and created patient safety organizations (PSOs) to collect, aggregate, and analyze confidential information reported by healthcare providers.[14]

All of these federal statues affect pharmacy practice, and therefore pharmacies are expected to be compliant.

STATE LAWS, RULES, AND REGULATIONS

Each US state and territory has authorities that regulate the practice of pharmacy therein.

Board of Pharmacy Act and Rules and Regulations: Every pharmacy service needs to be aware of its state pharmacy practice act, its rules and regulations, and any changes to the Act that usually occur once a year.[15] Who will be accountable for making sure the pharmacy permit, the controlled substance license and inventory, and the pharmacist licenses and continuing education are up to date?

Health Department Rules and Regulations: Every pharmacy service is covered by its state's health department's rules and regulations pertaining to pharmacy practice and providing safe care to patients.[16] Who will be responsible to make sure there is compliance?

State agencies concerned with controlled substances vary among states, but typically, the state board of pharmacy has authority over the distribution, storage, recordkeeping, and dispensing of controlled substances within the state.

EMPLOYMENT LAW

Pharmacy leaders and managers need to be aware of the laws, rules, and regulations concerning hiring, supervising, and terminating employees. A key to compliance with these legal requirements is the human resources department in the workplace, or a consultant who is an expert in this area of the law.

The *Americans with Disability Act* prevents an employer from discriminating against a disabled person.[17]

The *Age Discrimination in Employment Act* prohibits discrimination on the basis of age in programs and activities receiving federal financial assistance. It protects certain applicants and employees 40 years of age and older from discrimination on the basis of age in hiring, promotion, discharge, compensation, or terms, conditions, or privileges of employment.[18]

The *Fair Labor Standards Act* (FLSA) provides workers with minimum wage, overtime pay, and child labor protections. It protects most, but not all, private- and public-sector employees. In addition, certain employers and employees are exempt from coverage.[19]

The *Family and Medical Leave Act* (FMLA) entitles eligible employees of covered employers to take unpaid, job-protected leave for family and medical reasons with continuation of group health insurance coverage under the same terms and conditions as if the employee had not taken leave.[20]

STANDARDS AND GUIDELINES

In addition to complying with laws, rules, and regulations, pharmacies need to be compliant with the standard of practice, other pharmacy standards, and guidelines.

The Pharmacy Standard of Care: The accepted definition of the *pharmacist standard of care* is what a reasonable and prudent pharmacist would do under the same circumstances. What this means is that the practice of pharmacy, as carried out by its pharmacists, is not to be an outlier when it comes to patient safety.

Other Pharmacy Standards: Pharmacy organizations develop standards that allow the pharmacy profession to qualitatively and quantitatively measure the commitment to providing high-quality, reliable healthcare services and products. For example, "A pharmacist will collect and accurately record sufficient personal details and a complete medication history to establish a consumer profile when dispensing."[21] Such standards are usually written as a "should," rather than a "must"; nevertheless, as written by a national pharmacy organization, these are *quasi-legal* and can be used against those who may not be compliant.

Guidelines: Unlike a standard, guidelines are usually written as a recommendation, rather than a requirement, and thus have less weight. A *best practice* is a method that has consistently shown results superior to those achieved with other means. Best practices, although desirable, are considered guidelines, as a minority of practice sites may yet to be practicing in this manner.

PERFORMANCE

We manage best what we measure. Measuring healthcare quality involves the use of standards, guidelines, and performance indicators as benchmarks for desired performance, or measuring the effect of an intervention to see if the process, or the patient or economic outcome (or both) improve. Measuring performance means knowing the lingo:

Metric—What we measure. For example, one pharmacy metric may be measuring the extent of patient counseling by a pharmacist.

Benchmark—The measurement "norm" when compared to similar facilities. An example is 95% of patients are to be counseled by the pharmacist.

Compliance—Meeting a law, regulation, rule, standard, guideline, or best practice.

Intervention—Treatment, preventive care, other actions, or a test that seeks to improve health. An example is a pharmacist working with patients to improve medication adherence.

Process/Performance Indicator—A process or performance indicator is an intermediary measure between an intervention and an outcome. An example is medication adherence which lies between an intervention to improve a patient outcome and the outcome. For example, if 10% of patients are comprehensively counseled about the importance of taking their seizure medication, and the adherence rates in these patients rises by 20%, and the rate of seizures goes down 5%, the counseling is the intervention, the adherence rate is the process indicator, and the rate of seizures is the outcome measure.

In pharmacy practice, performance measurement concerns medication therapy—Is it evidence based? Is it safe? Is it timely? Is it effective? But, it can also be about measuring the process of care as in the example below:

There are several important healthcare performance standards and benchmarks critical to pharmacies that care for patients enrolled in Medicare Advantage Plans and commercial health plans.

MEDICARE STAR RATINGS

The *Five Star Quality Rating System* for Medicare Advantage Plans was put in place as part of an effort to help educate consumers on quality and make quality data more transparent. The star rating consists of 33 (accountable care) measures hailing from five different rating systems: HEDIS (Healthcare Effectiveness Data and Information Set), CAHPS (Consumer Assessment of Healthcare Providers and Systems), CMS (Centers for Medicare and Medicaid Services), HOS (Health Outcomes Survey), and IRE (Independent Review Entity).

Each of the 33 measures contributes equally to the Star Summary Score. Data to support these star ratings come from surveys, empirical observation, administrative (claims) data, and medical records. Rates and scores are calculated and stars are awarded on a contract level each year. This provides a means for Medicare Advantage patients to compare health plans based on quality.

Of importance to pharmacy, of the 33 metrics composing the star rating, 17 concern medication management.[22]

HEDIS MEASURES

The *Healthcare Effectiveness Data and Information Set* (HEDIS) is a tool used by more than 90% of America's health plans to measure performance on important dimensions of care and service. Altogether, HEDIS consists of 75 measures across 8 domains of care. Of the 75 measures, 29 concern medication management.[23] Progressive pharmacies will make achieving these ACO and HEDIS measures a priority for their clinical services.

OUTCOMES

Interventions (such as pharmacist review of therapy and recommendations for improvement) are used to improve outcomes. Outcomes are terminal events that can be divided into four areas: *clinical outcomes* such as morbidity, longevity, or mortality; *utilization outcomes* such as the number of physician visits, emergency room visits, and/or hospitalizations; *economic outcomes* such as the cost of various aspects of care or for all care; and *humanistic outcomes* such as quality of life (QOL), and patient satisfaction.

CLINICAL OUTCOMES

These concern the effectiveness of therapy.[24] Is the patient clinical status better, the same, or worse? There needs to be caution here. Many people measure intermediary or process indicators, such as laboratory results, thinking they are measuring clinical outcomes, and they are not. Laboratory results are not people. Does the patient feel better? Can the patient do more? Does the patient have less breathing difficulty? Has the number of seizures gone down? These are examples of clinical outcomes.

A validated instrument for measuring patient functioning is the SF-36, and when it is used in a "before" and "after" manner, can accurately measure changes.[25]

UTILIZATION OUTCOMES

For medication use, how does better medication management impact patients' use of physicians, emergicare centers, emergency rooms, and hospitals? Is there improvement in school or work days? Is a lesser amount of medication being used, or is the medication less expensive?[26]

ECONOMIC OUTCOMES

Based on utilization, is there a reduction in the cost of care?[27]

HUMANISTIC OUTCOMES

A patient's quality of life can be measured. Has it improved, stayed the same, or gotten worse? How satisfied are patients with the quality of their pharmacy care?[28]

Proving the value of clinical pharmacy services rests on well-designed "before and after studies" using these outcomes.

MEDICATION ADHERENCE

Medication adherence is a process or intermediary indicator, rather than an outcome measure. However, there is correlation between medication adherence and improvement in clinical functioning and reduced healthcare utilization.

A study evaluated the impact of medication adherence on healthcare utilization and cost for four chronic conditions that are major drivers of drug spending: diabetes, hypertension, hypercholesterolemia, and congestive heart failure in 137,277 patients under the age of 65.[29] For diabetes and hypercholesterolemia, high levels of medication adherence were associated with lower disease-related medical costs. For all four conditions, patients who maintained 80 to 100% medication adherence were significantly less likely to be hospitalized compared with patients with lower levels of adherence. For diabetes, hypertension, and hypercholesterolemia, high levels of adherence with condition-specific drugs were associated with lower medical costs for all the patients' treated conditions. For all four conditions, all-cause hospitalization rates were lowest for patients who had the highest medication adherence.

A key function of pharmacists should be to improve medication adherence.

THE JOINT COMMISSION

For pharmacists working in organized healthcare settings, such as hospitals, home health agencies, long-term care, and hospice agencies, The Joint Commission (TJC), previously known as the Joint Commission on Accreditation of Healthcare Organizations (JCAHO) standards apply.[30] It is beyond the scope of this text to go into all the TJC standards for pharmacy. However, there are several documents that discuss the requirements to pass the standards.[31,32]

TIPS FOR MANAGING COMPLIANCE

Pharmacy leaders in an organization are responsible for making sure the pharmacy is compliant with applicable laws, rules, regulations, and standards, and for measuring performance. But that does not mean they need to do it. Instead, they should delegate the function to a pharmacy compliance officer.[33] Besides routine compliance work, the pharmacy compliance officer needs to be concerned with fraud, waste, and abuse violations, especially if there is a 340b program.[34] Medication safety compliance may be improved if this responsibility is given to a pharmacy medication safety officer.[36–39]

SUMMARY

Full compliance with applicable pharmacy laws, regulations, rules, and standards is expected by the senior leadership of an organization, and the pharmacy leader is accountable for this. However, this function is best performed when the responsibilities are delegated to pharmacy compliance and medication safety officers. Meeting guidelines for medications use, such as compliance with accountable care and HEDIS measures, and improving patient medication adherence, should be the responsibility of the clinical pharmacy coordinator.

REFERENCES

1. Withrow SC. *Managing Healthcare Compliance*. Health Administration Press. Chicago, IL. 1999.
2. Wade R. *The Compliance Officer's Handbook*. 2nd Ed. HCPro. Marblehead, MA. 2009.
3. Joshua J, Peterson AM. Corporate compliance: An emerging issue for pharmacists. *Am J Health-Syst Pharm*. 2002;59:1874–1881.
4. The Drug, Food, and Cosmetic Act. U.S. Food and Drug Administration; www.fda.gov/regulatoryinformation/legislation/federalfooddrugandcosmeticactFDCAct/default.htm (accessed January 15, 2014).
5. The Food and Drug Administration Modernization Act of 1997. U.S. Food and Drug Administration; www.fda.gov/RegulatoryInformation/Legislation/FederalFoodDrugand CosmeticActFDCAct/SignificantAmendmentstotheFDCAct/FDAMA/FullTextof FDAMAlaw/default.htm (accessed February 10, 2014).
6. Controlled Substances Act. The U.S. Food and Drug Administration; www.fda.gov/regulatoryinformation/legislation/ucm148726.htm (accessed January 15, 2014).
7. The Prescription Drug Marketing Act of 1987. The U.S. Food and Drug Administration; www.fda.gov/RegulatoryInformation/Legislation/FederalFoodDrugandCosmeticActFDC Act/SignificantAmendmentstotheFDCAct/PrescriptionDrugMarketingActof1987 (accessed January 15, 2014).
8. Vivian JC, Fink JL. OBRA 90 at Sweet 16. *U.S. Pharmacist*. 2008;33(3):59–65. www.uspharmacist.com/content/d/featured_articles/c/10126 (accessed January 15, 2014).
9. U.S. Health and Human Services. The Health Insurance Portability and Accountability Act; www.hhs.gov/ocr/privacy (accessed January 15, 2014).
10. The U.S. Department of Labor. The Affordable Care Act; www.dol.gov/ebsa/health-reform (accessed January 15, 2014).
11. The Lewin Group. CMS Review of Current Standards of Practice for Long-Term Care Pharmacy Services; www.cms.gov/Research-Statistics-Data-and-Systems/Statistics-Trends-and-Reports/Reports/downloads/LewinGroup.pdf (accessed January 15, 2014).
12. CMS, Part D Regulations; www.cms.gov/Medicare/Prescription-Drug-Coverage/PrescriptionDrugCovGenIn/Part-D-Regulations.html (accessed January 15, 2014).
13. Health Resources and Services Administration. 340B Drug Pricing Program & Pharmacy Affairs; www.hrsa.gov/opa (accessed January 15, 2014).
14. U.S. Health and Human Services. The Patient Safety and Quality Improvement Act; www.hhs.gov/ocr/privacy (accessed January 15, 2014).
15. National Association of Boards of Pharmacy; www.nabp.net (accessed January 15, 2014).
16. Centers for Disease Control and Prevention. Public Health Resources: State Health Departments; www.cdc.gov/mmwr/international/relres.html (accessed January 15, 2014).
17. U.S. Equal Opportunity Employment Commission. Laws and Guidance; www.eeoc.gov/laws/index.cfm (accessed January 15, 2014).
18. U.S. Equal Opportunity Employment Commission. The Age Discrimination in Employment Act of 1967; www.eeoc.gov/laws/statutes/adea.cfm (accessed January 15, 2014).
19. Mayer G, Collins B, Bradley D. The Fair Labor Standards Act (FLSA)—An Overview. Congressional Research Service. June 4, 2013; http://digitalcommons.ilr.cornell.edu/cgi/viewcontent.cgi?article=2171&context=key_workplace (accessed January 15, 2014).

20. U.S. Department of Labor. Family and Medical Leave Act; www.dol.gov/whd/fmla (accessed January 15, 2014).
21. Pharmaceutical Society of Australia. Professional Practice Standards, Version 4. 2010; www.psa.org.au/download/standards/professional-practice-standards-v4.pdf (accessed January 17, 2014).
22. Centers for Medicare and Medicaid Services. Quality Measures and Performance Standards. 2013 ACO Quality Documents; www.cms.gov/Medicare/Medicare-Fee-for-Service-Payment/sharedsavingsprogram/Quality_Measures_Standards.html (accessed January 16, 2014).
23. NCQA. HEDIS and Performance Management; www.ncqa.org/HEDISQuality Measurement.aspx (accessed January 16, 2014).
24. U.S. Food and Drug Administration. Clinical Outcome Assessment Qualification Program; www.fda.gov/Drugs/DevelopmentApprovalProcess/DrugDevelopmentToolsQualification Program/ucm284077.htm (accessed January 17, 2014).
25. SF-36® Health Survey Scoring Demonstration; www.sf-36.org/demos/SF-36.html (accessed January 17, 2014).
26. Health Services Reports. The measurement of utilization in health care programs; www.ncbi.nlm.nih.gov/pmc/articles/PMC1615969 (accessed January 17, 2014).
27. Reeder CE. Overview of pharmacoeconomics and pharmaceutical outcomes evaluations; www.ncbi.nlm.nih.gov/pubmed/8846244 (accessed January 16, 2014).
28. Bungay KM, Sanchez LA. Types of economic and humanistic outcome assessments; www.accp.com/media/ppc11/pdf/chapter.pdf (accessed January 16, 2014).
29. Mann DM, Ponieman D, Leventhal H, et al. Predictors of adherence to diabetes medications: the role of disease and medication beliefs. *J Behav Med.* 2009;32:278–284.
30. The Joint Commission; http://Joint Commision.org (accessed January 17, 2014).
31. Strykowski, JM. Preparing for a JCAHO Survey; www.medscape.com/viewarticle/521248_print (accessed January 18, 2014).
32. Patton KA. Preparing the hospital pharmacy for a Joint Commission Survey; www.pppmag.com/documents/V5N11/p10_12_13_14.pdf (accessed January 18, 2014).
33. Fleming K, Boyle D, Lent WJB, et al. A novel approach to monitoring the diversion of controlled substances: The role of the Pharmacy Compliance Officer. *Hosp Pharm.* 2007;42:200–225.
34. Shane R. Detecting and preventing health care fraud and abuse—we've only just begun. *Am J Health-Syst Pharm.* 2000;57:1078–1080.
35. Saine D, Larson. Chapter 1. Medication safety officer: Getting Started.
36. Anon. Evolving titles in patient safety: medication safety officer: new and not-so-new responsibilities make up bulk of job. *Briefings on Patient Safety.* 2008;9:8–9.
37. Anon. Hospitals benefit in many ways when hiring medication safety officer. *Drug Formulary Review.* 2010;7:82–83.
38. Anon. Medication safety officer role adds value to hospital pharmacy. *Drug Formulary Review.* 2010;7:83–84.
39. Karpa KD. Medication safety officer: a new breed of pharmacist. *Drug Topics.* 2001;145:26.

Case Study*

The decedent's estate sues the pharmacy for negligent supervision of a pharmacist who obtained drugs from the facility that she allegedly used to kill her husband.

---

* Adapted from a case reported on in the February 2013 issue of *Pharm-Law E-News* from the American Society for Pharmacy Law. Case citation: *Wise v. Extendicare Homes, Inc.,* No. 1:12-cv-00100-JHM-HBB, W.D. Ky., 2013 U.S. Dist. LEXIS 16435, February 7, 2013.

Pharmacist June, working for independent pharmacy Smith's Drugs, allegedly took several controlled drugs from the pharmacy and used a lethal cocktail to kill her husband Jack. An audit of the pharmacy following Jack's death showed the pharmacy failed to implement an effective system to adequately control and account for controlled substances dispensed. Jack's estate has now filed a negligence action against Smith's Drugs as well as Sam Smith, who was both owner of the pharmacy and pharmacy manager, to obtain damages for wrongful death. Jack's estate sued Smith for negligence in failing to exercise ordinary care in hiring, supervising, and training June in her capacity as a pharmacist and failure to create and implement an adequate system to control and account for controlled substances and prevent diversion of drugs.

1. What was the pharmacy manager's duty in the case, how did he breach the duty, and was the breach the cause of the plaintiffs' damages?
2. What civil, criminal, and administrative charges could the pharmacist (June) be subject to?
3. What standard of care is a pharmacy manager held to when supervising his or her employees?
4. Were the injuries to Jack foreseeable to Sam in this case? Could a reasonable pharmacy manager foresee a potential injury or death due to a failure to properly supervise his employees or failure to properly implement an adequate system to control dispensing of controlled substances? Or is this injury too remote of a consequence to be foreseeable? Why or why not?
5. What hiring, supervising, and training practices could Sam have provided to meet the standard of care for what a reasonable pharmacy manager would have done?
6. What are some precautions Sam could have taken or specific procedures/systems/technology he could have implemented that would provide evidence that he had implemented an adequate system for control and accounting of controlled substances in his pharmacy?

Index